PRAISE FOR

Undertow: My Escape from the Funda
of The Way International

The Annual 2017 Florida Authors and Publishers Association President's Book Awards recognized *Undertow: My Escape from the Fundamentalism and Cult Control of The Way International* by Charlene L. Edge, in the category of Autobiography/Memoir, as a Gold medal winner.

"While a variety of controversies ended up surrounding The Way, the author's most astute portrayal concerns her participation in its research branch. ... A frank, in-depth account of one woman's struggles in a controlling organization." —**Kirkus Reviews**

#78 on BookRiot's list of "100 Must-Read Books About Life in Cults and Oppressive Religious Sects"

"In *Undertow,* Charlene Edge has written a brilliant and engrossing warning to the future by dissecting the past. There are really two books here: one is on a cult called The Way (one of the largest fundamentalist cults in America with about 40,000 followers [in its heyday]). The second book is an examination of the dynamics of all personality, religious, and political cults. By looking (from a heart-wrenching insider's point of view) at a misuse of power in one specific group, Edge has written a book that unpacks a far greater truth. What she exposes to bright liberating daylight is just how our political and religious worlds actually function based on the mesmerizing enticement of belonging to an in-group. This is a brilliantly written and timely warning against falling into the trap of thinking we're the self-proclaimed 'chosen' (be that religious or secular, left or right) as we exclude the feared 'Other.'"
—**Frank Schaeffer**, author of *Crazy for God: How I Grew Up as One of the*

Elect, Helped Found the Religious Right, and Lived to Take All (or Almost All) of It Back and *New York Times* best-selling author of *Keeping Faith*

"A magnificently written life story that sheds light on the enticing ways of cult recruitment and indoctrination that engender conformity, obedience, and loss of self. Nevertheless, thankfully, the seed of doubt grows, as the author strives for acceptance through hard work and deep faith. Edge's prose captures the essence of cult life and the personal devastation of having to acknowledge not only corruption and plagiarized teachings but also a 'sex ring' at the top levels of leadership. An important and must-read book—more gripping than a mystery. *Undertow* will sweep you away." —**Janja Lalich, PhD**, Professor Emerita of Sociology at California State University, Chico, author of *Bounded Choice: True Believers and Charismatic Cults*

"This thoughtful, beautifully written memoir is a window into the gradual but compelling pull cults have on unsuspecting and well-meaning people of faith. Edge's writing conveys images that invite the reader to a particular moment in US History and the fascinating development of a community seeking to impact the world as they perceived it. *Undertow* is an honest and affecting look at the way evangelical movements perceive their world and their duty in it. One gets the impression Edge wants to run back in time and tell that young, intelligent girl to reconsider her worldview. What Edge has created here is a welcome voice of reason for those who would be tempted by similar visions of evangelism and the accompanying claim that an original version of Christianity existed and could ever be accessible or fully intelligible to Christians today. The narrative she pushes against is one that continues to lay claim to evangelicals in our world. It is a worldview in which every moment is interpretable as a reaffirmation of 'us vs. world,' rendering a perspective

Undertow

and promulgated purpose that is hard to fathom if one has never experienced it. Edge's fascinating text gets us as close as one could hope to be. It is a worthwhile read, brimming with insight into a world many of us claim we could never understand. Edge lifts the veil on the power a community can have when discourse and ideology fuse."

—**Todd French, PhD**, Assistant Professor of Religion at Rollins College

"In *Undertow*, Charlene Edge manages to bring to life the inexorable, age-old struggle of light triumphing over darkness, of the search for truth in the misty range of a 'false prophet's' deception which she encountered firsthand as a research assistant in The Way International. While she was promised liberty, she found herself a 'servant of corruption' (2 Peter 2:19). Ms. Edge's heartfelt and earnest journey will leave you in awe of what the human spirit can conquer when it launches out in the search for truth. Well-written, compelling, and inspiring."

—**Kristen Skedgell**, author of *Losing the Way*

"How could a smart woman join a cult that asked of her everything, and took her all in the process? Charlene Edge walks us through the process with her new book, *Undertow*, which chronicles her involvement in The Way International, an Ohio-based 'Bible research' organization whose founder, Victor Paul Wierwille, was accused of multiple sexual improprieties, as well as plagiarism, before he died in 1985. As you read Charlene's story, you'll find yourself wanting to reach into the pages to pull the author out of harm's way. As she writes, 'We, the crippled, were sent to heal the stricken.' There is something in this book for anyone who has ever wholeheartedly embraced a questionable theology, only to find that what was meant as a salve eventually becomes a sword."

—**Susan Campbell**, author of *Dating Jesus: A Story of Fundamentalism, Feminism, and the American Girl*

"*Undertow* is a gift to young people and their families who want to understand the inner workings of fundamentalist cults. Charlene Edge's experience parallels much of my own twelve years as a follower of Victor Paul Wierwille's ministry. *Undertow* sheds light on the decisions, questions, and longings that she encountered, and ultimately worked her way through. In the words of Canadian author Matshona Dhliwayo, 'Books are kinder teachers than experience.' May *Undertow* be a kinder teacher to you than Charlene's seventeen years in The Way International were to her." —**Steve Muratore**, publisher of award-winning political blog the *Arizona Eagletarian*

"Charlene Edge's heartfelt and heartbreaking memoir takes us behind the scenes to reveal how easily a handful of religious charlatans betrayed the trust placed in their hands. The pain is palpable as Edge walks readers through her seventeen years of virtual imprisonment by cult leaders who twisted the Word of God to psychologically and even physically abuse thousands of young people at The Way International. *Undertow* is a disturbing reminder that abuse of power can and does happen anywhere."
—**Robert Ruff**, Emmy Award-winning television news producer

"A fascinating insider's account of day-to-day life inside a cult, which with its endless sacrifices, compromises, and increasingly convoluted doublethink, is not so unlike what an ambitious middle manager in any other large corporate enterprise experiences. With a novelist's eye for the telling detail, Charlene Edge describes the vulnerabilities that led her to join The Way International as a confused and emotionally needy college dropout in the early 1970s—and the growing disillusionment that led her back out into the world more than a decade later."
—**Arthur Goldwag**, author of *Cults, Conspiracies, and Secret Societies*

"Charlene Edge writes with clarity and sensitivity. This memoir on her experiences in The Way International will help readers understand the subtleties and complexities of cultic groups." —**Michael D. Langone, PhD**, Executive Director of the International Cultic Studies Association, editor of *Cultic Studies Review, ICSA Today*'s editor-in-chief, and editor of *Recovery from Cults: Help for Victims of Psychological and Spiritual Abuse*

"This well-written exposé of life in a Christian fundamentalist cult reads like a novel and portrays, in lucid detail, how the author was seduced into joining the cult. Through her vivid prose, she helps us understand how she lived with the founder's fantasies for seventeen years of her life. The story of how she got out is as illuminating as how she got in. It is a must read." —**Rita Bornstein, PhD**, President Emerita of Rollins College, author of *Legitimacy in the Academic Presidency: From Entrance to Exit*

"A tenderly written, intensely personal narrative about being swallowed alive by a cult. Charlene Edge's encounters with the abusive Victor Paul Wierwille and her firsthand observation of how The Way's Research Department twisted the Scriptures are enlightening and chilling." —**Karl Kahler**, author of *The Cult That Snapped: A Journey into The Way International*

"Charlene Edge has created a deeply human story of her conversion, commitment, disillusion, and disaffiliation from an evangelical Christian cult movement, The Way International. With balance and grace, she gives the reader a compelling portrait of the group's leader and his fraught relationship with his followers that stands as a warning beacon to all those drawn to charismatic prophets and their high-demand communities." —**Phillip Charles Lucas, PhD**, Professor of Religious Studies at Stetson University, author of *The Odyssey of a New Religion: The Holy Order* *of MANS from New Age to Orthodoxy,* and co-editor with Thomas Robbins of *New Religious Movements in the Twenty-First Century: Legal, Political, and Social Challenges in Global Perspective*

"The Way International was once one of the largest cults in America and had a worldwide membership of close to 40,000. One of those members was Charlene Edge and she writes of her seventeen years in the sect in her riveting book, *Undertow.* In fascinating and disturbing detail, she reveals how she was recruited into The Way while in college during a vulnerable time of her life. Her first-person accounts of meetings with cult leader Victor Paul Wierwille and later, the revelations of his psychological manipulation of members and sexual abuse of hundreds of women, are revealed against the background of her own growing doubts about the group and her commitment to it. A very well-written and compelling tale of delusion and the long path back to reality."
—**Jeff C. Stevenson**, author of *Fortney Road: Life, Death, and Deception in a Christian Cult*

"Charlene Edge's personal story, *Undertow,* is a wake-up call to moderate Christians (and everyone else) about the dangers of the respectable-looking kind of fundamentalism that conducts Bible study but in reality twists Scripture to produce self-serving doctrines, demands obedience to a cult-of-personality leader, warps believers' personal identities, and potentially damages members' long-term welfare. With nonprofit status, such cults are here to stay. Read *Undertow* and be warned."
—**Julia Scheeres**, author of *Jesus Land*

"Well written and compelling, Charlene Edge provides a cautionary tale about the dangers of absolute religious truth. She courageously tells the story of her journey into the depths of religious fundamentalism, and reveals the intellectual strength that ultimately led her to reason her way out." —**Yudit Kornberg Greenberg, PhD**, George and Harriet Cornell Endowed Professor of Religion and Director, Jewish Studies Program at Rollins College

"*Undertow* could be called 'The Great Mystery of The Way Revealed: How the Research Department Really Worked.' Every sentence rings true. In telling her story in *Undertow*, Charlene has also told mine. Holding degrees from the University of Toronto, having studied Hebrew, Aramaic, and Syriac, I taught and conducted biblical research for The Way International, albeit in a minor role, from 1976 to 1978. With remarkable clarity, Charlene tells her journey of recruitment, service, eventual disenchantment, and escape, which mirrors much of my own. I heartily recommend and endorse this well-written, captivating, engagingly told tale." —**Marty McRae**, former Eighth Way Corps member and former faculty member, Way College of Emporia

"*Undertow* sensitively portrays Charlene Edge's recruitment into a cult and her eventual escape. Her story is specific to her experience, but it is informative for all people who have been manipulated by a group, especially a fundamentalist one, and offers great insight on the difficulty of leaving. Her writing is magic, even exotic, making the reader identify with her and her struggle. The writing invites you into her life, and you are bound to come away better informed and a better person." —**Philip F. Deaver, PhD**, Professor of English and Writer-in-Residence at Rollins College, author of the Flannery O'Connor Award-winning story collection *How Men Pray*

"*Undertow* is a cautionary tale for all young people, especially those who are preparing to leave their familiar surroundings to go to college, join the Armed Forces, or move to start a new job. However, the same warning applies to anyone at any age who is going through any life change, such as the loss of a job, a divorce, or the death of a loved one. The names of high-control groups like The Way will be different, their teachings will vary, but the basic techniques of recruiting and mind control are the same. The extreme difficulty in leaving these organizations is evident in Charlene Edge's story." —**Marjorie Patton**, parent of a former Way Corps member who received successful exit counseling before Way Corps graduation

"This is a very personal and eye-opening exposé of the hidden world of life in a destructive group. It took great personal courage and strength for Charlene to break away and build a new life for herself and her daughter. A must read!" —**Patrick Ryan**, graduate of Maharishi International University, cult intervention specialist since 1984 at Intervention 101 .com, and contributor to *Recovery from Cults: Help for Victims of Psychological and Spiritual Abuse,* edited by Michael D. Langone, PhD

"Charlene Edge's *Undertow* shows how intelligent, even strong people, from all walks of life, can be sucked into a dysfunctional or abusive religious group or church, and once in the fold, how difficult it is to get out. I know because I was raised in a fundamentalist Christian church and school. When I started a support system for people leaving fundamentalism, that got me on *Oprah.* Afterward, I debated Jerry Falwell on *Today* and *Nightline* and exposed television evangelists like Jim Bakker and Jimmy Swaggart. I was amazed by the anguished, guilt-ridden, repressive, and tragic stories I became privy to. I wish everyone leaving fundamentalism could have the courage and the writing ability to bear witness against their religious bondage and testify as to how they broke free. The lure, the group dynamics, and The Fundamentalist Mindset are basically the same and are more important than the theological quirks of a particular group." —**Richard Yao**, author of *Freedom from Bad Religion.* Founder of Ex-Fundamentalists Anonymous and the new website http://exfundies.com.

"Edge has written a timely and compelling story about the power of words to seduce, to betray, and ultimately, in her case, to save. Avoiding tabloid cult tropes, Edge instead reveals, with maturity, honesty, and insight, the ways that fundamentalist groups twist the very words that honest seekers of truth believe. That she sought religious truth, worked in The Way's Research Department to discover the truth, and ultimately became a writer to tell the truth, strikes me as perfectly poetic coincidence."—**Robyn Allers**, author and journalist

Undertow

My Escape from
the Fundamentalism
and Cult Control of
The Way International™

CHARLENE L. EDGE

New Wings Press, LLC

Cover and interior design by Duane Stapp
Cover photo and interior photos courtesy of the Author unless otherwise credited
Back cover photo by Scott Cook
New Wings Press, LLC logo by Rachel Chase

Library of Congress Control Number: 2016914776

Permission requests can be made by contacting the Author at http://charleneedge.com.

Because of the dynamic nature of the Internet, any Web addresses or links contained in this book may have changed since publication and may no longer be valid.

ISBN: 978-0-9978747-0-9

Published by New Wings Press, LLC
527 Henkel Circle
Winter Park, Florida 32789

For information about special discounts for bulk purchases, send a request to the Author at http://charleneedge.com.

For Rachel
For Hoyt
And in memory of my parents, Anne and Joseph Lamy

Contents

PART 9: ESCAPE

Preface

In its heyday in the 1980s, The Way International was one of the largest fundamentalist cults in America, with about forty thousand followers worldwide.[1] Founded in 1942 by a self-proclaimed prophet, Victor Paul Wierwille (1916–1985), who marketed the group as a biblical research, teaching, and fellowship ministry, The Way still operates in the shadow of its dark history. I knew Wierwille personally. As one of his biblical research assistants and ministry leaders, I am a witness to his charisma, as well as his abuse of power and manipulation of Scriptures to serve his own agenda. I discovered his sexual abuse of women and chronic plagiarism. Today, those underbelly facts are hidden, denied, or otherwise squelched. The years of Wierwille's authoritarian reign and the chaos after his death provide the context of my story.

In 1987, after seventeen years of commitment to The Way, my life was a wreck. I rejected Wierwille's ideology, escaped, and resumed my education. At Rollins College, my essay "Somewhere between Nonsense and Truth" laid the foundation for "An Affinity for Windows," a short memoir in *Shifting Gears: Small, Startling Moments In and Out of the Classroom*. These writings are woven into this book. My recruitment story is included in Elena S. Whiteside's book, *The Way: Living in Love*.[2]

This book is a memoir. It is my recollection of events related to the best of my knowledge and ability. The story's crucial facts are true. Some events and conversations are combined in the interest of storytelling. Besides my memory and bits from others' memories, my sources include my extensive collection of notes, journals, letters, calendars, books, newspapers, photographs, and copies of *The Way Magazine*.

Names in this story that I have not changed, besides mine, are those of current or former public figures in The Way International: leaders at the state level or higher, Way trustees, and a few members of The Way's Biblical Research Department. For privacy reasons, other identities have been changed or are composites. I recognize that others' memories or interpretations of the events I describe herein may be different from my own. My book is not intended to hurt anyone. This is a recollection of life in a cult that in recent years has become a topic of public interest.

My title invites the question, what makes The Way International a fundamentalist cult? Here is the crux of my answer: Wierwille believed in scriptural inerrancy, a cornerstone of Christian fundamentalism. As the biblical scholar James Barr tells us: "It is this function of the Bible as supreme religious symbol that justifies us in seeing fundamentalism as a quite separate religious form."[3] The Way International is also a cult, or at least was while I was in it. I use the definition of *cult* I found on The International Cultic Studies Association (ICSA) website: "An ideological organization held together by charismatic relationships and demanding total commitment."[4]

Scripture quoted in this book is from the King James Version of the Bible.

Any errors of fact, interpretation, or judgment in this book are my sole responsibility.

I hope you enjoy reading my story.

Charlene Edge
Winter Park, Florida
October 2016

We do not receive wisdom, we must discover it for ourselves,
after a journey through the wilderness which no one
else can make for us, which no one can spare us …
– Marcel Proust

1

Hiding in Plain Sight

If they find out, they'll think I'm weird.

In the winter of 1987, my Sociology professor clutched a stub of white chalk, drew a pyramid spanning the height of the blackboard, and crowned it with an *X*. Thirty students, many half my age, surrounded me in a beige classroom. None of them knew my secret.

"Okay. Last week we discussed gender inequality in the workplace," Dr. Schaffer said. "Tonight, we'll examine autocratic groups and how they operate. My not-so-elegant drawing represents their hierarchical power structure. Religious ones are often called 'sects,' or 'cults.' By the way, I'm saying, s-e-c-t-s, not s-e-x."

When laughs died down, she said, "The leader is *X*." She underlined the *X*. "He or she dictates the group's beliefs and behavior."

Dr. Schaffer straightened her red print scarf and examined our faces one by one. Students rearranged notebooks and clicked their pens. Tonight's lecture was far from news to me, but I drew the pyramid anyway, mimicking other students, trying to fit in. Instead of *X*, though, I scribbled *W* for Dr. Victor Paul Wierwille, founder of The Way International, in its heyday one of the largest cults in America.

"Under *X*," Dr. Schaffer said, "I'll draw some little *y*'s and *z*'s to represent underlings. The *y*'s, right below *X*, report to *X* and oversee the *z*'s, who fill the pyramid's lower regions."

I was a *y*.

"The further down members are," she said, "the less status, power, and knowledge they have." She tapped the chalk on the *z* she'd drawn last. "This is the newest newbie."

Seventeen years ago that *z* was me.

Across the aisle, a young woman copied the pyramid in her notebook, filling it with ghoulish cartoon figures. But it wasn't funny. Each *x*, *y*, and *z* represented a real person.

In that lecture at a branch of The Ohio State University in Lima, I straddled two irreconcilable existences: one in a fundamentalist cult destroying me, the other in a college resuscitating me. My current situation? Right there on Dr. Schaffer's pyramid for all to see. The future? Nowhere in sight.

While safe in the warm classroom, I knew snow was amassing on Highway 75 and beyond that on Highway 29, which took me deeper into the countryside to home. I dreaded the dangerous return trip, but other things scared me more. The Way's compound, riddled with paranoia, was close to my house and less than an hour from campus down Highway 29. I worked there. I'd discovered what Dr. Wierwille had done. I saw what leaders he trained were doing.

"These underlings," our professor said, pointing to the *y* and *z* marks, "find something appealing about the group, like a sense of community where believers share the same values, a leader who claims special knowledge not found anywhere else, and promises of unique enlightenment or future rewards in the afterlife."

Yup. Wierwille promised he'd teach us God's true Word. Back then, I wanted that.

I shielded my eyes, leaned over my notebook, and retraced the *W*, digging my pen harder into the paper, monitoring my body language, avoiding any telltale move that might reveal I understood this topic better than Dr. Schaffer.

"To retain members," she explained, "the leader creates a sense of 'us versus them' to keep the group fighting a common enemy."

The Devil. That was our enemy. He used unbelievers and anyone who warned us against Wierwille, even our families. Only three years earlier I would have considered this professor one of those adversaries. Not now.

The previous week, we'd met in her office to discuss homework, and before I realized it, I'd blurted out, "I'm working at The Way International." That got her full attention. "But I'm trying to leave. I can't—" Then I cried and told her everything.

"You know, I've not had anyone from there in my classes before." Her oceanic tact put me at ease. "If you'd like, I'll teach one night about groups like it; some call them cults."

I wiped my tears, not knowing how to thank her enough. Her offer transformed her from authority figure to understanding guide. Her coal-dark hair, cut into a bob, reminded me of black-eyed Susans that grew wild along Ohio country roads. Spring would come again.

"Cults," she continued, moving aside for us to see her pyramid, "seduce people to join in a variety of ways." She scrawled the words *love bombing* on the board. "Recruits feel especially cared for during initial contact with the group. Members hug them. Make them feel they're in one big happy family. For a time, maybe they are."

I was eighteen when that happened, fresh from Young Life camp, sitting on a lounge pillow at The Way Inn Coffeehouse and listening to zealous Doug praise Wierwille's Bible class. These days, Way members betray each other.

Not far down the snowy road I would travel after class, confusion and suspicion were overrunning Way headquarters. Devious leaders vied for top positions and sent jolts of fear through the staff, causing untold anxiety attacks and rampant distrust about the organization.

"Progressive pressure is put on followers," Dr. Schaffer said, pointing to the chart, "to deepen their involvement and make more and more sacrifices to fulfill the leader's agenda."

That is the truth, Professor. I twisted a strand of hair; her eyes met mine.

She peered at students in the front row. "Many people give up marriages, careers, education, trust funds, and other religions to be accepted into a cult making irresistible claims."[1]

I'd done that. I'd strained ties with my family, broken off with friends, rejected an adoring boyfriend, abandoned a promising university education, and left the faith of my youth, but not once did I consider any of that a sacrifice.

"Think about this," she said. "A person's ability to make independent decisions and engage in critical thinking can atrophy, making it hard to leave, even frightening." She stood still, waiting as some students took more notes. Others leaned back, blinking in thought.

One student raised his hand. "I've heard about something like kidnapping. Parents hire people to take their kids from cults and un-brainwash them. It's supposed to change them back into who they used to be. Does it work?"

"That's called deprogramming," Dr. Schaffer said. "It can work sometimes. But it really is a criminal offense. Very controversial." She patted her hands together, sending chalk dust puffing through the air. "I don't think genuine change can happen through coercion, but some say it can. Some deprogrammers have been prosecuted, gone to jail. So remember that. A vital aspect of this issue, of course, is that cult believers have freedom of religion in America—just like anyone in a well-known church. This topic is complex."

No more hands went up.

"Loyalty," she said, "is the primary quality valued in a follower, you can be sure of that."

Yes. But now, as a traitor, can I escape before they find out? Before I'm thrown to the curb, penniless, like my friend John?

"Many people, even students like you," she said, *not* looking at me, "like to feel certain about God and spiritual matters. Cults offer certainty. That, you can count on."

On the drive home, nudging my car through the snowstorm, I leapt from one memory to another, ashamed that I allowed myself to get sucked into The Way, and that Wierwille used me to spread his propaganda. Dr. Schaffer, an unexpected humanitarian, held me steady for the moment, but I feared for my mental health, even my physical well-being. I'd discovered The Way's underbelly, bloody-black and swollen with greed, and nothing could make me stay. In the beginning, I only wanted to know, love, and serve God and understand the Bible. What harm could that possibly bring?

Understanding the I Ching, by Hellmut Wilhelm and Richard Wilhelm, informs us that the "hexagram Pi, Grace (Book of Changes, no. 22), ☲☶ stands for imaginative art, or song and image endowed with form." I wanted to use this hexagram in my book's design because without grace, *Undertow*—an image endowed with form—would not have been possible. ~ Charlene Edge

Part 1
Recruitment

2

The Midwife

"Jesus can mend your heart if you'll let Him," Judy said. "Come with me tonight, Charlene, you'll see." Judy, a cheerleader at our high school, was Protestant. I was Catholic with boyfriend problems. It was 1969, eighteen years before Dr. Schaffer's lecture about cults. My new girlfriend, Judy, was inviting me to a Christian fellowship for teens called Young Life. Founded in the 1940s, by 2015 it claimed to have reached 1.4 million kids worldwide.

"I don't know, Judy, I'm just not ready for that," I said. "I need to figure some stuff out before I go to any new church."

"It's not church, remember, it's a fellowship in my living room. You've seen the flyers." We were in the hall at James M. Bennett High School, leaning against lockers and whispering. Judy knew about my troubles. My boyfriend, a hotshot quarterback, had just dumped me. My father demanded I keep his ten o'clock curfew or be grounded. Catholic religion classes, mandatory on Wednesday nights, bored me to death. I'd been through eight years of Catholic school already, wasn't that enough? Besides, I more than resented the Church, I wanted out. A year earlier, the Catholic faith had deeply disappointed me when the worst of all possible things happened. My mother—religious, lovely, forty-eight years old, riddled with cancer—died. Priests said she died because God wanted her in heaven. They offered no relief for my angst, no *real* answer to my question: "If God loves me, then why this? Why do pain and evil exist in this world He made?"

"Excellent question," Father James said, "but we won't understand why until we get to heaven."

I did not want to wait.

Judy's meeting revved me up as if I'd chugged ten Coca-Colas. Kids, filling the floor space, stairs, and sofa, were happy, hugging, and laughing. Even football players I never would have guessed were "into the Lord" leaned against the walls, Bibles in their hands. The leader, a thirty-something Presbyterian minister wearing a golf shirt, tapped a glass to get our attention. He waved his leather-covered Bible and said we should read the Bible and pray to Jesus every day, speaking to him like He was our best friend.

Catholics didn't talk this way. The concept of Jesus as pal was new, and I loved it. Before long, I abandoned the Catholic missal and rosary beads of my parents' faith, and, as Judy's golf-shirted leader recommended, bought a paraphrased New Testament, *Good News for Modern Man*. To keep peace at home, I still attended Mass, but I quit questioning the priest and dismantled my altars to the Virgin Mary beneath pine trees in our backyard.

My full-blown Protestant conversion came one night at a Young Life retreat at nearby Ocean City. I broke out in tears as we sang "How Great Thou Art" and turned my life over to Jesus. I rushed to tell Judy. She threw her arms around me. "Praise the Lord, Charlene. You're born again!" Thus I began, without comprehending the serious shift I'd made, a journey into evangelical Christianity. Soon I transformed from a contemplative-but-disappointed Catholic into a frenetic believer zealous to live for the Lord. Jesus was my buddy, not a distant savior on a cross. The Bible was God's Word for me, not filtered through the pope. I read it for myself. Those things were different, but Young Life's core belief in life's purpose remained the same as what I'd internalized in Catholic childhood: to know, love, and serve God. For the rest of my senior year I rarely missed a meeting with Judy.

Before graduation in June 1970, I registered for a weeklong Young Life summer camp in Saranac Lake, New York, in August before we all left for college. I was headed for East Carolina University in Greenville, North Carolina. My married sister lived in Charlotte, close enough for visits.

"We call the camp 'College Prep,'" Judy said. "It'll pump us up for Christ." We knew college would tempt us with drugs, sex, and all manner of satanic influences, as Judy's leader said, doing his best to convince us we could not manage without College Prep. But before I would board the bus for Saranac, I had three months to earn spending money for college at my summer job at the beach.

I'm amazed my father allowed me to live unsupervised in Ocean City, the nearby resort town where I'd been born again. Perhaps it was a sign of those times that I felt safe renting a house with girlfriends from my senior class. We all found food-industry jobs, mine at English's Chicken and Steak House, a few blocks away, where I tended the take-out counter, selling donuts, éclairs, and coffee to the breakfast crowd, and coleslaw and fries with buckets of steaming fried chicken the rest of the day. I was thrilled to be away from home. I was at the beach. I was making money. I was free.

One day, despite my grimy white polyester uniform and equally greasy white tennis shoes, one of the busboys sauntered up to my counter and watched while I pulled my long blond hair into a ponytail and smiled at him. Rob. I'd heard he was a college man somewhere up north. Looking at him across that counter, I was struck first by the cowlicks that plagued his thick black hair and the popular John Lennon glasses that made him look intellectual. Soon I'd find out he *was* smart, and his passion for politics was nearly equal to his love of surfing.

"If you'd like, Charlene, I could try to teach you how to surf. What do you say?"

"I'll think about it." Thus we began.

Rob's patience as a surfing teacher was monumental, but I didn't practice. I'd rather listen to the Supremes on my portable radio and sunbathe while he caught a wave. Before long, I made no time for private talks with Jesus, my pal, or Bible reading every day. I stashed my *Good News* in the bottom drawer of my dresser, and Rob and I played in the ocean.

I admit I grew a little worried. Nagging guilt reminded me that my new love, a Jesuit-trained Catholic, enrolled in Boston College, was not born again and definitely not preoccupied with Jesus like Young Lifers were. But I couldn't help myself. I liked Rob. I started loving Rob. We talked about Christ and the Bible a few times and let differences fall aside. We spent lazy afternoons shopping for my bikinis and his surfboard wax. We ate crab cakes and fries under star-sprinkled nights while he inspired me with his plans for changing the world—the theme of our generation—and listened to my dreams of studying literature and art in college. In his apartment we played Van Morrison's "Moondance." It was as romantic as pop songs got that summer. Whenever I heard it, I thought of us.

One afternoon we spread our towels on the beach, planted Rob's Morey-Pope surfboard in a nearby dune, and slathered on Coppertone. When darkness covered the sands, we listened to the rushing pulse of our beloved Atlantic, and that's when Rob slipped off those John Lennon glasses and we slithered out of our clothes. His tenderness won me. My conservative mother was not there to warn me about moving so fast. Without her, I blundered into womanhood with no mentor, no wisdom. Life was beautiful.

Until I changed.

In August, my Young Life vow to attend camp boomeranged into our romance. Golf Shirt's wife called my Ocean City house to remind me about Saranac.

"I know the Lord wants you there," she gushed.

I claimed I had no cash.

"Don't worry about money, I've got scholarship funds for you." Evangelicals are practiced at overcoming wimpy objections. I soon boarded their bus for upstate New York, feeling conflicted but duty-bound, leaving a disappointed Rob on the beach. I'd be gone for a week.

At camp, shorts-clad ministers delivered breathless sermons threaded with warnings that we would harm our spiritual lives if we didn't find a Christian fellowship at college. They meant business about our need to keep studying God's Word, our only source of truth in this troubled, war-torn world. It was 1970. The Vietnam War raged on the other side of the planet and on our televisions. The sexual revolution surrounded us. The Women's Lib movement threatened traditional values. Thanks to the Beatles, Eastern meditation undermined Western-style religion. Hippies smoked pot and did LSD at rock concerts. Christians tried to be different. From a stage in the camp's Swiss-chalet lodge, students, weeping with joy, shared powerful testimonies about winning others to Christ, instantaneous healings, and what they called *speaking in tongues*. One woman said tongues was a gift from God, but not everyone receives it. "If you do get it, it is transcendent," she said. Without much pushing, I fell back into the old feelings I'd experienced at Judy's meetings: joy that my pal Jesus guided my every step and comfort that I had the Bible, God's Word to me.

I sent Rob a letter the day after I arrived at camp. I wished he were with me, I wrote, to see the importance of a Christ-centered life. I'd jumped to the conclusion that besides his being Jesuit, our relationship did not measure up to spiritually high standards because of our sexual shenanigans. In eight handwritten pages, I raved about what I heard at camp: "[Christ is] a living, breathing power who directs lifes [*sic*] given to Him and using [*sic*] those lives for Him." I was consumed with new rhetoric (and bad grammar) and bereft of self-reflection.

Leaders, praying over me, said I must find God's perfect will for me. I rededicated myself to "being a real Christian," pledging not to let anything, including my Catholic boyfriend, distract me. About midweek, a male friend of my cabinmate turned up and showered me with attention hard to deflect, even with my Rob only a few days in the background. Life was getting complicated.

"Come on, Charlene. Let's take a canoe out on the lake," Dave said. "It's gorgeous today and we need to get outside." We spent platonic hours hiking in the woods and listening, side by side, to motivational sermons in the lodge. With his friends, we shared mealtimes in the canteen. Dave, who fit the Young Life profile of wholesomeness and Jesus-love, symbolized what camp leaders called a "godly man." I thought I should give him a chance.

"You're a revitalized spiritual girl," one female leader told me. She reminded me of Glinda, the Good Witch of the North, in *The Wizard of Oz,* with her sweet smile and radiant face. "You should only date born-again young men committed to Christ." Catholics were off the list.

Camp ended. Dave said he would write. I returned to Ocean City where Rob waited for me. It's astounding how dramatic a change can occur in a vulnerable person in one week. I felt renewed, as if nothing bad could happen to me. God directed my every step. I floated on a carpet of peace, but when I met up with Rob on the beach, I shut down, unable to cope. We went to his apartment.

"Charlene, what's happened to you? You're so different. I mean, your body looks the same as ever, but your mind … it's far away. Look at me." His eyes broadcast worry, but I deflected it, overwhelmed, incapable of describing my experience.

We sat on his bed. He reached for me. "It feels like you're behind a brick wall or something. What's the matter?"

I *was* closed off. Besides my infatuation with Dave, which distracted me, I felt unattached to the material world and disconnected from Rob, as if I were still at camp awash in Young Life's version of Christ's presence. Some experts who study extraordinary psychological transformations might call my state *snapping*. People who snap feel blissful or high for a while after an intense experience, but many crash afterward, and some even spiral into depression or worse. I didn't. I kept my blissful, distracted, altered self for a long time.

Religious differences—and new flirtations—bring no end of tangled heartaches like the ones Rob and I encountered. True, we were young and driven by impulses and hormones, pleasures and pressures, but I sensed no doubt about what I thought it meant to obey God's will. My mistake was to misidentify religious bigotry as righteous belief. Camp people fed me Bible verses like this one to justify narrow-mindedness:

Be ye not unequally yoked together with unbelievers: for what fellowship hath righteousness with unrighteousness? and what communion hath light with darkness?
(2 Cor. 6:14)

Somehow, trying not to be mean, I found a gentle, low-tide moment and broke up with Rob. He urged me to write him letters, and although I didn't expect it, he would answer them. We left for our colleges thousands of miles apart, and when I reached East Carolina University, the euphoria from Young Life summer camp delivered me into The Way's hands.

3

Brought In

God could not answer my prayers fast enough at East Carolina University (ECU). I was blissed out and seeking more than college, ready for God to find me some Christian pals. One day someone slid a yellow flyer under my dorm room door. I picked it up and smelled mimeograph ink so fresh that it rubbed off on my fingers. Purple lettering read: "Interdenominational Christian fellowship this Friday. 7:00 p.m. Mendenhall Student Center. Join us."

This is it. A sign from the Lord!

I paced the room in overheated gratitude, waving the paper at absent roommates. If they'd been there, I would have asked, "Who's coming with me?"

That Friday night, I leapt up the stairs of the Student Center and landed in the room marked "Fellowship," not affiliated, I later learned, with any Protestant denomination. I sat in a metal folding chair in the back row and watched workmen roll an upright piano to the front. Students arrived and waited, as if in church. Soon a minister in a rumpled black suit and skinny tie bent himself like a hinge over the podium, and began reminding us of the importance of being Christian in the world gone mad with war, drugs, hippies, sex, and student demonstrations.

Fresh in our minds were the terrible Kent State University student shootings by the National Guard only months earlier. Every campus put up defenses. Risks were rampant. We needed Christ to save us. We needed peace through God's Word.

When the minister finished, I milled around the refreshment table with other students, but they seemed unfriendly, or perhaps they were shy like me. I overheard "Bless you" and "Praise the Lord" sprinkled in conversations, but no one said them to me. I floundered at the edge of the apparent in-group, which gathered around the piano to sing. I listened nearby, but after about ten minutes I left, disappointed, not fired up for Christ like I'd been at camp. I told God, as I marched back to my room, that He would have to do better than that. If He knew ahead of time how unfulfilling that evening would be, why did He send me the flyer?

The following week, I approached my dorm after class and noticed a girl sitting on the low brick wall by the door. Nearby, a small garden contained fragrant swamp jasmine that bloomed despite the change of season, and its perfume put a spontaneous smile on my face. The girl looked familiar; her red hair blazed in the afternoon light. She was reading a book.

"Excuse me," I said, and she looked up. "I'm wondering ... were you at that fellowship in the Student Center on Friday night?" I straightened my blouse to be more presentable.

"Yes." She smiled and put down her book, a Bible.

The Lord has brought me to this girl!

"I'm Debbie," she said. (Debbie is not her real name).

I introduced myself. "How'd you like it?" I asked. "The fellowship, I mean." I shifted my books in my arm, hoping she might say she'd hated it like I had.

"It was okay, but they were too uptight for me, you know, too fundamentalist."

I nodded as if I knew exactly what "fundamentalist" meant, but I didn't have a clue and I didn't ask, not wanting to get sidetracked.

"What about you?" Her slow smile matched her Southern accent.

"I didn't stay long. Felt out of place."

Debbie motioned for me to sit beside her on the wall, and I learned that she'd been in Campus Crusade for Christ, a group similar to Young Life in its goals of getting kids born again and living for Jesus. Her hometown was near the college, unlike mine. I'd been raised by devout Catholics, but her Protestant parents, she said, were not too serious about religion. She said she wanted a real Christian buddy and a Bible study group to join, just like I did. My heart raced. I went to that meeting Friday to meet Debbie. That was clear now. God had not forgotten me.

I saw the events leading up to this moment purely through the lens of Young Life's theology about my pal Jesus giving minute-by-minute guidance. When you're wearing that kind of interpretive lens, you cannot see through any other. It alarms me how single-minded I became and in such a short time. In the span of a year, Young Life's ardent message led me into becoming a fanatic? I hate to admit it, but that's the truth.

Debbie and I teamed up for Christ. We read Scriptures and prayed together. We talked to girls in our dorm about Christ's love. We taped colorful posters in our transom windows that read "Don't keep the faith, baby. Spread it." We preached to our dormmates that mainstream churches were part of the nation's evil establishment and put them down for having zero zeal for Christ and zero answers to our modern-day problems. We told anyone who'd listen that we needed to read the Bible and nothing else to know how to live for God—as if we understood all the Scriptures. We parroted phrases from our former high school Christian in-groups. We did not win anyone.

In America, we were free to believe whatever we wanted, but we failed to grasp an essential truth: such freedom does not always go hand in hand with enlightenment. Our enthusiasm for Christ was surpassed only by our ignorance of basic religious history. I could have learned at the library that in the sixteenth century an errant Catholic monk in Germany named Martin Luther launched a campaign to reform the Roman Catholic Church, which was rampant with corruption, and kicked off the Protestant Reformation, the effects of which I inherited in the evangelical Protestantism of Young Life. The Pope, who eventually excommunicated Luther, charged him with inciting Christians to reject the authority of Church leaders and replace it with the Bible, starting an era of *sola Scriptura* (only Scripture) that continues to this day. Protestant denominations continue to fight, reform, dissolve, reorganize, and spawn fringe dwellers like The Way, which Debbie and I were about to encounter.

The Way was not an isolated phenomenon in the Bible Belt of North Carolina. During the 1960s and 1970s, waves of young people across America grew tired of their parents' churches and joined new religious groups. Not all were Christian. Some sects originated in Asian religions. John Lennon, after a visit abroad, popularized Transcendental Meditation. Jesus freaks combined the love of Jesus with hippiedom. They, along with other marginal groups, fell under the umbrella of the Jesus Movement, which exploded all over America. Revolutions—religious, sexual, musical, you name it—inflamed our rambunctious era. Fundamentalist Christians spawned the most conservative sects, those that believed that the Bible is historically and literally true because God, not man, was the author. And because God is perfect, they reasoned, whatever He told men to write in the Bible had to be perfect, too. What followed was the belief in scriptural inerrancy, meaning a noncontradictory, error-free text. It can be as strong as a child's faith in Santa Claus multiplied by a thousand. Believers do not usually relinquish this belief—ever. Taken to the extreme, fundamental beliefs like inerrancy can lead believers to commit violent acts in the name of God, like bombing abortion clinics or worse. Fundamentalism, at its roots, means certainty that you are right. At that stage of my life, certainty appealed to me. In a chaotic world, believing in a God I could count on was the greatest relief I could imagine.

About a month after we met, Debbie and I returned to the Student Center for a second dose of that interdenominational fellowship. We sat side by side like matching bookends, watching as the same preacher with the skinny tie arrived at the podium.

"Please turn to First Corinthians," he said, "chapter 12. We'll read verses 9 and 10." He read them aloud.

> To another faith by the same Spirit; to another the gifts of heal-
> ing by the same Spirit; To another the working of miracles; to
> another prophecy; to another discerning of spirits; to another
> *divers* kinds of tongues; to another the interpretation of tongues:

Skinny Tie lifted his gaze then and looked around the room. "As Christians today, we no longer need those gifts," he said, "because we live in a different time from the apostles."

After the teaching, Debbie and I introduced ourselves to Skinny Tie and let him know we did not agree with him. Speaking in tongues and miracles were not dead with the apostles, I was sure. The three of us ended up at a table, drinking coffee, debating the issue. In the excitement, I failed to notice two guys taking seats at the other end of the table.

Skinny Tie assured us that prayer could be powerful, but miracles no longer happened, not like those Apostle Paul had performed. As for speaking in tongues, well, no one but the apostles had done that.

I did not know what to say. Never had I witnessed an instantaneous healing. Young Life members told me people they knew had been miraculously made whole, but I had not seen such miracles with my own eyes.

Along with the conversation, my coffee turned cold. I glanced around. That's when I noticed the two eavesdroppers.

"Hi, I'm Doug," said the one with curly hair. He introduced his friend, whose plaid shirt contrasted with Doug's T-shirt and jeans, perhaps indicating other differences between them. They moved closer to us and placed their Bibles on the table.

"If First Corinthians really says miracles and speaking in tongues are gifts that died out with the apostles," Doug said to the minister, "how come I can do them today?"

Oh my gosh.

The minister looked ready to pounce. "Son, I'm not sure you're familiar with these things—"

"I am. I've got a great teacher." Like a spy revealing state secrets, he swiped a hand through his curls and leaned in. "The gifts of the Spirit are not *gifts*," he said, "they are nine separate manifestations of one gift of Holy Spirit. The Greek text says so." He added something about the words being translated incorrectly in the King James Version of the Bible (he patted his copy), and that it took special research to learn this truth. I eyed my *Good News for Modern Man*. Compared with his leather-bound Bible, my paperback was a coloring book.

"That is just semantics," Skinny Tie said. He clamped his arms across his chest, crumpling his suit jacket.

A silent moment passed like ones I knew from playing chess with my father.

"Yes, you're right, sir. It *is* semantics," Doug said. "Semantics are everything when it comes to researching what the Word of God says."

Check.

I was dazed into silence. So was Debbie. So was the minister. We sat back in our chairs, inspecting one another across the chessboard. Doug took another pawn. He insisted, with the calm of a knowing professional, that miracles still happened because God was still in business.

Yes! I wanted to cheer.

He said believers today could operate the power of God like believers did in the Book of Acts. He was living proof. Not only that, he knew many other people who manifested the power of God.

Where were these people?

When I ran the hurdles in high school track, our coach would caution me not to jump the gun. She reminded us, at every practice, to wait until she fired a starting pistol before launching ourselves out of the starting blocks. Much later I wished she had been at that table with Doug. I could have used a cautionary voice telling me not to jump ahead, not to grab what seemed to be The Truth. In my eagerness, I failed to consider the possibility that the minister might know something worth learning, and maybe Doug didn't have the right doctrine. But Skinny Tie typified those denominational types that I'd been calling calcified. I didn't mind a young, good-looking guy interrupting and taking my side.

Debbie and I were like shy schoolgirls, smiling at Doug and at his friend Norman, who, in spite of his preppy plaid in-charge look, nodded in sync with sloppy Doug's every word.

The minister did not smile. "I understand where you're coming from, son," he said, his patronizing tone increasing, "but let me point out, I speak with some authority on the Scriptures. I've studied this topic and heard it taught by top biblical scholars, and the majority of them agree with what I'm saying." He slid his hands down the front of his crumpled suit.

"Well, maybe my teacher knows more than yours," Doug said.

Checkmate. What teacher? I could not sit still. Debbie wiggled in her chair. Doug held the gaze of Skinny Tie, whose eyes shifted from Doug to Debbie to me and back to Doug.

"Well, maybe that's so," the minister said. "You're welcome to think what you like, young man." He laid down his defeated king and shoved back his chair.

I couldn't stand it. *Who is the teacher?* I tapped my foot under the table. *Doug, tell us your teacher's name!*

Wound tight as tops, Debbie and I waited for someone to pull the string. To my delight, the minister stood up, murmured good evening, and left.

I suspect now that he realized his efforts were wasted on us. As the Bible warned, don't cast your pearls before swine.

"So," I said, turning to our curly haired hero, "who is your teacher?"

"Dr. Victor Paul Wierwille."

Debbie and I had never heard of Wierwille, so Doug began his story. Dr. Wierwille started The Way in the 1940s in Ohio. Since then, he built a ministry headquarters on the Wierwille family's old farm outside New Knoxville, Ohio. He called his ministry The Way because Jesus Christ said He was the way, the truth, and the life, and Dr. Wierwille, Doug said, was a follower of Christ. Wierwille's ministry was still small but growing fast because of the Bible class he taught called Power for Abundant Living (referred to as "the PFAL class"). Doug promised it would answer all my questions about healing and speaking in tongues. Like a Young Lifer on steroids, Doug repeatedly said the Bible is the Word of God, which resonated with me, an impressionable young girl. I gulped down Doug's words without any critical thinking, not pressing him to prove what he said. He was so sincere that I clung to his assertions, like "believing equals receiving," as if they were heaven-sent. His refusal to argue with the minister or grow impatient, like I usually did in challenging situations, impressed me. He possessed a *Jeopardy* contestant's confidence in knowing the answer and waiting his turn to reveal it.

Then Doug said something I'll never forget. "God's people are destroyed because they don't know God's Word." To prove it, he quoted this verse in the Old Testament:

My people are destroyed for lack of knowledge: because thou hast rejected knowledge, I will also reject thee, that thou shalt be no priest to me: seeing thou hast forgotten the law of thy God, I will also forget thy children. (Hosea 4:6)

"Christians are defeated because they lack knowledge of God's Word," he explained, tapping his Bible, "not someone's interpretation of it. We 'let the Bible speak for itself.'"

"That's right," said Norman.

Doug's bravado made his message about letting the Bible speak for itself sound logical. It was a long time before I realized that reading a text, any text, always involves interpretation. It is impossible for any book, even a sacred one, to "speak for itself." Humans apply meaning to what they read. I'd been reading all my life, but never thought about that. But ask members of any book club or literature class, and they'll tell you interpretation happens. You can't avoid it. But I could not resist Doug's conviction. The Bible was a special, holy book, after all, so I imagined if God wanted it to speak for itself, then He could make it do that. I had no understanding of how to challenge that ridiculous statement.

Debbie's eyes sparkled with conviction. She said, "I'd like to take this class."

I nodded and pulled my chair closer to the table.

"Great. Why don't you two come to the coffeehouse tomorrow?" Norman said. "It's at our Way Home. The believers would love to meet you, and you can fill out class registration cards right away."

"Sure," I said, watching Debbie smile and nod at me.

"Or better, you know what? If you want to," said Doug, "I can drive us there right now so you can see the place. Shall we go?"

Debbie gave me a look that asked *why not?*

"Fine with us," I said. God was opening the door, no doubt about it, and if we didn't take this chance, we might miss His plan for us to learn more Bible.

"It's a nice house right down the street. We run fellowships and classes there," Doug said. "And I live there with the leaders, a married couple. So does Norman."

Norman added that the house was owned by The Way and served as the outreach center of the ministry for North Carolina. That sounded important.

I'm astounded I swallowed Doug's claims so fast. To check on his ideas, I could have taken some time and hiked across campus to Joyner Library and found commentaries on the Scriptures, or books about theology, church history, or the history of the Bible. My parents passed on respect for books as if it were genetic material, so why didn't I go to the library? My mother practically raised me in one. She worked among the dusty stacks of Wicomico County Public Library in Salisbury where I sat cross-legged on the floor devouring Grimm's fairy tales like candy corn and later Nancy Drew mysteries. Nancy, the determined clue finder, was my heroine, right up there with Scarlett O'Hara in *Gone with the Wind*. I loved the musty smell in every Dewey-decimaled book I read. But Young Life's influence made me think that rather than learning from books, I must seek real live Christian teachers. So when these two Way followers showed up, of course the Lord had sent them. Any gut warnings against climbing into a car with strangers, especially males, and driving off campus were silenced by Doug's certainty—the sheer force of it compelled me to go. Within fifteen minutes, Debbie and I would find ourselves in no seeming danger in a well-kept house, unaware the threat was invisible.

4

Enticed

What happened at The Way Home surprised me at first, but by the end of that night I understood.

On the way there, I rode next to Debbie in the back seat of Doug's car, telling myself that the Lord set up this meeting with these guys. No matter that we'd met only an hour ago. No matter that the car rattled, creaked, and smelled of mildew. I gazed out the grimy window and watched dorms morph into bulky outlines against the darkening sky, crisscrossed by telephone poles. Lights twinkled on and off like fireflies, and I imagined students were getting ready to party. Even in the Bible Belt, what we were doing was unusual for a Friday night.

"We're here," Doug said. His brown eyes flashed in the rearview mirror.

A trim lawn wrapped like an apron around a white two-story house. It looked like a small-scale Southern mansion. Shrubbery, flowerbeds, and trees graced the yard. Debbie said how pretty it looked, how peaceful and tidy. We parked behind the house in a narrow lot and got out of the car. A large beech tree in the backyard rattled its sharp leaves above us as a cool breeze kicked up, making me shiver as I hurried to follow Doug through a door and into a neat kitchen. Norman snapped on lights. I'll never forget the shine on the stainless steel fixtures and the spotless sink. We trailed behind Doug through a chandeliered dining room, into a front entryway, past a carpeted staircase, and into a living room. A cat meowed somewhere down a hall.

"Everyone's out witnessing," Doug said. "They're all over town looking for hungry people like you to tell about the Word."

Debbie and I sank into a velveteen sofa across the room from an elegant fireplace. I looked around at the ornate vases, lamps, and silky drapes. Were these people rich? I felt small and poor, glad to be with Debbie, my ally. As much as I wanted to hear more Bible teaching, I could not imagine coming here alone.

Doug and Norman made themselves comfortable in matching chairs by the fireplace, as if ready to run a meeting. A grandfather clock in the corner ticked, ticked, ticked. Now what?

"Gosh, this is a beautiful place, and I don't mean any disrespect," I said, "but I thought Jesus's followers weren't supposed to be rich like this." I wasn't poor, but I'd grown up in a modest middle-class house.

"Oh, but the Word says we should be prosperous," said Norman. I was surprised that he, not Doug, took on my challenge. "It's right in the Bible." He waved his arms in a theatrical way, and to my surprise he quoted this verse:

Beloved, I wish above all things that thou mayest prosper and be in health, even as thy soul prospereth. (3 John 2)

In contrast to Doug's friendlier approach at the Student Center, Norman's quoting the Bible—no matter how applicable the verse—struck me as preachy, more like church than like Young Life's informal style. Conversation screeched to a halt.

I didn't doubt that God wanted me to be happy and healthy, but I didn't see the need to use that verse as proof. I didn't remember ever reading it, or if I had, I thought the Apostle John wrote it to a believer he knew, not to me. Way people were dead serious about the Bible being personal.

"Okay," I said, "I guess I had the wrong impression."

Debbie wasn't helping. She lounged on the sofa as if she were on vacation.

Doug picked up the slack and said the PFAL class would show us God's promises in the Bible, like the ones Norman just told us about, so we could claim them. *Claiming promises* was another new idea, a brand-new language. Could I learn it?

We all left the house and headed for a converted garage they called the Biblical Research Center. "We call it the BRC for short," Doug said. Inside, red wall-to-wall carpet and wood-grained paneling made it a serious study room. Fluorescent lights flickered above rows of folding chairs that faced a small podium at the front of the room. On the wall behind the podium hung a green banner with yellow letters that read The Word of God Is the Will of God. Norman said they held the coffeehouse in here, which explained a faint incense smell. While Doug and Norman grouped chairs together, I examined a countertop strewn with books, including *How to Enjoy the Bible* by E. W. Bullinger, *Babylon Mystery Religion* by Ralph Woodrow, and *The Myth of the Six Million* by Prof. David L. Hoggan.[1] I'd never heard of them. Evidently they mattered at The Way.

The four of us sat together near the book counter.

"First, I want to say you're invited to our coffeehouse in this room tomorrow night," Doug said. "You know, guitar players, singing, donuts, and of course, coffee." He grinned for the first time since we arrived. "Oh yeah, incense, too. It always smells like that in here."

Before he got started, he jumped ahead to invite us to come back on Sunday to hear Rev. John Lynn teach God's Word. John, The Way's leader for North Carolina, and his wife lived in the house and trained the college students who lived with them, all young men, to be Way leaders.

"Anyway, this room is mostly for biblical research and teaching. Biblical research, like Dr. Wierwille always says, is the heart of our ministry," Doug said. "He preached in a denomination before this, I think it was the Evangelical and Reformed Church"—Norman nodded—"but it didn't give him freedom to teach the Word like he wanted, so he left, and thank God he did."

That night, for the first time, I considered the importance of biblical languages to studying the Bible. We heard all about how Dr. Wierwille studied Greek, Aramaic, and Hebrew texts to compare Scriptures in one section of the Bible with Scriptures in another, and then implement certain methods to reconstruct the original Word of God.

"In-depth Bible study isn't available in every Christian group, you know," Norman said. "Some are only social clubs. They don't feed people meat of the Word like we do."

Debbie said that was true.

Doug chimed in to admit his skills in biblical research were minimal, but before he could develop them, his job, like every Way follower's, was to master the content of Wierwille's Power for Abundant Living class. They were supposed to learn that material before researching any new topics. Dr. Wierwille made that rule. Doug then revealed what first drew him to The Way—the kindness and generosity of the believers, not their Bible knowledge. He'd been a lost hippie on drugs, he said, and after a bad trip he needed serious help.

"The Way believers cared about me more than anyone I've ever known," he said, adding that he was living proof of the saying "People don't care about how much you know until they know how much you care." Then he opened his Bible and plunged into a sample of class material.

I'm not sure whether he intended to impress us with controversial topics, or just give an example of how Wierwille taught, but nevertheless his lesson shocked me. Using a Bible that included notes by E. W.

Bullinger, a scholar important to Wierwille, Doug showed us a photo-graph inserted in the back. It was of four concrete crosses with a fifth larger one in the middle in some kind of courtyard or cemetery. Doug said the photo proved a little-known truth about Jesus's death on Mount Golgotha. Debbie and I leaned over our desks to see. "The crosses are in France," Doug said. This was supposed to prove that people besides Bullinger, an Englishman, understood that four men, not two, were crucified with Jesus.

Four?

"Four bad guys," Doug said, "not two like most people think." He again reminded me of a *Jeopardy* contestant.

All my life I'd heard of only two thieves crucified with Jesus. Did the Catholic Church lie about this? To arrive at four, Doug said, you must know the Greek words for thief, robber, and malefactor. *Wow.* Learning the Greek language appeared essential to doing biblical research. I wasn't sure I could learn Greek, but if that's what I had to do to know God better, I would try. As the hour progressed, we learned that the four Gospels—Matthew, Mark, Luke, and John—*had* to "fit like a hand in a glove" because they couldn't contradict each other. They were part of God's Word and God's Word could not contradict itself because God was the author, and He was perfect. That sounded right and logical.

Under the deluge of Doug's rhetoric, I failed to think of examples of contradictions that I already knew about in the Old Testament. Even a cursory reading reveals the sort of God who changes His mind. "Thou shalt not kill" is a commandment, but verses abound with God ordering prophets of Israel to kill "pagans" when they interfered with His chosen people. Old Testament violence was one reason I preferred the New Testament.

Doug zigzagged around the Gospels, flipping back and forth to show that each gospel writer mentioned different thieves and robbers at the crucifixion. This teaching, called "Scripture build-up," he said, was

30

an example of Wierwille's biblical research method.

"Don't worry," he reassured us, patting his Bible. "You'll learn this stuff in the PFAL class and catch on soon." He confessed he wasn't the brightest student, but he could "work the Word." He gestured to some books on the counter behind us that he said we would need to buy—concordances, interlinears, and lexicons. I'd never seen such study aides before and they impressed me. Young Life meetings were shallow social gatherings compared with this serious biblical research fellowship. My appetite for more learning kicked into high gear.

One last surprise: the Trinity. Like my Young Life leader, Doug said the word "Trinity" was not in the Bible; therefore, it could not be true. He paraphrased what Wierwille taught: that the Trinity as a theological doctrine crept into the Catholic Church to ensure the divinity of Christ. The truth, according to Wierwille, was that Jesus was not "God the Son," he was "the son of God," half divine because God was his father; half human because Mary, a virgin, was his mother.

It was past ten o'clock, the adrenaline rush was over, and I was too tired to absorb any more. Debbie and I thanked our new God-sent teachers for the astounding Bible lessons, and we all climbed into Doug's clunky car to return to campus.

Many years later, I'd find a Way marketing brochure that confirmed Doug's words. In part, it read:

> As a research and teaching ministry, we are always open to learn more about the Bible. The Way Ministry has the freedom to change and to grow when something new is discovered in the Bible. No dogmas are imposed on an individual. The research is made available to those who wish to utilize it.[2]

If words were colored lights, the promises Doug made about research should have been neon red. But he made Wierwille's style of

31

study sound so inviting (and possible) that he distracted me from thinking critically about Wierwille's ministry. I let my excitement keep me from realizing what Doug did *not* say about their biblical research: he did not describe *how* they might change existing research whenever they learned more or discovered they were wrong. He did not cite any changes they ever made, and he did not guarantee they ever would make changes. If research were truly open-minded and transparent at The Way, these concerns should have been addressed from the start.

Over the years I heard numerous stories similar to Doug's—that love drew followers to the group. What drew me most powerfully that first night was wanting to learn the biblical research Wierwille conducted. It would not be long before I saw that these two forces could be strong competing beliefs: the first, to love one another like Christ commanded. The other one Wierwille put this way: "No one can know the will of God without knowing the Word of God. The Bible is the revealed Word of God."[3] Many of us translated that into doing everything we could to get more knowledge of the Bible, often at the expense of loving others— or ourselves.

Unaware of land mines ahead, the next night Debbie and I again jumped in Doug's rusted car, bound for more Word at the coffeehouse.

5

The Way for Me

In the BRC behind the house, Debbie and I grabbed cups of coffee and
followed Doug past the book sales counter, past a tray of shiny frosted
donuts, past rope incense stuck in bowls of sand, toward a low stage (the
podium was gone) to meet believers he wanted us to meet. We sat on
puffy pillows, and I ended up talking with a young wife and mother
who reminded me of the peppy movie star Doris Day. Dottie asked to
hear what the Lord was doing for me. I willingly offered up the high-
lights: getting born again, attending Young Life camp in New York,
learning that I might one day speak in tongues, meeting Debbie, and
running into Doug on campus.

"It sure looks like the Lord sent Doug and Norman along so I could
take the Bible class you have."

"You should," Dottie said. Then she shared her own story about
taking the PFAL class with her husband, Bob Moynihan, and how
thrilled they were with Way teachings. Dr. Wierwille makes sense, she
said. He teaches people how to study the Bible, not just take people's
word for what is in it. She smoothed her long hair and slipped off her
green Pappagallo flats, getting more comfortable on her pillow, and
chattered about the webbed relationships among the local Way believ-

ers. She was petite like me so we could easily look each other in the eye. "You'll come to see this for yourself, Charlene," she whispered, "but we are so blessed to be alive at this time. We have Dr. Wierwille, the man of God, to teach us the Word, the *true* Word of God." Her eyes sparkled with joy.

"Doug shared a lot of Bible research with us last night. It was amazing. But can you tell me how the ministry started? Doug didn't say much about that."

Dottie leaned back and crossed her legs on the pillow. "It's simple, really." She told me that in about 1942, Dr. Wierwille began a radio program in Lima, Ohio. His choir sang and he gave sermons. Soon he quit ministering at his church to study the Word and start this ministry. Later he put the PFAL class material together, taught it in person, recorded it on tape, and made copies so more believers around the country could hear it. A few years ago, he produced a color film of the PFAL class. Thanks to that, the Word was moving faster than ever. Even in Australia a Way fellowship ran classes.

Dottie flashed her movie-star smile and soon introduced me to a few girls my age. We sat back to listen to a performer, built like Mr. Clean, who played the guitar and sang along with a freckled young woman with hair the color of beach daisies. Someone said Mr. Clean was on the football team and had come over after that night's game against Richmond, a tough competitor. Suddenly, he stopped playing.

"Sorry to be the bearer of bad news," he said, hugging his guitar, "but we lost the game tonight." A moan swept the room, but the music resumed, and the freckled singer was so engaging that I didn't notice a commotion erupting in the back of the room until Debbie nudged me and nodded toward the door. Doug was coming in. Right behind him were two more guys. One wore a purple East Carolina University Pirates football jersey and a white sling on one arm. The other lumbered through the doorway like a fullback. Whispers flew carrying shocking news: the sling wearer, Gerald, had suffered a broken collarbone in the game, but just got healed right outside the coffeehouse in the parking lot. Earl Burton (the lumbering fullback) healed it.[1] *Instantaneous healing. Oh my God.* Debbie looked at me with big eyes. A miracle. Spontaneous healings *do* still happen. I knew Skinny Tie was wrong.

I didn't rush to meet Gerald. I felt awed like a new kid at the sidelines. Instead, I watched him move around and talk to people, then leave with Earl, his healer. Doug approached Debbie and me with his report of the miracle. "I saw it happen," he said. Apparently, Earl laid his hands on Gerald's shoulders and prayed aloud, describing broken bones mending in real time.

"Earl claimed the healing in the name of Jesus Christ," Doug said, "and it was done."

My heart leapt. The incident was proof that during the past twenty-four hours, God had plunked me down in the middle of a modern-day Acts of the Apostles with living, breathing people preaching the Word and healing the sick.

Not long afterward, the musicians announced closing time and groans of disappointment rumbled all around me. A few girls stubbed out the incense, leaving trails of smoke curling to the ceiling like candles in church. Debbie was talking with the guitar players, so Doug and I waited for her at the bookstore counter where Norman was clearing away the coffeepot and the empty donut tray. I was overcome with gratitude and unsure of how to express it to Doug. He and his friends were not only Christians who loved one another and wanted to love and teach newbies like me, they also were knowledgeable and powerful believers, more focused on using the power of God than any Young Life Christians I knew. They also seemed disciplined about outreach, since competition for young minds at East Carolina University was ongoing with popular evangelical groups like InterVarsity and the Fellowship of Christian Athletes. I was hooked.

Someone engaged Doug in a conversation, so I leaned against the counter and examined the items more closely than I had the night before. Wierwille's name appeared on many small pamphlets: "The Walk of Youth," "Christians Should Be Prosperous," "The Cry of Triumph," and "The Manifestations of the Spirit." Books included Wierwille's *Receiving the Holy Spirit Today*, and *How to Enjoy the Bible* by E. W. Bullinger, the author whose Bible Doug used to showcase five crosses. I was marveling at what I could learn when Doug came back and broke my reverie.

"Let me ask you something, Charlene. You're already born again, right?" I nodded. "You know you have the Holy Spirit inside you." I nodded again. "So, would you like to learn how to speak in tongues? It proves you are born again."

"What?" Fear struck me up and down.

"I can help you do it." He went on to say that speaking in tongues proved, beyond a shadow of a doubt, that a person was going to heaven, and nothing could change that. It was also perfect prayer. He smiled like a parent inviting his child to the circus, raised eyebrows and all.

Why does he have to spoil everything?

A girl grabbed him for a big hug, insisting she must talk to him, so he turned away again, leaving me devastated. Young Life leaders warned that if anyone claimed they could teach how to speak in tongues, watch out—it's a trick of Satan. Nobody could instruct another person to do it because, they claimed, it was a gift from God. Gifts are not to be expected. If that were true, Doug was a messenger of Satan. My escalating hope for the goodness of this group plummeted like a roller coaster off its rails.

I turned away from the sight of Doug and everyone else. If Young Life was right, I would have to reject The Way.

But I'd felt so sure God brought me here to learn what Young Life leaders said I needed: more Bible knowledge. I was serious about getting it. When the golf-shirted leader recommended I attend Wheaton College in Illinois, a Christian institution offering Bible studies, I wanted to go, but I was already enrolled at ECU; it was too late to switch. For a few seconds, I let myself consider that Young Life might be wrong. What if Doug *could* teach me to speak in tongues? If I refused his help and left The Way, I'd miss this loving fellowship and all this Bible knowledge within easy reach. How could this not be God's will?

Returning to the counter, Doug picked up where he'd left off, oblivious to my turmoil.

"Look, I'll bring you over tomorrow morning," he said. "We'll have a lesson out front under the trees about Pentecost and the Holy Spirit, okay?" I lowered my head, too confused to respond, realizing he interpreted my hesitation as fear of speaking in tongues, not as fear of *him*. I didn't have the guts to divulge Young Life's different ideas. By keeping my doubts to myself, I didn't have to defend them. I didn't want to face an argument I sensed I couldn't win. If Young Life was right, the Lord would help me figure out how to resist Satan's influence coming through Doug.

Debbie soon joined us, and Doug caught her up on our plan. She wanted in on the lesson, and her enthusiasm dispelled some fear. Her innocent smile made me think I must be silly. I should lighten up. She had a knack for keeping things simple when I tended to complicate them.

Looking back, it's clear her friendship was critical to my journey into The Way; I sometimes wonder if I would have continued with the group by myself.

When we returned to Cotten Hall that night, Debbie invited me to stay with her since her roommate was home for the weekend. I got my things from my room down the hall and sat on her roommate's bed while we talked about all the good people and great music at The Way and how the Lord led us there. We made popcorn in her electric popper, and the treat, along with Debbie's happiness, eased my worries. Before

37

long, a wave of lightheartedness emboldened me enough to tell Debbie my misgivings about being taught to speak in tongues. She shrugged them off.

"We'll be fine. We can ask questions," Debbie said. "Doug will help us, you know."

I pulled the covers around me on the bed, not so sure about this.

"He's really cute, isn't he?"

"Oh, Debbie, be serious. I'm nervous. I want to be open-minded to whatever the Lord wants, but how do I know what it is?"

"It can't hurt to go. We can always leave if we want to."

She switched off the lamp and moonlight overtook us, bringing more peace of mind with it. Echoes of laughter from down the hall bounced through the room, but they didn't stand in the way of sleep.

As it turned out, I wouldn't need the lesson the next day. That night I kept my habit of praying silently before I drifted off, but this time I asked God about speaking in tongues. Perhaps if it were His will, I could do it without anybody's teachings. I relaxed on the bed and prayed, and after a few minutes of silence I felt compelled to whisper aloud. Fuzzy images of the woman who suggested at Young Life camp that I might do this appeared in my mind. Soon my English words flowed into speech-like syllables resembling a foreign language. This was it—praise God, I was speaking in tongues! I spoke louder and louder. Debbie rushed over, sat on the edge of my bed, and grabbed my hand. Even with my eyes shut, I sensed her watching me. I felt lighter and lighter, as if I were floating above the bed, filled with peace. I cried for joy afterward, relieved and thankful, happy about finding The Way. Debbie wept and hugged me over and over. She said I looked ecstatic.

Doug called this phenomenon "manifesting the power of God," but I wonder now if it really resulted from the power of suggestion. Common among Christians is the problematic tradition of attributing the source of insights and inspiration (even speaking in tongues) to an entity called "God" that is separate from humans, when those insights may be coming from the imagination. Who can tell the difference? Does it matter? I do not know. To fundamentalists and evangelicals, it matters a lot; God is all-powerful, with a will we must obey. At the time, I assumed God gave me those strange-sounding words. But many kinds of religious or spiritual experiences happen, as the psychologist William James points out in *The Varieties of Religious Experience*. Sometimes it's hard to explain what they are. Most, I suspect, are mysteries we'll never understand.

I look back on my episode with tongues and wonder about its value. I liked it because it gave me a feeling of transcendence. Was it harmless? Yes, in that it made me joyful. No, in that it blocked rational thinking. It requires an altered state of consciousness—because of that, the phenomenon is often referred to as *thought-stopping*—and it is not always good or appropriate. In the coming years, Wierwille would encourage us to speak in tongues all the time—between thoughts, during conversations with others, and during times of prayer. To remind us to speak in tongues as much as possible, The Way sold red stickers in the shape of stop signs printed with the letters S.I.T.

Even though I didn't think I needed the lesson, I went to The Way Home the next morning with Debbie. We sat with Doug in lawn chairs under the tree out front. I was surprised when Earl appeared and Doug left to do chores, but by the way they handled the switch, I sensed Debbie and I were about to hear from a more experienced teacher. Earl said he'd never been a druggie or gotten into any real trouble. His big sin, as he described it, was his excessive love of football.

"I love researching the Bible and love teaching it more than playing a game like that …" he began. Debbie interrupted.

"Charlene, tell him about last night."

At the end of my story, Earl praised me for my bold believing, and went ahead with his teaching. Afterward, Debbie tried to speak in tongues, and Earl tried to help her, but she couldn't get the hang of it. It would be weeks later before she did. But the important part of that morning was how Earl stressed our need for the PFAL class. As soon as twenty people registered, he said, it would start. We signed up. We promised to wait.

6

Warnings

For the next couple of weeks, Debbie and I hitched rides to The Way
Home where Earl taught from the PFAL class material. I imagine he was
trying to whet our appetite for Wierwille's color film class. As the believers put it, Debbie and I held fast to the Word. As our parents would
have put it, we neglected college. But they did not yet know what we
were doing. We were too busy being perfect believers to call them.

As a tax-exempt, nonprofit organization, The Way did not require
payment for its classes; recruits were asked to offer a "minimum donation"—as long as the minimum was forty-five dollars. Otherwise, you
did not qualify to take the class. (In later years, the minimum reached as
much as two hundred dollars.) After twenty people registered, a start
date would be set. Twenty, I learned, guaranteed that rather than listening to Wierwille's voice on reel-to-reel tape, we would watch the coveted
16 mm color film of him teaching at a desk. We thought that watching
and listening would be better than only listening to a recording. Eye
contact with Wierwille, even on film, sounded vital.

Recruitment flew into high gear. Debbie and I cornered resident
advisors in Cotten Hall. Although one of them came to a fellowship,

neither she nor anyone else in our dorm wanted to take the PFAL class, despite our campaigning up and down the halls. No one cared to take another course, much less one about the Bible that cost money, didn't grant college credit, and didn't yet have a start date.

Mike, an ECU football star, always sat across the aisle from me in Spanish class. Despite his obnoxious flirting—flexing his biceps like Popeye as he leaned into the aisle—I got desperate enough to witness to him. One day after class, I took the leap and asked him for a chat.

"Sure," he said. His eyes twinkled with hope.

For the sake of the Word, I endured his brushing up against me as we walked out the door. In the autumn sunlight, we paused on the sidewalk. Red and brown leaves swirled over patchy campus lawns.

"What's going on?" Mike rubbed his crew cut and squinted at me.

"Look, Mike. I've been going to a Bible fellowship that's really great. We sing, pray, and hear a teaching from the Bible. It's at The Way Home—"

"Oh no, no thanks." He backed away. The twinkle in his eyes vanished. "I know those guys at The Way. Earl played football with me, and I heard all about their Bible thing. It's phony."

"What do you mean?" I took a step back, too. "Earl is a great believer. He teaches the Word all the time. He's serious about this. He gave up football for God."

Mike snickered. "He's just a smooth talker, like that Doug friend of his. Watch out. They're not teaching *true* Christianity, just their warped idea of it." He shifted his backpack further up his shoulder. Students hurried past, giving us worried looks but not wanting to get involved. He lowered his voice. "Look, I've heard their rap. Earl told me all about that power class, whatever it's called. After he took it, he quit coming to our Fellowship of Christian Athletes meetings. That Wierwille guy who teaches it, he's a con man for sure."

Birds flew out of nearby trees. Mike's attack threw me off balance. What should I say? I knew one thing for sure: *The Devil had sent Mike to thwart me.*

I let him have it. "I know those guys, and they're teaching God's Word, not their own ideas—but if you don't think so, then forget it."

"Think for one second." He held my arm, but in a gentle way. "Those guys are repeating whatever Wierwille says. He's suckered them in. That class they sell is bad news, honey, so just remember that they might sound like they know what they're talking about, but they don't. Don't get involved with them." He let go and looked me over as if he really cared.

"You're wrong, Mike. You're so wrong. I gotta go." Who did he think he was, bad-mouthing my friends? And he'd never taken the PFAL class, so what did he know? And he shouldn't have called me honey. Well, at least I didn't argue with him; Doug doesn't argue with people, he speaks The Truth, and The Truth needs no defense. I returned to my dorm.

Not a speck of light entered my head to make me see I was closed-minded. I'd only known The Way people about a month, but that didn't stop me from defending to the teeth something I knew little about. I'd heard a few teachings, spoken in tongues, and *felt* sure about God's hand on this group. Gerald's healing miracle *appeared* to prove God moved among these people. But I knew nothing about Wierwille or his ministry. I saw only what I wanted to see. I wonder now what would have happened if I'd seen Mike as a messenger from God to protect me, not a devil to trick me. But Mike's warning, a siren from shore, failed to reach me. I had already sailed fast into the storm.

1959. Charlene, age seven in second grade, celebrates her First Communion. Photo taken in the family's backyard in Salisbury.

1965. Charlene's family at their home in Salisbury, MD. Left to right: Charlene, Marie (her sister), and their parents, Anne and Joseph Lamy.

1966. Charlene, age fourteen in eighth grade, celebrates her confirmation. Photo taken in the family's backyard.

1969. Charlene at a hotel in Ocean City, MD, attending a Young Life retreat where leaders proclaimed she became born again.

2007. Cotten Hall dormitory at East Carolina University, Greenville, NC, where Charlene lived as a freshman in the fall of 1970. In November that year, she dropped out.

2007. The Way Home on Fifth Street in Greenville, NC, where Way leaders lived and trained college students and where Charlene first took Wierwille's filmed Power for Abundant Living class.

Part 2
Revolution

7

Snow Story

Less than a month after Mike's warning, at a women's fellowship in the BRC in Greenville, Debbie and I sailed further out to sea for the Lord.

"Announcement. Announcement. I'm driving to Headquarters real soon for a women's *advance*," Pat said. "Churches call them retreats, but we don't *retreat* from anything. We *advance* in God's Word." I liked Pat, John Lynn's wife; she and John served as North Carolina's leaders for the ministry. An imposing woman, I saw her as bold, a little like Sister Margaret Mary, my fifth-grade teacher, who only had to stand, ramrod straight, to get our attention.

"So who is going with me?" Pat spread her arms like a mother gathering children.

Six hands shot in the air, including Debbie's and mine. I was Dorothy in *The Wizard of Oz,* clicking heels to transport home. Even this early in my Way experience, Headquarters felt like my spiritual center. The man of God lived there.

The advance began on Friday the thirteenth, she said, next month. "Now, now. Let's not get superstitious." She cleared her throat. "Superstitions are of the Devil. Instead of them, we believe the wonderful promises of God."

She said we'd hear fantastic Bible teachings in Ohio and meet women from around the country, young and old, who stood on the Word.

"You don't want to miss this. Dr. and Mrs. Wierwille *both* will teach. Sign up tonight."

I marveled at how much God was doing for us, and so fast. I hadn't even taken the PFAL class yet, but I would soon meet the great man who taught it.

We left on Thursday the twelfth. Pat drove our little band of "women of God," as she called us, in The Way's station wagon from Greenville to the countryside of Ohio, my first of many road trips to that remote place. Earl sat beside Pat in the front seat. He was tagging along to visit his fiancée, who was enrolled in Wierwille's two-year leadership training program, The Way Corps. From Earl's description, it sounded like a disciplined and loyal Marine Corps for God. As soon as Earl graduated from East Carolina and completed training with Pat and John—which Wierwille counted as Corps training—he'd join Nancy in Ohio and they'd graduate together. I could see myself in the Corps one day. That was what I liked about this group. They had an organized way of serving God with their classes, goals, programs, training, and most of all their love and knowledge of the Bible.

We reached Highway 29 in Ohio. It was snowing, and as we got closer to "the farm," as Pat called it, a gauzy curtain of snowflakes covered the roads and frosted the rooftops of isolated farmhouses. We passed a sign for The Village of New Knoxville and soon turned down the road that still bears the Wierwille name today. On the corner, nailed to a post, was a green-and-orange sign that read "This is The Way Biblical Research Center." I sat up and paid attention.

Fields the color of pecan shells fanned out over hundreds of acres. The old Wierwille family farm, about half a mile down the road, Pat said, covered 147 acres. From this distance, buildings and trees, getting whiter by the minute, resembled a miniature village inside one of those snow globes with a smiling Santa spinning around a tiny hamlet with his giant sack of toys. By this time, Wierwille possessed the mythical status of Santa himself, bearing the Word like a magical gift.

"Dr. Wierwille should be here this morning," Pat said, turning into The Way's driveway. I strained to listen while she played tour guide. On the left was the Biblical Research Center (BRC), now veiled in icy flurries and the pale light of November. It was an oversized ranch-style house with a big parking lot. Built in the 1960s, it was used for Sunday services taught most of the time by Dr. Wierwille. "It was a prefab home," Pat said, "and they built the addition later." It provided the model for the Greenville Way Home BRC. Wasn't it grand that our fellowship was doing its best to imitate Headquarters?

Across the driveway was a two-story brick and shingle house, the refurbished original farmhouse where Dr. Wierwille lived with his wife and the two youngest of their five children; the older ones had already married. I squinted through the crystal streaks on the station wagon window to see the house. Several trees, their dark branches gathering snow, graced the lawn. The place looked normal and cozy but it wasn't what it seemed—inside lived the great man of God. It was hallowed ground.

Pat parked in the courtyard near the house. "Praise the Lord," she said. "I'm done driving."

I pulled on my coat and scarf and climbed out over the tailgate, stepping onto icy blacktop. I looked up. Smoke curled from the Wierwille's chimney. Dim sunlight peeked through the snowfall, creating a prism of lacy light about the house. Gratitude overcame me. Within minutes, I would meet Wierwille for the first time.

As we huddled on the blacktop against the wind, I wondered whether Wierwille would venture out to greet us. He didn't. My wool coat was on the thin side. I shivered. Snow was blowing around a cluster of outbuildings in the courtyard, tossing my hair in my face, sweeping scarves into the air. Behind us was the massive white barn I'd heard about. I could see dark tiles on the gray roof that read *A. E. Wierwille 1891*. The initials, I learned later, stood for the first names of Wierwille's grandparents, Adolph and Elizabeth, who'd built the farm.

Wierwille family history, I'd find out, was held dear by The Way community. It inspired tribal pride about Wierwille's heritage that in retrospect seemed more like worship of a guru's lineage. Followers viewed Wierwille's ancestors as protected by God for the purpose of bringing forth Wierwille to found this ministry. This belief was so strong that in later years, someone organized an historical tour that bused visitors to Wierwille's former nearby homes and churches, even to the old family graveyard where tombs of his grandparents were strewn with flowers. By the reverent tone in Pat's voice, I could tell she loved this homestead and the family who built it. It was still a working farm, she said, but it had a spiritual purpose now: it was the heart of our worldwide ministry. Dr. Victor Paul Wierwille and his older brother, Harry, transformed it into The Way, using much of Harry's money. Teachings emanated from here like shining beacons all around the world. Like Pat, I was smitten by both the peaceful country charm of the place and its spiritual significance. While she talked, though, I grew antsy to flee the cold. I edged toward the front of the group and coughed.

Pat steered us toward a shed. "This is where Doctor keeps his motorcycle." She pointed to a large cage behind the motorcycle shed, saying Wierwille's German shorthaired pointers usually stayed there in the summer. The dogs, too, would become part of my new family. Beyond the cage lay a frozen pond etched with ice-skate markings. Recent ones.

We approached the shed with its weather-beaten latch door covered in cracked and peeling paint. Ajar, it let out men's rough-edged voices, coughing, laughing. Pat swung it open and stepped through.

"Hey there, y'all. Bless you," she said.

Three men dressed in overalls and baggy green wool jackets turned away from a portable heater and looked at us. Furry hats covered their ears, gray stubble peppered their cheeks. Wide smiles broke across their faces. The man wearing a red-and-black checked scarf rushed forward.

"Pat. God bless." He hugged and kissed her. The two others waited their turn. In the hubbub, the rest of us shook snow from our coats, and I inched toward the heater. Glancing around, I saw the foretold motorcycle along a side wall. Across the room, a card table and a few chairs were scattered around, a television sat in the corner, and assorted tools were arranged on worktables, more neatly than any I'd ever seen in any garage. What struck me most was how the men spoke with Pat as if she were a long-lost daughter. Given that they were in that old shed and what they were wearing, I assumed they were the farm's maintenance men.

The only photograph of Wierwille in the Greenville Way Home was a formal portrait set on the book display counter. That did not match any face before me in that shed. Pat introduced the men as V. P., Ermal, and Uncle Harry.

"Doctor Wierwille, I'm so honored to meet you," Debbie said, giving the man wearing the red-and-black scarf her biggest smile. That surprised me, but even more astonishing was when she moved forward and hugged him. Then I recalled a few times when Pat caught herself referring to the teacher of the PFAL class as V. P. He was called Doctor by everyone else. The man of God was right there! Disguised as a farm worker. I guessed I was too tired from the trip or disoriented by the situation to recognize him. As it turned out, these men *were* maintenance men. Like wizards, they operated the behind-the-scenes machinery of the ministry as the Board of Trustees: Dr. Victor Paul Wierwille, president; Ermal Owens, vice president; and Harry Wierwille, secretary-treasurer and Victor's older brother.

I shook Wierwille's hand, but my misunderstanding embarrassed me. I couldn't do anything as personal as hug him. Pat declared we'd been on the road all night, so we headed for the Wierwilles' house with

Wierwille leading the way. By this time, Pat was calling him Doctor. Over his shoulder, Doctor said we'd find Dotsie inside.

"That is Mrs. Wierwille," Pat said, as I caught up to her. We entered the back door, and in the warm kitchen Dotsie bustled at the stove, stirring something that made me realize I couldn't remember my last home-cooked meal.

Mrs. Wierwille took care of herself. Dressed in a neat skirt, blouse, and sweater, with dark hair pinned in a French twist, she set down her eyeglasses and hugged us like family. The spotless kitchen was full of homey knickknacks on the walls and a gleaming coffeepot on the counter. Stained pot holders lay by the cooktop where I imagined she spent many hours. She'd raised their children practically alone, Pat once said, because Doctor was so overworked by ministry commitments. To assist the family, the Wierwilles employed a cook, Louise, who also helped with ministry events. She was in the kitchen helping Dotsie. We stayed long enough to say hello—no meal was offered—and then were directed across the driveway to the BRC, where dinner would be served at noon in the basement to visitors, staff, and Way Corps students. Earl went to find his fiancée. I was eager to eat.

We took a well-worn path to the BRC. Pat led us down a ramp and opened a door to the basement where we hung our coats on a rack in a lounge, filed through a multipurpose room, and pushed through swinging doors to a small dining room. Something sure smelled good. Roasting chicken? Three tables were set for ten. Until the meal was ready, we waited on old sofas and chairs pushed against the walls. A television sat on top of a refrigerator marked Corps Only. An upright piano stood in the corner. Across the room, a serving window opened to the connecting kitchen where Louise, like Houdini, appeared.

Over on the couch, a young woman combed her long hair and motioned to Debbie and me to come over. Naomi Bliss said she was in the Corps with Earl's fiancée, Nancy, and some others who would arrive any minute. Naomi's hair was wet. That surprised me, but not as much as when she leaned over, as if to find something on the floor, and swished her tresses like a horse shakes his mane. While upside down like that, she brushed her hair as she told us how wonderful the women's advance would be, but all I could think about was her personal grooming being inappropriate in the dining room. When she said she'd been a hippie before taking the PFAL class, I figured that explained a lot. She wasn't being rude. She was being her liberated self. I wondered how I seemed to her. Did I appear uptight or shy? In spite of Naomi's manners, I admired her commitment to learn God's Word. She'd given up her private life for this.

"Being in the Corps is the fastest way to learn the Word and how to teach it," she said, swinging her hair over her shoulders and sitting up. "By graduation, we'll know how to serve God's people and carry this ministry to the entire world." Her enthusiasm infected me.

Lunch—they called it dinner—was plentiful: roasted potatoes, baked chicken, green beans, cornbread, salad, and coffee. Debbie and I joined Earl and Nancy, a twenty-something with eyes that sparkled in a knowing way. She inched her chair close to Earl's, her shoulder touching his. He hardly took his eyes off her the entire meal. I envied them, so in love. Watching them lavish affection on each other, I felt a pang of homesickness for Rob, my surfing Jesuit—well, not anymore. It pained me he wasn't born again the way I thought I was. Part of me regretted we'd split up, but God's will for me was elsewhere. Maybe one day I would find the sort of love I saw across the table.

Sitting there, I couldn't help but study what covered the nearby wall: an oversized airline map of the world. Flight routes crisscrossed the continents in blue lines. I soon learned the map's purpose: to mark the outreach of The Way. Black ribbons, pinned to the map, stretched from Ohio to other states, to Australia, and to England where the ministry ran the PFAL class and fellowships. Across the top, large green letters read

"The Word Over the World"—their godly vision, and now mine. Earl explained the goal: "Give a man a fish, and he can eat for a day. Teach him how to fish and he can feed himself for a lifetime." The class didn't give people a list of things to believe, he told us, it taught people how to believe to receive the more than abundant life Jesus Christ promised.

Way followers were armed to their Bible-reading eyeballs with axioms like that. It's easy now to see the catchy phrases as marketing gimmicks. Wierwille, the self-proclaimed man of God, was no country bumpkin, at least in these ways. Flashy bright lights stand out in the crowd. My young self was enthralled.

Later, Pat told Debbie and me to hop in the station wagon for a ride to a house in the nearby town of New Knoxville where we would stay for the weekend. A married couple greeted us at the door. The old renovated farmhouse, owned by The Way, seemed the kind of place farmhands had moved antiques in and out of many times—scuffs and stains marked the baseboards. Dust swirled in columns of sunshine. I climbed the narrow staircase lined with floral wallpaper that reminded me of my Nana's house in Newport.

Here, the guest room, postcard old-fashioned, had a slanted ceiling, lacy curtains, and a colorful quilt on the bed. Glass-domed lamps painted with roses provided the only light. We rested that afternoon, ate another generous meal at Headquarters—a supper with dessert of warm apple cobbler and ice cream—and joined the first meeting upstairs in the BRC auditorium at seven o'clock in the evening.

When the student is ready, all sorts of teachers appear. The trick is to figure out which one to listen to. That weekend, I met two women who influenced my Way experience in dramatic ways. In fact, what they told me wove together the rope that tethered me to The Way for the next seventeen years. The first woman was Bernita Jess. An empty seat was beside her, a providential place. I sat down. As we waited for the meeting to start, she told me about learning the ancient language of Aramaic at The Way's summer school. I'd heard about Aramaic from Earl, but I told her I didn't know much about it. I hadn't taken the PFAL class yet.

"Well, Aramaic is vital to our biblical research," she said. "It was the language in which the original manuscripts of Scripture were written." With patience and great focus, she told me that Jesus had spoken Palestinian Aramaic, a dialect. This intrigued me, but I wondered why the Catholic Church never mentioned it, nor did Young Life leaders. Didn't they realize its importance? According to Bernita, The Way was dedicated to learning Aramaic, which made sense if we wanted to decipher the accurate meaning of God's Word. What she said drew me in, but it felt strange to be in the middle of Ohio with a homemaker old enough to be my mother, discussing an esoteric ancient language.

More homemakers and other teenagers surrounded me. I was now in a cloud of perfume. Several hundred women packed the auditorium that night seeking enlightenment and Bible knowledge, just like me. Among an active spiritual sisterhood, I longed to get to know them. This wasn't a church where people attended only once a week, but a thriving family with a common cause. It did not look anything like a church—no steeple, no vaulted ceilings, and certainly no stained-glass windows. Those were symbols of religious denominational greed, I would learn from Wierwille. In spite of the utilitarian purpose of the place, it did have a churchy communion rail and a podium, organ, and piano. Otherwise, it reminded me of the Knights of Columbus hall in Salisbury, Maryland, my hometown, where we crowded in for winter Christmas parties and scrumptious summer crab feasts.

The auditorium could have been a town hall. It seated about three hundred people in folding chairs. The downstairs rooms, excluding the kitchen, accommodated about one hundred more. That weekend, the space overflowed with chattering, hugging, kissing, Bible-carrying women—a jumble of ages and wardrobes. The youngest, about sixteen, sat alongside the oldest, a woman in her seventies who taught The Way

Corps about health foods. Wearing a flowered blouse and gathered skirt, she was still spry and proclaiming the value of unprocessed foods, like those in the Garden of Eden. But the featured speaker that weekend was Mrs. Wierwille, whose navy suit, plain but well-fitting, and neat French twist enhanced her authority. In her role as presenter, she was a proud lioness surveying her territory.

"Welcome, ladies, to the international headquarters of our wonderful ministry," she said. "This is our time to focus on being great women of God." Dotsie spoke in a serene and confident manner, nodding as she expressed how honored she was that we came to Ohio to meet one another and learn about our role as godly women. If she was playing a role, she did it well. I hoped I could be as poised one day.

Some older women were from the surrounding German farm towns and had been part of Wierwille's former Ohio pastorates but now came to Sunday services at the BRC. A large group of younger women was there from the dynamic, fast-growing fellowship in Rye, New York. Others came from California's Bay Area and from Wichita and Topeka, Kansas, where the PFAL class ran continually. Mrs. Wierwille announced news from each area, remarking on how the number of graduates was multiplying. About 500 people had taken the PFAL class that year.

After the news, she conducted the kind of meeting I'd grown accustomed to in Greenville. First we sang hymns from the blue *Sing Along The Way* songbook. Then we made monetary offerings, stuffing cash into baskets shaped like horns of plenty. During the worship service, attendees were invited to pray aloud for whatever they wanted. When individuals were called on to bring forth messages from God, they stood up in a trance we called "being inspired of God" and spoke in tongues, immediately interpreting into English. Others spoke a "word of prophecy" in English, also received by inspiration. Next, the fellowship leader taught a lesson from the PFAL class materials or on a topic like love or obedience. Afterward, more songs were sung, people were healed by the laying on of hands, and the meeting ended with coffee and refreshments. Wierwille instituted this order of service for all fellowship meetings, and Mrs. Wierwille stayed true to this pattern.

That night, she introduced a longtime Way follower to teach Proverbs 31:1–31 about being a virtuous woman. Such a woman possessed trustworthiness, strength, wisdom, and faithfulness—requirements important for a wife of a godly man. "She openeth her mouth with wisdom; and in her tongue is the law of kindness." I felt inspired to try harder at developing those qualities. Finding wisdom was our ultimate goal. I thought of high school track team practice, when, on cold windy days, I wanted to quit. But the goal of being first to cross the finish line kept me going. Wisdom became my new finish line.

Later, back at the guesthouse in New Knoxville, as Debbie and I readied for bed, the woman from the next room came swishing into our doorway wearing a puffy pink bathrobe and waving a nail file like a magic wand. Her name was Winifred, she said, but we could call her Wendy. Her story, like Bernita's enthusiastic tale about Aramaic, cemented me to The Way for years to come.

Like a busy elf at Christmas, Wendy emanated radiant joy. Her round face reminded me of Tammy Faye Bakker, the famous televangelist's wife, but unlike Tammy's ever-present black mascara, Wendy's makeup was gone for the night. We introduced ourselves, and the three of us crowded on the lumpy bed. Rosy lamplight danced on the walls. I giggled like the girl I used to be at slumber parties, curious and happy, only now I beamed with the thrill of being with like-minded women of God. After some girl talk, Wendy got serious.

"You know about Doctor Wierwille's revelation, right?" she asked.

"Maybe," I said, not totally sure. Neither was Debbie.

"Tell us," Debbie said.

Wendy began. Dr. Wierwille started The Way because he parted ways with his church in rural Ohio. He thought he lacked "the power of

God" to help people in his church, despite his earnest prayers. Apparently, he had not learned what he needed in seminary. After praying about this in his office one day, he said, he heard God speak to him—*out loud*. God said He would teach him the Word like it had not been known since the first century—if he would teach it to others.[1] Doctor could hardly believe it himself, he said, but that's what happened.

"That's why we're so special, so blessed to be here," Wendy said and waited for our reaction. Debbie and I were stunned. I then remembered Earl saying something like this, and Debbie agreed, but I guessed we'd been so busy and overwhelmed that its impact eluded us until now. Hearing Wendy gave me the chills. This was real, like a miracle, like God telling Moses the Ten Commandments.

Wendy said that to be sure he'd heard correctly, Wierwille prayed with his eyes squeezed shut and asked God to give him a sign to prove He made that promise. Sure enough, when Wierwille opened his eyes, his gaze fell on the window across the room in his office, and even though it was a sunny day, he saw snow so thick he could not see the pumps at the gas station across the street.[2]

Debbie and I were dumbstruck. Earl hadn't told us about the snow. From then on, I would call that claim of revelation "the snow story."

Wendy added a final touch. After that episode, Wierwille said he threw out all his theology books and studied nothing but the Bible.

For me and thousands of Way followers—including many who to this day follow Wierwille's teachings—that story established Wierwille as God's man, right up there with the Apostle Paul, the man of God for *his* times, according to Wierwille. Our man of God's unique revelation story, like Gerald's healing, sounded like a story from the Book of Acts, but taking place in modern times. I didn't even consider doubting it. I did not think it false, or ridiculous, or a lie to rope people into The Way. My vulnerability made room for the power of the claim. God talked to people in the Bible, why wouldn't He do so now? Without resistance, the snow story became the community belief that held us together the way the Christmas story binds other Christians. Without it, at least for me, Wierwille would have been another preacher among thousands. Wierwille's claim that God would teach him was not a vague one. It was Wierwille's piercing hook. On it, we hung our hearts. On it, we thrust our belief that Wierwille was God's man.

"Welcome, all you *bee-u-tee-full* women of God," Dr. Wierwille called as he strode to the podium. It was Saturday night of the women's advance, and his wife had just introduced him. Dressed in a striped suit, his hair slicked back, our man of God did not resemble the man in the motorcycle shed. Three hundred women stood up and applauded, overflowing with love and admiration. He invited us to take our seats and open our Bibles, his authority and energy emanating like rays of blinding sun.

"Ladies, God has entrusted us with spreading the accuracy of His Word around the world," he said, his smile flashing like a camera. "We must bring God's truth to every lost person looking for answers. By God's grace and mercy, we can do it."

His voice mesmerized me. Its cadence lifted me into a dream state that led me to belief. Bouquets of yellow flowers, gracing either side of the podium, beautified our teacher's presence. His steady confidence drew me to him like a fish on a line. I watched in awe as he pounded his Bible while reading verses. At the end, as he called us to dedicate our lives to the work of God, he also warned us. "Satan loves it when people turn away from God's matchless Word. We must stand together in this ministry that God has given us, manifesting the love of Christ, and speaking the Word. That's how we'll defeat the adversary. Remember, you are the apple of God's eye. Stand, and having done all—stand."

We rose to our feet, cheering and laughing and praising the Lord. I didn't worry about Satan. I bathed in comfort and bliss, enthralled, unable to concentrate on anything but Wierwille. He waved good night as invigorating organ music filled the room, enhancing the emotional crescendo of his words and fostering an atmosphere of commitment.

Debbie and I found the other ECU girls at the back of the room, and we rehashed the evening. Pat joined us and led us to the back door. Since we'd arrived, I'd seen she was close to the Wierwilles, imagining it was because she was a Way leader's wife. Wierwille himself appointed Pat and John as The Way's overseers of the North Carolina fellowships. Because of that relationship, those of us from Greenville were going to visit the Wierwilles at their house that night. I felt honored but I worried. Would I measure up as a strong believer? Would the man of God discern how little I knew about the Word? Would I say something stupid?

We stepped outside and buttoned our coats under stars covering a silky dark sky. The generous snow-covered lawns sparkled from lights on the roof. Streetlamps sent beams up the driveway. As we shuffled along like pilgrims to the Wierwilles' kitchen door, my heart pounded in anticipation. Inside, the aroma of fresh popcorn engulfed us as we left our snowy boots in the entryway. The Wierwilles greeted us like proxy parents trying to be real and relaxed; they had changed into casual clothes.

We settled down with cups of cocoa in sofas and chairs in their family room. Bowls of popcorn were passed around. Debbie and I were on a couch near Dr. Wierwille's upholstered chair. I listened to the animated conversation between Pat and the Wierwilles about the day's events and news of the Greenville fellowship. Doctor lit a cigarette (this startled me) and asked about John. When did he plan to run the next class? How were the students who lived in The Way Home? A television murmured, the volume set low, but it didn't seem to bother anyone. To hide my jitters, I hugged a pillow to my chest. Soon I finished my snack and noticed the conversation was still engaging everyone except Wierwille, who rested quietly in his chair and emptied a glass of what looked like 7Up on ice. I studied his face, the mole above his lip, his thick chin and large ears, his graying hair. His posture seemed perfect even sitting down, making him appear in charge of the room. Even wearing work clothes in the motorcycle shed, he was the rooster in the barnyard.

I was hoping for the slim chance of talking with him about the recent turn of events that changed my life. I took a risk. "Doctor, may I please talk with you for a few minutes?"

Looking a little surprised but agreeable, he said sure, snuffed out his cigarette, and led me from the family room down a hallway. I followed him into his office where he motioned to a wingback chair opposite his desk. Behind it, open draperies turned the plate-glass windows into a mirror. I saw us. Family photos were lined up like toy soldiers on a low credenza beneath the windows. The man of God swiveled in his leather chair as I pondered how to begin.

"Now tell me ... what's on your heart tonight, honey?" He tilted his head to the side.

Undivided attention flustered me, but I told myself never to forget this.

"I just wanted to thank you for teaching God's Word and tell you that I believe God has brought me to this ministry." I ignored my sweaty hands. What did I have to fear?

Wierwille's office manner differed from his dynamic podium persona. Here, he was more somber. He waved his hand for me to continue. I couldn't help but notice his Holy Spirit ring flashing in the lamplight. I'd seen those rings on sale in the bookstore and hoped to buy the women's version when I saved up. His left hand bore a gold wedding band.

"Doctor, I've been looking for answers, for Bible knowledge. Even though I haven't taken your class yet, I'm signed up for it and after hearing you teach tonight, I'm even more excited than ever to take it. This ministry is so great. I hope I can do my best to help spread the Word. The believers at ECU have been wonderful, teaching me a lot of the Word already. I'm so happy about all this and wanted to tell you myself."

He soaked it all in, nodding his head. I must have seemed hyper—I was—throwing this over-the-top enthusiasm at him, ignoring his tiredness. But there it was: my heart set out on a little cushion. Now I could relax.

Wierwille leaned back in his chair and ran a hand through his silvery hair. "Well, that's wonderful, honey," he said, looking pleased. "The Lord certainly has blessed us." He nodded in a thoughtful way, making me want to say more.

"Yes, sir. I just want to be the best woman of God I can be. I hope to marry a man of God and be a great wife, too." One night after a potluck dinner while I dried the dishes, Earl told me I would make a man of God a great wife someday, like Nancy would be for him. I'd taken that as prophecy.

"That's the most beautiful (he pronounced it *bee-u-tee-full*) thing any woman can say. You know, when I met you in the shed, I knew something had hit you like a ton of bricks." His hand slapped the desk.

"I guess God's Word has hit me."

"Right. We'll keep walking on the Word, then, won't we?" He slapped the desk again and stood up.

I would speak with Wierwille alone about a half dozen more times while associated with The Way. Either he would summon me to his office, or I would ask for advice at crucial moments, and feeling as if no other choices existed, I would follow what he told me. As I left his office that night, he gestured to the door standing ajar, assuring me I could talk with him anytime. I left the room ahead of him and joined the others watching late-night news on television. It was a minute or two before eleven o'clock.

Back on the sofa, I listened to the monotone of a newscaster. Then a different commentator appeared on the screen, his face a grim mask.

"We're sorry to interrupt the regular broadcast," he said, "but I'm here to report the following breaking news." His voice trembled. The papers in his hand were shaking.

"At 7:35 p.m. this evening the airplane carrying Marshall University's football team, the Thundering Herd, crashed."

It had flown from the airport in Kinston, North Carolina, and headed to the Huntington-Tri-State/Milton Airport in Ceredo, West Virginia. Everyone on board—players, staff, airline personnel, guests, and coaches of the Marshall team—was killed.[3]

We gasped, fixed in place like mannequins. I remember shuddering in shock, but after that, I don't recall what anyone else did or said for some time. The team that Marshall played that afternoon was ours, the ECU Pirates. We'd played in our stadium. At least one of our Way believers competed in the game. The newscaster relayed that despite the go-ahead, poor visibility caused the plane to crash into a hill where it burst into flames.

Doctor left his chair and turned off the television. I saw his face. It was unchanged from minutes before we heard the awful news. Perhaps he understood things in a spiritual way that I did not. He asked us to stand up and pray together. In a circle, we bowed our heads and joined hands. He asked God to comfort friends and relatives of the people who died, and the Greenville fellowship.

"Nothing the adversary can throw at us, not even this tragedy, can stop the Word from moving on the East Carolina campus. This is an outright attack against moving the Word at ECU."

He frightened me. *An attack on us?*

Overawed by his reputation, and inexperienced with his type, I did not recognize Wierwille's self-serving attitude as narcissism. Self-centeredness in the extreme, narcissism infuses the afflicted with an overestimation of their importance and abilities and an inordinate interest in their own problems. Our leader's abnormal and abhorrent interpretation of a tragedy like Marshall's, I'm ashamed to say, would become normal to me the longer I remained involved, the more cult-centered I became. Following Wierwille meant we believed that whatever evil occurred "out in the world" was directly tied to our Way world. Our so-called man of God was skilled, and became more so as years went on, at swaying our perceptions to match his. One of the best things about humans is also the worst—the ability to adapt to almost anything, even hurtful religious beliefs and actions.

Wierwille finished praying. I felt far away from everyone, even Debbie. We all seemed to withdraw into the protective shells of our own hearts. I imagined the Way guys in Greenville dragging around the house in a daze, shattered. I wanted to call them.

Voices began murmuring. Wierwille turned the television back on and more news spewed from the set, but I felt like I was outside, looking in through the windows. I asked Mrs. Wierwille's permission to use the telephone. Of course, she said, and led me to a table-top phone in the kitchen. I knew the telephone number since I'd called it so often.

"Hello?" a male answered—the coffeehouse guitar player.

"Hi, this is Charlene. We're at Doctor's house. Just heard the awful news. You okay?"

"Terrible." He sounded stuffy, like he had a cold. "Everybody is in shock."

I tried to be comforting but I felt lost. I assured him of our prayers and returned to the living room, where Wierwille was reminding the group that the Word was still the Word, and the born-again people on that flight would be raised from the dead when Christ returned to gather his believers and take them to heaven. Any minute Christ could return. The Second Coming could be tonight, for all we knew. That was supposed to give us hope, but that night it made those deaths seem like they didn't matter. Forget what might happen in the future with Christ, what about now? And what about the people who died but were *not* born again? What would happen to them? Young Life never talked about that, at least that I remembered. Catholics believed in a just God and said He'd take care of things like that. Wierwille's explanation of

Christ's return for the believers sounded haughty. Maybe I didn't understand what he meant, but I knew how I felt: horribly sad. The families of the dead suffered. I knew how grief-stricken I would be.

Wierwille, I knew, taught that feelings were not reliable barometers of truth. For truth, we could only count on the Word of God. It would take years for me to understand what he left out of that argument: that the Word is not so stable, either. It is subject to people's *interpretations.*

Chatter ebbed into whispers. Someone muttered, "The Devil's fighting this ministry. Tonight is proof." I cringed but felt compelled to accept that as true because if I didn't, the group would consider me a doubter and cast me out. The knowledge I assumed that every grad of the PFAL class possessed made them superior. So I succumbed to the pressure of groupthink dominating the room that night, clung to Wendy's snow story, and continued with the belief that God Himself directed the highly charged incidents leading up to my arrival at the women's advance. I rationalized Wierwille's cold comments about the dead as mysteries I could not understand until I took the PFAL class. My moments with Wierwille in his office secured a psychological knot, making it feel impossible to second-guess anything he said.

The next day we drove away from Headquarters with Pat at the wheel and the rest of us reflecting on the weekend. I might have looked like me, but I was not the same person returning to Greenville as the one who had left.

8

Revelation of My Own

My college history professor handed each of us, about twenty freshmen, a page of final exam questions and a blue book to write our answers in. I tackled the first question, but then, out of nowhere, a sharp twinge shot through my body like a flaming arrow. The course had covered tragic world events like World War II. The exam made me think about the pervasive evil throughout history, century after century, and I saw no end to it. The magnitude of darkness headed toward me like wildfire. I reeled in panic and fled to the haven of my obsession—the Bible. History made it obvious that the adversary, the Devil, was the god of this world. The Bible told us he was. The power of God in Christ *in me* was the only antidote, not political solutions. Terrible images flew from the storehouse of my imagination fueled by history and Wierwille's teachings: swords, killings, beheadings, Antichrists in black robes, and lies on every lip. I laid my pen on the desk.

The hellish scenes in my mind soon fell to embers. From the turbid ash rose other scenes of extraordinary events in my brand-new Way life: Gerald the football player's miraculous healing, my speaking in tongues in the dorm, my telling Dr. Wierwille in person that God brought me to The Way, my new desire to join The Way Corps. I grabbed the desk.

When I tried to refocus on the test, the questions swarmed like a school of minnows turning left and right. I blinked hard. I heard no voices, human or angelic. I smelled nothing but my own sweat. My classmates faded like blurred edges of a photograph. The lines in the test booklet beckoned me to write about the Word, so I did. I picked up my pen. It seemed to flow on its own across the paper, like automatic writing, condemning evil and praising the light of God to conquer it. My last sentence was Dr. Wierwille's fevered phrase: "It's the Word, the Word, and nothing but the Word." I stopped, exhausted, and closed the booklet.

I realized one thing. To serve God, as I believed I should, I must drop out of college right then, and commit myself full-time to The Way. That's what God had just told me; I was convinced He did. I must go and fight evil. I must. Relief spread over me, and I relaxed for the first time since I'd returned from the advance in Ohio. I must go back there. Dr. Wierwille received his revelation from God in 1942 when only twenty-six years old. Although I was only eighteen, I knew mine came to me that day. I collected my books and my purse, tossed my unfinished exam on the professor's desk, and walked out of that classroom to embrace a new life for God.

I returned to Cotten Hall and tapped on Debbie's door. She was inside studying, wrapped in a sweat suit, decked out with curlers in her hair.

"Charlene, what happened? Look at you. You're all red and blotchy."

We huddled on her bed, and I recounted what happened during my exam. The curlers moved like antennae as she tilted her head this way and that, absorbing my story. When I finished by announcing my decision to leave college to work full-time with the ministry, she stood up. "I'm going with you."

"Oh no, you're not."

"Yes, I am," she said, with the calm of a movie director anticipating the next scene.

"Debbie, listen to me." I pulled her back on the bed but she hopped up and paced the room. Her reflection in the full-length mirror patrolled back and forth with her. Her brows knit in scheming determination.

"You can't do that, Debbie. This is my decision. This revelation isn't for both of us. It's only for me." I had no idea what God wanted her to do, and I told her that. The last thing I wanted was to bear responsibility for her dropping out of college. Her parents would hate me. We spent at least an hour talking this out, but Debbie would not back down.

"It's meant to be," she said, and reminded me of something she'd told me more than once: the main reason her parents sent her to college was to find a husband, not get a degree.

I gave up, but not before making sure she understood that if her parents got upset, it wasn't my fault. Finally, exhausted, I left for my room.

November winds stirred leaves into twirling eruptions on the commons, and while watching them from my window, I speculated over what else the whirlwind of my decision might stir up. I felt as if a giant shell had broken open, and I'd stepped into another dimension, one sanctioned by God that other people would have to accept whether they liked it or not. I wasn't in a hurry to tell my family, or anyone else, not yet. I needed time to absorb the change myself.

The next day a resident advisor came to my room. My history professor had called, she said, and asked for me to report to his classroom immediately.

The history classroom smelled of chalk. Its color-coded world map, pulled all the way down, hid the blackboard. I greeted my teacher and sat in a front-row desk. He handed me my blue book and asked me to read what he'd written at the end of it: "Metaphysics is not acceptable as an answer."

I didn't try to explain myself. He would never understand me. Besides, I didn't know what metaphysics meant.

"You're a good student, Charlene," he said, with kindness I did not expect. "Tell you what. I'll give you another chance to take this exam."

"No thank you." For a second I felt bad. I realized he was trying to give me a break. But The Way's doctrines were strong, and they told me he was only a "sense-knowledge" man, unacquainted with the things of God—and God, I had no doubt, directed me to leave college.

"I don't need to retake it," I said. "I'm dropping out."

"Oh … I see." He shuffled papers on his desk. He asked me to reconsider. He waited and waited. When I shook my head, he asked whether I might make an appointment with someone in the college's counseling center. I could not grasp those words. What was he saying? Did he think I was crazy?

I lied and said I'd think about it.

That evening Doug drove Debbie and me to The Way Home for fellowship. As the car rolled down the familiar road, I debated whether or not to tell Doug my news. Debbie nudged me, but I hesitated. My professor's concern bothered me more than I thought it would. It was hard to shake off that he'd told me to see a counselor, so to ward off doubt, I plunged into telling Doug the story. He listened, steering the car with a steady hand, until he heard the part about my professor asking me to go to ECU's counseling center.

"You don't need any shrink," he hollered, pounding the steering wheel. "All you need is the Word. You're a child of God." His eyes flashed in the rearview mirror. "You're not crazy." He was disgusted in the way my father used to be by idiotic politicians.

I watched the trees whiz by. Doug's reaction, although supportive, disappointed me. He didn't think I was nuts, but he wasn't rooting for me, either. I was dropping out of college to work for God. Wasn't that worth shouting for joy over?

I sought out Earl to see what he'd say. Debbie came with me. Earl leaned forward in a chair next to me at the back of the BRC, and when I'd finished with my news, said, "I'm really happy that you—both of you—want to live for the Lord, but you should talk to John, our leader. He likes to counsel people before they make bold moves like this." Then he relayed the official word from Headquarters: God needed leaders in The Way who understood the world so they could influence it. College-educated leaders were best. A degree made you more credible. After college, we could reach businesspeople and politicians and influence them to make godly decisions. Earl's lack of enthusiasm for my great leap into God's work irked me, but out of respect, Debbie and I made an appointment with John.

We met John in his Way Home office. He was an ordained Way clergyman known for being "one of us." When we entered, he was leaning back in his chair with his feet propped on the desk. Dressed in a T-shirt, shorts, and tennis shoes, he explained he had a basketball game with the guys in the backyard after our talk. I started my story. He crinkled his brow now and then. When I finished, he lowered his feet to the floor.

"Right," he said, not smiling. "That is ex-act-ly what I heard from Earl." That habit of enunciating words to the extreme was standard John. Then he repeated the policy about staying in college to be a more effective leader for God. He said he sure hoped I wasn't telling my family that The Way put the idea of dropping out into my head. I assured him I was not. I realized he didn't want parents mad at him for their kids' rash decisions. I thanked him for the talk, but I left the office as suspicious of him as he probably was of me. He headed for his basketball game, and Debbie and I returned to the dorm more convinced of following God's plan.

Debbie reinforced my resolve. By this time, our influence on each other, perhaps on a subconscious level, entwined our decisions, making separation unthinkable. We were clueless about how our dream of working full-time with the ministry would play out in our daily lives, but that didn't matter. The Way, we knew, offered no jobs for us in Greenville or anywhere else, but that didn't matter, either. We quoted the verse about the lilies of the field having no worries. God took care of them; He'd certainly take care of us. After we took the PFAL class in December, we planned to set our sights on getting into The Way Corps. God would work out the details. Until the Corps started the next September, we would behave like first-century believers—praying, fellowshipping, and evangelizing. News of our dropping out spread like a virus around the fellowship. Before we went home for Thanksgiving, Betsey, a young teacher who had also taken Pat Lynn's road trip to the women's advance, offered us a rent-free room in her apartment. We could move in after Thanksgiving break. Naturally, we took this as a sure sign we were doing God's will. I found a ride to Salisbury with another student and geared up to speak to my father with the certainty my revelation inspired.

9

In My Father's House

I wasn't planning to tell anyone else, not even my family, about my history-exam revelation from God. Like my history professor, they might say I needed counseling. Instead, I would use Scripture, not my story, as authority for my new plan. We rode up Route 13 from Greenville to Salisbury, and with each mile I prayed harder for guidance, flipping through my new purse-sized Bible to find the right verse:

> "He that loveth father or mother more than me is not worthy of me" (Matthew 10:37). Perfect.

I went home to Druid Hill Avenue believing God was on my side.

Salisbury, the bull's-eye on the Delmarva Peninsula, lies between the mighty Atlantic Ocean and the crab-filled Chesapeake Bay. I grew up during the '50s and '60s when the town's population was about 15,000, half what it is today. Surrounded by unpolluted beaches, seafood restaurants abounded. The small town was home to many Roman Catholic families like mine. My parents paid for my eight years of Catholic school education at Saint Francis de Sales before the cold-water plunge into public school where "the other" outnumbered me. I learned to swim fast. Before long I wore the ID bracelet of a Jewish boyfriend, had several Episcopalian and Presbyterian friends, and had an English teacher, my favorite, who, I surmised, was an atheist. I branched out into extracurricular activities, trading Catholic May processions for homecoming dances and ballet slippers for running shoes. I joined the first women's track team at my high school and competed on the uneven bars for the gymnastics team. My awareness of the wider world grew as I watched the Huntley-Brinkley Report on our black-and-white television. In 1968, I was sixteen when televised footage of a grotesque and bloody war in Southeast Asia sickened me along with the rest of America.

That year, I felt pummeled by shocking, unpredictable, violence. In April, the assassination of Dr. Martin Luther King, Jr. In June, Robert F. Kennedy. Month after month, thousands of young men killed in Vietnam. Uncertainty about the future, a new sensation, left me disoriented. By November, a battle at home brought the worst unforeseen devastation of all: my mother's fight against ovarian cancer.

She lost.

When I was in tenth grade, most likely I was the only one in our family who did not realize the seriousness of Mom's illness. Dad avoided the topic. His severe introversion, coupled with his analytical training as a microbiologist, made him hesitant and ineffective in interpersonal relationships. He did not discuss feelings. When Mom fell sick, he left it up to her to tell me her status. Mom must have told me that she was growing sicker, that treatments were failing, but her words did not sink in. I was young. Everyone was immortal. My sister, Marie, seven years my senior, busy with her husband and first child at their home in Florida, was not available to advise me.

It's shocking how fast that kind of cancer spreads. But I did not imagine imminent death, despite the swollen abdomen that made my

75

mother look pregnant. She'd always bounced back whenever she'd gotten sick before, though I couldn't help but notice that she didn't go out in public much, not even to church. But did I comprehend she would die? No.

The summer before she passed, our small family received a gift of time thanks to Mom's love of the ocean: a peaceful week together at Rehoboth Beach, which enlivened Mom and fueled my assumption that she would recover. She spent some time alone with me while Dad escaped into paperbacks. One afternoon, she said, "Let's go for a walk."

I may have sensed on some murky level that her life was slipping away even as we stood barefoot in the warm sand, in the clear gentle waves. The tide was going out, and the heat of the day eased under a pink and lavender sky. Rhythmic undertow pulled against our ankles, sinking us deeper in the soft, darkening sand. Driftwood floated by. She told me a story.

For years before I came along, Mom said, she'd thought my sister would be an only child. She tried to have another baby but grew discouraged, thinking her time was up. She kept praying anyway. Seven years after my sister's birth, she conceived again when she was thirty-two, full of joy, she said, that God answered her prayer. "You were a special baby," she told me, her voice carrying a depth I'd never heard before that made me feel awkward and strange. We waded farther into the sea, letting it roll over our legs. She held her denim skirt out of reach of the water while I listened to her repeat how much she loved me. Perhaps she was saying good-bye then. I try to pull more of her words from the banks of my memory, but they've drifted off. The sea rolls in with a hiss, and I mourn.

Three months later she was dead.

She died the day before Thanksgiving. In her hospital room, my grandmother guided me to a plastic chair next to Mom's bed, took off my coat, and helped me sit down. One of my aunts patted my back. My father stood near the window, relieved, I think now, that the women were taking over. He'd been aloof with me for months.

She'd given birth to me in this hospital.

"Mom?" She didn't hear me, didn't move. The bleached sheets over her thin body were all that seemed real as I slouched in the chair not knowing what to do. I couldn't cry but thought I should. Lifting my head to look at the others was impossible. I studied my mother's waxen face for the slightest movement but saw none. Her eyelashes didn't even flutter. A tube from her mouth disappeared somewhere in a tangle of wires by the bed. I felt small and cold.

"Mom?"

My mother's doctor was not Catholic. My family, however, *was* Catholic with a capital C, and over the next few days they stayed true to their faith's view of death, telling me that Mom spent a good life serving God, and now she no longer suffered. Their intended comfort turned sour, however, when they added that God decided it was time for her to be with Him in heaven. This was not news. I'd heard this same idea when my father's mother died, but now was different. Now it was applied to my own mother. It repulsed me.

When we got home from the hospital, I ran upstairs to my room and threw myself on the bed, wailing, "Why God? You're supposed to love me, and you take my mother to heaven? Don't you know I need her?" A god who took mothers from teenage girls was no god for me.

For eons, people have agonized over the problem of death and evil in the world. If there is indeed a God of love, why does He allow bad things to happen? I feared a God that did this. What might He do next? Anything. The ground of certainty I counted on—that God loved me and would never hurt me—had opened like a gorge, and I was in free fall.

At Mom's funeral, I couldn't stop crying until we arrived home and I curled into her Boston rocker in a corner of the living room. Mom's youngest brother, Uncle Bob, said, "Here, dear, try this." He handed me a cup of something warm he called Irish coffee. He stood guard while I sipped the drink, hid my feelings from him, and blamed God for making me a motherless child.

Sometimes I think that if someone in my family had looked at me while I sat in that rocker and explained that, yes, it was terrible my mother had died of cancer but I could endure this sadness, I might have fared better. Or if someone had unhitched the wagonload of Catholic metaphysics attached to the inevitability of death, it might have helped. Perhaps if the physician had explained the medical reasons for her death, he might have eclipsed the influence of my family's theology. Perhaps if grief counselors had stepped forward, I might not have ripped the God of our Catholic tradition out of my life like an abusive father's image from a photograph. But no one sought a counselor, no doctor intervened, and no one disputed the Church. No one was able or willing to disentangle God beliefs from death. My family assumed I believed along with them. But they were wrong. Comfort was religion's duty to provide, and it failed me.

My mother's death sent me on a quest—on a subconscious level at first—for truth about death, life, God, eternity, and other great mysteries of our existence. At sixteen I was without a mother and a God, but vacuums do not remain vacuums. A year later something happened that makes me think I must not have dismissed the God of my Judeo-Christian tradition after all.

A new high school friend, Judy, came along with "Jesus answers." My vulnerability to her fellowship, Young Life, came from teenage heartache over losing my quarterback boyfriend and angst over my father's strict rules, but I suspect in largest measure it came from buried grief over Mom's death. I did not mourn her fully. I did not know how. I rushed back to regular life at school and kept a stiff upper lip, as my dad would say. But that trauma wounded me, and no distraction helped. Soon I tired of my father's increasing suspicion of every boy I liked, every party I went to, every penny I spent. I needed love. I needed support. Cheerful Judy came along with an easy crutch for the emotional cripple I was. With Young Life, she unwittingly led me back to the God of my childhood.

I returned home from college for the Thanksgiving holiday, grieving for my dead mother and facing my angry father, a widower of only two years. At the front door, he greeted me with a coldness I deserved after the hurried life-altering phone call I'd made from the dorm to tell him I was dropping out of college for God. In his eyes I saw a canyon of grief.

I climbed the stairs and set my things in my old room, absorbing the sight of my hand-painted antique bed. The curtains Mom made, with the purple-and-orange paisley design, still hung at the windows. Most things were where I'd left them before going off to college only three months earlier. The bulletin board nailed to the closet door displayed my drawings from high school. Knickknacks were covered in dust. I felt like a stranger in this room, as if I were looking through the wrong end of a telescope.

The feeling of being a foreigner continued when Dad and I met in the living room. On the coffee table in front of the couch where I sat, I placed my new King James Bible, smelling of leather and gleaming with gold-leafed pages, and some Way materials. Dad stayed across the room in his black vinyl armchair, a floor lamp shining over his shoulder. He looked worn and crumpled in his white shirt after another workday at the state's public health laboratory near the hospital. He was a respected microbiologist and the lab's chief scientist. I'd always admired him for helping people stay healthy. My mother would remind me, as I left the house with friends, to behave, because I represented my father. That made me feel proud, but also pressured, fearing my mother's wrath if I screwed up.

Dad wanted me to account for myself. I summarized my story, hoping my Catholic father would show even splinter-sized interest as I sprinkled my speech with Wierwille's phrases, like "the Word of God fits together with a mathematical exactness and scientific precision." I thought Dad, a scientist, would relate to "scientific precision," but applying that term to the Bible made no sense to him. He pursed his lips in that skeptical way of his. He didn't respond, so I launched another speech about manifesting the power of God, saying that speaking in tongues was one of nine ways to manifest God's power. The Catholic Church didn't teach anything about that, so I read verses from the New Testament to prove it. Still Dad did not respond. He watched me as if I were on television.

I opened Wierwille's book *Receiving the Holy Spirit Today*, and praised the research Wierwille said he did, hoping Dad would be impressed.

"Uh huh," he said, and removed his glasses to rub his eyes.

"Dad, I'm going to take the Bible class I wrote you about. It starts when I get back." He wasn't fazed. He was as rigid as the lamp pole next to him and just as uncommunicative. "And I want to work for The Way. I know you're not happy about my dropping out of college, but I have to do this."

Our black-and-white cat, Monique, sauntered into the room and settled in an elegant pose by Dad's pant leg. Now two sets of eyes stared at me. Oblivious to how self-consumed I was, I fidgeted with the silky black ribbon hanging from the bottom of my Bible.

"One more thing. I'm going to apply for The Way's summer school—"

"Oh no."

"But Dad, they've got real classes like Greek, Aramaic, and Keys to Researching the Bible. It's an actual school." I held up the book about the Holy Spirit. "It's a biblical research ministry, not a bunch of Jesus freaks running around like brainwashed robots." Somewhere I'd heard that awful label. "And I want to get into The Way Corps too, Dad. It's Doctor Wierwille's leadership training. It takes two years."

I omitted facts I knew we'd fight over: my history-exam revelation, my professor's recommendation I see a counselor, and my nonexistent plans for supporting myself while doing this work for God. Worst of all, I was blind to how I'd hurt my father. I imagine he thought me cavalier toward my college education, one he was paying for.

Now I see that Dad was at a terrible disadvantage. Evangelical Christianity and fundamentalism were foreign countries to my Catholic father. Also, at the time, there were few avenues for getting information about Wierwille. My father lacked evidence to convince me not to join, like that Wierwille manipulated Scripture and propagated what I later understood as bibliolatry—worship of a book, the Bible. Much later, I would learn from Rob, my surfing Jesuit boyfriend, that a few newspapers had published stories of parents complaining about Wierwille's control over their kids.

Dad's silence was a suffocating blanket, but his final pronouncement was worse: "Charlene, you're crazy."

He may as well have kicked me.

"This is all plain crazy," he said. He got up and quickly climbed the stairs, Monique bounding after him. I heard his bedroom door shut and that is when I cried.

Neither of us understood the impact on me of losing my mother. The trauma was as real as a gunshot wound and needed emergency surgery, but Dad had not known about the first-aid Young Life rendered. He knew I went to fellowships, but not that the teachings had sent me on a quest for Bible truth to heal me. Perhaps if I had shared my inner life with him, my jump onto Wierwille's speeding bandwagon might not have shocked him so much. But I had concealed my transformation, fearing Dad would have kept me from going to Protestant—with a capital P—Young Life meetings. Without divulging my born-again experience, I attended Mass and kept the true nature of those peppy non-Catholic fellowships with Judy a secret.

It occurs to me now that if my father could have considered my Catholic school indoctrination, he may have understood my radical behavior was a possible outcome for someone who took literally the Catholic dictate to know, love, and serve God in this world. If I hadn't already been accepted by ECU, I might have even taken advice Young Life leaders gave me to spend a few months in Switzerland at a place called L'Abri Fellowship—a Christian learning center run by Francis and Edith Schaeffer. There, I might have gained hope and enlightenment, but timing, circumstance, fate, S.A.T. scores, and Dad's money got me to ECU instead and ushered me into The Way. Now my father was so frustrated, all he could do was shut down and leave me on the sofa, reeling in the echo of "You're crazy."

How could I get through the rest of this visit? I ached for my mother, I cried for her. She would have understood this spiritual talk, I was sure. I longed to share it with someone who loved me.

On Thanksgiving Day my father and I ate turkey dinner with my mother's best friend, Theresa Knapp, and her family. The Knapps were as sweet as ever, but they were distant and jittery. I imagined Dad told them the reckless stuff I was doing. They kept up a superficial chatter about mutual friends, either confused over what to say to me or not wanting to get involved. For most of the meal, Dad did not look in my direction.

I was desperate for real Christian fellowship. To cheer myself, I telephoned a few Christian friends, who mentioned a coffeehouse at the Episcopal Church. Hoping I might run into born-again Christians I knew from high school, I asked Dad to borrow his car, and I drove alone to the church intent on witnessing for the Lord and telling anyone I could about The Way. The coffeehouse was in the basement of the old stone church downtown and far less welcoming than our Greenville coffeehouse. I smelled no incense. I heard few laughs. Orange lights put a glow on the walls. In a corner, a guy with a ponytail played his guitar and sang a Bob Dylan song. I sat at an empty table and looked around. There were no lounge pillows or free donuts, but a refreshment table against one wall, with a donation jar beside a punch bowl, looked inviting. A garish poster read Jesus Saves. About a dozen people were scattered about, smoking, drinking coffee, and tapping their feet to the music. After a few minutes I saw a familiar face. Janice. Her dark hair and ivory skin were unmistakable. The way she leaned sideways in her chair, as if something weighed down one side of her body, was also familiar. We'd attended Catholic school together. I saw her sit like that for eight years.

"Hi, Janice. Remember me? Charlene. From Saint Francis." I stood next to her table, holding the smile on my face as best as I could. She sized up my long hair and bell-bottoms; then she recognized me.

"Charlene. Gosh, come and sit with me." After general catch-up, I asked about fellowships around town and how she felt about the Lord. Without giving details, she said she was born again but still went to Catholic Church. *Ah ha. An open door.* I began my Way witnessing attempt, trying to guess what she might need to hear, and remembering what the believers at The Way Home said: everybody needs healing. To get her excited, I told her about the collarbone miracle at our coffeehouse in Greenville. She set down her drink.

"Charlene, I'll tell you this now. I am epileptic. That's how God made me. I'm supposed to be like this. You sure have funny ideas about healing people." She picked up her drink, and I sat in a flood of embarrassment. What could I say to that? I'd forgotten The Way's number one lesson about witnessing: don't assume anything. Ask people what they want from God, and then assure them they can have it. *Never* guess. Janice's problem was unknown to me all those years, which in itself was disconcerting. I apologized and tried to explain that God could still heal her if she wanted Him to. No sickness or health problem was too great for Him. But she shook her head. "I'm not sad about it. I have to suffer to please God."

"Janice, where did you get that idea?" That was rude, I knew, but her belief was as bad as the idea that God took my mother. By this time, I'd learned from Earl that the Catholic Church was wrong about that. He showed me the verse that proved it:

Forasmuch then as the children are partakers of flesh and blood, he [Christ] also himself likewise took part of the same; that through death he might destroy him that had the power of death, that is, the devil; (Heb. 2:14)

How plain could it be? I don't know if I was more relieved about God not having anything to do with my mother dying, or disgusted at my family for believing the Church's terrible lie.

At the time, that verse brought me endless comfort, even though it is a simplistic view written by someone long ago; scholars who study New Testament authorship can't say with certainty who even wrote it. But believing that the Devil, not God, killed my mother removed complexity from the situation. I did not consider what it cost me to believe it. That would come later.

Janice said, "I gotta tell you that I believe God made me like this for a reason." Her certainty that God would do this was as strong as my certainty He would not. Our conversation made me wonder whether I'd ever recruit anyone, convince anyone to give up crazy ideas like hers. Discouraged, I said good night and went to look for the minister Janice said ran the coffeehouse. The place was noisy and crowded by this time, but I snaked around the room and found him at the refreshment table. He was tall, with a trimmed beard and thick, dark-rimmed glasses that looked too heavy for his face. I introduced myself and got right to it.

"I wonder, have you ever heard of The Way ministry?"

"No, don't think I have," he said, pushing his glasses up on his nose. "Tell me about it." He poured himself a cup of punch.

"It's a Bible group. They've got a class you might like." I gave him the rundown, emphasizing biblical research.

"The Way teaches how to get back to the original Word of God," I said. I was doing it again, assuming I knew what my recruit wanted to hear. He peered at me as if studying a strange fish in an aquarium.

"That's interesting," he said, not sounding sincere.

"Yeah, I can't wait to take the class. I'm all signed up and—"

"It seems like a worthy goal," he said, "but I should tell you something. It's an impossible task, getting back to the original texts."

"Why?"

"Original texts were lost a long time ago. No one can ever know what they said word for word, but we can get close, and that's okay." He searched my face for a reaction, but I was lost. "We can still enjoy the Bible for its inspiration and moral teachings. We still have copies, you know, and—"

"I heard originals were lost, but can't we—"

"We can study lots of texts, yes, but keep in mind that they aren't literally God's Word, as you call it. Different men wrote Scripture in different languages over many eras." He gave me a weak smile. "And they wrote more texts that weren't included in the Bibles we have today. You know that, right?"

I'm sure he couldn't miss the shock on my face.

My Thanksgiving break was a pit of despair. My last hope was Dave, soon to arrive from Baltimore. Maybe he would listen. Our time at Young Life camp had been so sweet, it had even motivated him to visit me for East Carolina's Homecoming weekend. That was about a week before I met Doug and Norman from The Way.

When I greeted Dave at my father's front door, he said I looked better than ever. My father, when he shook hands with Dave, frowned at both of us. I imagined that having given up on me, he didn't much care about my boyfriends. He left the house to do errands.

I retrieved snacks and iced tea from the kitchen while Dave leafed through Way materials still on the coffee table. We sipped tea while I told him about the fellowship in Greenville. He listened quietly. He showed special interest in Wierwille's book about the Holy Spirit, so I bragged about my unique teacher, how he could "rightly divide the Word," and teach how Scripture fit together as a hand fits in a glove.

"What does that mean?"

"It means Scripture doesn't have contradictions since God is perfect, and He's the author of the Bible. We just think we see contradictions sometimes. They're not really there. You have to take Dr. Wierwille's class to understand all this." I gave him my biggest smile and then announced my plan to leave college and enter The Way Corps.

"That's big news, Charlene," he said, reaching for his tea glass. "But I'm astounded. Don't you want to finish college first? Don't you think you should? You could wait, you know." He set his glass down, avoiding my eyes. "Isn't that what those guys you met are doing? Why not wait like them?"

I didn't want to explain. My revelation from God was why not, but I didn't want to tell him about it. I feared he wouldn't believe me. And there was no way to prove it.

"I don't want to wait that long. I want what the Corps offers as soon as I can get into it."

"But aren't you jumping into this awfully fast—"

"Oh stop it, just stop it. You and Dad and everyone else says the same thing," I snapped. "Why can't you just respect what I want to do?"

"Hey, living for Christ doesn't mean you have to give up your college education—"

"It does for me."

"Hey, try and calm down. I'm just worried you think this group knows everything about the Bible. It takes a long time to learn what you say this guy teaches in only two weeks. Do you—"

"Take it yourself and find out."

"I can't right now. I'm busy with college and Young Life stuff."

"Fine." Believers warned me this might happen during vacation. Everyone I'd talked to so far was trying to keep me from The Way, even Dave, a born-again Christian I thought would understand. "Since you're not interested, then what do we do? This is my whole life now, Dave, can't you see? Everything I do is for The Way from here on out. Can you deal with that?"

We sat in silence a few minutes.

"Charlene, I liked you at camp, but you've changed. What can I say? You've made such big deal out of taking this class that I don't know how to relate to you."

"Yeah, well, the Word is all that matters to me. I thought you believed that too."

"I guess we have to live our lives the way we think best." He folded his arms across his chest. "I'm sorry to say this, but maybe I should bow out now. Is that what you want?"

"We'll have to see—"

The back door opened, and Dad rumbled around in the kitchen, signaling he was home.

Dave was so close I could smell his musky aftershave. He reached for my hand.

"Can't we give this some time?"

"I don't know." I was tense; I couldn't think. It struck me that it was wrong for us to fight over the things of God since we were both born-again Christians, but the self-righteous young woman I'd become was determined to stand up for the Word and what God wanted me to do.

I thought maybe I should forget about a romantic relationship with Dave, as sad as that might be, since, according to The Way, first and foremost believers must be like-minded on the Word; then romance could develop. Not the other way around.

"Maybe I'd better go," Dave said. "I've got a long trip home, and it's getting late. The highway will be jammed. Write me when you can, okay?" He leaned over and kissed my cheek.

I said I would, but I sensed he'd lost interest. Maybe he'd change his mind later, but I wasn't sure I could wait. We hugged at the door, and he left.

I looked around the room where I'd spent so many Thanksgivings, Christmases, birthdays, and, of course, Mom's wake. The bookcase held books I remembered from childhood. The rust-colored carpet was spotted from spilled drinks, and a faint path was worn across it from the stairs to the dining room. On the staircase wall, familiar drawings of songbirds in carved wooden frames ascended out of sight into the upstairs hallway. Every piece of furniture was in the same place it had been the day my mother died.

I had to get out of there.

Dave and I were through, I knew it, and I felt dejected and righteous at the same time. He was a spiritual, kind person who drove all that way to see me, but his beliefs didn't match mine. I'd done my job of making the PFAL class available, and if he didn't want it, then he was missing out. Any possibility that I might have been the person missing out, that I could rethink my decision and gain some perspective, was out of the question. Although Dave and I exchanged a few more letters, I never saw him again.

Dad marveled when Dave left early, but I didn't explain. I rushed upstairs and cleaned out my room. My upbringing instilled the good value of eliminating badness from my life, but that day I was crazed. Before The Way, I didn't think objects could be evil and unacceptable to

God. I did now. I yanked open dresser drawers and storage boxes, throwing into the trash can remnants from my "old man days"—jargon for our pre-Way lives. We rid ourselves of worldly possessions to symbolize our rejection of our former identities like moths breaking free of their chrysalides. I found a cardboard box and trashed Beatles records, T-shirts bearing my high school's name, glow-in-the-dark statues of the Virgin Mary, rosary beads, holy cards, prayer books, and school photographs. I tore up letters from my grandparents, pen pals, and cousins, and post-card mementos from summer vacations in Canada and Indiana. I shredded stories and poems I'd written and bagged up clothes for the Salvation Army—all to obey Saint Paul's command:

> …ye have put off the old man with his deeds; And have put on the new man, which is renewed in the knowledge after the image of him that created him: (Col. 3:9–10)

I now see that whatever talents we expressed pre-Way, like my art and poetry, were to be funneled into the service of Way propaganda, not enjoyed as my individual expression. Today I mourn what I did that afternoon—destroying keepsakes that testified to my early years on the planet. I wish I still had them.

That I was so sure my behavior was godly work is a testament to the power of religious belief. I left a trail of tears, not joy or understanding, not anything anyone in their right mind could be proud of. I alienated my father, upset an already suffering epileptic, estranged a kind boyfriend, and, without realizing it, hurt myself by ignoring what the Episcopalian minister was driving at—that Wierwille's claim of getting back to the original Word was impossible and unnecessary to having a spiritual life. The Bible needed to be accepted for what it was, not for what I wanted it to be. On account of this Bible mania instigated by Wierwille, the Thanksgiving message was lost to me that year. When my father mustered a good-bye from the front steps the morning I left to return to Greenville, I hoped I'd never have to return to his house again. I wanted only to take the PFAL class immediately.

Iconic welcome sign on the corner of Wierwille Road and State Highway 29, New Knoxville, Ohio.

Driveway entrance to The Way from Wierwille Road. Right: The President's Home, where Wierwille met with Way Corps in the basement Fireplace Room, and where Charlene took Aramaic classes with Bernita Jess.

Victor Paul Wierwille, founder of The Way International, posing at the podium in the Biblical Research Center auditorium at Way Headquarters, New Knoxville, Ohio.

Part 3
Addiction

10

The Class

The PFAL class would be the best Christmas present of my life. Debbie and I settled into Betsey's apartment, spruced up with greenery and red ribbons and bayberry candles alight on windowsills sweetening the air. Instead of worrying over things like sleeping on stained mattresses covered with sheets and blankets left over from college dorms, I ignored my self-induced poverty, terrible Thanksgiving, and grief over my mother to focus on what came next—taking the PFAL class and finding a job.

Part-time jobs, like Christmas trees, were popping up everywhere. I prayed to get one, doing what Earl told us: behaving as if I'd already received it, which was how to "claim what God promised." One of my favorite promises was: "Therefore I [Jesus] say unto you, What things soever ye desire, when ye pray, believe that ye receive *them*, and ye shall have *them*" (Mark 11:24). Wierwille called this concept *the law of believing*, making it sound as real as the law of gravity—when you drop something, it falls; when you claim a promise from God, you get it. If you don't, somewhere along the line you let doubt, worry, or fear overcome you. Wierwille would often say fear was sand in the machinery of life.

Soon a manager hired me to wrap Christmas gifts at a department store downtown. The only drawbacks were low pay and a smothering older coworker who reeked of perfume. I made the mistake of confiding in her about leaving college for The Way against my father's wishes, stupidly giving her the chance to voice worry after worry over my future. When I got my first paycheck, a cold you-are-scraping-by feeling flowed over me along with her worries, but I was thankful to have a job, any job.

On the first Sunday of that December, Debbie and I entered the familiar BRC behind The Way Home for the first session of the PFAL class. Exuberant believers hugged me as if I'd returned from a foreign country. Coffee simmered in an aluminum pot on the book display counter like it did for coffeehouses. Earl, organizing the PFAL class as part of his leadership training, sported a welcoming smile along with a new suit. He introduced us to grads of the PFAL class I'd never met before. Evidently, they were excited to see the film version produced in Ohio three years earlier. Debbie and I found our assigned seats in the front row—praise the Lord, the best seats in the house. Soon Earl stood like a master of ceremonies in front of a portable movie screen and laid down some rules. First, be on time and refrain from talking during the sessions. The next two were not so easy: no note-taking and no questions until the two-week class ended. The syllabus, he said, contained all the notes we needed, and as for questions, well, Doctor reworked the material for many years prior to filming it and incorporated answers to all relevant questions into this filmed version. Each session was built on the previous one, like a multistory house, so if we missed a session, we must listen to the tape before we could attend the next one. Rules were rules. I couldn't imagine missing a session, but worried I'd forget things without jotting them down. Oh well. No notes. No questions. Margins narrowed inch by inch.

Earl straightened his tie, the film rolled in the projector, lights dimmed, and a mirage appeared on the screen—Wierwille in a studio camouflaged as an office, wearing a dark suit and holding an open Bible.

I was so close I could see his eyelashes. He locked his focus on the camera, and I opened my heart.

"The first and most basic key for power for abundant living is that *the Bible is the revealed Word and will of God*,"[1] He spoke with practiced articulation. If we believed what he taught, we could receive power from God that would make our lives not just abundant, but *more* than abundant. As proof, he quoted John 10:10 in which Jesus said, "I am come that they might have life, and that they might have *it* more abundantly." If we didn't believe that, we'd forfeit God's blessings and allow the Devil to ruin us.

What I especially loved were the biblical research methods. They addressed a serious problem. It was common knowledge to Bible scholars, Wierwille said, that the Good Book was strewn with contradictions and riddled with copyists' errors. Over the centuries, translations were made from the ancient Hebrew and Greek texts of Scripture, and mistakes crept in. But Wierwille's research would reveal the original, non-contradictory, error-free Scriptures that God authored. For me, the snow story provided the only credential our teacher needed: God had promised that He would teach him the Word like it had not been known since the first century, if he would teach it to others. Doctor *had* to teach for God to fulfill that vow, and lucky me, I was blessed to be his student.

Our man of God would also teach us how to heal our broken lives. After all, the name of the class was Power for Abundant Living, not Power for Abundant Biblical Research. To fix ourselves, Wierwille insisted, we must overcome fear by trusting God, loving Him first and foremost, and treasuring the Word above everything else in our lives. He also said the only way to know God and His son, Jesus Christ, was through God's Word, the Bible. Wierwille cited Scripture verses to make these points. I felt certain that this class would put me on the road to a lifetime of researching the Bible *and* living abundantly. As long as I stayed faithful, I could not go wrong.

On the screen, an amber glass light fixture dangled from a chain near an easel that held charts printed with teaching points. With staged execution, our leader pointed a rubber-tipped rod at the charts when needed. On the shiny desk a vase held a red rosebud. A framed picture of Jesus—long brown hair, white skin—hung above a padded love seat where Wierwille, to avoid monotony, sometimes posed instead of sitting at his desk. This setting, tattooed on my memory, occupied my field of vision for thirty-six hours during two weeks as Wierwille filled me with his lessons, his eyes drilling into mine, his voice ringing through my days and nights and into all the years I was in the group. Like the lamp at the end of that chain, I hung on his words and lost myself.

What I did not see on that screen was a fundamentalist. I did not yet know what fundamentalism meant. Nor did I see a cult leader. I saw an informed, dedicated, and confident scholar. Even if I had wanted to turn away, it seemed impossible for me to shift my gaze. I was completely absorbed, unlike a few students who didn't show up for the second session. Rumors spread that they'd accused Wierwille of making up doctrines. The naysayers argued that life was more complicated than he described. Earl told them not to return.

I didn't argue at all. My hunger tethered me to every session. Just as Mrs. Jess had told me at the woman's advance, Wierwille referred to Aramaic words when he believed they were more accurate than the Greek text from which the King James Version was translated. Aramaic cast a spell that held me tight for years. It became the focus of my work at The Way.

At the last session, Wierwille led us through the steps of speaking in tongues. Students who had never done it before were initiated that night. A few were frustrated, so a graduate took them aside to help them. After that, Wierwille ended the class with a few admonitions. He directed us to put away all other reading material for three months and study only the PFAL class content, just as Doug described the night I met him. Wierwille also invited us to write him with questions—we should address the envelope to "The Teacher." He encouraged us to believe the Word no matter who challenged us, and to attend fellowships with like-minded believers. As motivation for us to spread the Word, he quoted Jesus's words from the Gospel of Matthew—"Go ye therefore and teach all nations ..." My heart swelled with determination.

When the film ended, Earl said we could retake the PFAL class for free anytime, anywhere. That was part of the deal.

"Ask God's help with understanding the material if you didn't grasp it all this first time around," he said.

I would do a lot of that. As I walked out the door, I peeled off the psychological label of novice and, in my heart, pledged my allegiance to The Way.

The weather turned crisp, cold, and overcast. I bought a new pair of gloves at the department store where I worked and continued wrapping gifts until I left for the holiday to visit my sister, Marie, and her family in Charlotte, about a four-hour drive from Greenville. Marie wrote to say Dad planned to drive down from Salisbury, so we would have a good old-fashioned family Christmas. I doubted that. Thanksgiving had turned into a nightmare that still continued, but I felt duty-bound to go and try to show Dad I loved him. When the time came, I hugged my Way friends good-bye, especially Debbie and Betsey, and hitched a ride with a college student going to Charlotte. By the time my brother-in-law met my ride at a gas station to pick me up, I was tired from traveling but more exhausted from Wierwille's rapid-fire lectures. They spun in my mind like the Tilt-A-Whirl at the end of the boardwalk in Ocean City. While I rode with George to their house, I told him I'd just taken a fantastic Bible class, but he didn't inquire, only nodded politely and talked about their dog's new litter of puppies and how big my little niece was getting. I arrived on their doorstep as a bedazzled Way graduate overstuffed with information. Dad and I didn't say much. Marie was cheerful but did not pry into my business. Witnessing to my sister would have been futile because I knew she still clung to the Catholic faith of our youth. Besides, I figured Dad must have told her his version of my recent radical behavior, and I didn't want to hassle with her over that. I kept my distance while she bustled about and cooked a festive dinner. We opened a few gifts, and I returned to Greenville in the same condition as when I'd left—caught in Wierwille's whirl of words.

Years later, my sister and I talked about that weird Christmas. She said I'd looked spaced out, and she'd feared I was taking drugs. She was sort of right. We often said we were high—high on the love of Christ and in awe of the Word of God. She said I seemed out of focus like a blurry photograph.

Sadly, no one in my family sat me down to talk about my plans, or hopes, or feelings. I was so jammed full of Way rhetoric that it would have been impossible to talk about anything personal like boyfriends or my dreams for the future. Only the Word mattered.

Back in Greenville, I repacked my suitcase, this time for another trip to Headquarters with Debbie. We'd heard about a New Year's youth advance designed for our generation. I could hardly wait to put hundreds of miles between me and my family.

11

No Defense

"God bless you," they said, hugging us like long-lost cousins. The Way Corps members we'd met in November greeted us at the back of the BRC. Some girls from Rye, New York, we'd met at the women's advance were already inside. Soon a crowd of about two hundred youths filled the room and waited for Wierwille.

"God bless and welcome to The Way," he shouted. He'd emerged from a side door that I knew led to a back room where he prepared for teachings. We clapped with happy abandon, releasing a river of excitement. If religion is the opiate of the masses, as Karl Marx wrote, then we were high on Christ's love at The Way. In bell-bottoms and sweaters, we sat cross-legged on the floor, clutching our Bibles, soaring at Wierwille's every word. Negative vibes from Christmas fell away from me, and I opened like a flower to assurances that only gurus like Wierwille can give.

"Tonight we're making history, kids," he thundered. "This is our first youth advance, your time to make a stand for the truth. Aren't you beautiful? You just shine like lights in the darkness of unbelief in our country and around the world."

Wierwille adopted his oratory style from old-time preachers. If he mastered anything, it was the ability to create the illusion that we had a unique mission.

After he blessed us in the name of Jesus Christ and repeated how *bee-u-tee-full* we were, pointing here and there around the room like a master of ceremonies, he barked out names of the cities we came from: Mill Valley and Alameda, California; Greenville, North Carolina; Wichita and Topeka, Kansas; and cities in Ohio, Illinois, Indiana, and Michigan. A busload of "saints" from New York, he said, was caught in a snowstorm. "Saints" was the Apostle Paul's name for his followers, and Wierwille revered Paul. While we waited for the Rye saints, Wierwille led rousing songs and invited people to share how the Word was spreading in their areas and report the number of people taking the PFAL class. The room buzzed with praises to the Lord for what He was doing in hearts and lives.

Before long, we heard a commotion in the hall and Wierwille stopped the meeting. A man bundled in a fur coat pushed through the swinging doors that led to the side entrance, shaking snow all over the place. "Bless you," he said. "And here come the rest of the New York saints." He sounded like an announcer. (I heard later that he worked as a radio disc jockey.) This must be Steve Heefner, overseer of The Way East[1], a group of fellowships in and around Rye. Behind him, cherry-cheeked students and hippie types came in, bringing cold air and loud blessings with them, smelling of cigarette smoke, patchouli oil, and wet wool coats. No matter. In my eyes they were famous, effective at winning over others, and I could see why. They hugged everyone in sight; their affection was indiscriminate. I felt a pang of jealousy. I knew that being an introvert was a disadvantage I must somehow overcome.

The saints streamed past me into the auditorium in a colorful blur. Winter coats came tumbling off. One guy took off a long coat, although first I saw his wide-brimmed hat.

Under it, his hair hung to his shoulders. He wore suede pants with fringe along the seams like Tonto's in the *Lone Ranger*, only these pants were turquoise. Maybe he's in costume for a play, I thought. Wierwille encouraged performances of Bible stories. Tonto smiled at me, then headed to the front of the room, toting a canvas satchel and a black guitar case. It wasn't long before Wierwille invited Tonto to sing a few songs he said he'd written himself. He performed with intensity, as if every note was a knock on heaven's door. After Wierwille finished teaching, since Tonto sat not far from me, we ended up introducing ourselves. He told me he was Ed (not his real name) from Rye, and his dad, a minister, allowed Way fellowships in his church. I told Ed I loved his music.

Debbie and I bunked that weekend in a trailer across the driveway from the BRC, but I didn't see much of her. Naomi, the Corps girl who had combed her hair in the dining room, was getting very friendly with Debbie, and I felt left out. Naomi was engaged to one of Wierwille's favorite young trainees, Johnny Townsend, and in my eyes that made Naomi a star. (They eventually became statewide leaders, also known as Limb leaders, of New York, and later California, and in 1986 Johnny joined the Board of Trustees.)[1] I never learned how this invitation came about, but Naomi said Wierwille selected Debbie and me to travel with him and some Way Corps members to Huntington, West Virginia, after the youth advance was over, to open up the area to the Word, with a focus on college campuses there.

"Isn't this great?" Debbie gushed, throwing her arms around me. "I can hardly believe Doctor wants us to go."

I couldn't believe it either, and I said so. "Debbie, I'm nervous. You know it's hard for me to witness to strangers."

"Don't be silly, Charlene. How can we refuse? It's an honor to be with Doctor. And we'll learn from watching the Corps in action."

I couldn't say no. This was what we'd dropped out of college to do. So we called Betsey, our landlord in Greenville, to say we'd return in a week or two. I repacked my pink suitcase while Debbie filled me in on what Naomi had told her. A Huntington believer was arranging great things, like a television interview and a couple of radio shows for Naomi and Doctor. Evidently, conducting this Huntington expedition was guidance from God. How could it be anything else?

We left Headquarters in several ministry-owned vehicles, including Wierwille's small camper he used for hunting trips. Our group included Howard Allen (Wierwille's right-hand man), Naomi, a few other Corps members, Debbie and me, and a leader from Kansas named Donnie Fugit, known for his witnessing talent and sensational guitar music. Wierwille often featured Donnie, a former druggie, to teach Bible accounts of people getting saved. He was a natural evangelist and drew people in with his emotional lyrics.

I soon figured out why Wierwille was keen on Huntington. The man who arranged the media publicity was a respected physician and a graduate of the PFAL class. He was convinced he found The Truth from Wierwille and flaunted his testimony in public. When I met the man—tall with a West Virginia twang—I imagined Wierwille loved his disarming boldness. He wasn't a hippie or a young student, but a professional that adults would take seriously. He was a walking billboard for The Way.

Over the years I watched Wierwille invite adults like that doctor to speak at meetings and coordinate events to lend The Way credibility. He was particularly solicitous of those involved in government. Loyal adults also served as solid financial supporters, perfectly respectable ambassadors for a growing nonprofit cult.

We checked into a musty old hotel in downtown Huntington. We girls shared a large room with extra fold-up beds moved in. It was dorm living all over again. For about a week we drove around to college campuses, especially targeting Marshall University, whose football team had died in the airplane crash only a couple of months earlier. People were still in mourning, vulnerable, perfect targets for the hope we promised. News stories of the heartbreaking incident still circulated. With our visit, Wierwille said, we brought spiritual healing to the students and faculty. God wanted us there for that reason.

With logic like that, I didn't question. It never occurred to me that we might be vultures, preying on people's vulnerability, selling them an easy solution to their pain. "Take this Bible class and you'll find peace of mind." Considering it now, I'm ashamed I thought this was acceptable behavior; I was infatuated with Wierwille's confidence, his claims that God was telling him what to do, his convenient spiritual justifications. Objections were out of the question.

Not only did we witness to strangers, but also close quarters at the hotel created chances for us to witness to each other. We called that "giving reproof and correction." It was supposed to encourage us to get back in fellowship with God when we were not acting in accordance with the Word, like being impatient, unkind, or negative. A brother or sister in Christ would let us know about our being off the Word so we could repent. We assumed we should accept any godly reproof. If we didn't, then we'd be even further out of fellowship, losing God's blessings. One morning, I circled the oversized coffee urn in the dining room, impatient for it to finish perking. Donnie, the Kansas evangelist, approached me, pushing his long hair back over his ears with one hand and holding a cigarette in the other.

"How ya doin' this mornin'?" he said, leaning against a nearby table.

I liked Donnie for his bold teachings but not his personal hygiene. He reeked of cigarette smoke. His shirt was flecked with stains.

I rarely spoke before 8:00 a.m.

"A watched pot never boils so speak in tongues, sweetie," he said, "and you'll simmer down." He lifted his chin and blew smoke off to the side. It drifted toward me anyway.

I nodded, mad about the smoke *and* the admonishment. Donnie's intentions were good, I told myself, but he was not helping. I wanted to ask him when he was going to quit smoking, but I chickened out because Wierwille, our example in all things, also smoked—he carried a pack of Kools everywhere he went.

Wierwille entered the breakfast area and asked us to sit in a circle of chairs for our morning session, a daily believers' meeting when we'd pray to meet people seeking The Truth. Donnie gave us a witnessing tip for the day: if a person's questions are difficult or accusatory, don't get defensive.

"The Truth needs no defense," Donnie said. "Sit and wait them out. Turn the tables and answer a question with a question. That usually puts doubters in their place."

With an attitude like that, I'm sure we came across as arrogant. Sometimes, not always, we were more concerned with one-upmanship than a desire to enlighten.

The week ended with our belief that the television and radio interviews were successful, and that we'd made inroads for the PFAL class to run in Huntington. Debbie and I convinced one high school student, who came to fellowships off and on, to take the class, and he wrote the donation check while we stood there and watched. I felt better about my outreach ability then, but my other attempts to communicate excitement to strangers on those campuses failed. I could be bold with family and friends, but stage fright overcame me when I opened my mouth in public. Breaking the ice felt forced and artificial, and over the years those feelings would grow. I couldn't change my introversion, and I couldn't alleviate my guilt over it. I knew the Bible verses that required us to preach Christ to others, and not being able to do that with ease was my secret sin.

Right before we left Huntington, an unexpected chance came my way. In the hotel's conference room, Doctor held an open meeting for the people we had contacted in town and at the colleges. To my surprise, he announced that the PFAL class would run at Headquarters beginning the following week (a class in Huntington did not materialize).

Anyone who wanted to make the trip to Ohio was invited to sign up. Way Corps members would conduct the sessions, he said, which would give them a chance to practice their leadership skills. Debbie, sitting a few rows in front of me, turned around to catch my eye. I knew that look, it said *Why not?* God had opened yet another door, and we'd be fools not to walk through it. That night Debbie approached Wierwille to ask permission, and we pooled our scant cash to pay seventy dollars each for room and board to retake the PFAL class at beloved Headquarters. Howard Allen offered us jobs manning the Snack Shoppe on Sundays and during class breaks to earn pocket money. For housing, Wierwille gave us his blessing to live in Trailer Six with the Corps women: Naomi, Nancy, and another young woman from the West coast. They had an extra bunk. We were in.

12

It Is Written

One afternoon I was alone in Trailer Six. Another winter storm blew over the farm, howling through cracks around the aluminum doors. Wrapped in a heavy sweater, I eyed The Way Corps application on the table in front of me—a combination of Peace Corps entrance questions and secretarial qualifications. I printed my name at the top, deliberate as Faust and just as convinced this transaction would bring me knowledge and power.

Anyone familiar with me then would have thought I'd already handed myself over. But that afternoon, like a prostrate novitiate, I bowed to Wierwille, hoping he'd consider me worthy to be a spiritual Green Beret, what he called his "Corps kids." I expected my witnessing trip to Huntington would count in my favor, along with my retaking the PFAL class. Besides, the Corps girls could vouch for me, having observed my obedience to Wierwille's command to put aside other books and magazines to study only the PFAL class materials. Even in my dreams, I saw Dr. Wierwille teach the Word.

The Way Corps motto was *It is written*, a phrase Jesus often said before he quoted Scripture. Every move Corps members made and every word they spoke was supposed to be in accordance with the written

Word of God, just like Christ. I yearned for that too.

I read the first application question: "What do you anticipate accomplishing by serving with The Way Corps?"

I wrote, "I anticipate being part of the honor and miracle of teaching His [God's] Word around the world."

Mimicking propaganda was such a habit that I'd forgotten how to speak for myself.

I listed my practical skills, like sewing and typing, and folded the paper into an envelope addressed to Dr. Wierwille.

Afterward, I covered my own stationery pages with slogan-filled letters to my father, sister, high school friends, and cousins. The wind blew harder around the trailer park. I paced the room a while before deciding on a long-overdue note to Rob, my former Jesuit surfer boyfriend. It was time I told him about The Way. I kept my letter short and stuck an eight-cent stamp on the envelope. Unlike some cult leaders who demand their followers abandon relatives and friends, Wierwille encouraged us to keep in touch with them. By our love we might win them. I sent my correspondence and waited.

13

Mantras and Marriage

Debbie and I were barred from Wierwille's private Way Corps teachings, but I soaked up every moment of the PFAL class, and hung around the Corps members, hoping they'd drop words of wisdom into my heart.

Earl's fiancée, Nancy, was my assigned Corps overseer. I liked her. She sensed my seriousness; she was serious, too. Her sincerity and discipline invited respect. Most days I worked alongside her, dusting and pushing a Hoover over the BRC auditorium's red carpet each morning and dressing up to attend the PFAL class in there at night.

One day on our coffee break, she gave a stunning directive I would never forget. She was dreaming of her wedding, another year away. She noted that fiancées, just like married women, had a duty to bring out the best in their men. When married, they'd raise children to continue the ministry, their grandchildren would carry it to their generation, and on and on. She could hardly wait to marry Earl. I yearned to meet my own future husband. That topic interested me, but it was what she said next that meant more. When we flicked off our vacuums for the day, she leaned over and said, "Remember this, Charlene. No matter what happens while you're in the Corps, just stay. Stay even if you don't understand what's going on. Doctor knows what he's doing. You'll be blessed."

She wound the vacuum cord around the handle and turned away.

Her words—"no matter what happens"—should have scared me to death or at least provoked me to ask for details. But I was not frightened, only intrigued, and did not think of challenging her. She was Corps.

I imagine now that her counsel may have been prompted by the failure of some Corps members the previous year. Wierwille dismissed them, called them the Zero Corps, and now he put pressure on Nancy's group to succeed.

Wierwille was always watching, like George Orwell's Big Brother.

As we left the BRC, Nancy tightened the screw. "You've made a commitment to God, Charlene. Don't break it."

"Just stay" became my mantra.

The PFAL class ended and I packed my suitcases again for a bus ride back to Greenville with Debbie. By then she'd also applied for the Corps. Until we were accepted (or not), we planned to serve in the East Carolina fellowship, get jobs in town, and stay at Betsey's apartment. But the best-laid plans did what they often do. Before we left Headquarters, we talked to a believer named Hunter. Hunter wore wrinkled shirts too big for his narrow shoulders, but despite his slipshod appearance, he was organized enough to run the Toledo fellowship. We met him when he'd attended some class sessions and Sunday night teachings while we were at Headquarters.

"Hey, you two, I heard you are really on fire for the Word. You went with Doctor to Huntington, right?" Hunter's eyes looked bloodshot.

I felt uncomfortable about being singled out. It seemed that Debbie and I were gaining a reputation for freelance witnessing.

"Our fellowship could use some help," he said, peering into Debbie's face. He was tall, but no taller than Debbie. "We've got some people ready to take the PFAL class. Only need a few more. Think you could drive up to Toledo and witness with us for a while?"

I stood still and asked God to guide us.

"I don't think so," Debbie said. "Tomorrow we're taking the bus to Greenville."

"You could ride to Toledo with me tonight," Hunter said. "My car is right outside."

When he added that a girl in the fellowship was offering us a room in her apartment and that hungry people waited for the PFAL class in Toledo just like everywhere else, I thought we should try to help. Wasn't this another open door? Hunter thought our mission should take about a week; he was optimistic. Debbie gave me that look. The three of us got in the car.

14

Blindsided in Toledo

Debbie and I spent the next week in the Student Union at the University of Toledo, walking up to students and reciting attention-getters we'd heard used by the Corps, like, "Did you know you have more power in you than Niagara Falls?" That got people's attention but not the kind I wanted. Some laughed as if I were a fool and said, "You're nuts." We did not win a single person. If I became adept at any skill during that time, it was the act of hiding my shame at failing. I'd let down Hunter, disappointed God, and often felt stupid. We believed "God has no hands but our hands" to spread the Word, but my hands seemed empty.

Debbie called Wierwille a couple of times to report our progress. He tracked our whereabouts to ensure we stayed on the outreach trail, but we were broke and running out of time to win anyone. We should have gone back to Greenville, but commitment kept us in Toledo and compelled us not to complain about washing our clothes in the bathtub and living on sandwiches, popcorn, and soup provided by local fellowship members. We were all grads of the PFAL class, and, right or wrong, that made us a family and family members help each other. Not once did I consider this freeloading or running away from my personal life. This ministry *was* my personal life.

Late one night, one of the guys in the fellowship telephoned and asked to come to the apartment where Debbie and I were staying.

"I've got some bad news. Gotta tell you in person."

We knew him well enough. He'd gone witnessing with us and visited Headquarters many times. Debbie brewed some coffee and we prepared ourselves for … we didn't know what. Within minutes he knocked on the door, and as always, when I saw him he reminded me of Eric Clapton with his long face and ragged beard. We all sat around in the living room.

"I hate to squeal," Clapton said, "but you should know something … Hunter's smoking pot again. With his old buddies."

Oh no. I was shocked, and Debbie, by the look on her face, was surprised, too. Pot was supposed to be a pre-Way habit. The Bible took its place. Hunter, of all people, as the fellowship leader, shouldn't be doing that. Clapton stared at the floor, not admitting he might be one of those buddies.

"He's dealing, too," he added.

Smoking pot was a definite no-no but dealing was ten times worse. God's Word was supposed to heal people from their drug trips, sex trips, and any other trips besides God trips. Those were Wierwille's *exact* words.

Pot wasn't all. Clapton also alleged that Hunter skimmed off the monetary donations he was supposed to mail to Headquarters. This made him a pothead *and* a thief! How could he do this? Wierwille described believers like Hunter, who turned away after being faithful, by quoting Proverbs 26:11: "As a dog returneth to his vomit, *so* a fool returneth to his folly." Hunter, once a good leader, now was a fool.

Eric left without any of us figuring out what to do. When the door closed behind him, Debbie rushed to the telephone.

"Doctor should know about this," she said. "He'll tell us what to do." Debbie's assurance in calling Doctor amazed me. She acted more confident around him than I did.

"Debbie, isn't it too late to call?" It was past eleven o'clock at night. "Why bother Doctor? Can't we talk to Hunter and try to straighten him out ourselves?"

"No way. Now, be still, will you, while I do this?" She frowned and pursed her lips. I knew the phone was ringing on the other end.

I can still see my friend by the window holding the heavy black receiver, waiting to hear Doctor's voice. Ever since Huntington, I'd sensed he liked her more than me, so if we *were* supposed to call him, I was glad she did it.

She greeted Wierwille and blurted out what happened. Across the room on the couch, I pulled a soft blanket up to my neck and watched her. Even from there I could hear Wierwille shouting.

"Yes, sir," she said and hung up the phone.

"What'd he say?" I clutched the blanket, watching her fall into a chair by the window.

"He said we've let him down." She heaved with sobs. "We failed. Spiritually."

"*We* failed? What are you talking about? Hunter—"

"We screwed up, Charlene." She sprang out of the chair and paced around the room, pulling the curtains shut.

"But *we* didn't do anything wrong. Hunter did."

"We're supposed to be on top of things, remember?" she snapped, wiping away tears. "Doctor trained us himself." Now *she* was shouting. "We're supposed to take charge spiritually. But we didn't see what was going on right under our noses. God was telling us, but we didn't listen."

Really?

"Remember, when we walk into a room we have to claim it in the name of Jesus Christ." Then devilish influences like pot would flee because the devil spirits behind them would see that the power of God was at our disposal. "If we'd been spiritually sharp," she said, "we would have heard God tell us about Hunter."

"I guess so …" I said, not wanting to argue. Debbie's words sounded reasonable, but were we actually in charge of Hunter?

"If we were truly Corps material, we would have known about Hunter smoking weed. Looks like we're not." She covered her face with her hands and cried harder.

Not Corps material? Wasn't that why we were running around witnessing here? To help people and prove we were Corps material? I clutched the blanket harder. Debbie straightened up.

"Doctor told me to go get that set of PFAL tapes Hunter has at his house. Pronto." She grabbed the phone again. "We have to bring them back to Doctor." She added, "He said if we think he'll ever allow us into the Corps, we'd better get those tapes, clear out of here, and drive back to Headquarters. Tomorrow. That's an order."

Panic seized me. What if he didn't let us into the Corps? What would I do? Where would I go? This was a storm out of nowhere.

We left for Hunter's house, Debbie behind the wheel of our borrowed car. I trembled next to her, trying to pray for Hunter but fearing for my own future in a way I could not have imagined only an hour earlier. I wrapped my scarf around my neck, shivering, selfishly focused on myself and not on how we might help Hunter. I didn't stop to think that Wierwille's main concern was his class tapes. So much for helping people.

We pulled into Hunter's driveway, and from the car, huddled in my coat, I watched Debbie on the front steps encircled by a shaded porch light. She knocked a few times until Hunter appeared and handed her a box. They spoke a few words I could not hear. Debbie walked back to the car holding the box like a tea tray, and in the shadows of the house, I caught my last glimpse of troubled Hunter.

The next morning, a bitter cold one in early March, I drove us in the borrowed car to Headquarters, about two hours away. Patches of snow lay on either side of the road. On the back seat, our suitcases lay on either side of the precious box. We didn't speak. I obsessed over my part in all this, dreading what was next, seeing my future spinning out of control like a midwestern tornado. Debbie relayed Wierwille's orders that we were to meet with him individually in the BRC auditorium as soon as we set foot on the property. "Separately," he'd told her. "Don't forget."

We arrived before noon. I was hungry, tired, and scared. I parked the car, and we trudged up the steps under the green awning. Debbie was to report to Wierwille first in the back of the auditorium. I must wait downstairs until they were finished. Nobody was around except Louise, the cook, who was in the kitchen fixing lunch for the Corps and staff.

"Hi, Louise," I called when I saw her. "How are ya?"

"Bless you, Charlene. Nice to see you." She waved from the serving window.

"I'm just gonna sit here a few minutes. Don't mind me."

I slumped into a greasy-smelling sofa by the piano. Within minutes, Louise brought me an apple and a cup of coffee without asking why I was there. She had an accepting manner—she didn't make comments or judge. The wall clock by the pay phone ticked off the minutes. When Debbie came down to get me, she looked more embarrassed than upset. Her cheeks were flushed. She nodded for me to get going.

Wierwille was in a chair by the display case that held copies of his old books, ones he said were out-of-date, like *Victory Through Christ*, his first. He glared at me. The auditorium was uncharacteristically quiet. Gray metal chairs were folded and stacked like an interlocked puzzle against the far wall.

"Sit down. Right there," Wierwille barked, pointing to the red-carpeted floor in front of him, as if I were Tick, his German shorthaired pointer. I sat down and noticed that his cowboy boots and flannel shirt looked worn and shoddy and his hair was rumpled. He rested his arms on his knees and twirled a Kool cigarette in one hand, looking eager for it.

"So. You doin' pot up there with those hippies?"

"No, sir." I inched away. "I don't do that. I'm scared to." I'd always been afraid of it, but I'd never talked with Wierwille about this before, so I put up with the question.

"Well, you let those guys get in your pants?"

"No." I slid back a few more inches. What *was* this? I wasn't in love with any of those guys in Toledo, and I told him so. "I have to be in love to have sex, Doctor Wierwille."

With that information, he softened a bit, but he still seemed hostile, far different from the kindly father I'd confided in during the women's advance about wanting to serve God. In his office, he'd been sympathetic. Here, he was mean, growling like a bullying factory boss. Disoriented, I wanted to crawl away, but I didn't. I couldn't. I could not bring myself to get up and leave, because despite this bizarre interrogation, I yearned to get into the Corps. I crossed my arms against my shaking body, and before I realized it, I was blabbing.

"I guess I should have paid better attention to Hunter," I said, "but I honestly didn't know anything bad was going on with him. I didn't see him smoke pot. I didn't see any pot around. And nobody was having sex that I know of, either."

Like a child falsely accused and wanting the moment to be over, I promised to do better, but in my heart I knew I was innocent. I promised to grow up spiritually. Somehow I rallied enough gumption to assert myself, emboldened by my mantra: Just stay. You'll be blessed.

"Doctor, I still intend to be in the Corps." My desire to learn God's Word from Wierwille trumped the likelihood of more ill-treatment like this.

"Oh, yeah? Well, I say whether you're Corps or not. Nobody decides that stuff but me," he snapped, flicking the cigarette as if knocking off ashes that weren't even there. He wagged his head back and forth in amazed disbelief.

"Okay, I'm puttin' you two on a bus back to Greenville." He pursed his lips. "John and Pat will handle you guys. They answer to me, don't forget. They'll report on you. You gotta *prove* you're Corps material. Got it?" He jerked his head for emphasis and jabbed the air with the unlit Kool.

In a confused mess of fear, exhaustion, anger, and a sliver of foolish hope, I vowed to do my best.

"Now get going," he said. "Move the Word like I showed you in West Virginia. Get outta here."

Wierwille's nephew, a farmhand, drove Debbie and me to Lima, a nearby town, where we climbed onto a Greyhound bus. In one hand I carried my suitcase. In my heart I carried shame. I took a seat alone near the back behind Debbie and stayed there for the whole long, terrible trip. A heavy snowfall blew in at the start of our thirty-something-hour ride to the only place I could call home—that spare room in Betsey's apartment. In the North Carolina mountains, our bus forged through a blinding blizzard, slipping and sliding around on the icy roads. I curled up on the stiff vinyl seat and cried, pulling my old navy blue coat, the one I'd worn to my mother's funeral, tighter and tighter around me. At one point we rounded a curve where no guardrail was in place, and I feared we'd slide into oblivion. My imagination went wild with images of me lying in a ravine below—because of someone else smoking pot in Toledo. How could God let this happen? What was I supposed to do now? Would Betsey still let us live with her? Would I have to go home and face my father?

The window I leaned against reflected my disheveled face. I was almost nineteen years old but felt much older. Half-moons of violet hung under my eyes and my pale winter skin, despite my freckles, made me look sick. I cowered in humiliation. Only a few months were left until summer school to prove myself worthy to Wierwille again, but I knew of no way to do it.

15

Addicted to the Ministry

I dreaded having to face them. John Lynn, our state leader, and his wife, Pat, were waiting in Greenville, ready, I was sure, with a cross-examination and a dose of "I told you so." I was totally frazzled after the nerve-racking bus ride through the blizzard, and riddled with angst over the awful session with Wierwille. I had no idea what the Lynns would do about Debbie and me. When the bus hissed into Greenville, I dragged myself and my suitcases into the parking lot where Earl met us. He said everyone makes mistakes (word got around fast), and tried to offer comfort. We got in his car, and he whisked us off to meet with John Lynn.

About four months earlier, John had questioned me about dropping out of college. Now he could blame me for my huge mistake. In his office, after awkward greetings, he said, "How about you two get together with some girls in the fellowship and start a women's Way Home?"

"Really?" Debbie asked.

"They're all ECU students, nice girls," he said. "Some have part-time jobs. All of them plan to attend Way summer school in a few months. Like I heard you want to do." Unlike us, these young women wanted to enter the Corps *after* college diplomas were in their hands. The idea was for us to study, eat, and witness together, and share finances and household chores. It didn't sound good to me—it sounded fantastic! We'd get jobs in town, and this living arrangement would inculcate discipline in preparation for summer classes at The Way, John told us. If we did well, the two of us might be admitted into The Way Corps next fall. John couldn't promise.

Debbie and I wasted no time in joining the girls in the move. It seemed the best hope for our rehabilitation. Even though we didn't know them—they'd taken the PFAL class while we'd been traipsing around Ohio—it wasn't long before I gained a sense of belonging and love again. I was glad this women's home was John's idea, not mine or Debbie's. After the Toledo failure, my confidence was shaken. By heeding John's advice, we would show Wierwille our compliance with his appointed leader. He couldn't find fault with that.

To lead our troop of young women in this endeavor to grow spiritually, John chose one, Felicia, and charged her with finding a cheap place to rent. Soon she discovered a freshly painted shotgun—a house with a hall running down the middle with rooms on either side. The place was okay: a tiny living room, kitchen, three bedrooms, and, for the seven of us, one toilet. The bungalow sat on stacks of concrete blocks over on Pitt Street, a dirt road across the river. Only one of us owned a car, which made it hard to get around. But we dealt with it. We could put up with anything for these last few months before we all left for Ohio.

Pat Lynn helped me find a job. Going with her to the women's advance had established a little bond that went a long way. She telephoned Jerry's Bakery, which supplied donuts for our coffeehouse, and the owner hired me for counter work. My bakery experience in Ocean City paid off. When I donned my old white uniform from that summer, I couldn't help but think of my surfing Jesuit.

After the move, John Lynn made a surprise announcement at a Sunday teaching: Dr. Wierwille was coming to town with some Way

Corps members, and he wanted John to host a youth advance as a spring break alternative for the hundreds of college-age Way followers looking for something to do. The minister of the church across the street from The Way Home rented us his all-purpose room, local believers prepared food, and Pat arranged housing for the out-of-towners from around the state and from Ohio, Kansas, and New York. Debbie and I were keen to see Wierwille again, hoping he'd recognize our godly transformation.

Surprises didn't cease. Around then my father called to say he wanted to visit. I was uneasy but the timing seemed perfect. I suggested he come the weekend of the youth advance. That way he could attend a reception held for parents to meet Wierwille and ask questions. Dad could hear for himself about our great plans for spreading God's Word and helping people. I also prayed for God to open Dad's heart to believe the Word and support me in the ministry. How could he refuse after hearing my teacher's vision and seeing me doing so well? I never thought to ask Dad for his weekend agenda. Did he have important family news? Did he want to apologize for saying I was crazy?

As if Wierwille's visit and my father's arrival didn't fluster me enough, angry student demonstrations were kicking up at East Carolina University. A couple of campus protests would soon overtake the college, each attracting several hundred students. Unfortunately, the protest on Saturday, April 3, coincided with our parent reception down the street. But we were too preoccupied preparing for our Way advance to pay attention to the confusing rallies out there in the world.

For our advance with Wierwille, we geared up to welcome about two hundred guests. For the meetings, someone made a banner with the weekend theme—"They have addicted themselves to the ministry of the saints" (1 Cor. 16:15)—and hung it above the stage in the church's all-purpose room. Although Wierwille did not say so that I recall, we understood that *the ministry* meant our beloved Way ministry. We took the hint that ours was an extension of Saint Paul's ministry and like Paul's followers, our aim was to become addicted.

The Saturday afternoon my father arrived, April 3, 1971, he checked into a motel near campus and drove to the dilapidated Pitt Street house. He was probably appalled by the shack where his daughter lived. When we stood in the street and looked it over, the wooden tinderbox leaned to the right, as if the next stiff wind might blow it down. The front steps were creaky boards laid across bricks. I coaxed my father inside, where my housemates greeted him with big smiles as he followed me around. His inner microbiologist must have been aghast—one bathroom for all these girls. We kept the place spotless, but still, he kept his hands in his pockets. He read the scraps of paper taped to the kitchen wall: "Love one another," "Work heartily unto the Lord." Dad said nothing. I showed him the room I shared with Debbie with the sheet nailed across the window and bragged about how our simple lifestyle was like that of first-century believers. He saw the one telephone (in the living room), and I told him we kept the line open each morning in case Rose High School called, because Debbie and I were on their list of substitute teachers. I worked at a bakery, too, I added, and hitchhiked there at three o'clock after subbing at school. No nod of approval came from my father.

At the parents' reception, when Wierwille shook my father's hand, two planets collided. These men were not only at theological odds, but also at polar opposites about life's purpose for me. Wierwille merely hugged me and said "God bless," then moved on to the next person in line. I thought his lack of personal interest meant he was testing my resolve to be Corps material without his coddling me. His inattention only made me want the program more.

Dad and I positioned ourselves on the velveteen sofa where I'd sat my first time in that house. Pat served us coffee and cookies. I could feel Dad's discomfort. His stiff body did not relax. He looked as glum as his gray suit, like a person killing time. Across the room, enthroned in a wingback chair, was Wierwille. He ran the reception like a meeting, taking charge, thanking the parents for coming, telling them about his ministry, and praising their children for their glorious commitment to God. His Holy Spirit ring flashed in the lamplight whenever he gestured toward us. A few parents nodded in appreciation, but not my father. No one else could tell, but I felt Dad's dislike of Wierwille, as deep as an old raging river. He swallowed hard when Wierwille, in his most sugary voice, said how thankful he was for "these tremendous young people" who boldly spread God's Word.

Dad and I were the first to leave. I felt embarrassed, darting out the door with him as if we were spooked squirrels running for cover. We got in his car.

"I want you to either come home with me tomorrow, Charlene, or get back in college." Dad did not take his eyes off the road.

"I can't, Dad."

We drove past the campus with its twinkling lights and he slowed down, observing the buildings and tree-lined avenues. The air in the car was thick with disappointment. I'd been wrong about this visit.

In the dim light of his stuffy motel room, I said as sincerely as I could that I did not want to come home or reenroll in college. I only wanted to go to Way summer school and then study God's Word in The Way Corps.

"That's it, then," my father said. He stood up. He did not shout. He did not plead or threaten. He turned to his suitcase resting on the bed, clicked it open, pulled out a letter-sized paper from the inside pocket, and held it on his lap. "You may as well not come back home."

After that sucker punch, there was nothing constructive to say. I stood up to leave, but Dad told me to sit down. He handed me the paper and told me to sign it. It was a statement promising to repay the money he was about to give me, the last of the funds my parents had designated for my college education. He could have kept it, but I suppose his conscience would have bothered him; he could see that I was broke. Although I feared I could never repay the money, I signed anyway, hoping he'd later change his mind. As I wrote my name, I wondered what my mother would have said about this cold treatment, but I couldn't bring myself to drag her into this.

Before we left the motel, I pleaded one last time for Dad to sponsor me in The Way Corps, should I get accepted. Wierwille required us to round up enough sponsors to cover the one hundred dollars per month it cost to be in the program. My pitch ended with what I'd heard Wierwille say in answer to parents' objections: our folks would likely pay for secretarial schools or trade schools, so why not a program to learn the greatness of God's Word?

"Charlene, I don't believe in this religion." Dad folded the paper I'd signed and stuck it back in the suitcase. "I can't support it." He wouldn't look at me, but to make sure I understood how bad he thought my decisions were, he added one more thing as he opened the door for us to leave. "You're going to wind up in the gutter."

At that, my heart withdrew its last bit of affection from my father, and I resolved to prove him wrong.

Dad dropped me off at the church with our youth advance inside, and I slipped into the back row beside my housemate, Felicia. Wierwille was on stage waving a Bible, working the crowd. At the end of his teaching, Felicia suggested we go down the street to the campus and witness to students at the rally. I was cold, so she loaned me her black crocheted shawl, and we walked to the grassy commons across from Cotten Hall, my former dorm. We heard rock music before we saw groups of students on blankets, sharing food and clapping as the music ended. The band started dismantling its equipment on the makeshift stage. At the edges of the gathering, some students prepared to leave.

"Hey, everybody, stay put for news from the administration coming any minute," an organizer shouted into a microphone. "Don't leave yet.

Our work's not over."

Then inspiration struck me. *Our work's not over, either.* I made a beeline for the wooden steps at the end of the stage, ran up, and whispered to the organizer, "I have to make an announcement."

He shook his head, but before he could ward me off, I grabbed the microphone.

"In the name of Jesus Christ, everybody listen up." I felt as if I'd stepped outside my body to act out a preordained task. A few students stopped where they were, turning to gape, holding their blankets and books. Most ignored me.

"God's the same today, tomorrow, and forever," I said, and I kept on talking fast, telling the crowd God loved them, scanning the startled faces for someone, anyone, who might be listening as I continued a stream-of-consciousness sermon about God and Jesus and love. As quickly as I'd rushed on stage, my reverie evaporated. I shoved the microphone back into the hands of the flabbergasted MC and took off, running down the steps to join Felicia, her shawl flapping against my arms, my hair streaming behind me in the dark. Then I heard it. Students hollered like cheerleaders. "Gimme an F!"

"F!" the crowd responded.

"Gimme a U!"

"U!"

"Gimme a C!"

"C!"

"Gimme a K!"

"K!"

"What's that spell?"

"Fuck you!"

I kept moving. Felicia and I ran down the street, away from the nasty jeers, and soon reached the safety of the church. Wierwille pranced back and forth on stage, snapping his fingers to guitar music and the splendid harmony from a three-man group, each one with dark brown, frizzy hair. Felicia later told the believers about what I did at the rally, and they praised me for preaching the truth. Whether Wierwille ever heard about it, I never knew, but my confidence increased so much after the episode that I quit vying for his attention. Anyway, he was too happily preoccupied with his Way Corps kids and his adoring leaders to pay attention to me.

The following Monday, April 5, 1971, I was famous. ECU's student newspaper, *Fountainhead*—whose tagline is "and the truth shall make you free"—published an article about Saturday's protest in its Daily Boycott Supplement that included this:

A blonde girl in a black shawl approached the microphone. "Jesus is powerful," she said. The crowd began to grumble. "You can see the power of God just like it was in the Christian Church during the first century. The name of Jesus is a powerful name and it works miracles." No one was listening. "God's the same today, tomorrow, and forever," she ended. "God loves you, and I love you. Thank you." Someone started chanting far out in the crowd, "Give me an F, give me a U ..."[1]

When the paper came out, word spread through the Way grapevine. I got more congratulations than I'd ever received for anything I'd ever done ... ever.

The next morning, Dad took me to breakfast at a local restaurant. Whether he meant to shame me or shake me out of my fantasy, I'm not sure. We ate fried eggs, bacon, and toast, and I listened to his account of the time during World War II when the Army stationed him in the Philippines and changed the direction of his life.

First, before the Army, in order to get some education after dropping out of high school to work in a shoe factory and help support his family,

Dad completed home study courses in bacteriology and chemistry. He wanted to become a scientist. When the Army ran an enlistment campaign, he joined and was assigned to Fort Getty in Jamestown, Rhode Island. That's where he met my mother, Anne Rochefort, a clerk-typist. They married in 1942. Later, the Army sent him to the Philippines to Quezon City near Manila on Luzon, a mosquito-infested South Pacific island, where he contracted malaria.

"I became so sick, the doctors said I would die," he told me. With a wife and baby (my sister) waiting back home, Dad said, "I asked God to spare me. I told Him that if He would save me, I'd dedicate my life to public health."

He recovered and kept his word. Humility was something I'd not noticed in Dad for a long time, but that morning I saw a man who'd humbled himself before God. He did good work for humanity and for the God he served, as I was trying to do. His laboratory job at the Wicomico County Health Department back home took on new meaning. A few layers of my resentment melted, but not enough for me to do what he wanted.

Before he drove back to Salisbury, we stood on the dirt road in front of my rickety house, its open windows seeping music and conversations. Cars I did not recognize were parked helter-skelter in the yard. A few guys attending the youth advance sat cross-legged on the porch smoking cigarettes, monitoring us like watchdogs.

Dad turned his back on them. "Charlene," he said, taking my hand, "won't you please come home with me?"

"I can't, Dad." I kicked some pebbles in the road, aggravated that he still didn't get the message. "I have work to do for God." Somewhere in my mind, like violin music in the background, were the words of young Jesus to his parents: "Don't you know I must be about my Father's business?"

Dad drove off. I climbed the front steps, greeted the kids on the porch, and inside found our living room packed with believers from New York. On the sagging couch was the guy in the fringed suede pants, strumming a guitar.

"Hi," he said as I sat down next to him. "Remember me? Ed from Rye."

We talked awhile, and I said I'd heard that his father, the minister, still offered his church's activity room for Way meetings. What I did not tell Ed was how jealous I was of his apparent good relationship with his father. I didn't mention my hurtful row with mine. Instead, I showed my new friend around our place and when we reached the end of the hall, he opened the screened door to the porch where we stood together in the sunshine and jasmine-scented air.

"You've got a great believer community here," Ed said, "like we have in Rye." We swapped stories about getting into the ministry, and then he shared the best news I'd heard all weekend: he was going to Way summer school, and he had applied for The Way Corps, too. I might see him in Ohio before long.

16

On the Beach

A couple of months later, I got a letter from Rev. Walter J. Cummins, Wierwille's biblical research assistant, announcing I'd passed the entrance exam for the Advanced Class on Power for Abundant Living. That class was mandatory for all Way Corps applicants. I was so excited my hands were shaking as I read the letter aloud to Debbie, who held another copy addressed to her. When I read the required reading list, I panicked. We barely had time to finish it before leaving for Ohio: many chapters in the Old Testament and a few books, including *Babylon Mystery Religion* by Ralph Woodrow, which revealed grotesque sins and transgressions in the Catholic Church, like priests fathering children and popes hoarding gold. Abuses of power abounded. Corruption reigned. After I read it, my rejection of Catholicism felt validated. I did not yet realize I'd swapped one authoritarian religion for another.

Debbie and I got ready to leave. I called Dad to say I needed things from home, and he said I could visit. When I left Greenville to go home before heading to Ohio, I felt a mix of joy and sadness as I said good-bye to everyone at The Way Home, to my coworkers at Jerry's Bakery, and to folks at Rose High School, where I'd been more of a babysitter than a substitute teacher. The hardest farewells were to my housemates, my sisters who nurtured me along to this success.

I boarded a bus with my banged-up pink luggage and rode north on Route 13 to Salisbury. Besides the need to retrieve some clothes and bedding, I felt like God wanted me to reconnect with my father no matter how unpleasant it might be. Wierwille cautioned us against alienating our folks, warning that parental ties were invisible forces that worked on us for good or ill. I would try harder to love. I would not pick a fight. But as I'd feared, my father's reception was frosty. For those few days, I made myself as small in his house as possible. Dad must have felt rejected, having his daughter under his roof yet so far out of reach. Like wary sparring partners, we hunkered in our separate corners, ate in different rooms.

While on the Delmarva Peninsula again, I wanted to see Rob, my old flame. It was hard to believe that only a year earlier I'd left him on the beach. I was not the same person as the girl he'd last seen, and I was nervous about what to say, how to explain my new self. It seemed too much to hope for, but I thought I might be able to win Rob over, since face-to-face talk should be more effective than writing letters. From our correspondence, I knew he was working again at English's, the fried chicken restaurant where we'd met, so we agreed I'd come to his apartment after his shift. Dad, amazingly, let me borrow his car and I took off, unsure of what Rob wanted, but knowing that all I wanted was to convince him to take the PFAL class. Nothing else.

Along Route 50 to the beach, familiar sights reminded me of past summers—billboard ads for surfboards, bikinis, Coppertone, and seafood restaurants. Soon blue-gray waters on either side of the road came into view, and the familiar arched bridge eased me onto the wide strip of sandbar where Ocean City gleamed in the sun.

At his apartment door, Rob seemed hardly changed. He still wore those great John Lennon glasses. Encountering him now from the stance of my Way worldview felt strange and awkward, as if we'd aged thirty years since being together. My perception of him as an unbeliever lay over him like a thick net, but tenderness rushed out from under it, startling me. He was gracious and held the door open, stepping back to look me up and down like he used to do.

"Charlene." He kissed my cheek and hugged me. "Let's go for a walk. Up to the beach." He steered me out into the sun before I could say anything. "It's stuffy in here," he said, "and I've been cooped up in English's all morning."

I was relieved we were outside. I wouldn't have to deal with those familiar feelings in his apartment, the double bed not far from sight. Before we reached the boardwalk, I heard the roar of the ocean and tension in my shoulders released. Rob was calm and friendly.

"I read your letters," he said. "Now talk to me about everything. Especially this Way Corps you want to join."

I couldn't think how to begin. His focused interest disarmed me. We soon reached the boardwalk and rested next to each other, leaning on the railing, our sights on the sea.

"Tell me about it." He moved close, his shoulder brushing mine. I launched into a quiet speech about the Corps and why I wanted to join it, and without pausing, rushed into saying he could take the PFAL class somewhere in Boston close to his college. Way fellowships were popping up all over the Northeast, and I could put him in contact with nearby believers.

We were facing each other when a breeze tossed a few strands of hair across my face and Rob touched me, gently brushing them away.

"Listen, Charlene, I've got to tell you something." He sighed. "I found a book by your minister."

"You did?"

"Yeah, of all places I found it in the college library. My *Catholic* college. I think the title was *Victory Through Christ*."

"That's Doctor's first book. There's a copy locked in a display case at Headquarters." It was kept like an ancient artifact. "I've never read it. Doctor says it's outdated and he doesn't sell it anymore."

A few surfers wearing wetsuits trudged across the sand carrying shiny waxed boards. As they paddled out to catch a wave, I thought of Rob's surfing lessons. We'd laughed so much during those sun-dazzled afternoons, splashing and kissing in the sparkling sea.

"I'd been trying to get information about your group, but it's scarce, you know. And I read part of that book, but it's just evangelical theology like so many other preachers write. Your minister takes the Bible so literally. Does he ever give you any information about the Bible's history?"

I bit my lip. "It's too bad you didn't like it." I shrugged a little to make him think it was no big deal and picked at a rotten place in the wooden railing.

"Remember that day we drove to Assateague Island? It was raining," he said. "We talked about the Bible, and I tried to explain that many things in it are situational—only for people at that time. They can't be taken seriously today. So. Are you shutting me out because I don't agree with your preacher?"

With familiar gentleness, he pulled me back to face him. He never liked it when I avoided saying what I thought. "Hey, sweetie, talk to me."

"I was hoping you'd think about taking the PFAL class, Rob. That's all. But since you don't like the book, I guess you wouldn't want the class."

"You're right. I'm not interested, but that doesn't mean I don't love God like you do." He gave a weak smile to show he was trying to be nice about this, but I didn't know what he was talking about. We didn't use the term *theology*. Theology was "religious," and we shunned religion.

Waves pounded the shell-strewn sands. To avoid Rob's eyes, I watched the wind sweep over the sea grass instead. Clouds gathered far down the beach, darkened hotels in the distance, threatened to come our way. I took a deep breath of the salty air, praying for God's guidance, sorry that Rob was so closed-minded. He'd never take the PFAL class, so I could never be with him. I shouldn't have come here.

"Look, I'm sorry," he said. "I'm worried. What's happened to you? You're so different, so serious." He inched a little closer. "I miss the fun Charlene I knew before. You're in there somewhere, aren't you?"

His words stung me, but I knew his concern was real. He moved behind me then, placing his sinewy arms along either side of my body, closing his tanned hands around the railing. He's trying to warm me, I thought, hoping to get romantic again. I felt weak, but I couldn't let myself love him that way, not now, not anymore, not unless he accepted the Word. With Rob's warm breath on my neck, I was tempted to cave in. I caught a whiff of his spicy shampoo and wanted to cry. My heart was so torn by his presence and the memory of what we used to have that when he pressed himself against my back, I felt arousal deep within me. I rested there in spite of myself, in between my love for Rob and the life I believed God wanted for me.

"Please don't run off to Ohio. Don't lose yourself in this Way thing, Charlene, don't believe everything this guy tells you, try to hear what I'm saying. Ministers like that are out for power over the rest of us. You'll suffocate."

"That's enough." I pulled away. "Doctor's not just another preacher. The Word is not theology." I cried above the ocean's thunder without realizing I was shouting. Slipping away, I ran toward the steps leading from the boardwalk down to the sand. Rob followed me, insisting that I didn't know enough about this group to give up everything for it. I marched faster, pushing against the wind that blew harder with every step. Sand gusts stung my legs, raindrops hit my face, but I pushed on. I was sure the Devil was using Rob, just like he used Young Life Dave, to trick me out of going into the Corps, but I would stand firm, as fixed as the concrete pilings under the boardwalk.

Rain let loose as we ran up the street to the parking lot by Rob's apartment and for a few seconds stood by my car. I was confused and avoided his eyes.

"I'm sorry if I pressured you, but I hate to see you drop out of college." He opened the car door for me, and I climbed into the front seat, tears burning my eyes. There was so much to say, but I couldn't seem to be daring enough. I thought that Rob finding Wierwille's book was a sign from God that he should take the PFAL class, but I couldn't tell him. Instead, I pulled the door shut and rolled down the window to say good-bye. I tried but couldn't break out of Way jargon and talk like a normal person. I felt an urge to cry, to cry hard, to let my heart break wide open and lay it all to rest, to tell Rob I couldn't forget him, would never forget him. He begged me to keep writing to him, to think for myself, but all I could do was nod and force myself to drive off and leave him alone in the street.

We would correspond for a time from our parallel universes, but I suppressed his prescient warnings, unaware that like shells from the depths of the churning sea, they could surface again.

17

Summer School

Debbie and I met up at Headquarters. The fragrant lawns were immaculate, but not for long, as hundreds of blissed-out believers traipsed over them, carrying sleeping bags, satchels, and Bibles. In the BRC auditorium, we lined up for registration. Older women—from Doctor's former churches, I guessed—handed us name tags, class schedules, housing assignments, and welcome packets stuffed with aerial-view postcards of the farm and plastic rulers imprinted in black script with "Learning is an exciting adventure."

We moved in. Along a dirt path to our assigned trailer were mulberry trees with bright green leaves. They'd been snow-covered in March when we last saw them. Memories of Wierwille sending us back to Greenville returned with a vengeance. But like the trees sprouting new life, I determined this summer was my fresh start with him. Today we returned in triumph, but I didn't dismiss the humble feeling about Wierwille allowing me back. It had taken a lot of effort to reenter his good graces, but I'd passed the rules of obedience and commitment in the Greenville women's home, and now I was here. Debbie and I could hardly stop smiling as we left unspoken what we both knew—with

God's help we'd met Doctor's challenge. Now we must keep up the good work to get into the Corps.

Inside Trailer Eight, our summer home, was a familiar sight—mattresses strewn on the carpet. A new living room, added on since last winter, smelled of fresh plywood and paint. I unpacked, adding what I'd picked up in Salisbury to what I'd been dragging around since dropping out of college: clothes, shoes, the PFAL class syllabus and books, my mother's sewing machine, a hair dryer and bouffant cap, electric curlers, Hush Puppies boots, bedding, an orange plastic alarm clock, a small tensor lamp, and an invaluable gift from Dad upon my high school graduation: a portable Royal typewriter. From a side pocket in my suitcase, I pulled out a silver-framed photograph of my mother standing with me in the backyard. We were dressed in Easter outfits complete with white gloves, straw hats, and black patent leather shoes. Our pink dogwood tree shimmered in the sun behind us. I was thirteen years old then. She was forty-five. Three years later she was dead. With all my heart I hoped Mom would approve of what I was doing, even though my father did not.

My mind was as fertile as farmland at The Way. Expansive cornfields and leafy soybeans lay in neat rows on the Wierwille homestead, forming a natural border around the compound. Wierwille would often say that God provided this peaceful setting away from the chaotic world to plant the seeds of His Word in our hearts and minds. Intrusions and distractions were minimized. We saw no television or movies. We heard no traffic. Unbelieving friends or relatives were too far away to bother us. We could focus on the things of God—and Wierwille. Most summer classes were expansions on topics from the PFAL class, like The Renewed Mind, Dealing with the Devil, Idioms and Figures of Speech in the Bible, and Keys to Biblical Research. Other classes were introductory courses on Greek and Aramaic, two languages in which ancient Biblical texts were written. We Corps applicants knew that even if we completed the classes, Wierwille still held the option of not accepting us into the Corps for whatever reason he might have. We were at his mercy. All summer he dangled the Corps carrot from a stick, and I did not let it out of my sight. I also didn't let Ed, my new friend, get too far out of sight, either.

Ed, the guitar player from New York, showed up like he said he would, bringing brand-new songs with him. We became close—not romantic yet, but headed in that direction. During classes and group activities, like softball games after dinner, barn dances on Saturday nights, and hillside sing-alongs, we formed an easy camaraderie, pairing up for barbecues in the courtyard and campfire fellowships with Wierwille officiating in the woods down Wierwille Road. For classes we arrived early and sat together. The only classes we couldn't share were Greek and Aramaic. They were taught at the same time of day, which meant that Wierwille split up his Way Corps wannabes, sending some into each course. The majority took Greek, including Ed and Debbie. I was assigned to Aramaic. I never knew Wierwille's reason for putting me in that class.

None of us could have known or predicted it, but if I had anything that could be compared to a calling during my time in The Way, Aramaic was it. One of the best things about Way summer school for me was that Aramaic class. We learned the alphabet, the bare bones of grammar, and a small body of vocabulary words. That summer was the first time Bernita Jess taught that class, and I got along well with her. Our lively conversation at the women's advance enabled me to ease into her personality. Bernita was a pin-curled, pear-shaped, studious middle-aged homemaker and mother—and a sometime-fuddy-duddy, although she was an inspiration, too, an unlikely one to be sure. I thought that if a midwestern woman like Bernita could study this ancient language to learn more of God's Word, so could I.

Our class, fewer than twenty students including a few in-resident Corps, met in the Fireplace Room in the basement of Wierwille's house. It was a large family room furnished with old sofas, tables, and chairs, and (no surprise) a large stone fireplace. We set folding chairs around, and Bernita, a combination of tutor, governess, and mom, went about her lessons, sometimes patiently, sometimes not so much. When she passed by my chair, I often smelled baby powder and heard nylon stockings shush, shush, shush. She usually wore pleated skirts, immaculate polyester blouses, and baggy sweaters with tissues hidden in the side pockets.

Aramaic was a secret I'd been waiting to learn. As Bernita told me at the women's advance, it was a Semitic language from Palestine, the land where Jesus had lived, and he had spoken a dialect called Palestinian Aramaic. That fact alone made studying the language feel like a sacred undertaking, especially since Wierwille said Aramaic was the language in which the entire Bible had originally been written. That differed from most scholars, I learned much later, who were convinced Greek was the original language of New Testament writings. For Wierwille, studying Aramaic manuscripts, as well as the more prevalent Greek texts, was essential to our attempt to reconstruct the original Word of God. Aramaic had my undivided attention.

The alphabet was almost calligraphic, like Arabic. Unlike our character set for English, Aramaic letters were picture-like symbols resembling familiar objects to the Eastern people who'd devised them long ago: a camel, a one-story house, a cane, a snake. Also unlike English, the written Aramaic language, like Arabic and Hebrew, was read from right to left. We often joked that we were reading backward. The vocabulary words we memorized were basic, like God, book, house, man, savior. Before the class ended, Bernita fed our anticipation for future research by filling us in on her current project: collecting microfilms of ancient Aramaic manuscripts. She said her teacher, Dr. George Lamsa, a scholar of the Scriptures who previously taught Aramaic at Way summer school, encouraged Wierwille to procure those microfilms from libraries around the world, and Wierwille delegated this task to her. She had already bought a microfilm of one of the oldest from the British Museum in London. Her work was so romantic and so intriguing that I couldn't stop thinking about it. It galvanized the rest of my years in The Way.

Bernita had another announcement. We were going to publish a much-needed reference book: an Aramaic-English concordance. For this, we eventually used the Peshitta Version of the New Testament (we called it "the Peshitta") written in Eastern Aramaic. Eastern Aramaic was called Syriac. Syriac is related to but not the same as Aramaic, but Wierwille preferred to use the term Aramaic, anyway. (This would become an important issue in my Way future). With such a concordance, she said, users could look up any word in the Aramaic New Testament and find its meaning in English, along with a list of all the verses in which the word appeared. Other concordances, like *Young's Analytical Concordance to the Bible*, had been in use by Christians for years already to conduct Hebrew word studies in the Old Testament and Greek word studies in the New Testament, but in 1971 no complete concordance existed for doing the same in Aramaic (Syriac). Many scholars, Wierwille said, wanted such a concordance. If we published it, we'd make history in academic circles—a goal Wierwille *loved*. A concordance would be useful not only for scholars, but also for unschooled believers like those in The Way. Lamsa convinced Wierwille to undertake this project. If we didn't, someone else would, and I think now that Wierwille was too competitive to let that happen.

When our class ended, fellow students returned their textbooks to Bernita, but I kept and paid for mine—a Syriac Old Testament, two Syriac versions in different scripts of the New Testament, a Syriac lexicon, and a Syriac grammar book. I didn't have the heart to let them go. I still have them, along with one I bought later, a Syriac-English dictionary edited by J. Payne Smith. Those books opened a door to the deeper mysteries of God's Word, I thought, and I couldn't make myself close it.

An unsettling event took place at summer school in August when Wierwille taught the Advanced Class on Power for Abundant Living to the entire student body—about two hundred people. It was not possible for any Way Corps applicants like me to not take it or to drop out and expect to enter The Way Corps. This class was the culmination of the summer—two weeks of advanced spiritual instruction about receiving personal revelation from God, healing people, performing miracles, and casting out devil spirits. Every Christian could do these things, Wierwille said; they only needed accurate teachings from God's Word. Some were from First Corinthians about the manifestations (or gifts) of the spirit: discerning of spirits, faith, miracles, and healing. We could see the lame walk, the blind see, and captives set free from any bondage when we prayed in the name of Jesus Christ. For examples of how to do this, we studied New Testament records of the apostles performing these mighty deeds. Those of us from ECU felt we'd witnessed miracles first-hand already, like when Earl healed Gerald's collarbone. We also listened to recordings of preachers sharing how they brought deliverance to God's people.

But one afternoon, Wierwille had a movie screen placed in front of the podium. Soon he appeared in the aisle, dressed in his customary white summer *guayabera* from Cuba, Bermuda shorts, and white patent leather loafers.

"Now I want you to learn something. The people in this movie I'm going to show you need deliverance. If you watch, you'll be prepared to deal with these things. Someone hit the lights. Howard, start the machine."

The film clicked in the projector, and on the screen appeared a sofa and a chair in a small room. Spotlights illuminated two women as they entered the scene and sat side by side on the sofa. They embraced. They kissed. They were naked.

Sickened isn't the right word for how I felt, but running out of the room wasn't an option. I had to keep watching because Wierwille was watching us. I was terribly confused, since more than once I'd heard our teacher use Bible verses to denounce people of the same sex having sex—they were depraved and damned. Wasn't it enough to know about these people? Did we have to see them in the act? I closed my eyes. Ed, sitting next to me, gave me a nudge, but I was too embarrassed to look at him.

From the back of the room, Wierwille called out, "You gotta see this stuff to heal homos like them." A spiritual battle was going on in that movie, he said, and we must keep what we saw in that context.

It wasn't easy.

Another character appeared on the screen—an athletic German shepherd. The women grabbed the dog and tugged him close. The poor animal struggled to escape but the women forced the dog into having intercourse with them. Wierwille laughed and hollered, "That mutt has more sense than those chicks," mocking people we were supposed to heal.

The film went on for several more minutes, and no one left—not one person. When it ended, I was sweating. Wierwille shouted from the back again, saying that if we were offended, then we weren't spiritual enough to handle ministering God's Word to sick people and casting out the devil spirits that made them act that way. He ordered us not to discuss the movie with anyone—even each other. It was private training meant only for Advanced Class students. Why our class did not unite and confront Wierwille says something about his cultivated skills of manipulation and our readiness to obey him. The film was a test of whether we'd follow or turn away. If I left, I would not get into the Corps. That was unthinkable.

I sat in silence.

Distraction followed distress—a common ploy Wierwille used to control us. The Advanced Class ended, and a couple of weeklong family camps swung into action. We were required to attend inspirational teachings day and night, morning Hour of Power fellowships, Devotion in Motion exercises on the lawns, arts and crafts hours, outdoor games, barn dances, and group sing-alongs. We had fun. We ate hamburgers with mustard and relish, and side dishes of coleslaw and potato chips; we drank free pop. Camps came with another, more important, benefit: close contact with adult believers from around the country who had money. A popular Way motto was "There are no strangers at The Way, only friends we haven't met yet." Corps applicants were encouraged to meet the families at camp, form relationships with the adults, and ask them to serve as monthly financial sponsors for our two-year Way Corps program. They were our new best friends.

After summer school ended and after all campers left, it was time for Wierwille's drumroll decisions about who would be allowed into the Corps. Praise the Lord, I made it in. So did Debbie. So did Ed. So did fourteen other young men and women from around the country. We lost one applicant, a girl I did not know well. She left abruptly after the Advanced Class, but I never heard why—I can now imagine—and at the time I didn't pay much attention. All I could think about was how God made my Way Corps dream come true. I would soon don the proverbial Way Corps Green Beret.

I'd qualified despite my "failure" in Toledo. Throughout the coming years, I sensed that Wierwille never forgot our ugly session before he ordered Debbie and me back to Greenville. I rarely felt completely comfortable around him. Sometimes I think he let me into the Corps because Debbie and I were inseparable. Perhaps he thought that if he rejected me I might make a scene or leave the ministry and turn against him, and

Wierwille didn't like scenes, much less turncoats, even powerless nine-teen-year-old women turncoats.

Before we officially claimed our Way Corps status, we had one more duty: to help produce the last event of the summer, a festival Wierwille christened the Rock of Ages. We called it the Rock. It was like an out-door youth advance to welcome back about a dozen summer missionar-ies Wierwille called Word Over the World Ambassadors (WOWs) and commission more who would commit to live and witness in assigned cities for one year. Right away I wanted to prove worthy of my upcom-ing Green Beret, so I volunteered to paint banners for the Rock festival. My biggest, in three-foot orange letters on oilcloth, stated our goal: The Word Over the World. When its paint dried, the work crew hung it across the back of a stage near a creek we called "the Jordan," behind the President's Home. That year, about 1,000 believers from around the country showed up for the Rock and many signed up as WOWs. Bands from New York and Ohio played Christian rock and roll. Ours was a mini-Woodstock, only with Bibles and without the mud, with Wier-wille and other dynamic teachers preaching the Bible, Way Corps mem-bers giving testimonials, and the audience filling lawn chairs and picnic blankets, singing, clapping, and cheering at all the right times. Excite-ment for spreading the Word over the world reached a new peak.

If Wierwille had not granted me entry into the Corps, I would have volunteered as a WOW and ended up in a faraway city somewhere, perhaps even overseas. How different my life would have been. I might have never left The Way at all. Committing to The Corps program was the road I traveled that made all the difference.

August 1971. First Rock of Ages music and Bible teaching festival behind the Wierwille home at Way Headquarters, New Knoxville, Ohio. About 1,000 believers attended. That weekend, Wierwille commissioned the first group of Word over the World (WOW) Ambassadors (missionaries for one year). Charlene painted the orange-lettered banner, "The Word Over The World."

PHOTO COURTESY OF THE BLADE SUNDAY MAGAZINE, TOLEDO, OHIO, MARCH 26, 1972.

2007. Charlene visits the East Carolina University campus commons, site of the 1971 student protest where her preaching escapade was described by a reporter for Fountainhead, the student newspaper.

Part 4
Leadership
Training

18

Becoming Corps

Science fiction writer L. Ron Hubbard is reputed to have said that if you want real power, create a religion.[1] He created Scientology. Wierwille created The Way. And like other religions, sects, or cults, The Way had a group of elite loyalists, The Way Corps. Before Wierwille started the Corps program, his followers, no matter how committed, were enmeshed in outside society, in their communities, families, and jobs. Way Corps devotees were willing to withdraw from those ties to focus on spreading Wierwille's teachings over the entire world.

On a sultry August day in 1971, after the Rock of Ages festival, I and other incoming Corps gathered with the First Corps (starting their second year of training) under leafy trees in Wierwille's yard to hear important instructions. Around that time, John Lennon's album *Imagine* was released, and we were imagining the Word over the world. Not much else.

"Living together in the Corps will teach you how to manifest charity," Wierwille said. "Most Christians can't live in peace, they fight all the time. If you can learn to live together with the love of God and get along here," he said, "you'll be able to love and help anybody with your ministry, anywhere in the world."

149

That scene reminds me of the Bodhi Tree where the Buddha experienced his enlightenment and taught his followers, like Wierwille was doing. But, as I would learn all too well, our teacher was as different from Buddha as you can get.

Our collective test began and we found out fast how seriously Wierwille took communal living—for us. He stayed in his house. The Second Corps women moved into Trailer Six, a familiar place to me, since I'd lived there the previous winter while retaking the PFAL class. It was a manufactured mobile unit anchored, like the other nearby trailers, into the ground. I carried my belongings from Trailer Eight, my summer housing, making my way through the newly added living room and into the bedroom. Surprise. Instead of the few mismatched beds from last year, five new identical wooden bunk beds—enough for the ten of us—were snug in a row, about two feet apart. Oh my God. How would we manage in here? For *two years*. The worst part was down the hall—one bathroom with one toilet. Ten of us. Ten young women and their hair dryers, toiletries, makeup, and other stuff. I'd had cramped quarters in Greenville, but this ....

Adding to the crowded, uniform atmosphere were the matching blue-and-green plaid bedspreads on the bunks, draped like flags over coffins. They sent a clear message: *personal identity does not matter here.*

Mrs. Wierwille, I found out, bought the covers to make the place look neat. It did. But it took me a while to make my peace with them; they smelled like the plastic bags they came in. I stuffed the flowery spread I brought with me into my suitcase, thinking I might as well be in a convent. The good thing was the bedspreads were of sturdy fabric, and would probably last the next two years without falling apart. I hoped I could hold up in here as well. God would have to help me. My mantra again came to mind: Just stay. You'll be blessed.

I made my way down the aisle between the foot of the beds and the row of five matching dressers side by side—one for every two girls—

with shelves above them. I dodged Corps sisters as they bumped around looking for the right bed. Name cards had been put on our bunks. I could smell the plywood boards used in place of box springs to support the mattresses. When I discovered my bunk—the last one, farthest from the bathroom—I was disappointed to find the card with my name on the top bed. *This is a test.* God must have told Mrs. Wierwille to put me up there because I needed to overcome my fear of rolling off top bunks. I'd never fallen yet, but you never knew. No one else was complaining about anything, so I kept quiet and moved into my assigned space. A built-in shelf in the headboard was perfect for small things like the photo of my mother and me in Easter outfits, my orange plastic clock, and my little tensor lamp. I stashed my suitcases in the barn, and put Mom's portable Singer sewing machine in a living room corner. When I was a preteen, Mom taught me to sew, and the sewing machine was one thing from my pre-Way life I did not believe God wanted me to abandon.

"Debbie," I called. She was standing in the aisle between two bunks.

"What?" She looked around the room before she spotted me. "Oh … you're so far away." It felt weird not to be bunkmates after we'd been close pals for so long. Some people even called us Mutt and Jeff (she was tall, I was short). But there she was, out of easy reach in the narrow room. I suspected Mrs. Wierwille separated us so we'd make new friends. My bunkmate was one of three fellow Corps sisters whose whole family was in the ministry. Debbie's bunkmate was the soft-spoken girl she'd become friendly with that summer. I'd spent most of my summer free time with Ed, not Debbie, and I'd felt a little guilty for abandoning her. But Debbie was happy that I'd found a boyfriend. In fact, she seemed happy about everything.

Trailer Six was designed for conformity and control, a perfect setup for a cult leader to regulate adherents. It was a contained environment on private property, out of shouting distance from mainstream society and law enforcement. A leader could make his own rules—and change them. Besides the rigid setup of bunk beds and dressers, and the limited personal space, there was no kitchen, television, radio, or telephone in our trailer—only an intercom that connected us to other residences and buildings on the compound. For occasional use, a pay phone hung on the wall in the dining room. We dropped off our outgoing letters at the Main Office, a trailer across the yard, for Wierwille's secretary to deliver to the post office in town. Incoming mail, a roll call event, was conducted at lunchtime.

To ensure his program was enforced, Wierwille assigned in-resident coordinators in each trailer. To remind myself of our goals, I taped the list of Way Corps principles he gave us on the wall alongside my bed.[2]

1. Acquire an in-depth spiritual perception and awareness.

2. Receive training in the whole Word so as to be able to teach others.

3. Physical training making your physical body the vehicle of communication of the Word as vital as possible. [*sic*]

4. Practice believing to bring material abundance to you and the ministry.

5. Go forth as leaders and workers in areas of concern, interest, and need.

These were nonnegotiable goals. Each task we did was presented as somehow relating to one of them. I now suspect that Wierwille wrote these after the Zero Corps failed in 1969. He must have realized he needed to clarify what he wanted from his "Corps kids" and get them to agree. He printed up the principles on small cards, as if they were verses of Scripture, and we each received a set to carry in our pockets. If we lived up to these ideals, we'd not only graduate, we might even receive what Wierwille called "gift ministries," described in Ephesians 4:11–13.

Wierwille was obsessed with cleanliness and order. The mobile units we lived in were fairly new and a maintenance man made sure the heaters, electricity, and plumbing worked. Our job was to keep Trailer Six neat and tidy, just like our lives. Biblical phraseology for this was "being good stewards of what God provided us." In secular language, that meant making sure everything was clean and in its designated place. A schedule was set up for who cleaned what every day. Despite the number of bodies and the amount of things needed to maintain them, our trailer usually gleamed. Whenever I opened the door, I smelled hair spray, deodorant, perfume, and disinfectant. Industrial-strength supplies were stashed under bathroom sinks. Kirby vacuum cleaners stood like robots in the closets. We hauled our laundry every Saturday to a laundromat in St. Marys, a nearby town, until a new office building with a laundry room downstairs was constructed across the lane behind our trailer. As we rotated in and out of the shower without turning it off, I learned the art of the three-minute body wash, including a shampoo. Getting dressed was a tight choreography of waving arms and high-stepping legs in the narrow aisles, clothes flying every which way. Sometimes in the crush, I bolted to the living room to tie my tennis shoes in peace before our morning run. Avoiding people often made it easier to love them. Every few months, Mrs. Wierwille changed our bunk assignments, which we understood was done to prevent us from getting complacent. It was also a good exercise in adaptation and obedience.

The living room was furnished with sofas, lamps, chairs, study carrels, and an extra-large closet. This addition was part of an expansion program to shore up the compound with office buildings and concrete block dormitories. We'd seen the architect's renderings, which included a huge dining hall, too. Given the ministry's exponential growth during the past few years, Wierwille projected it would mushroom in the future. I guess he'd been sulking at the evangelical sidelines long enough, watching in frustration as ministers like Jerry Falwell and Oral Roberts constructed their own universities. Our leader's competitive instinct must have flared like the Olympic torch whenever he heard those names. For the time being, until Wierwille raised more money, he had to settle for his family farm as a frugal center of operations.

Mobile homes were within his budget, housing staff as well as Corps. Bookstore operations expanded from a portion of the BRC basement into Trailer Eight. Trailer Five, called the Main Office, was workspace for Doctor's personal secretary and the ministry's pianist, Rhoda (married to his brother Reuben), and a few other secretaries. In the back near a 16 mm film cleaning machine, desks were crammed in a small area for Harry Wierwille, Howard Allen, and Outreach Coordinator Rev. David Anderson. A tiny room next to a tinier bathroom housed a tape duplicator where a Corps person organized the replication and shipping of the taped Sunday night teachings to hundreds of subscribers.

Trailers Six and Seven were each made from two identical trailers put end to end. In Trailer Six, where the two units met, a door separated Second Corps women in one unit from First Corps women—Nancy, Earl's fiancée, and Naomi, who had combed her wet hair in the dining room—in the other. The previous year, the third First Corps gal had run off with her boyfriend and created a hushed-up scandal. To fill the remaining bunks around Naomi and Nancy, a few female secretaries moved in, which made it convenient for them to work long hours for the Wierwilles and other Board of Trustees men.

Walking from one end of Trailer Six to the other was like touring one big happy college dorm with an added bonus—the residents were like-minded about God and how to apply what the Bible said to everyday life. With matching thoughts like bedspreads, we became friends, counselors, and substitute sisters, striving to love one another. I loved it. Like college roommates, we did our best to be kind, share, and put up

154

with one another's idiosyncrasies, knowing that if we couldn't hack it, we'd have to leave.

Groupthink, I'm sure, kept us on the accepted path, striving for harmony among ourselves. No one in Trailer Six failed at the task of being a good roomie. Our cause: more important than trivial concerns. Our goals: larger than life. Every single woman in that trailer entered the Corps with a heart that yearned to love God and others. I can say the same for the men. We'd all left our ordinary lives—as bakery clerks, high school teachers, art students, pharmacists, college students or job-hunting college graduates (two were psychology majors), and fellowship coordinators around the country—to come here. Together, we laughed, cried, worked, studied, cooked, ate, jogged, fasted, and prayed side by side for two years. We shared toiletries, notepaper, clothes, and rides to town. We shared secrets, too. It didn't take long before I thought I knew my Corps sisters better than my own sister. Living so closely together, how could we not read one another's moods? How could we not know one another's concerns? You'd think nothing could have gone unnoticed. You'd think nothing could have happened that should not have happened.

Our days began around 5:30 a.m. with prayers and a jog down Wierwille Road. Meetings ended late at night. Although the program challenged me, it didn't usually overwhelm me. I'd been on sports teams in high school. I'd held down a couple of jobs. I'd gotten used to this sort of discipline in the Greenville women's home. I adapted. That is not to say I didn't moan about rising early (I wasn't a morning person, and I still am not) or nod off during evening teachings, but discipline did not scare me.

For work my first year, Wierwille assigned me to assist the Outreach Coordinator, Rev. David Anderson, a clergyman ordained by Wierwille. My boss's faithfulness and love of the PFAL class was legendary. He'd raised a lot of money in the 1960s to produce the film of Wierwille teaching the class. He'd personally made sure lots of people took the class and afterward ran interference when they asked critical questions, convincing them to believe Wierwille's teachings and to remain faithful followers. My job included operating the clunky 16 mm film cleaning machine that spun, rattled, and hummed like an old refrigerator. Whenever films of the PFAL class were shipped back to Headquarters after being used in the field, I'd examine, clean, and repair them on this machine. Some films were in better shape than others. Most Way followers were inexperienced at operating film projectors, and often the result of their ineptitude was a sad thing to behold. Ripped sprockets turned yards of film into celluloid fringe. Once the damage on one reel was so extensive that I needed to cut out a major section and splice the filmstrip back together, which resulted in a loss of vital teaching points Wierwille had made. I broke down and cried.

"What's the matter?" David asked. He got up from his desk and came over to me.

"They've wrecked the film," I said, wiping my eyes. The damaged section I'd cut away looked like a snakeskin dangling from my hand. "That's God's Word … wasted." I cried some more. "All torn to pieces." I complained about how expensive the film was and that people should take better care of it. (Too bad I wasn't as careful to examine the *content* of the film.)

I also organized files and charts to track where each class ran, how many people were taking it, and the name of the local fellowship leader. I can't say I was pushed to exhaustion or traumatized by my work or the Corps program schedule. Sure, small things annoyed me, like having to report ten minutes early to all activities. My serious challenges were different.

One came in the fall when Wierwille required us to participate in a colon cleanse to rid our bodies of accumulated toxins we'd ingested.

This complied with principle 3 about physical training to make us fit to communicate the Word. The procedure was similar to what's done in preparing for a colonoscopy, only we cleansed for a couple of weeks, using products created by V. E. Irons, an innovator at the time. We could not quit the routine. Wierwille and his monitors were watching, although Wierwille himself opted out. I went from about 125 pounds—the extras gained at Jerry's Bakery in Greenville—to 89 pounds. I used safety pins to keep my jeans around my waist. I got sick. Some days I could not get out of bed. During the second week, I ate only saltine crackers. Others felt worse than I did. Former drug users said they hallucinated and relived bad trips, as traces of dormant drugs worked themselves out of their bodies. Can that really happen? Who knows. After the ordeal, I slowly regained weight and leveled out at around 100 pounds. The program accomplished the goal, but I don't know how safe it was. I feared having to repeat it the next year, as Wierwille planned, but as it turned out, I managed better the second time.

Another daunting hurdle was financial. Wierwille required us to solicit monthly sponsors. I had acquired a few during summer school and family camps. I juggled ten to meet the hundred-dollar-a-month requirement and worked hard at keeping them happy about getting their checks in by the first of every month. As Wierwille instructed us, I wrote inspiring letters to stoke their interest in the value of the Corps program and deepen their commitment to The Way. Just before Christmas 1971, despite my heartfelt letters and without giving a reason, one sponsor backed out. Stranded, I panicked, and night after night dropped to my knees in prayer.

One night, Ed put his arm around me and said, "I called my dad. He said he'd help you. He's sending the first payment today."

My greatest fear—that Wierwille would send me home—evaporated. Wierwille, of course, kept close watch on us, as did the in-resident trailer monitors, but he also appointed a First Corps couple to oversee our day-to-day activities. Del Duncan and his wife, Nancy (one of two Nancys in the First Corps), lived with their baby in a small unit across the yard from Trailer Six. I'd become familiar with them when Debbie and I were guests retaking the PFAL class. They were former California hippies, healed from drug abuse, they said; sincere people who embodied anti-establishment attitudes. Neither had a college education or any Bible training other than from The Way. As a consummate Way loyalist, Del was a combination of guidance counselor, minister, social director, rule enforcer, humorist, and prison guard.

"My credentials for this job," he'd often say, "come from being in the military, a motorcycle gang, a drug ring, and God's ministry. Not necessarily in that order."

Despite the seriousness of his job, Del had a knack of making difficult tasks, like killing and skinning rabbits and beheading and plucking chickens, easier by cracking jokes. Those survival skills were supposed to help us out if America fell into economic chaos—we could still eat. To the chicken, he said, "Hey, this is nothing to lose your head over!" Del often defused Wierwille's grumpy moods whenever someone did something wrong, like mowing down a sapling by mistake or failing to perfectly memorize a Scripture verse. If you complimented Del on his tie, he'd grin and say, "I knitted it myself." The program would have been more of a drudgery without him. He was one person who never gave Ed or me any grief over our growing love.

My friendship with Ed bloomed into romance. Living arrangements wonderfully facilitated relationships like ours because the men in Trailer Seven were only a few hundred feet from the women in Trailer Six. Before the Corps, Ed spent a year or so in college, but he disliked the academic world. He was interested in the performing arts and music but on his own terms. He taught himself how to play the guitar and the wooden recorder he carried everywhere, and he loved improvisational dance.

I loved ballet and modern dance, too, so dancing gave us something else in common besides The Way. At morning exercises, while Del led the men in military-style calisthenics, he delegated to Ed the task of instructing the women in yoga. Yoga was new to me and I loved it. Wierwille was firm about our getting physically fit to spread the Word and set an example of health and vitality. We were model believers in a showroom window. We must look our best. Del's challenge was to incorporate the Corps principles into our lives, transforming us into a lean, supreme, spiritual fighting machine.

The principles were fairly straight-forward to me except principle 1: Acquire an in-depth spiritual perception and awareness. That was vague. Even Wierwille hemmed and hawed about it. I imagined it had to do with a sensitivity I would develop after building up my inner spirit by speaking in tongues. I settled on the idea that I should follow Psalm 46:10: "Be still, and know that I *am* God." It seemed to me I'd been seeking still moments with God ever since my Catholic childhood. In our busy Corps program, recapturing that solitude was one of my greatest challenges.

It became clear to me years later that "growing your spirit" was incompatible with Wierwille's notion of the gift being a *complete* gift from God. How could it grow if it were complete already?

Principle 2 was more direct: Receive training in the whole Word so as to be able to teach others. I tried to absorb whatever Wierwille might offhandedly say about the Word at mealtimes, at spur-of-the-moment gatherings in the Fireplace Room or around a campfire, and at Corps nights, which were our weekly dress-up, sit-down Bible teachings in the auditorium. The previous winter, as a guest, I'd envied the Corps when they'd leave Debbie and me in Trailer Six and troop over to the BRC for those private teachings. Now God granted me the chance to hear them myself. I was not to mind other people's business; complain over trailer living and millet and liver dinners; or stress over girls using my hair dryer. I was there for the program and nothing else; I must keep my closeness with Ed secondary. Nothing should eclipse my purpose: learning the Word from Wierwille.

19

Literal Translations

On the first Tuesday night in September 1971, I sat next to Ed at the front of the auditorium for Wierwille's first Corps teaching that year. Our identification badges read Way Corps 2. Scents of Yardley lavender toilet water and Old Spice aftershave floated over the rows. Everyone wore their best outfits, leaving blue jeans and T-shirts stashed in the trailers. We dressed up for teachings because Wierwille said it showed respect for God's Word and the person teaching it—as if outward appearances always reflected inner realities.

The only non-Corps people permitted in these meetings were Rev. Walter Cummins, Bernita Jess, and Wierwille's personal research secretary, who lived with her family in a trailer across the driveway. Before the Corps was instituted, Wierwille had conducted regular biblical research sessions with those three trusted assistants. They were present for Way Corps teachings to serve as on-the-spot resources in case Wierwille needed them.

I ran my hand over the smooth leather of my Bible. Rev. Cummins soon emerged from the side door. We stood up as he made his way to the desk that replaced the podium on Corps nights.

"Please be seated, take your songbooks," he said, "and turn to 'Leaning on the Everlasting Arms.'" As ever, Walter's suit and tie were immaculate, his wavy hair combed back, and his eyes bright, but he was subdued as he led the song and the prayer service, possibly nervous over recently joining the full-time staff as Wierwille's biblical research assistant. His new duty was supremely important.

When he introduced Wierwille, we rose to our feet again.

"Please be seated," Wierwille said. He pulled back the chair and sat at the desk. "Take your Bibles tonight and turn to the Apostle Paul's first letter to the Thessalonians, chapter 1, verse 1." He read it aloud: "'Paul, an apostle of Jesus Christ by the commandment of God our Savior, and Lord Jesus Christ, which is our hope.'"

"Okay," he said. "Look at the word *Lord*."

I thought it as a simple title applied to Jesus, but Wierwille beefed up the meaning, and I transcribed his every word into my notebook, including:

Master, one who is ruler. It means supremacy, position of recognition. In Oriental custom, the wife speaks to her husband as "my lord." England gives [it as a] title of honor: Lord. It is a name signifying high position, like "elder" in the Old Testament and "bishop" in the New Testament.

Doctor was extremely detailed, like the First Corps said. The previous year, when he'd taught Acts, they said his teaching was excruciatingly meticulous. He would take each verse apart word by word and examine Greek meanings and nuances from Eastern customs, figures of speech, and facts from biblical archaeology. What surprised me was their report that Wierwille seldom consulted Bernita Jess about Aramaic words in deciding whether they brought forth more truth than the Greek text. That seemed odd.

After a few of these teachings, we recognized Doctor's pattern, especially the unique ending he always gave: "literal translations according to usage" (literals). These were a twist on the King James Version, supposedly giving the thought and intent of the original verses. To me, they *were* the original. Changing Dr. Wierwille's literals was as unthinkable as changing the Declaration of Independence. They were recorded on tape, transcribed, printed, and stored in binders. I believed they were the accurate Word of God shown to Wierwille by his heavenly Father. If anyone dared to challenge Wierwille's literals, they would be shunned—or worse.

20

Nothing Is Perfect

Nothing and nobody is perfect—a truism by this time I'd forgotten. In the fall of 1971, Wierwille took his Bible teachings on the road with his buddy and general manager of The Way, Howard Allen. They planned to visit fellowships in nearby states and afterward go hunting. We understood that Wierwille was undertaking official ministry business, and he was entitled to a little recreation as well. This sort of trip became an unquestioned tradition, like a sports team traveling for away games. Even though Wierwille left us in the trusted hands of Rev. Cummins, the absence of our man of God put more pressure on us.

"While I'm gone," Wierwille told us, "I'm charging you to hold down the ministry spiritually. Pray more, work harder, stay extra alert to guard against the wiles of the Devil."

We did. And we did it like soldiers pacing with lifted rifles in a watchtower. The Devil was always out to thwart us, even in subtle ways.

Wierwille was gone about a month. During that time, and many more times when Wierwille was away, Rev. Cummins taught at our weekly Corps meetings. Walter, as he let us call him, was only a few years older than most of us, but he was married with kids, making him seem mature beyond his years. His gray-flecked hair gave him that church-elder look. He'd earned that status. He'd been faithful ever since he was sixteen years old when he first took the PFAL class about a year after his mother took it. They'd lived in New Bremen, a nearby town, and became steadfast followers, so devoted that before long, his mother married Wierwille's older brother, Harry, The Way's secretary-treasurer.[1] That intimate tie to the Wierwilles no doubt helped Walter become a resolute believer. From the beginning, Wierwille took him under his wing like a son. Wierwille's older son, Don, was a grade-school principal during the '70s, not directly involved in the organization with his father. That came later. So Wierwille showered Walter with all sorts of special attention, mentoring his young trainee in every task related to the affairs of the ministry, especially its most important work: biblical research.

Walter was like a gentle young uncle, the kind of person who'd insist you take the last cookie on the plate. If you declined, he'd leave it there, just in case. Patient and self-deprecating, he loved to make puns. I liked him. After college, he'd taught high school English and mathematics while continuing under Wierwille's tutelage. Now, with Wierwille on the road, it was Walter's turn to tutor us.

On Corps night, October 5, 1971, Walter dove straight into the deep end of the pool and pulled us in with him.

"Tonight we're going to look at errors found in Greek manuscripts of Scripture." Walter may have mentioned the fancy name for this type of work—textual criticism—but I didn't care what it was called. Not yet.

"Somebody please check the doors. Lock them, okay?" he said. The only non-Corps in the auditorium were Bernita Jess, my Aramaic teacher, and Doctor's personal research secretary. They took seats in the back row.

Walter reminded us that Doctor mentioned in the PFAL class that some mistakes were made by translators and copyists. The topic did not disturb me when I'd heard it at that time because my impression was that Wierwille had fixed the parts of Scripture he taught. As for any additional mistakes lurking in translations, I imagined that over time

I'd be able to know a mistake when I saw one by using Wierwille's fool-proof methods.

In Aramaic class the previous summer, Bernita had also pointed out that scribes made mistakes, but she had not lingered over particulars. She simply said that since ancient texts were copied by hand, blunders happened. Monks worked in stifling rooms and grew tired or distracted, glancing back and forth from the source text to the fresh parchment or vellum (animal skin) on which they wrote the new copy. Dim candle or oil lamp light didn't help, either, nor did annoying flies. Some of the copyists, she said, didn't even know how to read. All they did was copy the words letter by letter. If they misspelled a word, they might not realize it. Bernita, like Wierwille, did not sound worried about these errors, so I didn't stress over them, either. Not until Walter, possibly making a big mistake, taught us about them that night.

On a blackboard, Walter drew two charts, one labeled *Unintentional Errors,* the other *Intentional Errors.* I copied the charts in my notebook.

"Unintentional errors include simple mistakes," he said. Under that label, he listed misspellings, added letters, deleted letters, and changed letters. He looked around the room, smiling, pleased he had our attention.

"A related inadvertent mistake is when a letter, word, syllable, or phrase occurs once, but it was copied twice," he said, tapping the chalk on the board. "Sometimes entire words were added or deleted. This can be more serious."

For each kind of slip-up, Walter wrote a technical term on the board, and I listed it in my notebook. He made sure to point out that most inadvertent mistakes didn't affect what the Bible said. Scholars translating the Greek texts had caught these sorts of problems like fish in a net before they swam away in the text. But there were other inaccuracies—deliberate ones. That's when I got nervous.

Intentional errors concerned Walter. No surprise. I looked around. His worry lines had transferred themselves to most faces in the room.

"These errors were deliberate forgeries," he said, "evil attempts to change God's Word for dubious reasons, even for money."

Money? Whoever altered the text had been up to no good. Tampering with God's Word like this was unforgivable, motivated by Satan. There were several kinds of these purposeful changes, including marginal notes transferred into the main body of the text, and dogmatic alterations, made when translators connived to make the Scriptures agree with their theology. In Catholic terms, this was as bad as a mortal sin.

Walter said, "Open your Bibles and turn to Matthew, chapter 28, verse 19." The soft rustle of turning pages filled the room like a rushing breeze. Walter read the verse aloud as we followed along:

Go ye therefore, and teach all nations, baptizing them in the name of the Father, and of the Son, and of the Holy Ghost.

Walter said the Greek text (he didn't say which one) stopped after the word *nations.* The rest of the verse, about baptizing, had been added by English translators to support their theology about the Trinity.

That added phrase was not italicized in the King James Version to indicate it was added. Without Walter having pointed out this deliberate addition, we could not have guessed it was not part of the Greek version.

I was too mesmerized to stop and consider how dependent we were on Walter and Wierwille to provide this kind of vital information.

Walter admitted he was still learning about these things. He always seemed duty-bound to tell us what he learned, not only from Wierwille, but also from the Greek classes he had taken years ago when he was in college, and the continuing study he did on his own. His analysis of textual errors impressed me. It sparked my imagination but it also raised new questions. Where were the Greek manuscripts Walter referred to? What more could I find out about scribes and translators? Would I ever learn what Walter knew?

It seems weird now to consider myself at nineteen, with no college education, being attracted to this esoteric study, while most of my girl-friends from high school were in college; dating or married; occupied with the latest fashions; engaged in politics, art, nursing, or a million other things. I must have seemed like a total oddball to them, at least to the ones I'd written to, describing my experiences. No one answered those letters. I was in another world, caught in a game of hide-and-seek for God's exact words. I wanted to get to the bottom of things; to chase down the truth; to know, love, and serve God by finding out exactly what He said. Walter's story of scribes adding the phrase about baptizing proved how important this study was.

If only I knew and understood more. If only I had more time to study these topics. If only I wasn't kept so busy.

I wonder now about how comfortable Walter was with sharing that unsettling information. Did he believe he'd ever find all the textual errors in the Bible? *And* fix them? Even if he read the Greek manuscripts himself, did he think he could identify all mistakes? How long would that take? [2] And most important of all, did he worry about any textual errors he might find that would make it necessary to change what Wier-wille had already taught as God's Word? When Doug recruited me, he'd claimed that the ministry changed when they discovered "new light" in the Scriptures. It didn't occur to me until years later that admitting that we should change an existing teaching—previously claimed as true and accurate—would harm The Way's credibility. Our believers made deci-sions about how to live their lives based on Wierwille's teachings. How did we possibly imagine admitting errors would work out?

I suspect Walter assumed that our fascination with textual criticism, if any of us had any, would not unsettle our rock-hard beliefs about our ministry's teachings. But perhaps to derail any potential worries, at the end of the night he added a cool disclaimer.

"Remember, we have plenty of Scripture to learn without getting distracted by scholarly matters, like minuscule errors in texts," he said. "Like Doctor Wierwille encourages us to do, we should master the classes he's already taught us before getting into studies like this." And he added one last caveat, one I'm willing to bet Wierwille gave him. "Listen, it's wise if you do not share this topic about scribal errors with immature believers. That includes your sponsors, the people you write to every month. They might not be able to handle it." That was code for saying Satan might tempt them to doubt what Wierwille had already taught. Satan, the great deceiver, could muddle people's minds with things like textual research. We must take care even with our own minds, especially while Doctor was away.

Walter erased his lists off the blackboard, and we left.

That session proved that research at The Way was a tangle of contradictions. Textual research was important, but not for everyone. Learning Aramaic was vital for research, but only a few learned it. Aramaic was the original language of the Scriptures, but Wierwille mainly used Greek as the source for the Word of God. Most Corps never became interested in textual research because they either considered it tedious and "geeky" or thought we should leave it to the pros: Wierwille and Walter. Some said only certain believers in the Body of Christ were called by God to do in-depth Bible study like Walter's. I wasn't sure about that. It seemed to me that if ours was a biblical research ministry, everyone should and would want to get down to the nitty-gritty with the Bible, like panning for precious nuggets in a river. I thought that was the reason we waded in, swishing the sand around, sifting to pull out the gold.

21

The Marriage Deal

In 1971, The Way competed with other groups who claimed to have gold, too—the kind found in personal transformation. In San Francisco, near our Bay Area fellowships, Werner Erhard conducted his first empowerment course: *est*. Participants, he claimed, could achieve, in a short time, a sense of personal transformation and enhanced power. People flocked to *est* like pigeons crowding in for bread crumbs—morsels of knowledge, power, and love—as we did to The Way Corps. After only two months in our transformative program, I knew more Bible, loved the Corps like family, and my platonic relationship with Ed made a left turn onto Lover's Lane.

One Sunday night about eleven o'clock in Trailer Six, Ed and I snuggled on the living room sofa, stealing a few private moments. A table lamp lent a soft glow to the room, and pale moonlight, streaming through the window behind us, shifted over the study carrels and blue furniture. On the other side of the wall, in the communal bedroom, our Corps sisters chattered like monkeys, opening and shutting dresser drawers and running the shower. Ignoring them, we kissed and cuddled. When I said it was time to quit and wiggled out of Ed's arms, he tugged me close again.

He whispered, "I guess we ought to get married."

"Huh?"

Not a romantic proposal, but there it was. We hadn't discussed marriage yet, but that didn't matter. I had a secret. I was convinced that God had already told me—about a month earlier down by the Jordan behind Wierwille's house, where I'd gone to pray about this relationship—that I would marry Ed. I had been tempted to tell Ed about this momentous revelation, but I worried he'd feel coerced, like most men probably would, even though God Himself was the one giving me directives. Or Ed would resent not being the initiator. I understood from the Bible that women should be subservient to men, not prime movers.

Most women hope for declarations like "I'm madly in love with you," "I can't imagine my life without you," and "Darling, will you marry me?"

I settled for a call to duty—"we *ought to*"—and said yes.

Over the years, I've wondered whether the proposal came along because we'd been fooling around (short of intercourse, due to the N.T. injunction against fornication) and Ed thought marriage was the honorable way to proceed, or because it just made sense to him given our beliefs. Choosing a marriage partner as a Way Corps member meant feelings should not dictate your decision. A spouse must be like-minded with you on The Way's teachings and loyal to the group—this was not negotiable. Falling in love was a notion from popular culture based on emotion and impulses of the flesh. Many Way Corps matches in the coming years resembled arranged marriages. Wierwille often said any two people could renew their minds on the Word to make their marriage work, regardless of differences in personality or temperament. Their Way-based common ground would keep them together. We would call these "ministry marriages." There were dozens.

Ed and I decided he should tell Wierwille of our engagement because Ed, as the man, was spiritually in charge of our relationship. We were only one step from fulfilling what the Word said about couples: "For the husband is the head of the wife, even as Christ is the head of the church: and he is the saviour of the body" (Ephesians 5:23). We were committed. Surely Wierwille would bless our vow. What better match could there be than one like ours, two steadfast Way Corps members dedicated to spreading God's Word together?

The next day, I waited outside Wierwille's motor coach while Ed went in for his man-to-man talk. The gleaming vehicle, dark blue and spotless, was parked in the President's Home driveway, where, as Wierwille often told us, he hibernated to study. It was a sunny day but still cool under a clear October sky. I pulled my sweater around me, for warmth as well as comfort. I worried about what Ed might say in there. It shouldn't take long. Any minute I expected to see him smiling as he carried Wierwille's blessing to me through those shiny metal doors. I paced around the courtyard. I daydreamed of walking down the aisle to Ed.

Soon I heard the clunk of the heavy motor coach doors, and Ed emerged. He was not smiling. He was pale and sullen. He came toward me, took me by the elbow, and steered me to the looming white barn across the courtyard where we sat on the steps.

"Doctor isn't happy about this," Ed said in a low voice. I looked directly into my lover's face and saw trouble there. "He kept saying we'll have to wait till after graduation to get married. No exceptions—"

"But we know that already. You didn't ask for an exception, did you?"

"No."

"Wasn't he pleased? Wasn't he even a little bit glad?"

"No, Charlene, he wasn't. I don't know why. Didn't want to press him. I said we knew we were supposed to wait till after graduation, but he was grouchy anyway."

Maybe Wierwille was testing our resolve. Or, more likely, Ed caught our teacher in a foul mood. I glanced across the courtyard at the motor coach and felt nervous. Maybe Wierwille was at a window watching us, suspecting we were plotting to run away. We heard that a couple in the Zero Corps left to get married, and a First Corps woman ran off the previous year with her lover against Wierwille's will. We wanted to prove we weren't like that. If we didn't, Wierwille might break us apart.

Wierwille's lack of enthusiasm for one of the biggest decisions of my life nagged at me terribly. I dragged around like a tired old woman hauling a basket of laundry. At least he hadn't forbidden our union. I now suspect he felt blindsided by our making this important decision without consulting him first. It was crucial for him to be in charge of us, to advise and lead us himself, and we had aborted his process.

Our Corps brothers and sisters, when we told them our news, acted glad for us, but I think they took a wait-and-see attitude, knowing our wedding bells could not ring until we finished the program. We had nearly two years to wait. And wait we would. We'd show everyone, including Wierwille, that our love was real.

I didn't interpret Wierwille's uptight reaction to our engagement as being inspired by God, although I thought everything he said was in line with God's will. Why not this? Because of my revelation as I prayed down by the Jordan. I believed in that revelation as strongly as I believed the earth made a path around the sun.

It pleases me now that despite habitually kowtowing to Wierwille, I opened my heart to an unlikely seed of self-empowerment disguised as my conviction that God told me to marry Ed. It incubated for years even in the cult's stifling environment. Tiny and fragile, the seed remained dormant through drought and starvation until, years later, I was ready to let it grow.

I carried on, not imagining that the wording of a marriage proposal is a lot like a weather prediction. It can tell you a great deal about what's in the making, but it can't guarantee things will turn out as you expect.

22

Those Doctor Moods

Anyone who ever knew Dr. Wierwille would be lying if they denied that his mood swings were sure signs he was troubled and destructive. One night about eight o'clock while we were in our trailers, Del called through the intercom. "Emergency meeting in the Fireplace Room in ten minutes." That room, in Wierwille's basement, was intended for privacy—whatever Wierwille said in that room, we were instructed to put in our "lockbox," a secret folder in our minds that we never opened again.

Wierwille was ready for us with bowls of popcorn and cold bottles of pop. "Somebody hit the dimmer switches," he said from his chair by the fireplace. "And close the door."

The recessed lights threw a distorting glow on everything. The shut door kept his family from disturbing us—even Mrs. Wierwille, who was upstairs. I sat in a corner on the floor, my back against the wall. In sagging sofas and chairs, or cross-legged on the floor, my Corps brothers and sisters looked like subdued children, brows and mouths drawn, ready for bad news, empathetic. Doctor rattled ice cubes in a glass filled with what we all knew was his favorite: Drambuie. His drinking wasn't secret. From what I saw, it was part of his daily routine. Like his mood swings. Nobody seemed to consider his drinking as a problem to address.

"Kids," Wierwille said, "the damn newspapers are after me again. They're sayin' I'm a cult leader. Nonsense like that. I only—" He choked up and shook his head, as if shaking out anger.

By this time, we were familiar with comebacks to the cult label: "One man's religion is another man's cult," "The Lutheran Church started out being called a cult," or "All new religions go through this stage."

Wierwille whined on. The source of his frustration was a recent newspaper article, an interview with a disgruntled former Way follower who made nasty accusations.

"He's out there stabbing me in the back, saying I'm a dictator. All I ever did was help that guy, and now look what he's doing to me. Blows my mind." He took a sip of his drink.

This guy, Doctor said, criticized him for excessive drinking, swearing in public, acting like a know-it-all, and womanizing.

"You know what the Word says about this stuff? 'All that will live godly in Christ Jesus shall suffer persecution.' Ain't that the truth? I've bled my heart out for thirty years teaching nothing but the Word, and this is the thanks I get. Kids, he's tearing down the greatness of God's Word I teach. The Devil is always after the Word, using people who focus on things of the flesh." He shrugged and lifted his arms in a gesture of surrender, and I watched nervously as his hand holding the glass of sloshing Drambuie almost hit the fireplace.

"Don't you forget, I run this ministry according to guidance from my Heavenly Father, not to please men, and I'm counting on you, my kids, to stand with me. Nobody sees the vision of this ministry like you do." With that, Doctor set his drink on the hearth by his chair and sighed loud enough for me to hear him in the back of the room.

He raged on and on, as adamant in his denial of womanizing as of being called a cult leader. I thought both criticisms were the outrageous lies he claimed them to be. He said that the disgruntled Way follower exaggerated his affection for female believers and misunderstood his

175

intention of following the example of the Apostle Paul.

"Just remember. Paul had women travel with him to do ministry work, loving them like sisters, not anything else. So do I."

The community belief was that when Way Corps girls traveled to out-of-town meetings with Doctor—while Mrs. Wierwille stayed home—or when he counseled women in his motor coach, he was doing the work of the ministry. To think otherwise was to think evil. Even as I watched Doctor raise the glass of Drambuie to his lips and heard the clink of ice, I felt honored he confided in us.

Before the meeting ended, he reminded us of our loyalty to him. "Hide this stuff in your lockboxes, kids—remember, we're a family." We understood his code. "No talkin' about this, even among yourselves."

I *did not* blame him for being upset, and I would not gossip about him, either, partially out of loyalty and partially out of fear someone might report me. No, what I *did* was worse. I acted as if the meeting never happened. Only the Word mattered, and he was my father in the Word. I trusted him, and that was that. The next month, I would hold tight to my Wierwille loyalty, even when I went home to my own family.

23

Family Disconnections

We had to face them. Our parents. It was Christmas 1971, and Ed and I left for the northeast, visiting my house first and his after that, hoping our families would be happy about our engagement. That would be our best gift. We loaded our suitcases into Ed's used Chevy van and climbed in. For gas money, we had saved a little from our monthly Corps allowance of $20 apiece (equivalent to $118.34 in 2015). Wierwille, with five children and a few grandchildren, knew the value of family Christmas. Sending us home was good public relations.

Dad didn't show much excitement about our engagement, mostly because we were in a religion he did not believe in, but also he probably thought Ed was an unreliable hippie, based on his long hair and turquoise suede pants. The two of them shared absolutely nothing in common. Dad golfed. Ed did not. Ed played ministry songs on his guitar. Dad was not into that. Dad read novels. Ed shunned fiction, as did I. Fiction told lies; we only wanted truth. There was no football or basketball banter. No male bonding took place. I suppose Dad was doing what he thought a father should do: stick to his guns and act accordingly—aloof.

I met up with a few high school girlfriends and witnessed to them, and although they listened politely, none were interested. Involved with

177

their college lives, boyfriends, and Christmas shopping, they could not relate to my Bible fixation. I considered them materialistic, unable to appreciate my newfound spiritual life. I must have been bizarre to them—why change your religion to live in a trailer on a commune in the middle of a cornfield and obey some guru in a suit?

A few days later, we arrived in Rye, New York, a quaint old town with historic stone buildings on rambling, tree-lined streets. Elegant homes with spacious lawns and winding driveways were partially shielded by sculpted hedges. A recent snowfall transformed Rye into an English village on a postcard—tidy and serene. Rich executives of companies like Revlon, Ed told me, lived in those fancy homes and protected their town with tireless ferocity: Kmart was forbidden to build within Rye's city limits. No cheap riffraff would pollute Rye's high-end ambiance. Even Ed's parents lived in a three-story stone mansion, but they didn't own it. It was church property, the manse next door to the church where Ed's father pastored. I was so excited to finally see Rye. The previous May, *Life* magazine had published an article about The Way's fast-growing fellowship in Rye, in which Ed's father was quoted expressing gratitude his son found the Lord Jesus.[1] The article made Rye's believers famous in our ministry.

We parked the van. Ed opened the back door of the house, and we stepped into a kitchen warmed by soft yellow light and the smell of fresh cinnamon bread.

"Hellooo, Eddeeee," his mother and sister called in unison from the kitchen breakfast nook. They murmured pleasantries as Ed made introductions, but their thin smiles betrayed hesitation. His mother stepped back to look me over, moving with alert deliberation, like the mistress of a grand old house in a Bette Davis movie.

"Welcome, Charlene," she said in a formal way. "Ed has told us such good things about you." She pushed her bobbed gray hair away from her cheeks. "We've been looking forward to meeting you ourselves." She extended a cool hand for me to shake. I felt bare, as she took in every detail of my appearance. Her eyes were as bright as a robin's, darting from Ed to me and back again. I recited my own pleasantries and stood there while Ed's older sister, Kathryn, who resembled their mother, said the same sorts of things. I wasn't sure if I was passing or failing a test. They invited us to take our things upstairs while they made tea, then we could all relax for a visit. Ed's father, the tireless minister I'd heard about, was at the church office next door. He'd be along soon.

Ed led me further into the spacious house. He breezed past everything he'd seen all his life, but I dawdled behind him to study the formal dining room, the stylish living room with red-and-blue oriental carpets and shelves overflowing with hundreds of books. An enormous Christmas tree stood in a corner, nearly touching the ceiling, its branches trimmed with lights, infusing the room with evergreen scent. Ed explained we would decorate it with ornaments and tinsel that night—that was their Christmas Eve tradition. Stately windows across the front of the room overlooked snow-dusted lawns and northern pines. Everything inside and out looked well cared for—and expensive. I felt a galaxy away from my modest house. Here, windowsills, stacked with cushions, were deep enough for a person to sleep on. Two Siamese cats were napping in one of them. When Ed and I reached the three-flight staircase, I whispered my surprise that a minister lived like this.

Ed replied, "The congregation is loaded."

On the second floor, we made a stop for Ed to stash his gear in his old room that he had shared with his brother. On the third floor, we placed my suitcase in a small bedroom overlooking the backyard. Ed told me their longtime live-in maid lived in the next room. Polished wood floors, with rugs scattered here and there, had a few creaky floorboards. In my guest quarters, doorknobs made of lovely faceted glass bejeweled each door. Antique furniture was set against striped wallpaper. A handmade quilt covered the narrow bed. I was charmed.

Downstairs as we drank tea with Ed's mother and Kathryn, Ed's father came through the back door, stomping snow off his feet, ushering in a blast of cold air.

"Well, well, we finally get to meet you, precious Charlene." He smiled and hugged me, holding my hands while I stood in front of him. He was not a tall man, yet he peered over his glasses set low on his nose. His warmth disarmed me. I smiled back into his friendly, round face and said how glad I was to meet him.

"How are you? How was the trip? Sit down and tell me all about it," he said. He didn't force a smile like Wierwille often did, or hold himself inside like my father did. He seemed more other-focused than Wierwille, who was usually more interested in what was on his own mind than what might be on ours. Ed's father listened carefully, like a good counselor, even as he puttered around the room, took a glass out of the cupboard, and opened the refrigerator. He nodded and murmured, poured himself a glass of water, and asked me how my father was.

"Oh, he's doing well. Pretty busy at the lab," I said. I explained a little about Dad's microbiology work for the Public Health Department. I lied and said our visit with him had gone well. He probably did not believe me, I was so tense, but he leaned on the kitchen counter across from me and nodded. Before long, he shared a little about his life. To protest Nixon's secret bombing of Cambodia, he had gone on a hunger strike, he said, and drank only buttermilk for a time. He declared that to this day he could not drink another drop of it; it brought back bad memories. He shook his head as if still concerned over that terrible episode.

At the time, Ed's father served in the Presbyterian Church, one of the largest established denominations in America. It bothered me when Wierwille condemned denominations, saying they only paid lip service to the Bible's commands and did not teach people how to use the power of God in their lives like The Way did. That indictment did not apply to

Ed's father except in the sense that he did not teach Wierwille's doctrines in his church nor was he active in a Way fellowship. He had listened to the PFAL class on tape, Ed told me, and even though he did not promote Wierwille's class, he was public about his gratitude for The Way's leading his son to the Lord, as he put it, and motivating Ed to give up drugs. He also offered The Way the use of his church's meeting rooms, particularly when Wierwille came to town to teach an Advanced Class. His integrity made him keep the room available in spite of the church deacons' growing dislike of Wierwille, possibly stemming from his statements about churches preaching lifeless doctrines. Wierwille went so far as to liken denominations to whited sepulchers, a derogatory term meaning they looked good from the outside but inside were rotten. The Gospels record Jesus applying that term to Pharisees, followers of a rigid school of Judaism at that time. With comparisons like that, Wierwille was lucky to have a relationship with Ed's father.

Ed's brother, William, arrived later that day from college. Coming in the back door, he exuberantly greeted and hugged his family. William nodded politely at me and shook my hand. I liked his energetic handshake. His eyes, like mine sweepers, sought out everything in the room. He carefully unpacked his satchel on the kitchen counter and tossed a book to his sister, challenging her to read it and discuss it with him. William was still a teenager but on a vastly different path from ours. He excelled in his college studies and graduate school for him was a given. Ed had warned me his brother was not interested in anything The Way offered; neither was Kathryn. I hoped I'd simply show them I loved Ed, set a good example of a Way Corps person, and offer kindness when I could.

At dinner, the gregarious family held forth on hot topics that I knew nothing about—ones most Americans would have been familiar with, like the raging Vietnam War. I watched and listened while they lobbed political topics like tennis balls back and forth across the table. William was more than upset about the Vietnam War, he was livid. He said that

President Nixon had finally withdrawn some troops—that was news to me—but not enough or fast enough. Kathryn voiced her views on women's rights—drastic changes should happen soon. What was she talking about? In my world, single women should marry and married women should have babies and mind their husbands. Ed's father posed a question, but I didn't hear it. I was stuck trying to absorb what I'd already heard. Was our country in the terrible mess this family said it was? Wierwille was right. In this country, if we were going to have peace, people must get back to believing the Word of God like the Christian settlers of America who had made Jesus Christ their Lord. Wierwille said it was up to us to save our country, and that night's conversation proved the urgency of our task.

More bad news came just before dinner ended. William wanted to discuss the Pentagon Papers. I gathered they revealed scandals about the government discovered by brave and daring journalists. I tuned out the conversation, knowing I wasn't supposed to get worked up about politics, I was supposed to speak for God, but I was lost in this sea of ideas with no paddle to navigate. How could I know what God wanted in these particular political situations?

Soon Ed's father snuffed out the candles with a silver wand, and I felt snuffed out, too. It was impossible for me to form godly opinions about anything they'd said, and that made me worry about my inability to connect with this family. I couldn't bridge the many gaps in our experiences. The only way I saw of developing relationships with my soon-to-be relatives was by following basic biblical dictates of kindness, patience, and love.

I don't recall anyone in that house mentioning our engagement. I got the impression they were taking the same wait-and-see approach as everyone else we told. Things could change during the next two years. Why get excited?

I did watch Ed's mother closely until we left, hoping to get to know her better. She was about the age my mother would have been by this time. As a social worker, her concerns for humanity were strong, as were her political opinions, which I saw when she debated with her husband at meals, something my mother never did. The previous summer Ed had told me the shockingly sad news: she had cancer. Lucky for them, unlike my mother's, hers was in remission, and naturally they all hoped it would stay there.

As I observed her those few days, I saw no hint of a sick woman but rather an energetic one who tried to make me feel welcome, although I distanced myself with my ideology. It's a shame I lacked the ability to open up to her; she didn't know I admired her self-assurance and quick wit. Surely we could have found more in common if I had told her about my mother, but I could not bring myself to talk about Mom.

Instead, I focused on principles we were learning in the Corps from Dale Carnegie's *How to Win Friends and Influence People,* like "Be a good listener." If we listened closely to others, Wierwille promised, people would be more likely to listen to us talk about God's Word. But I never got around to discussing the Bible. No door opened for that. Ed's family must have been close to losing patience with the simplistic fundamentalist views we absorbed from Wierwille, watching how our obsession with the Bible retarded our ability to learn about the world in which we actually lived.

Late on Christmas Eve, after we decorated the tree, we trailed over to the church for a midnight service. At the door, ushers handed out lit white candles encircled with cardboard wax-catchers. I followed Ed to his family pew and looked around, realizing I'd not seen the inside of a church since I was in high school. Being in one with hundreds of people singing Christmas carols brought to mind Catholic midnight masses when I was a child. The familiar sight of red poinsettias lining the aisles cheered me, although I felt as though my outsider status must be show-ing like a slip hanging below the hem of my dress.

That night in the little third-floor room, I couldn't sleep for thinking about Ed's mother. She had not taken the PFAL class. As a sociologist, she probably evaluated our ministry differently than Ed's father, but I did not know enough about her field to understand her perspective. Ed told me that one day while his Dad was listening to the PFAL class tapes in his home office, she had overheard Wierwille's voice and later re-marked, "That man is paranoid."

Ed dismissed her comment, calling her a typical outsider, and natu-rally I agreed. I've often wondered over the years why Ed's parents did not address Wierwille's paranoia with Ed, especially when he applied to enter the Corps, putting him in close daily proximity to the man. Per-haps his father's joy over his son finding purpose overshadowed his mother's cynicism. But even if they had tried, I imagine they could not have stopped Ed from getting deeper into Wayworld, just as my father could not have stopped me.

We left Rye with lovely Christmas gifts and memories, but in my heart I ached for more—a world in which everyone believed exactly what I believed. Estranged from my own family and with tenuous ties to Ed's, I rode alongside my fiancé back to Ohio, eager to rejoin our like-minded community where I believed everyone loved me.

In March, I got the surprise of my life: my father remarried. A few months earlier, I'd gotten a letter from Dad telling me about his be-trothed, a childhood sweetheart from Manchester, New Hampshire, where they'd grown up. Thanks to a mutual friend, they reunited forty years later. "Can you come for the wedding? I'll pay for your ticket," Dad wrote. I was so happy that he asked, that he had not disowned me after all, that I rushed right over to Del's trailer to get permission. Del, our Corps coordinator, was playing games with his son.

"Of course you can go. Your father is getting married, and God bless him." he said. "You should be there."

I booked a flight. All went smoothly at the wedding—I liked my new stepmother—but I felt awkward among so many strangers, and uncomfortable about trying to win anyone to my ministry. But I was to feel much worse than uncomfortable when I returned to Ohio.

"Doctor's mad you went," Ed said. "Go see Del right away."

Del had overestimated his authority. He did not clear his decision with Wierwille. When Doctor noticed I was missing, he was furious, as if I'd gone AWOL. Del took the heat, I learned from Ed. I felt awful, but Del said, "Don't worry, Charlene. I handled Doctor. I'm glad you went."

Del, my secret hero, knew how to smooth things out. Neither of us imagined that heat like that would flare again.

24

Me, Lazy?

Those Wierwille moods, which I thought made him bold in the Lord, invaded our psyches and our privacy. One evening after supper in September 1972, the start of our second year in the Corps, Ed and I strolled across the courtyard to the big white barn, desperate for private time. We were engaged. We were a couple. We were in need of a hideaway and found one in the barn—a small, temperature-controlled storage room for old 16 mm films of Wierwille teaching. Within minutes, we heard *click, click, click* behind us on the blacktop. Turning around, we came face-to-face with Wierwille. He had his German shorthaired pointer, Tick, with him.

"Sit," Wierwille ordered. Tick obeyed immediately. Our leader looked us up and down like a general inspecting troops.

"You two. In my office. Now."

Before we could answer, he tugged Tick's leash, and the two of them turned and marched toward the President's Home, disappearing under the trees, kicking up yellow and orange leaves on the lawn. Ed and I followed, but I dragged my feet, disappointed our romantic interlude was canceled, learning again that walking felt harder when I sensed a reprimand coming. Did he know about our hideaway and disapprove?

Had we done something else wrong? I racked my brain.

Like the rest of the Corps, we'd recently returned from summer vacation after playing host to hundreds of believers at summer school and family camps and cleaning up after the Rock of Ages, which had become the Super Bowl of the ministry. Afterward, we'd helped with graduation for the First Way Corps and a few weddings, including one for Earl and Nancy, my mentors, who were assigned as Limb leaders of Ohio. When we were free to go, Ed and I had driven straight to his parents' Rhode Island beach house and sunbathed away our stress, sleeping late and hanging around in their breezy cedar-shingled home overlooking the mighty Atlantic. We didn't talk about The Way much. Ed's father had just attended the Rock of Ages. He'd seen the joyful crowd of about 3,000, and sensed the hope in our hearts for spreading the Word around the world. He was more than well acquainted with The Way—at least, what Wierwille let people see. Wierwille was a master at keeping financial matters, leadership issues, personal relationships, IRS investigations, and business dealings wrapped in secrecy, cherry-picking what he would make known and when, if at all.

In Wierwille's office, Ed and I perched on the edge of chairs across from his desk. Tick lay on the floor. The curtains were open, and I could see the neatly trimmed bushes and mown lawns (Ed had helped mow them) sloping away from the house toward the road. Beyond that, a neighbor strolled around his farmyard. The sky, the banner over all, was robin's-egg blue.

Our leader gave us a penetrating gaze in a good imitation of General George Patton, one of his heroes. More than once, Wierwille required us to watch *Patton*, the movie depicting the gruff military man. The point: stay tough if you want to accomplish your goals.

Almost two years had passed since I'd been in this office during the women's advance when I expressed my desire to become the best woman of God I could. God knew how hard I'd tried. Did Wierwille?

"So, Ed. I phoned your father this morning." Wierwille rocked in his leather chair, holding a scowling gaze on us. His face, lined and puffy from exhaustion after managing the summer events, was also deeply tanned from countless outdoors hours.

"Thanked him for comin' to the Rock. Real good talk he gave, dontcha think?" The slow rhythm of Wierwille's voice told me he was warming up to something.

Wierwille had invited Ed's father not only to visit the Rock but also to be the guest speaker on Saturday night. As a supportive church minister who attributed The Way with getting his son off drugs and giving him a purpose in life, Ed's father had been a crowd pleaser, as expected. I have no doubt that Wierwille intended for him to lend respectability to our ministry and persuade skeptical adults to contribute to The Way. Ever the ecumenical clergyman, Ed's dad obliged, since like the rest of us then, he did not consider The Way a cult that could harm anyone. He also didn't think Wierwille's dogmas were too outrageous to complain about, at least to his face. From the podium at the Rock in front of those 3,000 expectant believers, Ed's father admired our enthusiasm in spreading the message of the Lord Jesus. He praised God for us. Noticeably, he did not praise Wierwille's teachings, since he did not agree with most of them, but he lauded us for helping lost young people to find the Lord. In a flood of spotlights, he peered into the throng of attentive faces, young and old, and finished his friendly speech with the benediction: "May your tribe increase."

The crowd went wild. Kids and adults jumped to their feet, clapping with reckless abandon and waving peace signs. To hear this good man affirming such wonderful things about us in public made me proud. He would soon be my father-in-law and he understood and loved me.

The Rock was a really big deal that year. Wierwille had hired a professional filmmaker to produce *Rock of Ages 1972*, a documentary about the ministry with a distinct focus on the festival. In the film, viewers saw

Wierwille preaching to thousands of happy faces and heard earnest voice-over testimonies from people of all ages and religious backgrounds, including Way Corps members, thanking God for our ministry. Along with those glowing reports, Ed's father's speech, captured in that film, became a portable tool for distributing Wierwille's message.

In Wierwille's office, our father in the Word told us that Ed's father had remarked on the phone that Ed and I were so tired when we got to Rhode Island that we were only interested in sleeping late, lounging on the beach, and keeping to ourselves. We lacked joy, focus, and vigor, he'd said, and he'd questioned whether we were keeping up in the Corps. Was it too demanding? Were we overworked? Were we eating enough? What was going on?

"So, you guys were awful lazy up there," Wierwille summed up. "Have anything to say?" He tapped a pen on the desk. The lines on his brow grew deeper.

Ed launched our defense. We'd been worn out like everyone else after summer classes, camps, weddings, the Rock, and cleaning up after the Rock, all while fulfilling our Corps duties. But Wierwille wasn't listening. His face reddened, his lips pursed. Before Ed could finish, Wierwille let loose. He threw accusations across the desk—we'd set a bad example, we'd failed to act like Corps, we made his training look bad. He didn't dare mention how he wanted to impress Ed's parents, since he counted on them for valuable public support, the use of their church, and the financial aid Ed and I received from them.

"How's come you blew it like that?" Wierwille sneered. "You're Corps, damn it. Act like it." He slammed his fist on loose papers and sent them sliding across the desk. Whatever we did on vacation, he said, or anywhere else, reflected back on him and the Word he taught. It was no use trying to stand up to him. Like Patton, he always won.

"Now get going." He waved us off like flies.

We crept out the door and retraced our steps to the barn, where we made our way to the one-room hideout and fell silent, subdued after Wierwille's harsh reproof. The lone lightbulb hung above us from a wire. The air conditioner hummed. Smells of hay made Ed's nose turn red. Barn wood—some of it commandeered from railroad ties—surrounded us like old friends. I shoved a few boxes together to sit on, feeling awful, and asked Ed to sit with me, but he was too distraught. He paced, asking what we'd done wrong in Rhode Island. He kicked an empty box against the wall and sputtered, "Why didn't Dad talk to us about this? Why's Doctor such a jerk?" Why, why, why. Ed ran his hands through his hair in frustration. "He doesn't see what we go through around here. He treats us like kids." Ed spat out the bitter words, circled the tiny room again, and reached behind a stack of boxes for his stash—a bottle of apricot brandy. Alcohol was forbidden (for us) on the property, but Ed didn't care. He sat down with me and handed me the bottle. We took a few swigs, and I did not feel guilty at all, too upset to realize the obvious answer to his last question: Wierwille treated us like kids because we encouraged it with our compliant behavior. True, he often made us feel special, loved, even trusted, but without anyone to hold Wierwille accountable or take him to task, he'd trapped us in adolescence in a pseudo-family in which he held the power. Our situation was a tangled mix of his condescension, our weakness, and our parents' obliviousness. We rationalized Wierwille's calling us "my kids," not taking it seriously until, over time, it took its toll and damaged some of us, if not all, by putting a large dent in our ability to take responsibility for ourselves.

Ed sounded off about Wierwille to me in private, comparing Wierwille to his dad. He'd say things like, "In Dad's church, courtesy is important. Wierwille just hands out criticism." True, Doctor's humiliations were awful, but I feared that Ed's bitterness, gone unchecked, could be bad not only for him, but for me. The worst thing that could happen? Ed would leave the Corps or provoke Wierwille to kick him out. For Ed, like me, returning home spelled failure. He'd already dropped out of college and tried living as a hippie. If he quit the Corps, he had nothing.

Despite Ed's discontent with Doctor, he was lured by principle 5: Go forth as leaders. He aimed for a leadership position after graduation, which meant he'd be away from Wierwille and could run his own show, taking center stage somewhere in the field. As a trained performer, he knew he'd be good at it. Perhaps, too, he thought he'd prove to his father that he could help people without attending a traditional seminary like his father had done. Maybe Ed thought he had to remain in the Corps because we were engaged—he knew I would stick to my vow to remain in the program. Maybe all of these factors compelled him to stay. I'm not sure.

Under the bare lightbulb, I asked Ed to focus on the good things Doctor was doing. I tried to tamp down my panic. "He's teaching us the Word all the time. We can't learn it anywhere but here. Right?"

Exasperated, Ed nodded, knowing he couldn't argue with that. He believed it as much as I did. I'd heard him say it to strangers. He wanted the Word, but not the teacher.

"Think of the practical things we're learning," I continued, watching Ed's face to make sure he listened. "Like how to run a ministry, organize meetings, conduct classes, and teach." I stood up and walked around, thinking of what else I could say to calm him. "We need to know all this, Ed. Besides, don't we always say this ministry is the best thing going?" Ed called The Way the best ministry going in his witnessing speech he gave in nearby bars and shops. I'd even heard him say the PFAL class changed his life. The previous year, he had convinced a former prep school friend to apply for the Corps, telling him he'd learn what God wants us to know.[1]

To break any thread of resistance Ed clung to, I rattled off a list of privileges. Wierwille invited teachers to enlighten us on a variety of topics: biblical archeology, Old Testament history, Christian etiquette, public speaking, physical fitness, wilderness survival, song-leading, office management, health foods, and automobile maintenance. He loaned us his personal copies of books showing God's help in times of crisis, such as George Muller's story of how prayer saved his orphanage. Wierwille showed us how to set up budgets; lead meetings using *Robert's Rules of Order*; conduct weddings, baby blessings, and memorial services; operate film projectors and tape recorders; and dole out counseling on any topic, from marriage to flossing teeth.[2] We were God's one-stop shop. For emergency survival, Del taught us to skin rabbits and behead chickens so we wouldn't starve if America ever fell into chaos—Wierwille was paranoid that the government would one day persecute fringe groups like ours, and we'd have to live off the grid.

I'd internalized exactly what Wierwille wanted. I'd become an extension of him—a sold-out recruiter, re-recruiting my own fiancé. Ed didn't outright say he wanted to leave, but that day I think I yearned for him to stay more than he did.

I suspect I was more submissive to Wierwille than Ed because of the Toledo incident. To survive that, I'd returned to Greenville as a contrite follower, anxious to start over, clinging to the belief that Doctor, the man of God, must have been right about my failure. As for the recent Rhode Island incident, I believed the same thing. Ed and I must have let the Devil trick us. Conveniently, this mitigated Doctor's maddening behavior—he was not mean, he spoke for the Lord like a bold Old Testament prophet reprimanding disobedient Israelites. I was looking through a screen door and calling it glass. I could not see the holes.

More than anything, I wanted to keep my relationship with Ed on an even keel. He would be the head of our union pretty soon. I must support him in times of stress; this was one of them. I'd been studying Proverbs about the attributes of a virtuous woman. I'd also been reading the secular books Wierwille explicitly assigned to Corps women: *Fascinating Womanhood* by Helen Andelin and *The Art of Homemaking* by

Daryl V. Hoole. They reinforced Wierwille's attitudes about married women—they should be submissive to their husbands and bear children. At the time, I was unaware these beliefs were being upended by the Women's Liberation Movement, kicked off by Betty Friedan's seminal book, *The Feminine Mystique*.

We left our barn hideout and fell back in line like good Green Berets. I compartmentalized my tug-of-war with Ed and Ed's tug-of-war with Wierwille, and kept our conflicts in a closet. I must keep moving. The First Corps had left after graduation for assignments around the country and handed us a legacy of loyalty. Like oversized clothing, it challenged us to grow into it. The continuation of The Way depended on us. I chanted my mantra—just stay, you'll be blessed—hoping my relationship with Ed would improve. It gave me hope I could do the surprising job Wierwille had just given me: assisting Bernita Jess with the Aramaic project. The honor bowled me over.

25

The Aramaic Dream

It was a crisp September day in 1972 when I opened the flimsy door of the old Main Office trailer and stepped into a dream. The previous year I had cleaned 16 mm films of the PFAL class in this trailer. This year it was repurposed as the Biblical Research Department for two: Bernita Jess and Walter Cummins. The smell of coffee brewing in the tiny kitchen greeted me, along with a faint hum in the rear of the unit. In front of me, bookshelves replaced my film cleaning machine and the secretarial desks; those had been moved to a new office building behind the trailer park. The place was as quiet as a library.

"Mornin', Charlene," Bernita called. She waved from an area near the rear window. When I reached her, she enveloped me in a hug.

"Come, look what we have." She guided me to a boxy machine, the source of the hum, positioned by her desk. "It's a microfilm reader printer."

Displayed on what looked like a television screen was a microfilmed page of an Aramaic manuscript, two columns of elegant script. Bernita pressed a button. The machine whirred. A few seconds later, below the monitor, a printout of the page slipped into an output tray.

"The paper's a little slippery. See?" Bernita said. She carefully lifted the page and handed it to me as if it were a silk stocking. "Isn't it wonderful?"

"Yes," I said, smelling the fresh ink. I examined the text and recognized familiar Aramaic words, like the one for God. Bernita had given us sample microfilm pages during our summer class, but this page on this particular day was a personal gift.

"We're in the groundwork stage of the project," she said. "I'll tell you the details later. First, let's pour some coffee. I brought donuts today."

Research was not simply a job. Bernita considered it a calling of God. To me, it represented the ongoing realization of God's initial promise to Wierwille—that God would teach him the Word like it had not been known since the first century if he would teach it to others. That revelation gave our Aramaic dream its power and gave me a case of the jitters.

While my Corps sisters worked as secretaries, bookstore clerks, magazine layout assistants, and cooks, I worked at the center of the ministry's purpose. Why? I had no idea, except for believing it was God's will, and I related well to Bernita—she could be moody sometimes, but I worked around that. She knew I'd kept my Aramaic books because I was still interested, so maybe she requested me as her assistant. She never said. In any case, I was exhilarated but took serious stock of myself. I had only a few months of college to my credit and no more education in Aramaic (technically, our work was in Syriac, a derivative) than the basics Bernita taught. I surely couldn't read it fluently, and suffixes, possessive cases, and verb tenses often confused me. But my neophyte status didn't seem to deflate Bernita's confidence in me. Perhaps curiosity and loyalty compensated for my wobbly skills. I vowed to do whatever it took not to disappoint Bernita, Wierwille, or God.

If dreams are contagious, Wierwille caught this one in 1957 from Dr. George M. Lamsa, a theologian from what is today known as Turkey. Lamsa taught Bernita and others at Way summer school. He was best known for his translation, *The Holy Bible from Ancient Eastern Manu-*

scripts, first published in 1933. Wierwille sold that in our bookstore.

Perhaps because Wierwille was characteristically contrary to mainstream scholarship as well as theology, he adopted Lamsa's views on Aramaic, like the belief it was the original language of Scripture.[1] Lamsa further convinced Wierwille to acquire microfilms of the oldest Aramaic manuscripts for research at The Way, a task delegated to Bernita.

Early in this manuscript hunt, Wierwille made one critical mistake that would frustrate his researchers and provoke scholars to mock him. He assumed, since he was not a scholar, that because Estrangelo was the oldest *script* (like a font) in which the Aramaic and Syriac languages were written, then all manuscripts written in the Estrangelo script must be the oldest in existence, the closest to the long-lost original texts. But this was not necessarily correct. Manuscripts written in the oldest script did not always indicate the oldest content. Syriac was written in three scripts—Estrangelo, Nestorian, and Maronite. (Bernita used the term Jacobite instead of Maronite, unaware that Jacobite was considered derogatory.) Manuscripts in each script were passed around Near Eastern churches at different times, and used by different sorts of believers.

By the time I worked with Bernita, she had contacted museums, monasteries, universities, and libraries all over the world—including the British Museum in London, the John Rylands Library in Manchester, England, and the Peshitta Institute in Leiden, The Netherlands—and ordered their catalogs of Aramaic and Syriac manuscript holdings. A gray file box with neatly printed contact information on three-by-five-inch index cards sat on her desk. Way funds, from tithes and offerings, were allocated to realize the dream.

Bernita's space in the Biblical Research Department reflected her dedication and organizational skills. Pens, pads, folders, and in/out trays were arranged on her desk. Her family photos had not one speck of dust. Research books and manuscript materials were squirreled away in a couple of antique bookcases with glass drop-down covers, beautiful pieces of furniture I coveted. An IBM Selectric typewriter was on a small table, and near it, the magical microfilm machine. Not only had Bernita kept plugging away in Aramaic studies and teaching summer classes, but also her marriage made her a pillar of the church.

Sometime in the 1960s, Bernita married George Jess, the Director of The Way Corps. His role was to pray for us daily, support Wierwille's plans, serve as the farm's caretaker, and coordinate outdoor tasks for the Corps, like mowing lawns and trimming trees. I loved his gentle "bless you" whenever I passed him on the driveway. Wierwille depended on the devoted Jess couple to instill their unwavering commitment in young believers like me. Bernita's age and demeanor, along with her interest in helping me, cast her as a mother figure.

"Here, Charlene, this desk is for you," Bernita said, pointing to a new study carrel. I set my books from Aramaic class on the shelf, the gold lettering along their spines facing outward. They would become my sources for resolving a major problem with this dream project: the difficulty of locating verses in the manuscripts on microfilm without chapter and verse numbers or punctuation. We had to insert the chapter and verse numbers and punctuation ourselves. First, we printed the microfilms, roll by roll, creating stacks of those sheer pages of the Old Testament in Estrangelo script from the fifth century. Bernita handed me Genesis.

I opened my hardbound copy of the Old Testament printed in a typeset adaptation of the Nestorian script. The benefit of using this Nestorian Old Testament was that it had chapter and verse numbers and punctuation already inserted, as well as vowel markings. I had read enough Syriac words to recognize the alphabet letters in each of the three scripts, even though the design of each letter in each script was somewhat different. So I used the Nestorian Old Testament as the example for where to pencil in the chapter and verse numbers and punctuation on the Estrangelo copies. Occasionally the microfilmed manuscripts in the Estrangelo script differed from the Nestorian and Maronite texts. Any differences could be important—Wierwille would decide.

Part of the Aramaic dream was more personal. I had four hours a day in the quiet of a library away from noisy offices and from Wierwille himself—he often made me nervous. Sometimes I felt guilty over how happy I was to be out of the claustrophobia of Trailer Six and the hubbub in other departments. Some days I let my imagination drift to images of robe-clad monks bent over tables in candlelit mountaintop monasteries, sweating over parchment or vellum, dipping slender instruments in inkpots, and swatting off flies.

"Watch for fly specks," Bernita said, "you know … those teeny drops of fly poop on the pages. They look like dots above some letters and can fool you into thinking a word is plural."

I suspected that scribes must have felt frustrated sometimes—they were flesh and blood like me, and this was tedious labor. What did they think about while they wrote? Did their task become, like mine often did, a meditative experience? I easily forgot the time as I worked. Did they? Did they consider who might ever read their writing?

Our little task was integral to the big project. We inserted those chapter and verse numbers and punctuation marks to locate what we wanted to study, but eventually someone would enter those microfilm manuscripts, after they'd been put into code, into a computer database and include our inserts. For that, Bernita developed a system of transliteration (not translation), assigning a letter of our alphabet to each Syriac character. That produced the code used for the content of our Aramaic publications. Throughout the year, I gained invaluable lessons in the importance of going slow and the sabotage of haste.

We had to be accurate. If we weren't, we would be guilty of changing the text of Scripture, although unintentionally, which would displease God and disqualify us for rewards in heaven. I didn't permit myself to think about failure. Only perfection. Wierwille did not accept less.

26

Do or Die for Doctor

"Okay, shut the doors," Doctor said from his desk in the auditorium. "Del? Is everybody in?"

"Yes, sir," Del, our coordinator, called out from somewhere behind us. Wierwille counted on Del to carry out even his smallest orders.

"Good. Stay back there. Nobody else gets in." Wierwille looked over our heads at Del. "This is lockbox night. Got that?" He glanced at us. "You know what to do."

Lockbox, we knew, meant that whatever he said was secret. We could not talk about it, even to each other.

Our teacher slumped like a man besieged. One of the First Corps girls trotted out from the side door carrying his usual cup of coffee. He waved her away.

"Kids, the adversary is tearing up Kansas. Alan—I ordained him— well, he and his wife are fighting. Can't believe it." He shook his head. The issue, he summed up, was loyalty to the ministry. Alan Canter, the Kansas Limb leader, was not a Corps graduate. His offence: refusing to mail donated money to Headquarters as Wierwille's organizational structure required. Canter argued that the Bible, in the Book of Acts, said each fellowship should keep donations to further its local work. He was on the brink of splitting off to form his own ministry. His wife was in an unimaginable quandary.

Wierwille had no tolerance for insubordination. He would say, "If God says 'Jump,' you don't argue, you ask 'How high?'" We believed Wierwille's Way Tree organization was revelation straight from God: our modern ministry could not function exactly like the first-century church, so God allowed Wierwille to adapt the Word to our culture. Sending money to Headquarters to distribute seemed the perfect solution.

A couple of things could happen. Wierwille could fire Alan. Or Alan could disassociate from us—but that meant turning his back on God's ministry. Faithfulness to The Way and faithfulness to God were intertwined like one grapevine with another.

Fear snaked through the room. I felt the crisis in every muscle.

"If Alan leaves," Wierwille said, "I have no choice but to follow what the Apostle Paul told his disciple Timothy to do with leaders like this." He quoted the familiar verse.

Holding faith, and a good conscience; which some having put away concerning faith have made shipwreck: Of whom is Hymenaeus and Alexander; whom I have delivered unto Satan, that they may learn not to blaspheme. (1 Timothy 1:19–20)

This topic scared me to death. We viewed the Kansas conflict—and every argument—as a spiritual fight requiring spiritual warfare. We prayed for Alan and his wife and Way believers in that state. We tried to visualize good and peaceful fellowships, despite our alarm at Satan's attempt to destroy God's ministry and cause confusion in the Body of Christ. This episode especially upset those of us in the Second Corps, soon to graduate and be sent to "areas of concern, interest, and need." If

the Kansas couple left, none of us wanted to replace them after this ca-
tastrophe. We burned with questions. Would Alan calm down and obey,
would Wierwille dismiss him, or would he leave the ministry? What
would his wife do?

A few prominent Way leaders had already left their posts, including two
Way clergymen and their wives—Steve and Sandy Heefner (featured in
the *Life* magazine article about Rye, New York), who had overseen The
Way East, and Jim and Judy Doop, in charge of The Way West, primar-
ily the Bay Area fellowships. Those areas were our fastest growing—and
our wealthiest. But those coastal leaders had not left because they chose
to. Wierwille claimed he had to relieve them of their responsibilities
because they were not faithful to the Word—we heard no details. Years
later, I learned it was for the same reason Alan had: Wierwille wanted
them to send believers' donations to Headquarters instead of using the
money to further the work of the local ministries.

Wierwille dismissed those leaders right after he instituted The Way
Tree policy that Alan objected to. It was hard to accept that the Devil
had deceived all of those esteemed believers, but apparently disloyalty
could happen to any of us if we weren't spiritually sharp—although in
the depths of my heart, I could not imagine that I'd ever turn my back
on the ministry that taught me the accuracy of God's Word after all I'd
been through to remain faithful. As a deterrent against attrition, Wierwille usually quoted the Apostle Paul:

> But avoid foolish questions, and genealogies, and contentions,
> and strivings about the law; for they are unprofitable and vain.
> A man that is an heretick after the first and second admonition
> reject; Knowing that he that is such is subverted, and sinneth,
> being condemned of himself. (Titus 3:9–11)

After Wierwille fired the Way's leaders on each coast, he installed fierce loyalists in those vacated positions. First, he appointed a thoroughly loyal couple from the Greenville fellowship, Bob and Dottie Moynihan, as New York Limb leaders. Wierwille had recently ordained Bob. Dottie was a model clergy wife—cheerful, supportive, and an undeterred *help meet*, a term used in Genesis 2:18 to describe Eve. Dottie was the Doris Day look-alike, an Eve in Pappagallo shoes, who had facilitated my recruitment.

Around the time Wierwille fired the Heefners in The Way East, he installed a first-ever Limb leader for Massachusetts, a believer named Christopher C. Geer. Geer, a highly motivated follower from Rye's fellowship, had proven his loyalty as the Branch leader for Westchester County, New York, as well as The Way East's general manager and handyman, a job patterned after Howard Allen's duties at Headquarters. Geer had also managed bookstore operations for that area. He had a calculating finesse that became his trademark. It's been said that he studied Wierwille's personality and style, from tone of voice to one-on-one interactions with people, and ingratiated himself to his "father in the Word" every chance he had. After the Massachusetts assignment, Geer and his wife entered the Seventh Way Corps, and he became Wierwille's bodyguard, valet, and eventually his confidant. The Geer-Wierwille connection was locked and loaded. And it fired at all the appropriate times.

Despite Wierwille's damage control in The Way East and The Way West, some followers were upset and left the ministry, like tornado survivors choosing to reconstruct their lives elsewhere. During the upheaval in Rye, Ed had worried about his father's reaction—would he continue to let The Way use his church's activity room? But his dad was focused on his own pastorate; he did not get involved in Way matters, and the church kept its door open to The Way for a time. At Headquarters, in the wake of this split in the Body of Christ, as we saw it, sadness laced our hearts together for weeks as we prayed for healing. The incidents were red flag warnings—obey or else.

A similar loss had more directly impacted me the previous year. One day I reported for work to clean films. My boss, Outreach Coordinator Rev. David Anderson, was at his desk. The next day, without saying good-bye to me, he was gone. To my astonishment, another clergyman from the field arrived immediately to take over: Rev. Johnny Townsend, the fiancé of my First Corps sister Naomi. I careened around for weeks, confused. When I asked Del what had happened, he parroted the official explanation: pride and the Devil's deception had made David believe he knew how to run the ministry better than Wierwille. Granted, David had often been overly excited about new ideas, but he was also an innovative leader, and he loved God and His Word like the rest of us. I took it hard but hid my conflicted feelings, even from Ed. One slip of Ed's tongue could throw me in the hot seat—my fiancé didn't watch his words as carefully as I wished.

I worried over my part in my boss's situation. If he truly had been tricked into deceit, how had I missed it? Had God warned me but I hadn't listened, like in Toledo? Confidence in my spiritual judgment shook me to the bones but no admonishment came from Wierwille. Over time, I quit analyzing the incident, although I was sorry I'd had no chance to hear David's side of the story. I wanted to find him, but digging up details was dangerous. If I got caught, I might be sent home. With no straight answers, I pulled a curtain of denial closed.

"Kansas is so hot for the Word," Wierwille continued, "but Alan can't lead now with a marriage in trouble … my heart just breaks. Kids, I guess it's up to you to stay put for God and move this ministry. These two sure ain't gonna do it. Why can't people make up their minds to stand on the Word, come hell or high water?"

I thought Wierwille might cry. He tapped his Bible with his forefinger.

"So, what does the Word say wives should do if their man with a ministry trips out?" He thrust his chin out, daring us to answer. *Tripping out* was our term for leaving the ministry.

"Turn to Acts 5:29," Wierwille said, and read the verse aloud. "'Then Peter and the *other* apostles answered and said, We ought to obey God rather than men.'"

Wierwille's question hung over us like a loose light fixture—one ill-timed shake and it would fall. One wrong answer and Wierwille would yell.

"Well?" Wierwille demanded. "What does the Word say? Read it," he shouted. He yanked his tie loose, unbuttoned his collar, and looked around the room, expecting someone to speak up. I bowed my head, confused because the surrounding context of Acts 5:29 was not about marriage. It was about the apostles preaching Jesus's resurrection in spite of the high priest's command against it. The apostles had resisted that order, saying they should obey God rather than man. They would preach because God wanted them to. What did this have to do with marriage?

"What should the wife do?" Wierwille slammed his fist on the desk. "Leave, if necessary!" By this, he meant that the wife should leave her husband. Our teacher took the general principle of obeying God and applied it to Alan's wife. He deduced that wives must obey God whether their husbands did or not, and obeying God meant obeying the Word, and obeying the Word meant sticking with The Way, because The Way taught the most accurate Word of God.

I still have my notes from that meeting. What I did not record is how I felt. My gut churned at the words "leave, if necessary." I felt sorry for that wife—her situation was my ultimate nightmare. I'd thought about it a million times, whenever Ed complained to me about Wierwille. I feared Ed might leave, that the Devil would tempt him. Even though we weren't married and Ed wasn't ordained, we had made a lifetime commitment to the ministry and each other. What would I do if I were that Kansas wife?

Alan left us, his wife went with him, and Wierwille wasn't the only one let down. I let myself down. I caved in to Wierwille's use of Scripture out of context to justify his opinions, and in doing so, I set my own trap.

27

Missing Rose

I hated the limelight. But it was unavoidable at the August 1973 Rock of Ages, because Wierwille focused his brightest spotlight on the Second Way Corps. The following week we would graduate, and Wierwille could hardly wait to introduce us to the thousands of believers from around the United States (and a few other countries) who came to the Rock. He was going to announce our fulfillment of Corps principle 5: Go forth as leaders and workers in areas of concern, interest, and need. I was proud to graduate yet dreaded the flurry of attention. Hiding away with manuscripts in my study carrel that year acclimatized me to anonymity and quiet.

Rock-and-roll music primed the audience for Wierwille. Dynamic in a white linen suit, he strode to center stage, grabbed the microphone, and yelled "God bless you." The crowd rose to its feet, cheering and dancing as if to beating drums. Wierwille's face, flushed red with excitement, matched the carnation in the lapel of his suit.

Soon, he coaxed his Corps kids to file up the stage steps. I drew my long dress—green with white polka dots—to the side so I wouldn't trip. The smell of fried chicken from a nearby food tent drifted toward us, and

I yearned to be on a picnic bench eating instead of paraded on a stage. I clung to Ed's sweaty hand and squinted into the glare. Adults, teens, grandparents, and young couples with fussy children leapt from their camping chairs and blankets, clapping and laughing in the summer evening, creating a blur of faces and colors across the green fairgrounds.

Wierwille praised our accomplishments, especially conducting the PFAL class in towns where he had sent us the previous winter—a test of our believing. He had divided us into teams and arranged for us to live with believers whose fellowships needed help. It felt like a Toledo replay, only it turned out better. Ed and I were sent with two others to Peoria, Illinois. That our father in the Word had sent us together boosted our confidence about getting married and was a sign that Wierwille authorized our engagement. On stage, he announced what we already knew— he was sending Ed and me to Los Angeles as Area Coordinators of Southern California.

"Next week these two are getting married," he cried, and cheers went up. "Then they'll carry the heart of God's Word and The Way ministry to California." He grinned like a proud father. The many West Coast believers clapped and hollered. We waved and nodded as if we'd won an election.

But the night was bittersweet. What most people in that audience did not know, and Wierwille certainly did not mention, was that after our winter test, one of our Corps sisters left.

Rose's departure was suspicious and abrupt. At the time, she and I were bunkmates—she had the top bed. Rose was an introvert like me but far better at recruiting strangers. Her brown eyes peered into people's hearts when she talked with them. I loved that about her. She took her time when she had something to say. I admired that, too. Then one day, my marvelous Corps sister climbed into her bunk, curled up on the plaid bedspread, and faced the wall.

"Rose, you alright?" I patted her shoulder. "Rose?" No response. "What's wrong, Rose?" I was trying to coax a stone to talk. I couldn't tell whether she was angry, sad, afraid, or what.

Our in-resident trailer monitor relayed orders from Wierwille. "Don't pry into this," she said. "Doctor is handling Rose. We are not to interfere. She's got serious spiritual problems."

Soon Wierwille's grown nephew arrived at the trailer, the same steadfast workhand who had delivered Debbie and me to the bus after our failed Toledo episode. "Doctor told me to drive Rose to the bus station as soon as she's ready," he said. "He said to tell you Rose can't perform her Corps duties anymore," he added, glancing around the room at us, "so she's going home. Tell anybody in there to vacate the bedroom so she can pack her stuff."

Dumbfounded, we stood like dressmaker dummies in the living room, duly intimidated.

Fear had the upper hand that day, and we had learned a thing or two about it from Wierwille himself. In a notebook, I had written his words: "Anyplace God's presence is, there's no fear. Fear is a way you can get people to do stuff. Love is [the] true way to get people to serve out of free will."

If Wierwille was right about fear, God had left the trailer.

With Rose missing, our Corps graduation ceremony was a farce. We had failed Rose, which meant we'd failed at loving one another, which should have been Corps principle 1. Instead of fighting for one of our own, like real Green Berets, we pretended Rose never existed. So did Wierwille. But Rose, our phantom limb, did exist. Somewhere.

After Doctor announced all the assignments, we had to sing.

"Show 'em you're Corps," Doctor laughed and snapped his fingers, commanding the crowd to join in, waving his hands like a bandleader. We belted out one of his favorites, "Got a Reason for Living Again," as if we had lost any reason to live before believing in him.

28

Going Forth

We were now qualified to save America, or at least California. On August 30, 1973, we graduated from the Corps, and the next day Ed and I said our marriage vows. As we had requested, a local jeweler inscribed "GOD" on the outside of our gold wedding bands and on the inside, "The Word Over the World." Wierwille and Ed's father performed our wedding ceremony in the BRC auditorium.

I asked my new bunkmate, Christy, to be my maid of honor instead of Debbie. For reasons I still don't understand, Debbie and I had drifted apart. I'd been involved with Ed, while Debbie's friendship with the soft-spoken girl had deepened during our training, and often she was evasive, busy with projects Wierwille gave her. Christy and I had bonded over late-night chats, trips to town, and morning jogs. I liked her earnest desire to do the right thing and her ability to admit her faults—she was easy to love.

Using my mother's sewing machine, I sacrificed sleep to create a white lace wedding dress, and I carried yellow roses and daisies—my mother's favorites. The staff stylist set my hair in pin curls, and over the swirls, I carefully slid a wide-brimmed white hat. I felt like Jackie Kennedy.

As pleased about getting married as I must have appeared, the flurry of the past few weeks—the Rock, Corps graduation, and then wedding preparations—left me with a confused mix of joy and sadness. I was exhausted. I missed my mother. I believed she would have been happy for me, but I felt her absence in a way I hadn't in a long time. A girl needs her mother on her wedding day. My stepmother filled in as best she could, but our bond was unsteady. I remained a motherless child.

And we mourned another loss. The previous month, Ed's mother passed away. We were sad, but when Ed flew to Rye for the funeral without me, my sorrow doubled.

"You don't need to come, I'll handle this," Ed said, and brushed off my protests. I was floored and felt shut out. But my feelings were not supposed to count. Ed must know best. At least his mother had not objected to our marriage, as far as I knew. We'd last seen her at Christmas (the second and last one I shared with her), and we were grateful for that, but we missed her sorely at our wedding. Ed's father, sister, and brother carried their fresh grief like black roses down the aisle. But we had to proceed. California believers were waiting for us.

Ed's father was a solemn model of courage in the face of his abysmal loss, performing our ceremony with grace alongside Wierwille. When we turned and faced our families and guests in the auditorium, I felt relief that we'd crossed one more threshold in God's plan. Before nightfall, Ed and I drove away in a new green Chevy, bought with a recent inheritance from my grandmother, pulling a U-Haul trailer loaded with wedding gifts. Now we were official spiritual Green Berets, trained by the best.

Trailer park at Way Headquarters, New Knoxville, Ohio. Charlene lived in Trailer Six from 1971 to 1973 with other Way Corps women. Accommodations included ten bunk beds with matching bedspreads and one toilet. Men had similar housing.

1971. Second Way Corps members at Way Head-quarters learn to kill and pluck chickens in the courtyard by Wierwille's house. Center: Charlene with long hair.

1972. Wierwille holds informal teaching in the BRC auditorium at Way Headquar-ters with First and Second Way Corps members and others. Left of center: Charlene, with long hair swept back from her face, seated, her side facing the camera. Right: Wierwille, standing, resting his foot on a chair. Display case in the background contained some of Wierwille's books, including Victory Through Christ, which Rob, the surfing Jesuit, found in his Boston College library.

1972. Stage and audience at the Rock of Ages festival at the Shelby County, Ohio, fairgrounds in August. Way believers from 30 states attended: about 1,700 on Saturday and 3,000 on Sunday. Wierwille invited Charlene's future father-in-law, a Presbyterian minister from Rye, NY, to be a guest speaker. A professional documentary company filmed the event.

PHOTO COURTESY OF SIDNEYDAILYNEWS.COM.

1972. Charlene carrying a drink cup at the Rock of Ages festival. Believers sit in circles for fellowships on the lawn.

1972. Charlene in the living room of Way Corps Trailer Six at Way Headquarters during the Christmas season. Ed proposed marriage here the previous year.

1973. Charlene and a Way Corps sister in the BRC basement dining room at Way Headquarters, New Knoxville, Ohio. The Word Over the World banner and airline map wallpaper impressed Charlene when she attended the women's advance in November 1971.

1973. Second Way Corps members pose with Wierwille backstage at the Rock of Ages festival where moments later, on stage, he introduced them and announced their assignments. Charlene, wearing a long polka dot dress, stands left of Wierwille, in white suit. Second row, first on left: L. Craig Martindale, future second president of The Way International.

1973. Rock of Ages festival. Charlene designed the green and yellow bunting for the stage.

1973. Charlene and Ed marry in the BRC auditorium at Way Headquarters. Wierwille and Ed's father officiate. Way staff, Way Corps, and family members attend. Left: Rhoda Wierwille (wife of Wierwille's brother, Reuben) on piano. Right: Dorothy Owens (wife of Ermal Owens, then Vice President of The Way) on organ.

Part 5
On the Field

29

California Shocks

In 1973, the year we went to save California, American troops withdrew from Vietnam, the Supreme Court ruled on Roe v. Wade, and the World Trade Center in New York became the tallest building in the world—major events with monumental consequences. We viewed our Way activities as similarly significant, only ours were more important—they affected the spiritual world, not this earthy realm.

Life in Los Angeles was sketchy at first. Wierwille had arranged temporary housing for us with a couple in Anaheim, grads of an early PFAL class. I'll never forget their generosity. They opened their hearts and their home, close to Disneyland, and oriented us to the gargantuan area, advising Ed to buy the spiral-bound paperback Thomas Guides to navigate the complex roads. Ed and I explored the city. I was struck by the gigantic white Hollywood letters planted on a hillside and the red Japanese bridge in the gorgeous Huntington Gardens. As we looked for a place to rent, I was overwhelmed by the convoluted traffic jams, towering cacti, and unending San Gabriel Mountains—we were not in cornfields anymore. We found a three-bedroom apartment on Los Robles Avenue in Pasadena, not far from the sprawling Fuller Theological Institute—we considered it a competitor. Stately palms, taller than telephone poles, lined the street right outside our front door.

One night we drove to the famed Mulholland Drive, parked on a cliff overlooking the vast City of Angels, and got out to pray. Behind us, automobiles honked their horns as they sped past. I caught a whiff of honeysuckle. Above nearby flat-roofed houses, stars seemed close enough to pluck like oranges from trees. Police sirens from distant streets pierced the silence. As we stood gaping at millions of twinkling lights in the sky above and the valley below, Ed prayed aloud for God to bless the people of the city, claiming it in the name of Jesus Christ—a ritual prayer to ward off the Devil and open doors for reaching those who needed us.

Looking back, our efforts now seem more like a tissue carried off in the wind.

We were finally running our own ministry. Sudden independence from Wierwille felt like straps had been unbuckled, freeing our atrophied arms and legs. We organized our home as married grownups. We determined how and when to eat, spend money, and work. Ed was thrilled, I knew, to run his own show, which in retrospect seems silly, since we had to follow Wierwille's rules: submit weekly reports, mail donations to Ohio, and most importantly, run the PFAL class on a regular basis. Without Wierwille's watchful eyes on him, though, Ed let go of his annoyance over micromanagement. We were happy.

The L.A. area was a newly designated Branch on the Way Tree, the work having been started the previous year by WOW Ambassadors who had run a few classes. The WOWs had left after their year of service before we showed up. We also watched over a couple of smaller Twig fellowships in San Diego. As long as we remained faithful, the fellowships would grow and we would climb the ministry tree.

The five Way Corps principles still guided our behavior—we got up early, donned sweat suits, and jogged a few miles. I cooked healthy meals using recipes from the grandmotherly woman who'd taught us about natural foods. We scheduled time to study the Word, and we taught believers in their homes and ours. Saturdays meant informal fellowships and picnics in parks or at the beach. Sunday mornings meant training sessions in our living room for fellowship leaders. Sunday nights meant dress-up fellowships, open to the public, in rented halls like the Masonic Lodge or an inexpensive hotel banquet room. We rarely let a night go by without a meeting. Once in a while we enjoyed a date night; as newlyweds, we needed it.

We lived for a year in that Pasadena apartment, on the street with those elegant palm trees. Wierwille had trained us to think of our home as a showcase for the ministry, a haven from the world, a place where order and cleanliness must bless people, so I dusted and swept and polished everything nearly every day. You never knew when someone might drop by. In January 1974, someone did.

Rob, my old flame, the surfing Jesuit, rang the doorbell. We'd kept in touch through letters, as we'd promised, but when he wrote to say he was in San Diego and could drive to L.A. to visit me, I panicked. I was married now and Rob had refused the PFAL class, so what was there to talk about? I felt sure I'd mailed him my wedding announcement—could it have been lost in the mail? The only acceptable reason for me to see Rob now would be to attempt—one more time—to recruit him. I explained the situation to Ed, who said sure, invite Rob over, and I did, convincing myself that my former lover must be ready to believe the Word.

I greeted Rob at our front door, unsure of what to expect. He looked the same as ever as he peered through those John Lennon glasses and entered the living room. Believers, milling around, were instantly on alert, like radar tracking his presence. Ed was running the first PFAL class since we'd come to L.A., and it was intermission. Students drank coffee and nibbled cookies and fruit.

Rob and I sat on the sofa like skittish teenagers at their first dance and attempted a private conversation, surrounded by suspicious gawkers. Romantic feelings I'd had for Rob were repressed beyond retrieval by this time, replaced by the secure knowledge that I had married a man of God. Ed breezed into the room, I made awkward introductions, and the two of them mumbled a quick greeting. The only common interest they had was me, and Ed sure wasn't going to compare notes about me with Rob.

My nervous state must have interfered with my ability to process whatever Rob said, because whenever I recall that fragile conversation, all I remember is that Rob hadn't changed his attitude about The Way. I marveled that our paths had crossed once more—he had enrolled at UCLA, not far from our apartment—but we remained a galaxy apart. When the PFAL class break was over, he graciously wished me well and left. I thought I would never see him again.

A few months later, Ed and I rented a charming house on Benrud Street in Monrovia, a town nestled against the foothills of the San Gabriel Mountains, which afforded us more privacy and parking space. I remember that house well. It was the site of an unimaginable and significant coincidence that haunts me to this day, but at the time it failed to change anything.

Ed took off one night to teach a fellowship at a houseful of believers in Arleta, just north of us; some had applied for The Way Corps, others for the WOW Ambassador program. Part of our job was to inspire believers to make those commitments. Sometimes I made this trip with Ed, but that night I stayed home to prepare for a children's fellowship the next day.

A few hours later, Ed returned. I was in the living room, drawing a colorful poster for the children.

"Look at this," he said, tossing a gray paperback book on the coffee table. "You won't believe it. On the way home, I stopped at that church we drive past all the time, that small one with the name Stiles on the sign. The Osborne Neighborhood Church, remember?"

"Of course." The first time we saw that sign we'd been surprised to see the name Stiles. Wierwille often recounted the story about J. E. Stiles, a minister he'd met at a Christian convention in Tulsa, Oklahoma, in 1951. After the convention, Stiles had apparently coaxed Wierwille into speaking in tongues—a vital turning point for our teacher.[1]

I put aside the poster and picked up the book. The cover read *The Gift of the Holy Spirit*, by J. E. Stiles. Ed was in the kitchen opening the refrigerator. Bottles clinked.

"You mean," I said, standing up, flabbergasted, "Stiles wrote this? *The* Stiles? Ed?"

Nothing.

"Ed."

"What?"

"I didn't know Stiles wrote a book about the Holy Spirit. Did you?"

"Nope," Ed muttered over his shoulder.

"Doctor never mentioned this," I said, turning it over in my hands. "Not ever." I opened it and examined the front pages as Ed opened a bottle of Coca-Cola. I often teased him about being addicted to it, not realizing I was right.

"I glanced at it," Ed called to me. "It's not accurate, you know, it's real religious."

We used that term, as Wierwille did, to describe uptight orthodox Christians and their ideas.

"Did you buy it at the church?"

"Huh?" Ed was tearing open envelopes from the daily mail.

"How did you get the book, Ed? Did the church have a bookstore or what?" My husband rarely forked over details.

Ed sauntered into the living room, gulping his Coke.

"I went in the church and knocked on the first door I came to. A man named Larry came out, said he was the associate pastor. A nice guy." Ed said that when he told Larry about the connection Wierwille had to Stiles, Larry said he'd never heard of Wierwille.

"Oh, yeah," Ed added, "He did say that Stiles would jump on a plane at the drop of a hat to minister the Holy Spirit to somebody. Guess that's what happened when he met Doctor."

I listened in amazement while my husband told me that he and Larry had traded phone numbers in case either of them wanted to attend the other's fellowship. Before they'd said good-bye, Larry had retrieved a new copy of Stiles's book from the church's supply and handed it to Ed as a gift. On the inside cover, Ed had printed Larry's name and telephone number, and a phone number for the church.

The first page read: "Price: $1.50. Reprinted 1970. Order from Mrs. J. E. Stiles." A post office box in Burbank came after her name. I scanned pages filled with thank-you letters sent to Stiles from thrilled readers of the book, and flipped through a few chapters. Chapter One: "Have You Received the Holy Spirit Since You Believed?" Chapter Two: "Holiness!" We didn't use that term. Chapter Three: "The Body of the Holy Spirit." Stiles referenced Jesus as the "second person of the blessed Trinity" so I shut the book. Why waste time reading wrong doctrine? I stuck the paperback in our bookcase, considering it a minor piece of Way history, and returned to making posters. I had no idea at the time how significant that unassuming book would prove to be, about a decade later when I returned to Headquarters.

Near the end of our first, rather unspectacular year in L.A. (we'd run only one PFAL class), Wierwille ordered the Corps in the field to return to Headquarters for meetings, later known as Corps Week. I was happy because I would have the chance to see Bernita Jess, my Aramaic mentor. We were able to chat briefly in her tiny trailer office where I had worked with her, but my schedule mainly kept me focused on the reunion of the First and Second Corps, as well as the graduation of friends in the Third Corps, to whom we'd passed the proverbial Corps baton of commitment. The Fourth Corps, the largest group ever, was also there. Wierwille had all his Corps kids to himself before thousands of believers descended for the Rock of Ages.

On August 8, a few days into Corps Week, we gathered in the BRC auditorium, where a television had been set up, and witnessed an announcement that would transform our entire nation. The president of the United States, Richard M. Nixon, resigned.

Ed and I didn't own a television, and we hadn't kept up with the Watergate scandal. I understood just enough to know Watergate involved grave misdeeds by people in government—but I didn't realize the scandal included the president. I looked around and saw my Corps family frowning at the television. I was worried, too, but I had little interest in politics. We were supposed to be busy with God's work, not the affairs of this world. Wierwille was riveted to the television screen, but I didn't see what difference Nixon's resignation made as long as we kept spreading the Word. God would take care of His people no matter who lived in the White House. We couldn't let the Devil distract us from our goals. The Way was gaining traction lately and in a few days Wierwille planned to ordain more men to serve God. Ed was to be one of them.

The clergymen-to-be were the ten men of the Second Corps, including Craig Martindale, who would become the second president of The Way in 1982. Some of them had family members arriving for the ordination service, but Ed's couldn't come. They had an important ceremony to attend in his father's church. Our mismatched schedules didn't bother us until a few days after Nixon resigned, when Wierwille pulled Ed aside in the dining room after lunch. Wierwille looked casual and friendly in shorts and an untucked summer shirt, but he glared at Ed and his face darkened. I stood by, examining my fingernails.

"So your father's gettin' married again," Wierwille said. He raised his voice over the clatter of plates and silverware that kitchen staffers in white aprons were clearing away.

"Yes, yes, he is," Ed said. "To a wonderful woman, a longtime friend of the family—"

I glanced up. My husband cleared his throat, looking wary about Wierwille's reaction. I knew that Ed had mentioned his father's second marriage in his last report to Doctor.

"Well, that's *reeeeal* nice," Wierwille said. "And you're leaving today for the wedding, are you? Flying up there to Rye?" He peered into our faces. I saw my reflection in his glasses.

"Yes, sir," Ed said. "But we'll be back in time for ordinations."

Behind the kitchen doors, a plate crashed to the floor. Wierwille frowned but held his piercing gaze on us.

"Okay ... well ... good." Doctor nodded like a person absorbing baffling information he couldn't sort out while Ed and I stood there like kids hauled before the principal. Wierwille started to turn away but spun around and thumped his finger on Ed's chest.

"How's come you don't tell your father you won't go to his wedding unless he comes to your ordination?"

Our mouths flew open. Ed chuckled like someone had tickled him. But Wierwille was not teasing. He didn't even twitch.

I knew Ed wouldn't make this demand on his father, even with Wierwille's challenge. His father simply couldn't come. We understood that.

Without waiting for a reply, Wierwille pursed his lips and shrugged, turned his back on us, stomped down the aisle, slung his arm over the shoulders of the nearest Corps man, one of Ed's closest buddies, and guided him through the kitchen's swinging doors. Faithful Tick scampered after them.

Doubts flared inside me. Were we doing something wrong? The old feeling of being caught between Ed and Wierwille pulled me this way and that.

Ed kept muttering, "I can't believe he said that."

The entire time we were away toasting the happy couple, Wierwille's intimidating comment ran through my mind like numbers through a ticker-tape machine. I didn't dare remind Ed of it, but I dreaded what Wierwille thought of Ed's defiance. But maybe he was angrier at Ed's father, a fellow clergyman, who hadn't made it a priority to attend his own son's ordination.

As usual, the world revolved around Wierwille.

Our visit in Rye was rushed and awkward and over before we knew it. Right after the champagne and cake at Ed's massive stone house, we flew back to Ohio, arriving before nightfall.

The next night, Wierwille ordained Ed, along with the others, at a ceremony in the BRC. The lights were dimmed, and the organist and pianist played hymns like "A Mighty Fortress Is Our God." One by one, Wierwille laid his hands on the head of each Corps man who knelt before him, and by revelation from God (supposedly), spoke a prophecy stating that man's ministry or ministries—Ed was proclaimed a pastor and a teacher.

The service was thick with tenderness and gratitude, as misplaced as that now seems. The emotional effects of lighting, music, singing, praying, and ceremonial garb deepened our commitment. I cried thinking about everything Ed had overcome to reach this point in his life: drugs, the loss of his mother, confusion over his life's purpose, even humiliation by the man blessing him that night. Being married to Ed meant more now; it was a spiritual job with increased responsibility. Sitting with clergy wives, I watched intently from the front row, imagining what Ed's father would have thought about this. The ceremony was couched in Way jargon: a Way clergyman was sworn to serve God's people in the household. If he ever left, he would suffer the loss of God's protection. Ministers held a position of honor, and my husband was willing and thankful to take it on despite his dissatisfactions with the man who ordained him. The title of reverend was a family issue, also. I think Ed felt he had achieved equal status with his father. How could his father not be proud of him now?

Nearly a year after Wierwille ordained Ed, we crossed another threshold—into parenthood. Rachel was born. Her little round face, tender smile, and gurgles brought us joy beyond joy. With the help of Ed and loving friends, I soon adjusted to being a mom. What I loved most was the time I spent nesting with our baby, the light of my life. I'd fulfilled my ultimate woman-of-God role. It was June 1975, and we'd rented a hilltop house on Kaweah Drive in Eagle Rock, the fourth residence of our L.A. assignment (the third was a large house in Monrovia). The Kaweah house was sunny and comfortable and often full of believers who cherished Rachel; we were never short of a competent and loving babysitter.

Our living room picture windows gave us a view—very distant but interesting—of the Rose Bowl Stadium on one side and the sprawl of Santa Monica on the other, but after Rachel was born, I didn't spend much time looking out windows. My focus, my greatest pleasure, was her.

If she had not come along, it's highly likely I would have remained tethered to The Way, unable to leave it. As the years unfolded, this would become clearer and clearer.

Ed was a full-time minister, although he helped with the baby when he wasn't traveling around Southern California to teach fellowships and run classes. The work I did for The Way, even as lightweight as it was, took a backseat. Occasionally I conducted women's fellowships near our house. No long-distance Aramaic tasks were available—few people were involved with the Aramaic project at that time—but I stayed in touch with Bernita. I missed her motherly interest in my daily life. I still had my books, but no time to use them. Aramaic study felt like a lost cause. Any free time I had was spent teaching basic lessons from the PFAL class, a nonnegotiable directive from Wierwille.

Sometimes I felt lonely at night with the baby when Ed was out doing the work of the ministry. That year, one young wife in the fellowship had become my friend, and we sometimes kept each other company. Ed and I had no social life except an occasional dinner with her and her husband, but they were leaving to enter the next round of Way Corps training, joining about 300 others at the Way College of Emporia in Emporia, Kansas, our new property designated for that purpose. The training had become more expansive, with more classes and a hunter safety program. Wierwille, an avid small-game hunter—mostly quail—owned several guns. Guns had been regular features around Headquarters for years.

About a month after Rachel was born, our lives changed again with only one telephone call. Usually, to get ministry information to and from Wierwille, Ed relied on our Limb leader, Del, who lived in San Leandro in the Bay Area of Northern California. Sometimes we flew up for weekends and stayed in his ministry-owned house with him and Nancy. Our visits fell into a routine. Nancy and I would prepare simple dinners, like linguini with pesto, Caesar salad, and white wine, and we'd sit around the kitchen table drinking with our husbands and discussing ministry business. As Way Corps graduates, we could now drink alcohol, but the limit imposed by Wierwille was two drinks (we sometimes had more). On one such trip, we learned that Wierwille wanted the First Corps back at Headquarters that coming August for a full year. They'd been in the field for three years. It was time for a reboot.

Back in our Eagle Rock home, Ed found me in Rachel's room changing her diaper. "Got some news," he said. "Doctor called a minute ago, asked if we'd replace Del and Nancy next year. Be the Limb leaders."

"Oh my gosh, Ed. Are we going to?"

His voice prompted Rachel to coo softly. She was making motions to let me know she was hungry. I needed to nurse her, but she must wait. I had to listen to Ed.

"Somebody has to take over," he said, "and we're the most likely Corps. I went ahead and said yes. Couldn't imagine you wouldn't want to."

"Of course I want to, honey," I said, pulling plastic panties over Rachel's cloth diaper. "It's a huge blessing," I added. Ed was ordained; we had no choice but to do it, whether I liked it or not. Ed returned to his home office down the hall, and I settled in the rocking chair to nurse Rachel and think about this change.

Our new job would be a privilege, but with it came more responsibility. Demands on Ed's time and attention would increase—there would be more meetings, conferences, and teachings to prepare for and deliver. The Limb office in San Leandro was miles from the leader's house—I might feel isolated. The reality of moving once again began to sink in—I dreaded packing. We'd just settled into this house before Rachel was born. I'd have to repeat the process within a month, *and* with a new baby. I prayed this transfer would be the last for a long while.

One of Wierwille's directives was to travel light. We left our furniture—even my parents' maple bedroom set—in our house in Eagle Rock for the Corps graduate filling our position. I'm sorry we let go of that heirloom. Nevertheless, material things were only that—unimportant compared with spiritual values. We packed our belongings in Eagle Rock and unpacked them in San Leandro in the Limb home that Del and his family had vacated a week earlier. We inherited the furniture, the car, even the hummingbird feeder hanging outside the kitchen window. Everything at the house was owned by the ministry, including the Corps who lived inside.

30

Climbing the Way Tree

Ed's position as Limb leader boosted his ego and our paycheck and opened more opportunities for him to counsel and teach people—exactly what he'd always said he wanted. His dedicated wife at his side and his young child in his arms gave him confidence as the head of a growing family. He'd earned the respect and love of the California believers, several hundred by this time—everyone said so. His pre-Way training as a performer made his Bible teachings animated and motivating, stirring people to commit to The Way. As an ordained clergyman in a position of trust, he endeavored to nurture God's people, pray for the sick, and help troubled believers. He conducted fellowships and classes. Together we held an advance for couples, teaching about Word-based marriage, the roles of men and women of God, and child-rearing. We were complimented on our good example. God had made my dreams reality.

Ed's promotion signaled he was a valuable leader and that Wierwille trusted him, but while Ed's responsibilities increased, mine were usually unnoticeable. A local woman supervised the children's fellowships here; I had run them in L.A. In the office, Ed's full-time secretary doubled as office manager. A local believer managed bookstore operations. About a dozen workers in a Way Corps preparatory group, Fellow Laborers, helped with conferences and special events. They lived in apartments above the Limb office; a few of the girls loved to babysit Rachel. I held an occasional women's fellowship and planned the annual women's spring advance, but with less to do, I stayed home with my baby most of the time. Soon my daily routine became … well … routine. In the fall, I decided to change it. Ed was busy, with little time to think about what I did, although anything ministry-related was fine with him.

First, I reached out to Bernita Jess. Along with the Aramaic project, she was also responsible for The Way's home-study lessons that graduates of the PFAL class were required to complete before taking the Advanced Class on Power for Abundant Living. The lessons were simple questions about the class material, like recounting what Wierwille taught about four crucified with Christ and the "law of believing." Each state had a person who graded these lessons and mailed the results to Bernita, so I took that job for California, glad that at least we had this connection. Conveniently, I could do the grading at home while my baby napped.

I also ventured out. Before Christmas, I decided to visit UC Berkeley, where a few students who were Way followers conducted an off-campus fellowship like the ECU arrangement in Greenville where I was recruited. By now, I was twenty-three years old. I hadn't been on a college campus since Wierwille had bused us to The Ohio State University in Columbus in 1972 to watch a film series by Kenneth Clark, *Civilization*, which acquainted us with Western architecture, philosophy, archeology, and fine art. I suspect Doctor intended it to provide us with chit-chat material when recruiting.

A few Way believers at Berkeley had made a specific commitment to spread the Word on their campus as College WOWs (like Word Over the World Ambassadors, but College WOWs remained at their colleges). I called their leader.

"We would be thrilled to have you visit whenever you can," he told me.

One day I did. I arranged a babysitter for Rachel and entered a time machine back to college. The College WOWs opened their hearts to me about goals and projects. I lent support as they invited people around campus to that evening's fellowship. Their coordinator, a Way Corps applicant, invited me to audit his Business class. After that, I attended a class with the only female WOW, and we laughed while rushing across the sprawling campus to be on time. These students were motivated and intelligent, like those at ECU who had recruited me, but they ran their fellowship without micromanagement, unlike the students at the Greenville Way Home under John Lynn's watchful eyes.

My new college friends escorted me up Sather Tower, known to most as the Campanile, for a pleasurable 360-degree view of the tree-dotted campus and the surrounding city, famous for its hippies. The College WOWs said they often climbed the tower and claimed the city for Christ, as Ed had done in Los Angeles. I marveled at the old architecture and the lovely bell chimes. That evening at the Berkeley Way Home—similar to our women's house in Greenville—we shared a meal of flavorful vegetables and bright green lettuce from their backyard garden. Wierwille encouraged self-sufficiency like that, but I'd never had success growing food. Afterward, in their living room, I taught about love, the most important thing. I ended the day feeling invigorated, happy, grateful that those Berkeley believers treated me not as a Limb leader's spouse, not as a tag-along wife, not as a superior Way Corps graduate, but as their sister in Christ. They were tender. They cared about me.

On the drive home, I felt a shadow lifted from my heart. Before I'd arrived at Berkeley, I hadn't realized the shadow was there. It wasn't a worry about Rachel. I'd missed her that day, but she was in good hands. As I drove into San Leandro, it hit me. I had not missed Ed all day. In fact, I'd felt relieved to get away. What a pitiful state to be in, I told myself as I pulled into our driveway.

The public success Ed and I enjoyed as Limb leaders continued into the summer of 1976. Americans were preparing to celebrate the 200th birthday of our nation. While America was maturing, so was our ministry. That year Wierwille purchased two large properties: a ranch in Gunnison, Colorado, and a sanatorium in Rome City, Indiana, converted into a Way Corps training location for families. He also bought an airplane from Exxon of Libya for $750,000.[1] Money was flowing in. In 1976, Way records showed $5.8 million in assets.[2] Wierwille's nonprofit organization was making him rich.

Early that summer, Ed traveled around California for a few months with the Fellow Laborers to recruit people for the PFAL class. This effort was in response to Wierwille's dictate to do everything we could to spread the Word over the United States by the Fourth of July. Across the country, every believer was challenged to save America by that date; otherwise, Wierwille believed, a secret devilish group, possibly Communist, would commandeer the United States government, implement a new Constitution, and persecute anyone who challenged its authority. As outrageous as this sounds, we believed it. "They" had a list of organizations that would oppose them, Wierwille said, and he was certain we were on it. To ensure our teachings survived, we had to survive. If there were such a takeover, we couldn't let our ministry collapse. We'd keep it alive underground. Influenced by popular conspiracy theorists (I know now), he ordered the Corps to stockpile dried food, buy .22-caliber rifles, and make contingency plans in case we were chased into hiding. We prepared.

I was terrified. We could be captured and coerced into handing over names of Way believers—an idea Wierwille put in our heads—or jailed for our beliefs. We might be driven into the woods to live by our wits. Thank goodness we'd learned to kill rabbits and behead chickens in case

America fell into ruin. Ed bought two rifles and stashed them on a high closet shelf. I prayed we'd never need them.

Curiously, with a shopping spree like Wierwille's that year—the properties and the airplane—he must not have been overly worried about a government takeover.

We wondered how we would know whether we'd spread the Word over the country by the Fourth of July.

Wierwille's answer: "When the PFAL class is run in at least one city in every state of the Union." We were fast approaching that goal when disaster struck my family.

31

A Graceless Fall

On a June morning in San Leandro, I watched green hummingbirds hover at their feeder outside our kitchen window. Rachel played on the floor with pots and pans. The phone rang. I picked up the receiver and said, "Hello."

"Charlene? It's Anna." Anna was Ed's secretary. She was with him and the Fellow Laborers on their two-month witnessing tour around Central California, part of Wierwille's call to get the Word over the country by the Fourth. They rented tents at KOA campgrounds and held fellowships, like old-time revivalists, in neighborhood parks or at the beach.

"What's going on, Anna?"

"It's ... well, Ed left this morning." She started crying. "He took off with somebody, and I don't think he's coming back. I'm so—"

"Who? Who is 'somebody'?"

When I heard the girl's name, humiliation burned through me like wildfire. What a fool I was. I'd believed Ed when he'd promised, a week earlier, to give up the young woman. Even Wierwille had gotten involved. The Way leader for the United States, who had been in our area when Ed told me he was leaving me and wanted a divorce, had informed

Wierwille of the breakup. Those two had berated Ed into repentance and we tried to move on. I hadn't questioned Ed when he leaned close and whispered, "Do you want your husband back?" It was strange he did not speak of himself directly, that he didn't say, "Will you take *me* back?" I should have paid more attention to what he was *not* saying, like, "I'm truly sorry. I know I've hurt you. Will you forgive me?" But to be fair, I didn't reach out to him, either. I was too numb. His standing in the ministry and our family stability depended on my answer, so I immediately whispered yes without insisting on a heart-to-heart talk, without asking him to explain, if he could, his apparent sudden unhappiness with me. Nor did we seek counseling. We already knew what to do: renew our minds and obey the Word. Instead of dealing with our crisis, we steered ourselves through the motions of a united couple. Ed went back to his Fellow Laborers, and I'd assumed he sent the girl home as he'd promised.

Rachel had left off playing with the pots and pans and moved on to the alphabet magnets on the fridge.

"I'm so sorry, Charlene," Anna said. "What do I do now? Bring this group home?"

"I'll call you back. I need to call Doctor Wierwille," I said and hung up. This was partly my fault, I knew, since I'd not sensed my husband was only biding his time until he could resume his liaison. Now Ed had run away.

The Second Corps was scheduled to return to Headquarters in only a month. Wierwille wanted us back for a year, like the First Corps. The last thing I wanted to do was report this terrible turn of events to Doctor—he'd hit the proverbial roof. But I wanted to get it over with. I dialed his office right away.

"What? Damn it all," he yelled. "I thought you guys got straightened out."

I didn't know what to say.

Wierwille huffed into the phone. "I'm puttin' Johnny Townsend on a plane. He and Naomi are taking over for you guys anyway. Just be sooner than normal. Shoot. He's gotta do damage control."

"Yes, sir." I heard him swearing under his breath.

"Tell me. Do you want that husband of yours back?"

"Yes, sir." I wanted to love my husband. I thought it was God's will.

"Okay." He hung up.

The next few weeks were hell.

I turned my attention to Rachel, wondering what we would do, where we would go if Ed stayed away for good. What would God have me do? Would Doctor tell me what I should do? Perhaps Johnny would guide me, or maybe I'd offer to go home, back to my father's house. God might even direct me to go there. Dad and Gabrielle, my stepmother, had visited us only a month earlier, and the experience had been sweet. We'd had a little party for Rachel's first birthday. When we set a chocolate cake on her high chair tray, she stuck her hands in the icing, smiling, endearing her to her grandfather forever. Many years later, he would write, "What made me able to eventually accept this loss [of me to The Way] was my marriage to Gabrielle. [Then] you married and along came [Rachel]. I could not help but feel closer to you from then on."[1]

Ed had driven home from his summer outreach program for Rachel's birthday, but afterward made excuses and left without staying overnight. Now I knew why.

How had such blindness and duplicity plagued my marriage? A more self-aware woman would have known her marriage was in trouble. Of course I was responsible, but The Way lifestyle clearly engendered dependency on an authority, usually veiled as God's Word. In that patronizing system, I was without discernment, bereft of a capacity to rely on my own feelings and form independent judgments. That is too high a price to pay for involvement in any group.

For the next few days before Johnny arrived, I wandered around the house wrapped in my bathrobe, my hair a mess. I rarely ate. Rachel, my little cooing anchor, comforted me with her warm little body, the smell of her soft skin, her chatter. We peered out the kitchen window and watched the hummingbirds drink red juice from their feeder. She'd point and jabber as some stared back at her. I rocked with her in her nursing chair and sang to her by day; by night, I slept on the sofa, wondering whether I'd forever sleep alone. Too exhausted to cry, too anxious to sleep, I lay awake listening to creaks in the house and the neighbor's dog barking at nothing.

Unknown to me until later, Ed had driven to San Diego with his girlfriend, where they stayed at her parents' house. Wierwille tracked them down through Way connections and ordered Ed to board the next flight to Emporia, Kansas, where he was teaching The Corps. Amazingly, Ed complied. I'll never be sure of the real reason Ed flew to Emporia. Guilt? Maybe. Perhaps his girlfriend accepted the reality of Ed's distraught wife and his baby at home and kicked him out after Doctor called. Maybe Wierwille made a deal with him, promising Ed another chance to become a big Way leader if he repented.

After Emporia, Ed flew home. I won't say he returned to me because I know his heart was not in it. Mine was not in it, either. I was in a carnival house, bumping into one distorted mirror after another.

Evidently, besides Doctor, other Way leaders confronted Ed in Emporia, grilling him with no shortage of foul accusations and assertions that he was not in love with that girl.

"If you think divorce is an option for you, you're dead wrong," one said, according to Ed.

"You get your damn butt back to California and patch things up with Charlene. Make that marriage work. No excuses," another said.

"You committed yourself to that marriage, Ed," said The Way Corps leader, "and you're clergy. Both are commitments for life."

Like polite guests, we took turns in the kitchen. Like the estranged couple we were, we slept on far sides of the bed, kept our eyes down while dressing, and spoke only when necessary. Ed had said he was sorry. I had said he was forgiven. Now we had to forget. Wierwille had not taught us how to do that.

I was weak and unsteady, my heart as broken as any bone could be. What woman truly mends from such a breach of trust, no matter how hard she tries, no matter what the Bible says? I kept telling myself "I can do all things through Christ which strengtheneth me." But I didn't feel like I could.

Why didn't I call another leader's wife to advise me or console me? I could not talk about this. Only a few believers knew of our estrangement, and I didn't want anyone else to find out. People might devalue any good Ed and I had done in California. Besides, I thought I must protect the reputation of the Corps. Many believers wanted the training, like those wonderful students in Berkeley. I couldn't let my personal failure color their estimation of Wierwille's program.

I had no idea how deceptive that thinking was. The truth was that the Corps training did not transform people as many expected—my troubles were evidence. We were blind to how the program trapped us in a codependent relationship with Wierwille. And for me, it added another unhealthy relationship: with Ed. I fit myself into Wierwille's plans and Ed's confused issues, distorting my sense of my own identity and of reality in general. But at the time, I still believed God wanted me to be married to Ed.

When I asked Ed what I'd done to make him want to leave me, he said, "Nothing. It's not your fault."

With no hint of how to improve the relationship, I accepted the reunion as if it were real.

Our replacement leader, Rev. Johnny Townsend, the apple of Wierwille's eye at the time, had arrived while Ed met with Wierwille in Emporia. Johnny was a Way propaganda professional. He immediately put out the word that Ed and I were leaving early for Ohio to join the other Second Corps at Wierwille's request. If I was excited about anything besides my sweet baby, I was excited about returning to Headquarters, my only real home. To my relief, I was reassigned to work on the Aramaic project with Bernita Jess. I imagined she had a box of new pens ready for me on my desk.

I'm still struck that Wierwille, known for kicking people out of his ministry for less serious mess-ups than Ed's, gave my husband another chance. Was it because he was ordained? Because I wanted Ed back? Because Wierwille cared about what we could do for his ministry? Because we had a baby? Because Ed's father supported The Way? I never asked. We packed ourselves into the station wagon and drove to Headquarters.

32

Boot Camp Again

Nothing was certain. We arrived at Headquarters and learned the First Corps waited for us in Wierwille's basement—without popcorn and soda. Wierwille had charged them to counsel us and examine our commitment to the marriage and the ministry, but in truth they interrogated Ed. They already knew where I stood. As wily investigators, they extracted promises from my husband that he would be loyal to me and to Wierwille, no matter what. No one enjoyed that meeting, but evidently it worked. Their report satisfied Wierwille.

Our family was assigned to a four-bedroom, two-bathroom trailer with two other Second Corps couples. One had a girl Rachel's age. With people around who loved us, if our marriage couldn't be restored here, I thought, it couldn't anywhere. Not only did supportive friends ease our tensions, the peaceful countryside meant we were far from stresses and temptations of the world—especially Ed's old girlfriend—and immersed in clean air under baby-blue skies. Most importantly, we fed on Wierwille's personally delivered Corps teachings again. The idea was to mend ourselves so we could resume our ministry of outreach to others. Ever since I had met Ed, his goal had been to help people.

Without a college education or any specialized training, which he had no interest in acquiring, Ed saw Wierwille's ministry as his avenue for helping people. His assignment this year was to join the growing Way Productions performers where, even without those old turquoise suede fringed pants, his talents fit best. While in the Corps, he had acted in plays depicting Bible stories—he could be riveting—and he wrote, directed, and produced a play based on Elena Whiteside's book *The Way: Living in Love*, which told the stories of many of us in the First and Second Corps. When I was happier. Before the failures and the indiscretions.

Immersed again in the pioneering Aramaic project that I believed was my calling, I learned new things from Bernita. The project's current phase required that she teach me to transliterate the Aramaic words from the manuscripts into a special code she developed. That meant filling rows of little squares printed on letter-sized paper using green ink pens. Page after page, the tedious work demanded my full concentration. Even one Aramaic letter incorrectly coded could be as disastrous as the difference between *bean* and *bead*. Accuracy depended on my clear eye and steady hand. If I thought about that too much, I freaked out. Mistakes meant I had changed God's Word.

The first couple of months were busy and productive. Rachel had baby friends in morning day care. Like all the mothers, I only worked mornings. I thought Ed and I were healing. I sensed Wierwille's approval. We were off to a great start.

Three months later, Ed was gone. On a morning in mid-November, the time of year when corn stalks dry and split apart in the wind, trouble broke our hearts again and sent us spinning backward. I trudged to Bernita's office as if carrying a suitcase full of rocks. Bernita had relocated to the Data Management Services trailer to facilitate entry of our coded manuscripts into a computer database. To reach her, I had to walk past several staff, and I'm sure they saw my tears that morning as I tried to slink by them unnoticed. I opened Bernita's door.

"Hi, Charlene—" she said, looking up, a green pen in her hand.

"Bernita ... something's happened." I slumped in my chair opposite her.

"Oh, dear."

"Ed left. Doctor told him to go."

Her hand flew to her mouth.

"We've had problems, Bernita, serious ones ... marriage problems ... for months. Doctor told me I could stay here with Rachel." I choked back tears.

My mentor fixed her gaze on me, motionless as a sphinx, waiting for more. Surprising both of us, I reported my sad story as if describing someone else's problems, some other woman's confusion. I recounted the scene in Wierwille's office the previous morning after Ed told me—relaying no reason—that Wierwille had ordered him off the property.

"He's been with another girl, honey," Wierwille had said, setting his glasses on the desk. "I can't have things like that going on around here." He rubbed his eyes. "Go ahead and sit down."

I collapsed into the nearest chair, feeling like the world's biggest fool. Didn't Ed care at all about Rachel and me? I was humiliated, afraid, disgusted. What was I supposed to do? Leave with Ed? Every bone in my body said no. But what did God want? Did God expect me to stand by my husband who acted like this? I couldn't speak. I only stared out the window over Wierwille's shoulder and watched tree branches tossed by the wind, losing more leaves. It was November and winter was coming.

I had no capacity to consider that perhaps I, not God, had dreamed up the idea of marrying Ed to begin with. Had my belief about God giving me a personal revelation been true? I wasn't sure now. Before I left the office, Wierwille told me I could remain at Headquarters if I wanted, but I should keep this breakup quiet until Ed left the next morning—he'd given him twenty-four hours to clear out. Wierwille would inform the Corps later.

That night, Ed and I huddled on opposite sides of the bed in the dark—an impossible arrangement, but there was nowhere else to go.

"This is it, Ed. I want a divorce." I watched shadows flicker across the ceiling for what seemed like an hour.

"Do you think … sometime later," Ed whispered, "that … maybe we could get married again?"

"No!" I recoiled at how crazy that was, how out of touch Ed had become. He did not recognize that he had hurt me over and over with no apparent remorse.

Like any marriage, both spouses create whatever they have together. Both of us had issues and traumas we'd brought with us to The Way. The serious problem was that its dogmas did not address our wounds, but merely plastered them with band-aids. Our troubles persisted for years without proper treatment, and finally festered into infection. Ed's emotional development had been stunted by a variety of factors, including addiction and psychological issues from childhood. They remained with him even after his recruitment to The Way, affecting him as much as a physical injury, as much as my mother's death had affected me. Way teachings exacerbated the problems. Our simple belief that the Devil killed my mother did not put me any closer to reality, but I was closer than my husband. He did not seem aware that he had trashed the last bit of trust I had in him.

Before I had told Bernita the news, Ed drove our car away from the farm. He did not tell me where he was going. He made no provisions for me or for our child. I guess he assumed The Way would take care of his family for him indefinitely. Meanwhile, for reasons still a mystery to me, the young woman Ed had been with was allowed to stay. I didn't have the nerve to ask Wierwille why. Every time I saw her pretty face, I looked the other way.

Unimaginable as it is now, Wierwille did not counsel Ed and me before ordering Ed to leave. If Wierwille had been a loving Christian leader, he would have required a session to clear the air. He would have held Ed accountable for his family's welfare, and not allowed him to leave me in the lurch. I should have demanded it, too, but I had given up, and Wierwille was probably glad to be rid of Ed, a wild card beyond his control.

Bernita absorbed my news with the silence of a confessor holding back judgment, but she couldn't hide her dismay. She reached for tissues in her pocket and handed me one.

"I'm so sorry, Charlene." After a quiet moment, she added, "This must be so hard for you, I know, but try and remember one thing: where there's life, there's always hope." She hugged me then, and I felt a measure of motherly comfort. I knew her message ran deep.

Before Bernita came to The Way and married George Jess, she had been a missionary and then married a Methodist minister. Unfortunately, he had been killed in a tragic car accident that left her to raise their two small children. She understood the pain of loss better than most. In my crisis, she counseled me to remember that although Ed might be gone, he was still alive, and so he might return and we could learn to love again. I didn't have the heart to tell her that was the last thing I wanted.

Bernita and I regained our bearings, and she accepted my situation with professional grace. My job became a surprise avenue of healing, a combination of mentorship and motherly love as she brought homemade baked treats to the office and gave me educational presents, like comparative readings of the New Testament and William M. Thomson's *The Land and the Book*. In the sanctuary of her office, we picked up our green pens and resumed the tedious but necessary coding—a meditative task that calmed me. I gave my whole heart to the work, and it gave back to me, absorbing my attention, my problems, my pain.

33

Wit's End

Life was different. Life was the same. I fell into a new category: quasi-single married woman. Daily routines without Ed changed little. Each morning I settled Rachel at child care and trekked to Bernita's office by 8:00 a.m. Mothers were granted free afternoons with their children—a perk I now realize was a great gift—but other benefits were lacking. I had no checking or savings account, no health or life insurance. We received a small monthly allowance. Housing and meals were provided by financial gifts from the tens of thousands of believers around the world who kept the lights on. Occasional extra needs were evaluated one by one by Wierwille's brother Harry, the secretary-treasurer. After I told my father that Ed left, he sent money once in a while, as did Ed's father. I'm sure neither of them realized how close Rachel and I were to asking them for shelter if Wierwille had not let us stay.

Wierwille had ways of testing people's loyalty—kick out the husband, see what the wife does.

At Headquarters, I felt safe and provided for. Meals were generous and served family style. By this time the number of staff and Corps had increased to over one hundred, so we ate in the BRC's downstairs all-purpose room instead of the smaller dining area by the kitchen with the airline-map wallpaper. At noon, we had hearty meals of millet, roast chicken, and green beans from the farm's abundant fields. Always well fed, I gained weight and felt better. Wounds from the summer and fall were healing. Tension eased.

At work, sunlight melted snow crystals on the windowpane next to my desk, sending specks of bright yellow across photocopied pages of manuscripts and sending me back into daydreams of dedicated scribes. The manuscripts stirred my curiosity about their origins and their mysterious journeys in and out of clay jars, churches, monasteries, and caves. My imagination was sparked. My determination to see this project to its completion was empowered. Working at it, I felt valued. Without it, I feared I would flounder. When I wasn't in the office, I often felt like Wierwille's charity case, a problem he had not bargained for. Mine was an inconvenient presence. Perhaps my specialized work made up for that. I couldn't tell.

As much as the farm was a serene and protective environment, the outside world was a dangerous place. By this time, Wierwille's defensiveness about his ministry was mounting. He faced outside criticisms about his hunter safety program in Emporia, Kansas, for The Way Corps. At Headquarters his increasing paranoia manifested one winter day when he announced he was riding up to Minnesota to teach at a statewide meeting and he required the Second Corps to go with him. He wanted the strongest believers he could round up. Bad publicity had circulated about him in that area, and he wanted to thwart it with the Word.

I arranged for a babysitter and our Corps piled on the motor coach, a few of the men carrying guns under their trench coats like Mafia hit men, bulky holsters strapped to their bodies, as Wierwille wished. They held regular target practice at a hill in the back of the compound—I'd watched them once—at a safe distance from housing units, children, and prying local citizens' eyes.

In any context, I should have been alarmed. I should have thought, "Why does a man of God need armed guards?"

In 1982, I had attended a small research fellowship meeting during which Wierwille had said, "I'm not afraid of those Jews who are out to get me." I have no knowledge of any actual threat, but I do know that Wierwille's selling of the book *The Myth of the Six Million,* which denies the Holocaust, was evidence of his anti-Semitic attitude. He blustered about dozens of other things, too—the IRS, cult deprogrammers, upset parents, the preachers in New Knoxville. Wierwille would say, "The Devil has his boys after me, but they won't get me."

His bodyguard brigade on the bus back in 1977 was evidence that guns in The Way had other purposes besides quail hunting.

Meanwhile, divorce was on its way. In the spring, during a rare telephone call, Ed reported to me that California no-fault divorce papers were in process. (He had gone to California because he knew a few believers there who would offer hospitality no matter what his situation and help him find a job.) We had nothing else to discuss and hung up. I should have sought legal advice, but lawyers were worldly—and expensive. All I could think of was ending the farce of our marriage. Make it official. Motherhood without a husband wasn't easy, but I managed with the help of caring believers. I did learn, though, that it's possible to feel lonely even among well-meaning people.

I kept hoping a deep emptiness I felt would go away. As absorbing as my work was, it could not love me. Wierwille encouraged me to date. God knew I'd tried with Ed. God understood I was a healthy young woman who enjoyed male attention and hoped for a happy marriage someday. No one tried to give me false hopes about Ed. Not even Bernita.

On a June afternoon, the telephone rang in my housing unit. It could have been the wail of a fire truck for all the panic it caused. A Corps sister answered and said Doctor was calling for me.

"Hello, Doctor."

"Charlene. Can you come by my office in a minute?" His voice was unusually soft. "We need to talk."

I combed my hair and put on a clean blouse, all the while scouring my behavior for failings, but I couldn't identify anything serious. Rarely did I speak to Doctor one-on-one. I asked my Corps sister to watch Rachel and rushed out the door.

Every month or so, Wierwille mailed a letter to Way Corps members to share his heart, announce upcoming events, and keep us like-minded with him. He'd sent one recently, especially directed to former Corps who'd left the program. The letter was the first of its kind. Usually when Corps abandoned the ministry, Wierwille accused them of caving in to the Devil's temptations and turning against him, the man who bled his heart out for God's people. This letter was different. Amnesty was declared. Doctor had tracked down these traitors to say he loved and forgave them. It was now possible for his prodigal children to come home, which meant come back to Way fellowships wherever they were.

I arrived at Wierwille's office and took a seat across from him. He was on edge, clearing his throat, forcing a smile. He lit up a Kool.

"Honey, now is the time to tell you that your Ed has been calling me."

Every bit of oxygen flew out of my body.

"I was surprised like you," he said, a sheepish look on his face.

I did not think we were surprised in the same way. This had been brewing and he had hidden it from me?

Ed had not called me for about a month, nor had we signed divorce papers. He kept saying they were in progress. I kept saying hurry up.

"He says he's had a change of heart, honey, a real miracle," Wierwille said. "He wants back in the ministry, but I wanted to see if he was spiritually cleaned up before I told you. He's supposed to call in a few minutes. Asked me if I thought you might talk to him."

That's when I heard blaring sirens in my head. Doctor swiveled his chair to the side and glanced slyly over his shoulder at me.

A talk with Ed was not what I wanted, especially with Wierwille sitting right there, but I was outmaneuvered. What on earth would I say?

The window behind Wierwille framed a section of the farm across the street. Dogs in the grassy field were running this way and that as the farmer tried to steer them through a gate.

"Guess the Word says we ought to forgive, right?" With that, he swiveled around to the front and shot me a look that I knew, from all my time around him, carried ultimate authority. "I'll put you on a plane for California. You guys should work on your marriage out there."

I was in shock. If I agreed, my dream of working with Bernita on our project, my desire to learn Greek from Walter Cummins—an offer he'd recently made—and the chance to live among believers with Rachel as part of God's plan for me would vanish like the smoke from the end of Doctor's Kool.

The telephone rang. Wierwille picked up the receiver, greeted Ed, told him I was there, and covered the mouthpiece with his hand.

"I think you've got your man back." He motioned for me to come around to his side of the desk and handed me the phone.

"Hello?"

"Hi there, Charlene ... how are you?"

"Okay."

Wierwille remained in his chair, but turned toward the window.

Ed hurried to admit his call must be a surprise to me, but he wanted to say he was sorry and was ready to return to the ministry and to me, if I wanted that.

I hoped to hear him say he loved me, but he didn't. I wanted him to ask how I felt about him, but he didn't. Perhaps those things were too much to expect. My head spun, overwhelmed by this *Twilight Zone* situation. Surely I could have said no, I didn't want to reunite. But I didn't. I might have asked for time to think things over, but in that moment, the pressure to do what was expected of me felt like a vise holding me motionless while these two men turned the screw.

If I refused to forgive, I would displease God and relinquish the chance to mend our family. I would also go up against Wierwille. How could I live with myself then? Rachel's future, as well as mine, lay in my trembling hands. My little Rachel had no voice in this. What would she want? Didn't she deserve to have her father in her life? I might not be in love with Ed anymore, and he might not be in love with me, either, but I could not believe he did not love his daughter. Love was getting extremely confusing. Was it a feeling? An action? An omitted action? Was it all of these or none or more? Could I act in a loving way without feeling love? If I did, would that make me a hypocrite or a person obeying God, who said to love? Feelings come and go, Wierwille always said. God says to forgive. Ed was asking for forgiveness. How could I not give it?

Ed kept talking. And talking. And talking. He said he'd felt bad when he read Wierwille's letter and God had worked on his heart to want us to be a family again. "Don't you want that, too, Charlene?"

About a month later, with my duties completed and my suitcases packed, an orange sunset streaked across the Ohio sky as one of my Corps sisters drove Rachel and me to the airport in Dayton. My purse held airline tickets to San Francisco—paid for with a loan from the ministry—pink lipstick, sixty dollars in cash, snacks from Louise in the kitchen, and my brown leather purse-sized Bible. My baby bag was jammed with supplies for Rachel. I was twenty-five years old, returning to my mixed-up husband who was attempting to repair his life. Our daughter had recently had her second birthday. She was walking and stringing words together in simple sentences. While we rode in the car, her blue eyes shone into mine, and I cried. I had gone around the farm that day saying good-bye to my patient and supportive trailermates and to the men I had dated, whose tenderness had been a gift. I thanked Walter and Bernita profusely for the job offer in research. I was sorry to decline, but they understood I was leaving to take care of my personal life. Perhaps Bernita felt happy that love, or at least hope, had carried the day. Lastly, I said farewell to my bittersweet experience as a single mother. In reversing that status, I was more than cautious. I was scared, as if following a shadow through a dim alleyway, trusting it to sense turns and obstructions, to show me where I belonged. With Rachel in my arms, I stepped aboard the plane, and we flew into the vast black night.

34

A Rabbit Hole in London

The moment I spotted Ed at the airport was as eerie as San Francisco fog. I barely recognized him. He'd grown a beard—the first one ever—and wore a green-and-gray checked shirt I'd never seen. Rachel woke up in my arms as I approached her father, and he forced the ingratiating smile of a guilty man.

"Hi, Charlene. Long trip?" he asked, peering into our child's face. He offered to carry the baby bag. Strangers probably didn't sense we were man and wife. Our innocent child, fragile as a silken thread, held us together. Surely she must have felt my hesitancy. At two years old, what does a child register if not the immediate emotional condition of a parent?

Ed drove us through the undulating city streets in a car I had never seen, either—an old blue Ford convertible. A California believer had donated it to the ministry, he told me, and the Limb leader, Rev. Johnny Townsend (our replacement from the previous year), gave it to him after our old car died. We arrived at the townhouse Ed was housesitting for a couple of months, owned by a believer's relatives who were traveling abroad. Believers here were generous, although using a stranger's furniture and belongings added another layer of uneasiness.

Our reconciliation was as unsteady as the tectonic plates below us. Day to day shifted in tone. What could I discuss without rousing Ed's defenses? Did he truly want me back? Did I really want to be there? Agreeing to this arrangement had been an abstract idea for weeks, and I needed time to absorb its actualization.

Some people considered our reunion a miracle. One woman, a singer in Way Productions who did not know us well, said: "Gee, it's so romantic, like he's been away in Vietnam, and he's finally coming home."

What if I had said no? What if I'd rejected Wierwille's reconciliation plan? It's possible I could still be in The Way; I would have remained at Headquarters. I could have continued believing I worked for God. I could have raised Rachel in the narrow-minded, repressive beliefs I held. I might have delivered myself to another Way clergyman and kept my help-meet status. I might still be asleep in the concrete coffin of fundamentalism.

Ed and I kept our "don't ask, don't tell" policy from the previous year, especially about any love life we had while apart. I didn't want to know. Ed never asked. Why burden each other with knowledge that would hinder what little ability we had to repair the pile of damage we already faced? We reassured each other of our health; that was it. Sometimes I was ashamed of my romances; at other times I knew they'd done me good.

It was a long time before I realized a hard truth—if Ed and I had been truly interested in healing our relationship, we would have sought counseling and retaken our vows, but we never discussed it. Our Achilles' heel, repeatedly torn, left a deep and tender scar. With a collage of unresolved issues, resuming sexual relations took a long time. I busied myself with Rachel and functioned in a more compartmentalized way than ever, with Ed in one box, our child in another, and private memories locked inside myself. I shelved our missing year like a heavy winter coat. When I felt lonely, sometimes I took it out of storage, tried it on, turned this way and that, reminisced about how it used to fit, how free I had felt without Ed—it was impossible to un-remember. Some recollections facilitated survival. Others helped me appreciate Ed, and what I sometimes viewed as his courage in returning to me.

I often felt our resumed domesticity put Ed's nerves on edge, especially about providing for our family on a carpet cleaner's income—his new skill. With Rachel so young, we decided I wouldn't take a job. To pass the time, I read a lot of Bible and found fulfillment in a bit of long-distance work for Bernita, although I was not on the ministry's payroll. She mailed me manuscript pages, along with a supply of coding sheets and green pens, and I worked at the chopping block kitchen table while Rachel napped or played on the floor. The work was a good distraction from my stress over the future, money, and sex. The Aramaic project, my treasured task, saved me again.

Ed and I knew we wouldn't be in San Francisco long, not only because the townhouse owners would return, but because annual Way Corps assignment letters were being mailed, and we expected to be sent elsewhere. Ed hoped for reinstatement as a high-end leader because he was a sincere prodigal son, but in July when our letter arrived, we were both bitterly disappointed. Wierwille's decision for us: Twig leaders, Bakersfield, California. Twig leaders did not receive Way salaries. Most of the time, neither did Branch leaders. Twig leaders served at their own pleasure.

Bakersfield, ugh. It was a roughneck, dirty desert town in the middle of nowhere. We'd been the leaders of California, and we knew Bakersfield had only a tiny fellowship of about four people who did not often meet. Was this punishment? Cowboys, tumbleweed, dust storms, and lackadaisical believers. But if we wanted to stay involved with The Way, we had to move there, pump some life into those people, teach their flailing fellowship, and recruit any new folks we could. We, the crippled, were being sent to heal the stricken.

But one day I gained a new perspective. Before we moved to Bakersfield, the Way's travel agent called the California Limb office and left a message for Ed to call him. As it turned out, I returned the call.

"How would you and Ed like to go to London?"

"London?"

"Doctor is going to ordain our leader for England next month at the European WOW festival, and you're invited."

"Whoa."

The festival would be at Alsager College, he said, near the town of Crewe. I had no idea where those places were but that didn't matter.

"A group of us are flying over … mostly clergy and wives. We've chartered a plane and hope you can go."

"Are you kidding? We'd love to, but I need to check with Ed. We're pretty broke right now … and what about Rachel? Can we bring her?"

He said sorry, but children were not allowed. Maybe I could find a babysitter. The good news was that the ministry would pay for our flight, transportation, and housing for the event, and even put us up for a few days after that at a hotel in London. We'd have to pay for meals and incidentals, like sightseeing.

When I sprang the news, Ed was thrilled. This gesture made him feel that Wierwille and the clergy in the inner circle accepted him again. We made arrangements immediately. Money for moving to Bakersfield transformed into money for England. We would save for relocating later, Ed told me. A married couple in the fellowship offered to babysit Rachel; the wife not only was very caring, but she was also a nurse. I wrote to Bernita to explain that the trip to London would interrupt my work. The mailman delivered a reply from her right away. She regretted she couldn't go to England herself, but she was enclosing a letter to the Director of the British Museum's Library asking permission for me to see their Aramaic manuscripts. I leapt for joy.

I was Alice in Wonderland. On September 13, 1977, after the ministry's ceremonies at Alsager College, I was in the famous British Museum Library, at the time part of the main museum in the heart of London. Ed walked me to the Oriental Students Room, then left to explore other exhibits.

The room's expansive ceiling and elaborate wood paneling lent an air of antiquity. Smells of musty books and furniture polish awakened memories of visiting my mother in Salisbury's library. I browsed around some artifacts until I got up the nerve to speak to the clerk behind the reference desk. His face, ruddy and round, shone from under a layer of hair combed flat to his head. I introduced myself and handed him Bernita's letter, watching his face as he read it. Bernita described me as her Biblical Research Assistant for The Way, and stated it would be valuable for me to examine Aramaic manuscripts firsthand since we were producing Aramaic reference books. He smiled, and in an elegant English accent, asked me to wait at a reading table.

"I'll be a few moments," he said. With Bernita's letter in hand, he scurried down a narrow hallway like Lewis Carroll's rabbit, his spiffy blue blazer tight around his middle. I took a seat and waited.

From sunny California to foggy England, there I was, a stay-at-home mom transformed into Aramaic researcher. Three years earlier in Bernita's office, I had read this museum's list of manuscripts in a copy of William Wright's *Catalogue of the Syriac Manuscripts in the British Museum, acquired since the year 1838.* Never did I think I'd ever lay eyes on them.

About ten minutes later, the chipper librarian reappeared, rolling a cart bearing several tomes of crusty vellum pages between dark brown bindings. He lifted them off the cart and set them like infants on the table in front of me.

They *were* real.

"Please be careful," he said, bowing toward me. He glanced at his watch and recited the Library's policy that I must not take the manuscripts out of the room. "You have an hour to examine them. Exposure to light and air expedites their deterioration. Enjoy." He handed me a ticket in case I wanted to return the next day and left me alone with the treasures.

I examined a volume that contained the first books of the Old Testament—Genesis, Exodus, Numbers, and Deuteronomy—written in Estrangelo script. Turning the pages, I prayed I wouldn't damage them. God help me if I did. This was a priceless ancient text known as Add. 14425—one of the oldest known dated manuscripts of Scripture in the world, written in 464 AD in Amid, a city located in present-day Turkey.[1] Each page was covered with a protective layer of wax, but through this smooth film words were unmistakable. In some of the margins were squiggles of notes, some in red ink. I remembered Rev. Walter Cummins explaining how copyists incorporated marginal notes into the text, and wondered whether these had later been added by mistake. In other margins—or even in the middle of a page—were decorative markings in diamond shapes and swirls, intricate and beautiful. I was awed. These were the actual words someone had written 1,513 years ago. Most women my age would have gone shopping at Harrods while in London, but I preferred poring over these old, decayed books.

On the tray were other manuscripts, called psalters—collections of Psalms for devotional use—and lectionaries—portions of the Bible read on certain days of the year. These folios, although providing insight into ancient worship services and practices, were not important to us. We worked only with texts of the Holy Scriptures like the precious Add. 14425. Nevertheless, examining them made me breathless, as if they were holy relics. I thought of my mother, who, a few months before she died, handled a relic of Saint Anne that our priest loaned her, saying it might heal her.

I heard the clerk scuffle down an aisle toward me. My hour was up. I closed the manuscript covers and gazed around the room to fix this scene in my mind forever—the walls and carved ceiling, the artifacts preserved in glass cabinets, and the stacks of antique books against the walls. I vowed that no matter what challenges might plague me, any Aramaic work I could do to help uncover God's Word was worth my efforts. Opportunities like this did not come to many people.

The polite librarian laid the volumes on the cart and whisked it away, leaving me as dumbstruck as Alice after her most fantastical dream.

1974. Ski vacation in Squaw Valley for some Way Corps grads. Front row: Charlene is second. In back row are Wierwille, Del Duncan (California Limb leader), Howard Allen (Wierwille's pal and general manager for The Way), and far right is Ed on skies.

1976. The California Limb leader home in San Leandro. Rachel celebrates her first birthday with Grandpa Lamy as Charlene (age 24 and far too thin) looks on. Ed had left the party to rejoin his Fellow Laborer group on their witnessing campaign to save America by the Fourth of July.

1977. Charlene and her recruiter Doug (from the ECU Way Home and also a Second Corps grad) on the lawn of Ball State University, Muncie, Indiana, where the Second Corps and hundreds of Way believers attended the Power for Abundant Living (PFAL) class that Wierwille taught in person.

1982. Charlene and Bernita Jess in the biblical research team's office adjacent to the library at Way Headquarters.

1982. Biblical research conference at The Way's Indiana Campus in Rome City, Indiana. Seated, front row: Rev. Walter Cummins (Director of The Way's Biblical Research), Mrs. Wierwille, Wierwille, and L. Craig Martindale (then Director of The Way Corps). Standing, second row: Bernita Jess (behind Rev. Walter Cummins) and Charlene (behind L. Craig Martindale).

1983. Charlene and Ed (a Way clergyman since 1974) pose with Mrs. Wierwille, Wierwille, and George Jess (Bernita's husband and First Director of The Way Corps) in celebration of a decade of service by the Second Way Corps.

Part 6

Research
Regained

35

Paradise Offered

After London, my dream of Aramaic work faded. I was exiled from Headquarters, sent to the field with Ed, with no marked pathway back. In-residence Corps people were assigned to help Bernita at Headquarters. Ed and I did our duty in Bakersfield, and then Wierwille sent us to Oxnard, California, and after that across the country to the Tampa Bay area in Florida. By 1982, we were in Orlando. All the while, we conducted a Twig fellowship and struggled to keep our shaky marriage going. Ed, banished from paid Way positions, took sales jobs to support us. Feeling stuck on the bottom rung of the ministry and in uninteresting sales work, he lost motivation. By 1983, our Twig in Orlando consisted of three grads of the PFAL class and no new recruits. For part-time work, I cleaned houses. For free, I coordinated Way children's fellowships. By now, Rachel was nine years old—a good student and talented ballet dancer—and my husband was a frustrated man who drank too much.

We were stuck. Way leaders nagged Ed with a quote from Proverbs 18:16: "A man's gift maketh room for him," insinuating that if Ed used his gift ministries effectively—teaching and pastoring God's people—more believers with their monetary gifts would make a full-time ministry job possible for him. Since that hadn't happened, it was Ed's fault—and his help meet's.

For years, Ed had watched his peers succeed as dynamic leaders. The most dramatic case was in 1982, when Wierwille retired as president of The Way. He spent a year preparing Way followers for this change. He said it was time to move the responsibility of The Way onto the shoulders of a younger man, so he trained and appointed L. Craig Martindale, one of our Second Corps brothers, to replace him. This was accepted as a positive transition, one certainly approved by God or else Wierwille would not do it. When Craig's induction ceremony was held at Headquarters, attended by thousands from all over the world, a new era began—but not for Ed. In his eyes I saw anxiety over being left in the dust.

I was anxious, too, but for different reasons. While in Tampa, we had weathered another separation. Leaders told us to quit fighting over our stupid problems. Like Winston in George Orwell's *1984*, I felt trapped in a life designed for someone else, living out my pain and hoping for an escape hatch to appear. In the fall of 1983, in Orlando, I finally summoned the gumption to create an escape hatch of my own.

One day I approached my friend Mary Ann, the wife of Rev. John Hendricks, Limb leader for Florida. They were Fourth Way Corps graduates and highly respected. Mary Ann and I sat at a table in her sunny kitchen.

"I've been thinking Ed and I need a change," I said. "We aren't growing, you know? Our marriage feels stagnant. We're not recruiting anybody, either. Maybe we should move to a different town. Make a fresh start. What do you think?" I held the cup of coffee she'd poured me and took a sip. Wierwille and the leaders he trained often moved troubled underling leaders, hoping they'd do better someplace else.

"I understand," Mary Ann said, "but your problems are in the past now, so—"

"Not to me," I said. "Ed is so down about being only a Twig leader. He wants more to do, but he can't make it happen. He accuses me of not forgiving him for our first split-up, and maybe I haven't. He's got patterns. We fight about how to raise Rachel—he says I'm too strict. And money—we barely get by. It's hard to focus on ministry outreach when he gets home from work. Maybe if we—"

"It's hard to know what to do," Mary Ann said, nodding in sympathy. "I see that." She stirred her coffee and kept her eyes from meeting mine, brushing aside her glossy hair, glancing at her children playing nearby on the Italian tile floor—they lived in an expansive and expensive house. The ministry paid the rent. From the kitchen window, I watched palm trees sway in the breeze alongside the swimming pool. A shimmering blue Orlando lake lay beyond it.

"Look, we'll figure this out, but you've got to believe God has an answer," she said.

I was sick of these speeches.

"Anyway, I thought you were doing better these days," she added. "You seem so happy when I see you running children's fellowships."

"I am happy with the kids, but that isn't enough." I suspect most people in the group never would have guessed I was so disheartened. On the surface, where most people in The Way tended to look, I was an active, committed believer, married to a Way clergyman, mother of a loving, talented child, and an all-around faithful volunteer.

If I'd been brutally honest with Mary Ann, I would have admitted I was bored and tired of trying to be my husband's perfect help meet. I scrubbed people's toilets for pay and assisted Ed with our fellowship, where we sang the same Way songs, repeated the same approved Bible lessons, and listened to tape-recorded teachings by Craig Martindale, the new president. Rather than engendering zeal for God, that repetition wore me down. I missed the excitement of my initial Way days in Greenville when I first took the PFAL class. But I couldn't tell Mary

Ann how I really felt. She would think I was negative.

"I'm not sure what to say, Charlene, but I agree that sometimes we need a different situation to bring out the best in our ministries." She took another sip of coffee, leaning a little closer out of earshot from her kids. "This seems like one of those times. But as much as I wish I could tell you something today, I've got to talk to John. He's the spiritual leader here, not me. God will give him guidance." She leaned back in her chair, satisfied with her diplomacy.

"Right," I said, but I felt let down. Mary Ann could never comprehend how I felt, never know the shame I endured over our setbacks year after year. According to ministry beliefs, we'd created our own problems. We'd let Satan tempt us. We should renew our minds and claim God's promises of abundance. But what about God? He loved me, so why didn't He tell me what to do to improve my life? I'd been praying, I'd been "going to the Word," but a cloud of confusion engulfed me.

I put on a smile and thanked Mary Ann for our heart-to-heart talk, but I broke down and cried in my car on the drive home.

The next time we met with our Limb leader, John Hendricks, was in his home office overlooking the swimming pool. Before he said a word, I wondered whether baring my heart to Mary Ann had been a mistake, and I was going to hear about it now. Out the bay window, I saw her sitting by the pool as her children played in the sun. Farther out, a motorboat swished by on the shimmering blue lake.

"You know," John said, "you guys are Corps, God's best." He leaned on his elbows, folded his hands, and smiled. "Mary Ann and I understand how you might, you know … need a change in perspective. Recharge your spiritual batteries, so to speak, like Doctor says. We all need a boost once in a while, right?"

"Sure," we murmured. Ed blinked faster and faster, a nervous habit since childhood.

"And I understand how important it is to strengthen your marriage, too."

Oh brother, I thought. Would Ed think I'd been complaining about him?

"Let's see, you've been together for … well, for so long and have been so faithful … to the ministry." John cleared his throat, leaning forward a little more. Built like a fullback, he filled the entire chair. He smoothed the long sleeves of his blue Ralph Lauren shirt—heavy on the starch—that emphasized his clear blue eyes, eyes that glanced around the desk.

"So, a change seems to be in order, don't you think, Ed?" He cocked his head to one side, waiting.

I wanted Ed to take the lead, but he didn't say anything, only kept blinking. I was anxious about what was coming next from either of them.

To my amazement, John asked, "Why don't you two apply for jobs at Headquarters?"

Headquarters? He might as well have said Paradise, for all the promise that place held for me. Immediately I yearned for Bernita and the Aramaic project—for years I wondered whether I'd ever work on it again. But because of what happened the last time Ed and I had lived there, I never thought that as a couple we'd be invited back. The look on Ed's face told me he was thinking the same thing, but John made it sound possible.

"You'll be surrounded by dedicated staff people and have plenty to do," he said.

"Gosh. It would be like going home," I said. "Several friends of ours work on staff." I thought of Debbie, my old pal from college, who worked there with her husband.

Ed said, "Sure."

John said he would recommend us for any jobs we could do, from mowing grass to washing dishes. *Oh*. That didn't sound so thrilling, especially to Ed, who saw himself capable of greater responsibility, if only Craig, the new president and our Second Corps brother, would believe in him.

John was quick to admit those were menial tasks, but we'd have the joy of living at the hub of the ministry. Loyal workers like us were needed. As time went by, we could prove ourselves worthy of promotions. Although I wondered whether Craig would ever trust Ed with more responsibility when hundreds of other Corps with unstained résumés were now available, Ed and I were appreciative of the suggestion, and we said so.

The three of us slumped in our chairs as the possibility sank in. Leafy branches close to the window filtered in sunshine, making Ed look brighter than when we'd arrived. Later, he'd tell me that not only was the idea of working with believers appealing, but a predictable salary, instead of the fluctuating income he earned from sales commissions, would be a relief. He also hoped to get involved with the ministry's theatrical productions, which had become more professional. As for me, I'd be more than glad to do whatever work was needed. Helping Bernita again seemed almost too much to hope for—she had other helpers now. Perhaps I'd be assigned to the Children's Fellowship Department, since I was experienced with that.

"So, Ed," John said, "how does this sound to you?"

"It sounds fantastic, if they want us." He'd come alive. "I'll bet Rachel would like being around her Way friends whose parents work there, too."

We mailed job applications immediately. Right before Christmas, John telephoned Ed.

"Walter Cummins and his family are coming down to Disney for the holidays. Would you two like to join all of us for dinner?"

We said sure. Over the years, I'd done my best to maintain my connection with Walter and the research team, attending research conferences and communicating about progress on the Aramaic project. One year, I even assisted Bernita in teaching an Aramaic class to the Corps.

Over the pleasant seafood dinner at an Orlando restaurant with Walter Cummins and his family, John mentioned that Ed and I had applied for jobs at Headquarters for the coming year.

"You did?" Walter turned to me, his eyes bright with possibility. "That's wonderful." He tapped his fork on his plate. "Charlene, maybe you could work with us again in the Research Department."

"I'd love to," I said. "If you need me, I'm ready." I glanced at Ed, but he picked at his food, half listening.

Walter smiled affably, saying he was pretty sure Bernita and the research team could use my help to finish the Aramaic concordance. He assured me he'd check with Bernita as soon as he returned to the office. I felt excited, but I didn't want to raise my hopes, which is not to say I didn't ask God to make it happen.

In the spring of 1984, we received our annual Corps assignment letters. John's idea had been prophetic. As Walter anticipated, I was to join the Biblical Research Team and work with Bernita. I was thrilled. Ed was assigned to the Shipping and Receiving Department, menial by comparison. I did not miss the disappointment on his face. He was anxious to get promoted as soon as possible.

As we'd hoped, Rachel was happy, excited about seeing her Way friends in Ohio; she'd met many at summer camps for Corps kids. She would attend public school with them in New Knoxville. I thought our relocation would enhance her spiritual life and shore up her strength to obey God's Word, since she would be hanging around with believer children, not the worldly and materialistic ones who surrounded her in Florida.

We readied to leave for Ohio, the state whose motto is With God, all things are possible, and said good-bye to our friends, especially my girlfriend Tillie, who'd helped me pack. She had volunteered to "go

WOW"—join our missionary program—that year, so she was also leaving Orlando. At the upcoming Rock of Ages, she would find out where she'd be sent. I would miss her, but we promised to stay in touch.

Soon after Ed and I finished packing, as we'd done every year of Rachel's life, The Way's moving truck arrived. The driver and his helper loaded our boxes and furniture and took off for New Knoxville. In the trunk of our car, I set my tan plastic file box where I kept irreplaceable photos and Way correspondence for safekeeping. I hid its key in my purse. Our things on the truck would be stored in a warehouse at Headquarters until we found nearby housing. We'd asked for that arrangement rather than accepting trailer accommodations on the compound, explaining we preferred more privacy. That request to live off Way property proved more helpful than we could have imagined.

As our little family drove away from Orlando, I did not look back. I imagined nothing but a pot of spiritual gold at the end of a Way ministry rainbow. My whole life led up to this, I was certain, beginning in Catholic school where I was raised to know, love, and serve God, the life purpose that led me to The Way. And my Aramaic dream was continuing after all; the research team needed me. Besides the official assignment letter, I had received a thoughtful note from Frank, one of the researchers. He expressed how glad the team was that I would join them, and remarked on my close relationship with Bernita and my love for Aramaic studies. Frank, not Bernita, appeared to be my assigned welcome wagon representative. He signed off by saying he would fill me in on lots of news after I got there.

36

The Hub of the Word

"You ready?" Ed asked. He opened the glass front door of the Headquarters office building, an enormous structure with a colorful farmland mural painted across the front. It featured Bernita's husband, George Jess, sowing seeds over the farmland. With diligence and kindness, George had maintained the farm for years and, as the first director of The Way Corps, dutifully prayed for us and supported Wierwille's vision of the Word Over the World.

"Sure," I told Ed and stepped inside.

It was August 1984, and we began our first day as staff in the Outreach Services Center (OSC), a business hub alive with hundreds of dedicated worker bees. The Way Builders, craftsmen who lived at or near Headquarters, had built the huge OSC building, longer than a football field. In the lobby, a receptionist smiled from a desk as tall as a judge's bench. Ahead of us were two uncarpeted staircases: one up, one down. We knew which way to go. We'd meet each other at the noon meal in the vast dining room.

Since 1976, when we'd last lived on the compound, Headquarters had undergone changes in leadership, staff, and appearance. The most significant leadership transformation was in 1982, when Wierwille retired and appointed Craig Martindale, our Second Corps brother, as president. Before Craig, a blond six-footer, entered The Way Corps, he'd been a college football player in Oklahoma and a charismatic leader in the Fellowship of Christian Athletes. During our Corps training, Wierwille gave Craig major responsibilities, such as overseeing the WOW Ambassador program. After graduation, Craig ran The Way Corps program at The Way College of Emporia. Ordained on the same night as Ed, Craig was married now and had a couple of children. He and his family lived in a log home, the Corps Chalet, in the woods across Wierwille Road from the OSC building. He used the ministry's airplane, motor coaches, and every other resource Wierwille had accrued. Not for a second did anyone doubt Craig's loyalty to Wierwille. In his book, *VP and Me* (not for sale to the public), Craig likened their pseudo father-son relationship to that of the Apostle Paul and his disciple Timothy. During the 1980s, Craig's book was read aloud to the in-residence Way Corps.

What Craig did not control was biblical research. Wierwille, at his retirement, left Rev. Walter J. Cummins in charge of that. Walter, loyal to a fault, had the experience and patience for research. Craig did not. Craig was the promotional front-man, he trained leaders for outreach, and, along with the other members of the Board of Trustees, he ran the organization.

This division of power between Craig and Walter would cause some of the worst trouble I would witness.

Also in 1982, Wierwille made an extraordinary decision that in one way or another affected all of us: he added an arm to The Way Corps program. He commissioned his loyal confidant and former bodyguard and valet, Christopher Geer—a former Massachusetts Limb leader who was now a Seventh Way Corps graduate and ordained Way clergyman—to establish a Way Corps training center in Gartmore, Scotland.

Because Geer would live in Europe, not many US Way Corps, much less any regular believers, came to know much about him, but the Geer-Wierwille relationship was always locked and loaded, at the ready. For anything.

By August 1984, when Ed and I arrived at Headquarters from Florida, the number of staff had swollen to about six hundred. It was dominated by Way Corps members, since that designation implied the highest level of allegiance. As for the compound, more structures had sprung up in the cornfields, including a modern dormitory and a busy hub, the aforementioned Outreach Services Center (OSC), nothing less than a small city under one roof. Upstairs was home to the library and research room, where I was assigned. Also up there were offices for the Board of Trustees, Way Publications, Architects and Builders, a Translations Department, Legal Counselors, a Credit Union, an Accounting Department, and a workroom for Interior Design. Downstairs, in full view of the lobby, was a welcome area with sofas and a stone fireplace, and offices for *The Way Magazine*, The Way Bookstore, the Printing Department, a Post Office, Video and Tape Recording, and Way Productions (the music division). A commercial-sized kitchen supplied daily meals in a dining hall that seated about eight hundred people and also served as an auditorium while The Way Builders constructed a new auditorium across the street. On the opposite end of the building from the dining room, straight down the main hall, was Shipping and Receiving, where Ed would work.

With new buildings, personnel, and equipment, a group called Bless Patrol—The Way's private security police salaried by The Way—protected Way property and everyone on it. Bless Patrol members had completed Deputies' Training Courses at the Shelby County Sheriff's Department and were granted Auxiliary Deputy Sheriff status that applied to Way properties in Shelby County, Ohio, only. This training granted them open-carry peace officer privilege; they were armed with handguns.

How did we pay for this expansion? In 1984 alone, The Way reported $27.1 million in income.[1] Believers around the world, in gratitude
for learning God's Word, flooded Wierwille's organization with money.

Soon after we arrived, Craig met with Ed and me under the trees on
Wierwille's lawn to discuss our assignments.

"If you work hard as *real* Corps for about three years," he said,
"then we'll send you back in the field—maybe as full-time leaders
again, who knows?"

Three years—agreed. Our little family retrieved our things from the
warehouse, settled into a refurbished farmhouse nearby, enrolled Rachel
in public school, and opened our hearts to receive our spiritual boost.

Under the receptionist's gaze, Ed and I said good-bye to each other in
the OSC lobby. As I climbed the steps, I felt more and more tense. I
worried this job might be beyond my abilities (a fact most everyone on
the team probably knew). With Frank's letter and Walter's enthusiastic
response at our dinner in Florida, I was somewhat encouraged. But
more than their belief in me, something else pushed me up those stairs:
certainty that God wanted me there. Odd things happen when you believe you are chosen.

I also worried about whether I looked okay to work in an office, but
it was too late to change. Before leaving Florida, I'd trashed my housecleaner wardrobe of grimy T-shirts and sweatpants and scoured consign-
ment shops to piece together modest outfits, keeping in mind the
male-dominated team. That first day, I wore a gray skirt, a cotton blouse,
and black high heels. I pinned back my long hair. I wasn't wearing glasses yet, but in a few months I would be, and they would complete my
"research-geek" look, as staff friends would teasingly say.

I entered the carpeted research library, opposite the Board of Trustees suite. To my left, behind a checkout desk, a set of wooden folding

doors hung open like stage curtains pulled to either side. Behind them was the research team's room. The aroma of brewing coffee, mingled with the stuffy odor of books and close quarters, overtook me. Male voices drifted out of the room, and I caught a glimpse of Frank in the doorway. His shock of red hair, slicked back from a high forehead, and his short stocky figure made him unmistakable. He caught my eye and waved me in.

"Hey, Frank. How are you?" I glanced around as the five other young men on the team swiveled toward us from their desks. I felt my face turn red at interrupting their work. I already knew them, but they all looked so official and important in this room.

"I'm doing great," Frank said. Like the host at a reception, he brought me into the room and gestured to the others. "We're so blessed you're finally here, right, guys?" They nodded their heads all at once. Looking at me, he added, "You'll help us get some work done around this place," and laughed. "Let me reacquaint you with these gentlemen." They made their ways around the bulky conference table in the middle of the room to greet me. Each, I knew, worked on a specific topic supervised by Walter Cummins, our boss: Greek New Testament, Gospel Harmony, Eastern Customs, Old Testament History. Joe Wise, the only one wearing a tie, teamed with Bernita on the Aramaic project. Joe was completing his master's degree at the University of Chicago, learning Syriac and early church history for credentials needed to do this Aramaic (actually Syriac) work. After our greetings, we gathered around our version of the water cooler—the glass coffeepot simmering in the corner—and within minutes, their easy camaraderie dispelled my feelings of intimidation. With smart and caring colleagues like this, I could hardly wait to get started. Besides the separate projects we did, I knew we would work as a team to help Walter prepare teachings for The Way Corps each week, which were still a sacred ritual; Walter, having succeeded Wierwille in delivering God's Word in detail to the Corps, was our high priest.

Chatter petered out and everyone started back to work. Joe approached me near the wooden folding doors where I sipped my coffee, studying the pretty golden patterns.

"They're birch wood," Joe said. "Don't keep out much noise, and don't keep in much either, but they're okay." Like a protective brother, he towered over me, his hands in his pockets, his tie loosened now.

"I guess you know," he said, "the work around here is tedious, but we try to have some fun, too." His eyes sparkled behind his glasses, and his friendly style put me at ease.

"Yeah, Joe is our social director," one of the guys chimed in. "He sets up movie nights and pizza and stuff. Believe me, we're glad he does. We'd go crazy if he didn't get us outta here once in a while."

Joe walked back to his desk and Frank, heading out the doorway, said he'd show me around in a minute, right after he got back from dropping off materials to his wife, who worked in another office. I set my purse on the desk that he'd pointed out as mine and looked around. Bookcases were stuffed with many versions of Bibles, a multitude of reference books, and stacks of papers. Against the opposite wall from me, three desks were side by side; one was Joe's. On the other side of the open door, Alvin, the librarian, and John Schoenheit, who specialized in Old Testament History, busied themselves at their desks. I was grateful to be among such dedicated workers. For so many years, I had wondered whether I could or would ever return to the most important work I thought God wanted me to do in this ministry. Finally, here I was!

I marveled at the changes in this department. Since my first days with Bernita, thirteen years earlier in the old office trailer, and later in the Data Management Services trailer, this research endeavor had grown steadily. Now there were more researchers engaged in more projects. The two most significant ones at the moment were the Aramaic concordance and Gospel harmony research, an attempt to fit the four gospels together in one narrative, eliminating apparent contradictions. One of Walter's assistants on that most prized project was John Schoenheit, who had become Walter's good friend.

John had always struck me as overly optimistic, but his enthusiasm could not be beat. Unimaginably, John's legendary idealism would one day be his downfall at The Way.

Across the room, the beloved coffeepot sputtered atop a dorm-sized refrigerator beside a heavy metal door. Above that was a red Exit sign. What some people never guessed when entering the OSC's lobby was that a cavernous warehouse ran like a spine along the back of the building. It housed furniture, farm equipment, lawn mowers, staff belongings, stage materials for the Rock of Ages, portable lighting, bicycles, golf carts, and anything else that didn't require refrigeration. Rows of tall heavy-duty metal shelves held smaller items in sturdy wooden crates. A few downstairs offices opened into the warehouse, and several on the second floor had fire escape stairs leading down to it. Our exit door connected to those stairs. I'd soon learn I could take that staircase to reach my car parked out back. If I was late for work, that staircase was a quick way in. My footsteps would echo through the space, with its dark rows of storage shelves. Sometimes bats flew through the huge open doors at each end, and sparrows flapped against low-hanging lights. Once in a while I'd see one of those sparrows lying in a dusty corner, having lost the struggle to find its way out.

Our back stairs also became a shortcut to the Printing Department below our room. Its back door was often propped open to let ink fumes escape, as well the loud *thump, thump, thump* from the black German printing press, running at all hours, pumping out thousands of copies of *The Way Magazine* and other materials, symbolizing industriousness underway all over the building.

At my desk, I stashed my purse in the lowest compartment and finished my coffee. Frank returned from his errand.

"I haven't brought my Bibles or Aramaic books today," I said. "I hope that's all right."

"Oh sure," said Frank. "Today we'll just get you settled in. Don't want too much information overload the first day, right? Only a little," he grinned again, but I felt a layer of tension rise. Where were Bernita and Walter? Their offices were on the other side of the library, down a short hallway. When I asked about them, Frank said neither was in that morning.

"Let's take a little stroll to orient you to the rest of the neighborhood," he said. He escorted me back out the way I'd come and into the silence of the main hallway.

"Hey," he whispered, steering me along, "I gotta say again how glad everybody is that you're here." He shut the door behind us, and I heard the click of an automatic lock. With a slight scowl, Frank held out a metal key, warmed from his hand. He told me it was my own key to the library and cautioned me, in Humphrey Bogart fashion, to guard it with my life.

"We must protect the Word," he said. His cryptic message struck me as odd. It was jargon, I knew, for defending Wierwille's research, but what could possibly threaten it here?

"Doctor trusts us so much, you know?" I nodded without being sure I "knew" in the same way he meant, but I imagined he was warning me to be loyal, unlike a few past researchers who had forsaken the ministry about six years earlier and been branded as deceived by the Devil. They did not protect the Word.

"When we heard you got this assignment, we were thrilled," he whispered as we neared the Board of Trustees suite. T. J., Craig's loyal assistant, was headed inside. Tall, suntanned, and sporting khaki pants and a striped button-down shirt, T. J. nodded to us, but his glance was full of suspicion. I didn't know him well, but I'd seen him at Corps Week for years, tagging along with Craig, nodding at his every word like a perpetual yes-man, like Chris Geer did with Wierwille. T. J. disappeared like a ghost into the Trustee suite.

When I turned back to Frank, he was frowning. What was going on? Where was the joy I'd seen moments earlier? I thought of the note he'd sent me before I'd left Florida, intimating that the team truly needed me. A door slammed, and he glanced furtively at a woman who was leaving the ladies room next to the library. We remained quiet until she disappeared into the finance office at the end of the hall.

"You know, I've always admired your commitment," Frank said. "That's exactly what we need on the team right now. You love the Word, and you're an experienced leader. The rest of us on the team don't have much experience as leaders in the field. We're too new ... and we hardly know Doctor Wierwille. We rarely, if ever, worked with him doing research like you did when you were in the Corps."

Current team members graduated from the Corps *after* Wierwille had run the program.

"Doctor is like a distant grandfather to us," he said, looking down.

"Right. I guess he would be." They had missed the chance of being around Doctor to observe how he researched the Word. When I was in the Corps, we'd meet in the BRC and Doctor would consult with Walter and Bernita and others. They would look up Greek words, figures of speech, and Eastern customs, and search for the accurate Word together as we watched and listened in. Those days were long gone.

"That experience helped you learn to trust Doctor's scope of the Word, didn't it?" By that he meant what Doctor referred to as his "big-picture understanding" of how "the whole Bible fit together like a hand in a glove." It also included Doctor's ability to see things God showed him in the text of the Scriptures that the rest of us could not see. Frank's words aroused my nostalgia for the old research days.

"Sure did," I said. "But that's such a long time ago. I'm a little rusty."

That didn't matter to Frank. It was true I was the only current team member besides Walter, Bernita, and Alvin, a Third Corps grad from 1974, who had worked with Wierwille in the old days. Alvin was not technically a research team member, but he assisted Walter with many projects. Our personal contact with Wierwille had sealed our loyalty to his ministry in a manner not available to Corps who came after us. But newer Corps were needed and along the way they'd proven they were trustworthy. Only loyal Corps grads were invited to be on the research team.

"There's another important reason we need you," Frank said. "To help Bernita."

"How?"

"George has been sick for a long time. You know that, right?" George Jess was Bernita's husband, once the beloved Director of The Way Corps.

"Uh …"

"I'm sorry to have to tell you this, but George is seriously ill. His doctors don't expect him to live much longer." Frank's hands began shaking.

I barely heard him ask me to keep this secret, I was so shocked. Sadness swept through me as I tried to grasp the awful news. George was only in his sixties—too young to die, younger than Wierwille, who then was sixty-seven.

"I'm not sure what's wrong with George, but he's unconscious," he said, "confined to the hospital in Indiana where our Way believer doctor and Corps grad nurses are caring for him. Bernita's there right now."

"I see."

"So we need to help her. We are asking you to drive her to visit George every week. Her life has split in half." Understandably, Bernita had fallen behind at work, Frank explained. The stress had pulled her off the concordance project for months. Joe had stepped in to organize the massive, complex project. Weekdays and weekends blended together for him. Wierwille expected the concordance to be published by the following August; since the founder of the ministry had been waiting decades for it to make history and give him the special credit he sought from biblical scholars worldwide, he was impatient. Even in his retirement, this project was still his Aramaic dream. We had one more year.

"When we found out you wanted to come on staff," Frank continued, "Walter talked things over with us. Given the whole situation, you were perfect for this job." It was no secret that I'd worked with Bernita the longest of anyone and circumnavigated her moods well—at times she could be fussy and obstinate, but we loved and honored her as our teacher.

"Don't you agree Bernita would welcome your help?"

"Of course." How could I refuse? My heart ached for Bernita, but memories of my mother dying in a hospital surfaced like broken shells washing ashore.

"Thanks," he whispered. "This means a lot."

I had a splitting headache. Frank's news made me feel as if I'd been spun around a hundred times. Joining the team intimidated me, but caretaking scared me, and I resented being put in this role. I hated hospitals and barely tolerated having to be in one for my own baby's birth. But I must respond to this unavoidable duty; Bernita's adult children lived far away. Bernita had uplifted me when Ed and I separated years ago; now it was my turn to aid her. The concordance could wait for my input, although without an in-depth knowledge of Syriac, what could I possibly add? I was only a displaced housecleaner dressed up in research clothes.

Frank assured me that I'd work on the concordance as time allowed, but my immediate focus was Bernita. I assured him that I'd keep this matter to myself. Death, we were taught, was an enemy. When it was not due to old age, we considered it an attack by the Devil. When I was recruited at college, I told Earl about my mother passing away and that the Church said God took her. That's when I learned the verse about the

Devil as the "author of death." According to The Way, sickness like George's and my mother's meant they failed to believe God for healing. That made them weak. George was the first case of a beloved, too-young-to-die staff member, so it shocked me he was not going to recover, but we had to face it. Sometimes people did not believe as strongly as we thought they could or should. Since George was a public figure in The Way, news of his imminent death would distress and disappoint the entire ministry. The situation blanketed me in sadness and fear for Bernita's future.

Whenever I drove Bernita on the depressing pilgrimage to see George, I reminded myself this duty was a service to God just as much as working on the concordance. At Headquarters, work and personal issues were more closely entwined than in the outside world. We were a family. But I felt conflicted about being pulled off the project for this personal agenda. After all, I believed that working on the Aramaic project was God's most important plan for me.

37

Not So Good

Isaac Newton told us that a body set in motion stays in motion. I think a moving mind does the same. A remark can start it going, even a whisper can, and associations leap like monkeys from one branch of thought to the next, and before you can swing back around, before you realize how far you've gone, you're tangled in a mess of jungle vines. That describes what happened to me one day in mid-November 1984 when our team met with Walter.

Bernita insisted she and I attend this meeting and delay our visit to George, who was still in the hospital. At the conference table, she sat to my right; another team member sat to my left. The rest of the team circled around the table with books and papers stacked at their elbows. Walter clicked the folding doors shut, set a pipe in a glass ashtray by his pile of books, and took his customary seat at the head of the table. "Let's get started," he said, and read Ephesians 6:11 aloud, the verse we were to examine that session: "'Put on the whole armour of God, that ye may be able to stand against the wiles of the devil.'"

Within minutes, I faced a problem that not only would mushroom into outlandish proportions in the ministry, but also signaled the first shocks of a psychic earthquake that sent me careening out of Wierwille's psychological grip.

The problem really began in 1971 around a campfire in The Way's woods down Wierwille Road at Headquarters. Doctor was "sharing his heart" with some of us in the Corps about Ephesians. He claimed that military words in chapter 6 "had to be wrong," although he admitted he did not have textual evidence to prove otherwise. He said he just *knew* that the military imagery in that chapter *should be* athletic imagery. Why? The Father (God) told him, he said. Besides, to Wierwille, Christians were not soldiers of the Lord; they were athletes of the spirit. Granted, the phrase *armour of God* may be a metaphor, but Wierwille took it literally. As many fundamentalists do, Wierwille cherry-picked which verses to believe literally, which ones to accept metaphorically. Military terms were for Old Testament times, he said, when God's people, the Israelites, fought pagan nations. God's people today, the born-again Christians, should be associated (as they are in other New Testament sections) with athletic imagery, like running a race to win crowns in heaven. It wasn't long after that campfire that Wierwille sent Walter Cummins overseas in search of Greek texts to prove he was correct. Walter never found such proof.

Ten years later, in the article "Ordained of God" in *The Way Magazine,* July/August 1981, Wierwille put his belief in print: "God has called all of us to be spiritual athletes. The great record from Ephesians 6 does not picture believers as soldiers with military armor, but rather as athletes of God."[1] Wierwille's personal belief was made official Way doctrine.

But Wierwille was wrong.

On that November day in 1984, huddled at our conference table at our meeting with Walter to examine the highly charged issue, a lot of double-checking went on to verify—and it did—the definition of the Greek word *panoplia,* translated in Ephesians 6:11 as *armour.* It turned out that *panoplia* had nothing to do with athletics. It meant hardcore military gear, including a shield, sword, lance, helmet, greaves (shin protectors), and a breastplate.

Added to that, in his own PFAL class, Wierwille pointed out that the context of any word gives understanding about its meaning. Ephesians 6 was about how believers must be protected, and a military metaphor made that point.

Long minutes passed. Tension piled up like snow on Wierwille Road. Walter paced the room, and I shook with distress at the blatant change Wierwille had made to Scripture. None of us looked at each other. Eyes down, we examined our shoes so Walter could have space to think. He was in charge. The task of resolving the dilemma was his, not ours. He had to teach this verse to the entire Way Corps. Would he stick to Wierwille or to the text? More silent minutes passed. The wall clock's ticking sounded surreal, the coffeepot steamed in the corner, my mind felt hazy and numb, and that's when it happened. The team member beside me leaned in close, and in the fashion of a Shakespearean aside, said:

"I love Doctor Wierwille, but sometimes his Greek isn't so good."

From then on, nothing was the same for me.

My knee-jerk thought was: *What the hell do you mean? Doctor's the man of God. God is teaching him the truth!* But I sat silent.

I shut my eyes to block those words from reality—words I would later call "The Comment"—and shield myself from their blinding truth. Flashes of fear zigzagged behind my eyelids like spasms of red, bursting and exploding. Despite my defensiveness, I knew it was true. The evidence was right on the table under my nose. But it was the strangest sensation to hear my colleague's words out loud. What he said was unthinkable—that our man of God was incompetent—but that message did not match his tone of voice or emotion. He seemed unruffled, as if intellectually critiquing a painting in a gallery, not our man of God's doctrines that we were supposed to build our lives on. He might as well have added: *This is the way it is in research. This is why only loyal Way*

Corps grads like us are on the team. You'll get used to it like I have. We cannot let these things undermine our commitment to the basics of the Word, to Dr. Wierwille, or the ministry. Walter will handle this tricky issue and all others. That's his job. Don't interfere. You will only cause trouble for yourself.

So much for being a biblical research ministry.

My mind's eye pictured a rubber raft approaching to carry me back ten minutes to a safe place before I heard The Comment, but the raft bobbed out of reach and left me floundering in my new reality: I could not trust Wierwille. Disorientation took over. The coveted raft drifted out of sight. What would I do? How had I not admitted that Wierwille changed and twisted Scripture to serve his agenda? The answer, clearly, was that I believed that Wierwille's snow story validated whatever he said: "God told me He'd teach me the Word like it has not been known since the first century—if I would teach it to others." That claim justified whatever Wierwille taught.

The thought of having endured years of intimidation to stick with The Way—and my unsatisfactory marriage attached to it—crushed me. I'd done all that for this?

I was a typical black-and-white thinker, a person who bought into Wierwille's "all or nothing" fast-talk. The realization hit me: I must stop my life immediately to check everything Wierwille ever taught. Sure, it's impossible to do, but I was accustomed to extremist thinking. Either the Bible is God's Word or it isn't. Either you stand with the household of The Way or you don't. You either have fear or faith, belief or doubt—and doubt, according to Wierwille's fundamentalism, was of the Devil. Wierwille had drummed into us that Eve's doubt in the Garden of Eden— from listening to the Devil—ended in separation from God. Using the story of Eve, Doctor effectively scared many of us out of doubting his teachings. How silly it now sounds, yet that's exactly what he did. That day in the research office, though, I knew in my heart that my colleague was not devil-possessed. Sincere and helpful, he was oblivious to how

The Comment affected me, and I kept it that way. I never told him. If I had, he would have felt abysmal, but it wasn't his fault that Wierwille's Greek wasn't "so good." I had received a favor I could never repay.

Then and for years afterward, I struggled to be honest with this moment. During my time in The Way, I had attended private biblical research sessions and often witnessed Wierwille change the text. He did not always claim divine revelation as his authority. Instead, he would say things like, "I know there must be a text in the world someplace that backs this up; we just haven't found it yet." This was backward, I know, but he made it seem acceptable. He ignored the proper course: first you have a text, then you teach what it says. Somehow Wierwille steered us into accepting his authority rather than the authority of the written words. (Many ministers practice this sleight of hand, but he was a master.) Because there were several Greek versions of the New Testament and a Syriac one (the Peshitta NT), which sometimes differed from the Greek, we would acquiesce to Wierwille's decisions about which text was accurate. But how did he know? I never questioned his skimpy-to-nonexistent training. Deference became such a habit for me that I did not in the slightest way suspect it was wrong to follow Wierwille without question. It didn't *feel* wrong. I'd done it for years—until The Comment.

The spoken word is often more powerful than we realize, bringing into immediate conscious awareness what might be floating around in our heads. That day—perhaps because I was ready to hear it—The Comment pierced my bubble of Wierwille-awe and made his act of changing the text *feel* wrong. An irreversible shift took place and awakened me to respect the written texts for what they said, not what Wierwille wanted them to say.

On the surface, though, what difference did it make if we said the text referred to *soldiers* or *athletes*? Not much … except it made us wrong about what the Bible said. And knowing what the Bible *really meant* was supposed to be our sacred mission. However, that mission was becoming suspect.

In 1985, about a year after that research meeting with Walter, the problem of armor and athletes would become expensive and embarrassing when the new president, Rev. L. Craig Martindale, spent thousands of dollars—donations from Way believers—on a musical production that starred him as the man of God performing alternately as dancer and athlete. Craig, a former football player, was a spectacular flop in this role. The show portrayed believers as athletes of the spirit—in tights, executing ballet and karate moves as they fought incarnate devils. The costumes cost a small fortune, as did feeding and housing the professional dancers (Way converts from New York). Worst of all, Craig's laughable talent show distracted him from his presidential duties, which ticked off Wierwille. Meanwhile, those of us in the Research Department across the hall from the Trustee suite would roll our eyes as we watched any respect for what biblical texts actually said being tossed out.

At The Comment meeting, Walter paced around the conference table like a caged dog. We waited for his decision. Was it going to be athletes or armor? Killing time, we flipped through our Bibles, moved books around, straightened papers. Walter's cherry tobacco smoke floated in circles around our heads. Finally, I heard Walter take a deep draw on his pipe. "We'll set this aside for now."

The meeting ended and likewise my certainty about Wierwille. When I stood up, I wobbled like a newborn kitten. Why couldn't I be like the rest of the team, who accepted the disturbing situation with calm and continued with their business? No one showed the slightest sign of a nervous breakdown like I thought I was having. To manage, I knew I had to repress The Comment and stay the course. My family and my job depended on my composure—and my silence. I must think of Bernita, too, and her husband, who now lay dying.

38

Dust to Dust

For many Americans, November 1984 unfurled a carpet of bright promises as President Ronald Reagan, for whom Wierwille encouraged us to vote, was reelected in a landslide victory—but I paid no attention. I was mourning. One night in Bernita's new mobile home (across the driveway from Wierwille's house), my mentor sat in a new powder-blue chair, nodding at her grown children across the room, dabbing her eyes with tissues. Two nurses sat on the sofa next to me. The calming scent of hot herbal tea filled the air. Everyone was riveted to the closed-circuit television in the corner, waiting for the meeting to start. Soon Wierwille, dressed in a formal black suit, appeared onscreen, sitting behind a desk in the OSC auditorium. This event was personal for Wierwille; otherwise, Craig would have officiated.

About six hundred Way Corps members filled seats in front of Doctor. Others gathered in their trailers on the compound, watching television monitors, and hundreds more stationed around the United States and abroad listened by telephone.

As fast as a judge slams his gavel on the bench, Wierwille flung a heavy plastic bag, gray and bulging, on the desk. "This ... is George Jess."

I gasped, a reaction I'm sure Wierwille aimed for. The nurses who had attended George in the hospital burst into tears. Bernita was quiet. She pulled another tissue from her sweater pocket and leaned back in the chair. Whether she'd given permission for this grotesque performance is something I'll never know. I couldn't ask her such a question.

Wierwille evidently wanted to shock us with an unavoidable truth about life—death. His gesture delivered finality in a way that no amount of Bible teaching could. Physical death is decisive. There is no bringing life back. Not immediately, anyway. The Word of God, Wierwille reminded us, promised that at any moment Christ could return for the living believers, raise the dead believers, and take us all to heaven. That's why we did not say believers died. We said they *fell asleep*—because Christ would wake them up when he returned. The first time I'd heard this theology—the night Marshall's football team died in the plane crash—I'd felt bad for the dead nonbelievers and their families. By now, however, I was desensitized and cared only about Christ's return for believers. We would see George Jess again, and our reunion would last forever. In the meantime, we must spread the Word over the world. George would want nothing less.

A poem by Jack Gilbert, "Michiko Dead," likens grief to a heavy box carried by a man who continuously rearranges the way he carries it—from his arms to his shoulder and back to his arms—so that he never has to put it down. [1] Bernita had outlived two husbands now (the first was the minister who died in a car crash). She bore the load of both. We knew it would be some time before she resumed working. Meanwhile, Joe assigned more tasks to me. Despite our burdens, we must meet the August deadline.

39

Research and Loyalty

"I want you to read this, Charlene," Frank said, handing me a folder marked Confidential.

I set it on my desk and opened it: one typewritten page with signatures at the bottom.

"I'll give you a copy, too." he said. "It's in response to a dispute that happened in the Satellite Research Group."

Frank went to his desk and left me sipping my coffee, reading the document, titled "Household and Family."[1]

Before joining the Headquarters research team, I'd participated in the Satellite Research Group. Consisting of about fifty serious believers from around the country, many with degrees in biblical languages, it met annually with the Headquarters research team. I remembered hearing something about a dispute over Doctor's distinction between the meanings of *family* and *household* in the Bible, but I had been in a different focus group studying another topic. These terms were used in our ministry to denote a hierarchy of Way believers—being in the household of The Way was better than being only in the family.

Near the top of the paper, Wierwille's definitions for *family* and *household*—common knowledge in our ministry since the 1970s—were stated. He used *family* to indicate genealogical descent, and he used *household* to mean people under a common roof. By those definitions, people could leave a household but could never undo familial bonds. This distinction was used to buttress the idea that if you were active with The Way and obeyed Wierwille's teachings, you were in the household. If you left our ministry, you were out of the household, but you were still in the family, because you were a born-again child of God—you could never lose that status. The permanence of being born again was Wierwille's theology based on letters in the New Testament attributed to the Apostle Paul.

This topic was a sore spot with me. Ed had left The Way household more than once, and to regain that status had been difficult. I lived in the shadow of this household/family debate.

Wierwille's distinction evidently upset members of the Satellite Research Group—two researchers in particular. I remembered hearing they objected to Wierwille applying these terms only to *his* ministry, not all Christianity, and they did not see a difference in the two terms as used in the Bible. The words functioned, it seemed to them, as synonyms.

The page I held in my hand described what happened next: a compromise instead of a research conclusion was reached by the people who wrote papers on the topic. The paper did not describe the compromise, and I never heard what it was. However, Walter and the Headquarters research team continued to agree with Wierwille's definitions.

At the bottom of the page was Walter's signature, as well as signatures of the Headquarters research team on staff at the time. A note stated that Bernita was not present to be able to add her signature. It was possible her absence was deliberate. She was famously independent, picking and choosing what she did, answering only to Wierwille. She and Walter respected each other, but I never heard him tell her what to do.

This "Household and Family" statement—on only one page—revealed a vital moment in the department's history, and it made me a little sick. The two researchers from the Satellite Research Group who ignited the dispute—by writing papers questioning Wierwille's use of the terms—were not novices. They were longstanding, loyal figures in the ministry: his private research secretary of more than twenty years, and his eldest daughter, who edited most of his books. Along with everyone else in research, I respected both women. It frightened me to think that they of all people would go up against Wierwille. They had worked on countless biblical research projects with Wierwille and alongside Walter for more than a decade. Had they felt so sure they were right that they took this stand?

I've since recognized a more important aspect of this incident. It could have upended Wierwille's credibility. That these women, among the most adept of Wierwille's researchers, reached different conclusions from Wierwille about the distinction between *family* and *household* suggested there might be a serious flaw in his work, making it impossible for people to replicate his results (his interpretations), which he called the accurate Word of God. Only one example is needed to put truth-claims in doubt, and those two women gave one.

If Walter had agreed with those women and confronted Wierwille, it's highly likely there could have been a huge blow-up. Wierwille might have even "released" Walter. Walter had to make it clear he and his team agreed with Wierwille. He had to kill the issue. If it had been broadcasted in the ministry, it's possible that Way followers, who made decisions about how to live their lives based on Wierwille's teachings, might have turned away and taken their financial support with them, realizing the accuracy of Wierwille's Bible teachings was in doubt if Wierwille's closely trained and loyal researchers couldn't come up with the same doctrine as Wierwille when they followed his "foolproof" methods. Millions of dollars in donations could have evaporated. The Way as we knew it could have collapsed.

To maintain the status quo, Walter and his team extinguished the firestorm before it spread. Thus, the paper—in effect, a loyalty oath—was signed. Wierwille's private research secretary and his daughter let the matter go, I heard, for the sake of the unity of the ministry. "Keeping the unity of the spirit in the bond of peace" was a mantra derived from the Bible and invoked when differences erupted. Once highly respected, the two researchers no longer visited our department unless Walter invited them for a specific project. Later, the ministry's official view of *household*—begun by Wierwille—was reflected in *The Way Magazine*, which began publishing "A Believer's Pledge of Allegiance" that stated: "I pledge allegiance to the one true God and to His Son, Jesus Christ, and to His Word for which we stand, one household under God, indivisible, with liberty and love for all."[2]

The message was loud and clear.

Wordlessly, I returned the folder to Frank and kept the copy he gave me. We never again discussed it.

During Thanksgiving break, our family ventured out to visit Ed's father and stepmother at their house in Rhode Island. We enjoyed a lovely dinner and kept conversation light, only mentioning the ministry in terms of our new jobs and how we liked them. Rachel chatted about friends and school. She'd adjusted well—her personality was far more outgoing than mine, thank goodness—and she was making good grades and taking dance lessons from a professional on staff. Ed's family was easier to be around now, and I imagined it was because of Rachel. She endeared herself to everyone, especially her grandparents.

Being away from Ohio was a welcome break, but it brought our marriage and the emptiness I felt to the foreground. My work schedule gave me little time with Ed. I'd tell him about milestones with the concordance, but I kept research problems to myself. I could trust no one. When Walter requested team members to publish articles for *The Way Magazine*, I fretted over mine, which was about studying the PFAL class materials, trying to word it to hide my misgivings. Ed's interests lay elsewhere. He was finally doing something fun with people he liked after those stressful, boring sales jobs in Florida. His nights were filled with choir practice, ballroom dancing rehearsals, and performances with people I barely knew. He had reestablished himself as an enthusiastic and committed Corps grad eligible for another leadership position. We had moved further apart, but we maintained the fiction that we were happy together, hoping things would improve. I hadn't yet heard that doing the same thing repeatedly but expecting different results was insane. At least Rachel brought us both much delight. We would soon need that more than ever.

40

The Emperor's New Text

Where was Wierwille when we arrived in 1984? He inhabited the shadows. I observed him only from a distance—driving a golf cart with his dog beside him, dining in the OSC with his wife, teaching an occasional Sunday service. We had no idea how much influence he wielded behind the scenes. Despite retirement, Wierwille appeared in the spotlight at the two-day grand opening of the Word Over the World (WOW) Auditorium on March 16–17, 1985. (The auditorium has since been renamed the Prevailing Word Auditorium.) More than four thousand people from the United States, thirteen other countries, and four continents packed the auditorium—costing millions of donation dollars—and filled the OSC building across the street, where more seats were available and closed-circuit television monitors broadcasted the program.

What many outsiders were horrified to learn was that The Way had another ceremony that weekend: a book burning. The ritual was begun by Doctor and held annually in memory of his brother, Harry Ernst Wierwille, the first secretary-treasurer, who passed away in 1977. "Uncle Harry," whose birthday was March 19, was memorialized with a bonfire to "burn the chaff"—books, paintings, music, or anything considered remotely inspired by the Devil. Like the Florentine priest Girolamo Savonarola during the Renaissance, Way followers publicly torched suspect objects on the pyre, believing they could live for God better without them.

On Sunday night of that special weekend, hundreds of Way clergy, including Ed, processed in black robes down the aisles of the gleaming auditorium—its brass railings shining, its stage full of flowers, its organist pounding the keys—to pay tribute to The Teacher. I would never forget that day, not only for the festivity, but because later Wierwille blamed his leaders and the research team for something we did not do.

The next day, Monday, Walter entered our research room and snapped the folding doors shut. He didn't greet us or relax to smoke his pipe.

"Listen up. Last night, Doctor met with me, Craig, and the cabinet." The cabinet consisted of department directors, like Walter. "Doctor let us know we blew it yesterday. We were not spiritually on top of it. All of us, you included, missed too many details."

Me?

Apparently confusion and ineptitude plagued food services and seating arrangements for the thousands who'd come to hear the Word. The Devil, Walter reminded us, was the author of confusion. Apparently, he'd crashed our party.

That Sunday evening I had taught a group of children for an hour. That was my assignment. Food and chairs were not.

"Along with the rest of us leaders," Walter said, knocking his empty pipe on the table, "the group in this room is to blame."

Shock must have registered on all our faces because Walter said, "You all know what I mean—we failed spiritually." He spat out the words.

This was a Toledo fiasco rerun, a failure at Ed's parents' house rerun. Wierwille flung the same vague charge—failing spiritually—at people whenever he wanted a scapegoat. Once, when it rained at the Rock of Ages, Wierwille blamed the thunderstorm on The Way Corps being "out of fellowship with God," causing God to withdraw his protection and his sunny skies.

In the past when wrongly accused, I would have cowered in false guilt. This time, I guess I'd reached a boiling point in my dissatisfaction with Wierwille, his ministry, his bad research, his control and intimidation. I snapped.

I wish now that I had said what I was thinking: *This is bullshit.*

"You're supposed to be the most spiritually mature people in the building," Walter ragged on. "Doctor has entrusted this group with the Word, and we're to protect it and walk by the spirit of God better than anyone else." He paced in front of the bookcases, shooting us stern looks. "We're spiritually responsible for what goes on around here."

It was flattering to be deemed so spiritual, but it was absurd to think we had the duty he described.

"Doctor Wierwille gave our group more freedom of thought than anyone else in the ministry," Walter continued, "and along with that privilege is responsibility. And we blew it."

Wait a minute. My gut felt the punch. Wierwille didn't give us freedom to think. God gave us that freedom. What Wierwille had given us, I realized then, was fear of speaking freely and thinking critically. In The Way, freedom of speech was a lost civil right. I later surmised that Walter meant our team, in the service of doing research, could ask a few more questions than the average believer without being reprimanded, but that only went so far.

"We all blew it yesterday, including me," Walter said and unsnapped the doors. He trudged out like a defeated general and headed for his office with Bernita trailing him. I clutched my tacky Florida coffee cup with the palm trees on it. Joe scanned his desk as if looking for a misplaced binder clip. The others remained silent. No one made eye contact.

From that day onward, I was finished with taking seriously any intimidating remark.

≡≡

But intimidation was not over. One day in April, Walter and Craig appeared with Doctor in the auditorium for a special Corps meeting. Doctor said they were going to clarify the research on athlete and military imagery, which Craig and Walter had been butting heads over. Wierwille moderated. Walter read the Greek word for *armour* in Ephesians, which Craig publicly taught as *athletic gear*. In this, Craig was only following Wierwille, who had taught this since the '70s. That day, Wierwille played the diplomat to show he was open-minded to what Walter said was "more light" on the topic. Within the hour, Wierwille brokered a deal, which, as far as some of us on the team were concerned, contained a small victory wrapped in a large disaster.

"We do not have Greek textual evidence in Ephesians for athletic terms," Walter said, "only military terms." A minute passed with Wierwille hemming and hawing.

"But we still might find it," Walter added.

We might find it? A mysterious text we hoped would verify our belief? When? Where? Meanwhile, we're okay with teaching whatever we want the text to say? As far as I was concerned, that day Wierwille made it public that he did research backward. Astonishingly, no one balked (out loud). He was the man of God. He decided what the Word said. The meeting ended. I laughed to keep from crying. This was straight out of "The Emperor's New Clothes."

In truth, over the years I'd been as bad as Walter. I'd colluded with Wierwille by going along when he said textual evidence might materialize *after* the supposed "truth of God's Word" had been taught. I'd believed—like I believed the moon orbits the earth—that God granted my teacher special knowledge that overrode texts.

To deny that out loud now, at this point of my journey, would have meant getting kicked to the curb without pay, losing every Way friend I had—my *only* friends—and being seen as deceived by the Devil. Was speaking the truth worth the risk? No.

Not yet, anyway.

Dissenters can survive in an oppressive place like Headquarters, as authors like Viktor Frankl know better than anyone, by being inconspicuous. Blend in. Bide your time until an emergency exit opens.

Soon afterward, Dr. and Mrs. Wierwille traveled to Gartmore, Scotland, to inspect the European Way Corps being trained by Rev. Christopher Geer, Doctor's former motor coach driver, valet, confidant, and armed bodyguard, who for more than a decade had bowed to Wierwille's every wish and even trained Doberman Pinschers as attack guards. Since Geer had lived overseas for some time, newer Way Corps and staff did not know him like some of us from the early 1970s who were well aware that Wierwille trusted Geer like no other. When Wierwille returned from that Gartmore trip in mid-May 1985, he slunk deeper into the shadowy background. Then one day in late May, research problems and every other difficulty fled our minds like dogs running scared.

41

The Call that Changed It All

Early Tuesday morning, May 21, 1985, Ed and I were in bed asleep when the telephone rang. Ed jerked awake and grabbed the receiver from the bedside table.

"Hello? ... Oh no!" My husband hung up the phone and turned to me. "Doctor died."

"What?" I rubbed my eyes.

"He passed away. Last night. He's dead."

Ed's boss had delivered the news and reported that Corps and staff members were to attend an 8:00 a.m. meeting in the auditorium. Bring our children. We were a household in crisis. Headquarters was closed today.

We'd heard that Doctor was sick but not that death was imminent. A few years earlier, he'd had an eye removed and replaced with one made of glass, but he had remained active. Recent rumors said he was mysteriously weakened. No one dared accuse him of not believing God's promise of health, or voiced that Satan was gaining power over our man of God.

I felt conflicted. Half of me was sad—anyone's death is a loss—but half was relieved. I felt as if a hundred-pound satchel had fallen off my back. Wierwille could no longer propagate incorrect teachings. That was callous of me, I knew, but I couldn't help it.

It did not occur to me then that his teachings would live on and on, promoted as indisputable truth. Even as I write this.

Hauling myself out of bed, I tied my robe around me, wondering how his death would affect our department. Our team existed at the pleasure of the man who started this ministry, and now he was gone. Could Walter bear up under know-it-all Craig Martindale? We had lost the man whose dream had made the Aramaic concordance possible and who was our best advocate for its success. Granted, he ill-treated Ed and me more than once (I did not yet know of his widespread sexual abuse of women), he was a bully who drank too much, and his research was a mess. However, Craig Martindale did not comprehend the significance of the concordance like Wierwille had, nor did he have the faintest notion of the expertise it took to produce it.

I was disgusted with Craig, my Second Corps brother. His humility, which he'd shown during our Corps training, had been washed away by the attention showered on him, especially after becoming president. From what I saw of his swaggering teaching style on Sundays and his condescending attitudes in the dining room, that humility had been gone a long time. This hadn't registered with me clearly before I'd joined the staff, although I'd heard Craig rant angrily on Corps nights when we listened in by telephone, and I saw his increasingly arrogant style at the Rock of Ages year by year. But Ed and I had been on the fringes, not in regular contact with Craig and other leaders we'd once known personally. I was well aware that Wierwille had shaped Craig in his own image and likeness. I blamed him for setting the pattern for the narcissistic leadership I now saw in Craig, which wasn't leadership at all. It was domination.

Rachel was awake when I sat on her bright yellow-and-pink bedspread. The telephone's ringing had awakened her, so I told her of Doctor's passing. We must hurry and leave for the meeting. I held her close as I spoke. My child was only ten years old.

"Mommy, I don't want to see all those people crying."

I didn't want to, either, but I had no excuse. Ed agreed to let Rachel skip the meeting and go to school instead—a decision for which we later took criticism. Even Rachel's Way friends made disparaging comments to her.

In the auditorium, people were sobbing all around me. It didn't take long before I cried, too. I wept for the Wierwille family's loss and how everyone there was so upset. I tried to think of good things Wierwille made possible for me, like public speaking class, healthful eating instruction, and my work with Bernita. Memories of other deaths streamed through my mind—especially George Jess's and my own mother's. I missed her sorely that day.

Ed didn't seem too worried over Wierwille's passing, but it was getting harder to read my husband. We were sitting side by side in velvet-covered seats at that early morning meeting but we were shut in separate realities. Ed still clung to the dream he might be promoted. Doubts plagued me night and day. Wierwille's so-called "accurate" teachings were not what I'd thought, but I didn't trust Ed's discretion enough to confide my upheaval. He blabbed things when he shouldn't—not always deliberately, but thoughtlessly. The walls at Headquarters had ears. We could get fired, kicked out, and publically ostracized if I spoke against Wierwille, and I wasn't going to let that happen. I wanted to finish the Aramaic projects. I wanted to protect my family.

On stage in the auditorium, Craig Martindale stepped out of Wierwille's shadow and into his new existence. Howard Allen and Don Wierwille sat with him, their faces strained. As Craig eulogized the first president, he donned more fully the mantle of power Wierwille had set upon his shoulders. For a while, he reminisced about his experiences with Wierwille, but I half-listened. I'd heard them before.

Finally, Craig announced plans for the memorial service and led us in prayers for the family and the ministry around the world. I prayed for my own family, too, wondering how we'd go on if Ed wanted to be a leader in a ministry that I could not wholeheartedly support. If we returned to the field with positions in the limelight, we'd have to promote Wierwille's self-serving, fundamentalist teachings. At Headquarters, I didn't have to do that. It was easier to hide in plain sight.

Wierwille's burial service was on the front lawn of his house at the ornate new Fountain of Living Waters, a multilayered stainless steel water display made by a Way believer artist. It cost a fortune. (The official memorial service would be at the next Rock of Ages.) At the top of the monumental structure was an enormous shining steel Bible, glinting in the sun, inscribed with The Word of God Is the Will of God. Trees and shrubs added softness to the scene as the man who founded The Way was buried amid the bubbling pools and artistic stonework. Colored lights shone and Way hymns were piped in from hidden speakers. Staff and Corps employed at Headquarters—about six hundred—gathered at the edges of yellow and white flowerbeds. Few words were said. The sounds of water splashing against steel filled many silent moments.

As the event ended, I ran into my old friend Debbie from ECU, who worked on staff with her husband. Our paths rarely crossed. As we hugged near the fountain, I felt a pang of hypocrisy. I knew what she would think of me if she could read my mind: I was disloyal and possibly deceived by the Devil. Disbelieving Wierwille's teachings was as serious to Way loyalists as committing a mortal sin is to Catholics. Maybe worse. My friendship with Debbie had wilted long before this, and she, like most Way people, was oblivious to behind-the-scenes research cover-ups. She would definitely reject me, or even report me, if I revealed I no longer believed Doctor was our "father in the Word." (Debbie is no longer associated with The Way organization, but as of this writing, she still reveres Wierwille.) I was sad about our estrangement, but I kept silent about my defection. She had her own life to live.

Denial was rampant about lots of things, most of all Wierwille's cause of death. We heard through the grapevine that he died of a stroke. Many years later, I saw a copy of his death certificate on the Internet and learned the cause of death was cancer.[1] Why weren't we told that? Wierwille taught that cancer was caused by devil spirits. That stance made telling Way believers the truth problematic. His cancer was one of the biggest secrets I encountered in The Way.

People wept for weeks. Wierwille's photograph, hanging in an office, would bring on sudden grief. The sight of a close friend would trigger tears. It was impossible to step outside Wierwille's legacy, even in our computer room, where a framed drawing of his family tree hung on the wall. Wierwille's name was on most every publication. His wife and other family members worked on staff among us. To avoid overt mourners, I entered the OSC through the warehouse and climbed the fire escape stairs to the research door. But there was a problem with that: I had no key. Only security personnel—Bless Patrol—carried keys to those warehouse doors. If no one was in the research room to hear me knocking, I had to turn around and retrace my steps, wasting precious time. And time *was* precious. We had until August, about three months away, to finish the concordance. If we missed the deadline, scholars around the world would scoff, and Way believers at Corps Week and the Rock of Ages would miss the chance to buy the concordance at its grand book launch. The Way bookstore's goal of selling thousands of copies nipped at our heels.

42

Book Baby

It was August 1985, time for the concordance to be born. One day, we had a birthday party. In the research room, Joe leaned on the conference table, examining galley proofs. The book's introduction gave directions on how to use it and included helpful information about the Syriac language. We deliberately designed our reference book for use by scholars and non-scholars alike.

"Good thing people can buy the dictionary supplement, too," Bernita said. "That'll help with looking up words till the interlinear is done."

That was the next book in the Aramaic project—a Syriac-English interlinear of the Peshitta NT containing each line of the Syriac text with its English translation inserted below it, thus the name *interlinear*.

Bernita stood beside Joe, dazed by the realization that the concordance was almost finished. It represented fifteen years of her life and many of his, including his course work (on his own dime) at the University of Chicago. Despite my growing doubts about Wierwille, I was proud of this publication—a Way-theology-free reference book. About a week earlier, Bernita and I had reviewed the front matter, including Joe's overview of the history of the Peshitta NT; this was a team effort. We had asked a few non-research people on staff to give the concordance a test run, and incorporated their feedback, too.

"Even the pronunciation guide is in there," Joe said. "You guys like it? Any last-minute comments? Snide remarks?" He rolled up his shirt-sleeves and loosened his tie, smiling as if his basketball team had just trounced the opponent. I'd never seen him so happy. Bernita either. Around the room other team members voiced their admiration for our slam dunk. My heart swelled with joy.

"Too bad nobody will know who did this work," Bernita said. Her face held stories in the lines around her eyes and mouth, anecdotes about her many Corps helpers over the years. Usually Wierwille's name appeared as the author of Way publications, regardless of who did the work, like the recent *Jesus Christ, Our Promised Seed*, written by several on the team. The concordance was different. Wierwille's name did not appear on it. But neither did anyone else's. An inside page read "Edited by The Way International Research Team."[1] In the preface, Joe did his best to acknowledge contributors, noting that the book was a "… work by numerous individuals," but that was as close as Walter would permit to giving anyone credit, even Bernita.[2] A shadow crossed her face. The book's editor may as well have been Anonymous.

Before we signed off on the proofs, we had one final issue to clear up. I'd learned about it from the current team who had been aware of it for years, as had Walter—Wierwille's mistranslation in the PFAL class of Jesus's words *E-li, E-li, la-ma sa-bach-thani?* The King James Version (KJV) offers this translation: "My God, my God, why hast thou forsaken me?" (Matthew 27:46). However, Wierwille taught: "My God, my God, for this purpose was I reserved, for this purpose was I spared."[3] This unusual translation—which we knew was based on George Lamsa's interpretation—was recorded in the PFAL class, leading people to believe it was accurate and it meant Jesus fulfilled everything God required of him to be our Savior.[4]

But it was wrong, and it was not a minor point. It was one of Wierwille's defining teachings. Depending on which translation you chose—"why hast thou forsaken me" or "for this purpose I was spared"—Jesus is portrayed as a different sort of Savior.

In the KJV, as Jesus hangs on the cross dying, he asks God why He has forsaken him. Many scholars assert he was likely quoting verbatim the lament in Psalm 22:1. But Wierwille did not believe Jesus would ask God, his Father, why He would leave him, because other contexts in the Bible indicate God would never leave Jesus. On this topic, Wierwille allowed his beliefs, based on other sections of Scripture, to supplant the textual evidence in this section of Scripture.

Surprisingly, not long before Wierwille died, he changed his mind and taught a small group of Way Corps members that those words of Jesus meant "Why was I spared?" But this change, not announced widely, still did not reflect what was in the Peshitta NT text, which, when properly translated, said: "For what purpose have you *left* me?" Users of our new concordance would discover this and realize the ancient text was different from Wierwille's PFAL teaching. Questions would fly.

It all seems so tiresome now, but at the time it was a critical issue in The Way, and still is today. The controversial verses and their specious translations presented an undeniable instance of sloppy research left uncorrected that misled believers about what the Bible said. I was upset.

One day, I went to Walter's office to discuss the issue. "Maybe Lamsa just misled Dr. Wierwille," I said, using my mildest tone of voice. Practically every hair on Walter's head stood on end.

"Look, Charlene, I believe Dr. Wierwille was more spiritual than any of us."

I should have expected that reaction, but I was shaken. After mumbling that I understood, I left Walter's office with the discomfiting feeling he had his eye on me now. My comment—although not a direct criticism of "our father in the Word"—had revealed my willingness to doubt. Walter had just glimpsed a startling new version of me emerging from a thicket of denial.

Later, Joe and I met with Walter to make sure he understood the problem this verse posed for users of our concordance. We sat down in his office and he puffed on his pipe while Joe again stated the predicament.

"Well, isn't that part of research?" Walter asked, nodding to solicit our agreement. "Aramaic is part of it. Users need to learn how to work the Word."

I clenched my teeth. "Work the Word" was jargon for using Wierwille's Bible study methods; it was the clichéd response to pesky questions. Feeling patronized, I left Walter's office with Joe, kept my mouth shut, and tried to forget about *E-li, E-li*.

Not long afterward, a box of shiny blue concordances arrived in our research room. We gathered around it like awed kids discovering treasure. On each book, the gold-leaf title gleamed in the office lights: *The Concordance to the Peshitta Version of the Aramaic New Testament*. Wierwille had insisted on putting Aramaic in the title, but it was erroneous. The version is in Syriac, not Aramaic, and scholars—the people Wierwille yearned to impress—knowing the difference probably laughed.

Despite the title, the celebration began. We signed each other's copies as if they were high school yearbooks. In mine, Bernita wrote, "Thanks for continuing to stand with us as we complete this project—interlinear & lexicon. Bless you much, Bernita Jess." That and similar expressions of affection and thanks from the others moved me to tears. Every page of that concordance was covered with our love, and I could not have felt more honored. Who could know the book's ripple effects, how it might benefit people all over the world? Despite setbacks and challenges in our personal lives, we had the joy of sharing this accomplishment. We were proud and imagined Wierwille would have been, too—even without his name on the cover. We drove to town for lunch at Adolph's Restaurant, still the best place for burgers, fries, and warm cherry pie crowned with vanilla ice cream. Happy birthday, concordance!

In August, at Corps Week and the Rock of Ages, the concordance would be on sale in our bookstore. That year, sixteen thousand people were expected at the Rock of Ages. *The Way Magazine*, anticipating great interest, had published an article about how to use our new publication, including diagrams and photographs.[5] Marketing ramped up.

That summer I felt the letdown that comes after finishing a book. Frank, having completed his assignments for Walter, left to spread the Word in another state. Bernita took some time off, and Joe, with Walter's blessing, drove to the University of Chicago to complete final requirements for his MA in Near Eastern Studies. That left just me and a few others in the office. I kept busy. I prepared Syriac research topics for the next group of graduating Corps, compiled notes for Walter's upcoming Corps teaching on 2 Thessalonians that fall, and swept aside persistent doubts about Wierwille's research.

At home, summertime brought changes, too. Rachel played with friends at the compound. In the evenings, Ed practiced his choir and dance productions for Corps Week and the Rock of Ages. With more quiet and solitude at work, I fell into doing a lot of thinking and writing notes to myself. Soon I directed my writing elsewhere.

At a Sunday service, Craig Martindale promoted our new concordance, but the way he lauded the publication threw us into a tailspin. He repeated the same glaring claim Wierwille had made that our Aramaic concordance was the first ever produced. Wierwille had gone uncorrected because, well … he was Wierwille.

It was midsummer and I was the only one from the project who heard Craig's ill-informed pitch. Tapes and videos of that service—carrying the wrong information—would be mailed the next day to tens of thousands of believers all over the world. I had to do something.

Since Craig was my Second Corps brother, I thought he would listen if I corrected him, so I sent him a friendly letter about the man in the 1700s, Carolo Schaaf, who produced a *partial* Syriac-Latin concordance for the Peshitta NT.[6] (We remarked on Schaff's in the Introduction of our concordance.) I also mentioned that others had made *partial* Syriac concordances for the Gospels. Even though our concordance was not the first *ever* produced, we could proudly say it was the first *complete* Syriac-English concordance for the Peshitta NT, and the first with a numbering system that would allow laypersons, as well as scholars, to use it. I sent Craig the letter, copied Walter, and waited.

In the auditorium at the next Corps meeting, Craig reprimanded our team for not telling him the correct information sooner, accusing us of hiding in our ivory tower. Thankfully he didn't mention my letter, but I felt terrible and apologized to the department for stirring up trouble. Joe advised me to keep my head down, forget Craig's remarks, and focus on our next book: the interlinear. But Craig's antagonism had rattled me. So had Walter's response to the *E-li* issue. I felt trapped like the lone sparrow I saw flying around in the warehouse. But I wasn't flying in any sense of the word. I was clinging to a skinny branch.

Summer 1985. On a casual Friday, Charlene (age 33) is at her desk in the biblical research team's office at Way Headquarters. Background: the door to the staircase leading down into the warehouse.

Winter 1986. Charlene and Bernita Jess pose with Joe Wise at his graduation from the master's program in Near Eastern Studies at the University of Chicago.

Part 7
Doubts

43

The Chaplain

In about 1978, a Way believer witnessed to my sister, Marie, in Connecticut, and soon she took the PFAL class. She called me afterward to say she'd arrived "home." We felt much closer then, but soon believers approached her to sponsor them in The Way Corps. One hounded her for money she didn't have, so she dropped out of The Way and returned to Catholic Church.

Growing up, my sister and I were not close. We were seven years apart, too many to bridge. But in December 1985, I wrote one of the most important letters of my life, and it was to Marie. It was also the 44th anniversary of the attack on Pearl Harbor. In the remote farmland of Ohio, I hunkered down at my desk, caught in my own raging battle. I was at war with myself over the ministry problems I saw, and like many a soldier trying to stay loyal to the cause despite my doubts, I felt compelled to seek a chaplain who could help me gain some peace. Marie and I had not seen each other in years, but I sensed she might be that priest. She had firsthand experience with The Way.

December 7, 1985

Dear Marie,

As I work here in research, I am constantly confronted with

questions—questions about the Bible, about what is taught in the Power for Abundant Living class, about how we do things in the Way ministry. Sometimes I don't know why. All I know is that when I took the PFAL class I had been looking for answers to questions like "Why did Mom die when I felt I needed her most?" "Is speaking in tongues available or not, and what good is it?" and many more. That class had more answers than I [had] found up until then so I stuck around. I wanted to learn more so I kept taking more classes and went into the Corps … There are enough truths I do agree with that we teach that I am willing to put things I don't agree with or understand on the back burner and teach and share the truths I am convinced of.

Having been committed for so long and having influenced so many others to commit to The Way, I felt guilty about my doubts but unable to deny them. A hostage, I couldn't pack up and go. We were being paid—about $30,000 per year—but moving money and savings did not exist. If we left, other pressures, worse in my view, would come. Leaders would demand I explain my change of heart. Ed most certainly would blame me. We would be seen as deceived by the Devil and ostracized by everyone we knew and loved.

After writing Marie, I made a deal with myself—I would stick with the ministry because, although grossly flawed, it was still helping people to some degree. What did I expect of Doctor or any man or woman, anyway? That they know every little truth perfectly?

I did not mail the letter. I was too paranoid about admitting, even to my sister, that I'd turned. If I mailed it, I could not take it back. My sister might ask questions I wasn't ready to answer. Perhaps I'd mail the letter someday, but not now. I stuck it in my file box, and drove to the office.

44

Trust and Trepidation

I had questions only Joe could answer. One spring day, I found him in the Rare Book Room, a mini-library opposite Bernita's and Walter's offices, where Wierwille's personal books were kept, along with items from Bernita's old trailer office: the microfilm reader printer, microfilms of Aramaic manuscripts, file cabinets, the Selectric typewriter. A small conference table had been moved in, and that's where Joe hibernated to translate the Peshitta New Testament for our upcoming Syriac-English interlinear. Joe needed peace and quiet. I needed his advice.

I was in charge of Corps students writing research papers. They had to finish them to graduate in June. Many such papers were written every year, not only by in-resident Corps, but also by members of the Satellite Research Group and our research team. This year, my advisees were to use our new Syriac-English concordance to conduct word studies—they'd choose a word, like *love*, and from the verses in which it appeared, they'd gain insight into its meaning and write about it. Way believers were accustomed to this pattern of examination, called a word study, in Greek and Hebrew. It was time for them to do it in Syriac.

I opened the door and greeted Joe. "How's it going in here?" I knew he was well on his way through translating the Gospels.

"Tough." Reference books and computer printouts were spread like giant paper fans across the table.

"Got time for a question?"

"Sure, take a seat." He set down his pencil. I closed the door and sat at the table. His expression told me to start talking.

"Corps research projects. I'm worried. One student wants to do a word study on *love*, comparing its usage in the Syriac text with its usage in the Greek text. You know how much trouble that'll cause. He'll see the problems—"

"Yeah."

"What do you think I should do?"

Joe and I had burned through many hours discussing instances in which the Peshitta New Testament (in Syriac) was different from the Greek New Testament. A perplexing example was the word *love* that my student wanted to study. The Syriac and the Greek words for *love* did not correspond perfectly. They couldn't. Greek had four words. Syriac had only two.

This discrepancy invited a host of questions, but primary among them was: Which text represented the original Word?

"Let's have your group conduct their word study only in Syriac," Joe said, "and not make comparisons with the Greek. Otherwise, they'll get confused to no end. Nobody has clear answers about the differences in these texts … yet. We don't know enough about the history of the Peshitta."

"Good, they'll have their hands full learning the concordance numbering system, anyway."

I was becoming more comfortable approaching Joe with questions, and he assured me he didn't mind them. He was the family's tolerant retriever; I was the new puppy sniffing out corners, chewing old shoes. This year, our second of working together, Bernita was usually in her office, and Joe and I developed a good rapport. My curiosity also grew about what he'd learned at the University of Chicago.

One day I overheard him talking with another team member who also attended the University of Chicago but was taking this year off to work with us. Joe didn't notice I was eavesdropping as he mumbled to his friend over by the coffeepot. I heard only snippets:

"… about the Gospel of Mark …"

"Q."

"… source for Matthew …."

That's all I picked up. As I carried my tacky Florida cup toward the coffeepot, they changed the subject.

"So, what's Q?" I asked.

"Oh, it's not that important," Joe said and shrugged it off with a smile.

"But I heard—"

"Hey guys," Joe raised his voice, calling to the others around the room. He whispered to me, "Later on that."

"What do you say we see a movie tonight?" Joe asked. "It's Friday night, remember? What'll it be?" Even before I joined the team, Joe had been initiating regular social events.

Someone piped up, "How about *Revenge of the Nerds*? I have it on tape. My house. Seven o'clock."

"How fitting," I said.

They laughed that off, but Joe had succeeded in distracting me, and I forgot about Q.

Sometime later, I found Joe working in our computer room, typing his translation into the database. Joe and I took turns at this task. He kept typing as I started talking, continuing an earlier conversation, as if picking up a stitch in an ongoing knitting project.

"So," I said, "about the different Syriac and Greek words for love—"

"That again?"

"Yeah. I wanna know. Doctor taught the four Greek words for love to show how precise God was in telling the writers which word to use.

But what if the Syriac, with only two words for love, really reflects the original text? Why did Doctor choose to teach only the Greek?"

Joe stopped typing, turned toward me, and gave me his undivided attention. "I don't know why, but most ministers do. It's more dependable."

"But if we're supposed to teach the accurate Word, how do we know which text is right, which one contains the real truth? Greek or Syriac? Or even Latin, or that other one. What's it called?"

"Coptic. It's Egyptian, remember?"

"Right." I'd never seen a Coptic text.

"We know Wierwille went with the Greek, but we don't know why. I think a lot of stuff died with Wierwille, like reasons why he did things that no one can explain now."

Joe hesitated, as though he wanted to say more. I insisted he say what was on his mind.

"I guess I have trouble with a lot of Wierwille's stuff, especially circular thinking."

"Meaning?" I shut the door. We were out of earshot from the research room around the corner, and we were whispering, but if anyone walking past overheard us, I feared we'd get in trouble, like any conspirators would.

"Well, think about it. Doctor believed in the inerrancy of the original text—no mistakes, no errors, no contradictions—and to prove it, he did gymnastics to make it seem like the whole Bible fit together. Then he said 'See? The Bible is perfect.' But it's so-called perfect because he made it look that way. He never proved the whole entire Bible is inerrant, like he said it must be. And he never said which Bible was supposed to be perfect. You know, you were Catholic. Catholic Bibles have more Old Testament books than Bibles used by Protestants."

"Huh … you're right … I didn't think of that …." I felt ridiculous.

It had taken me all these years to come up against this simple question?

Joe sat back in his chair. He was in teaching mode now, ingrained in him from his years of teaching high school and coaching basketball.

"You sure you want to talk about this? It can be disturbing—"

I nodded.

"Okay. Doctor worked from the assumption that the books in the King James Version are the only God-inspired ones. But different canons of Scripture exist in different versions of the Bible, and writings by apostles and other people in the early church were in the first canons used by Christians. Wierwille doesn't investigate them. The fact is, the question of which books, letters, psalms, histories, and all the rest were considered Scripture has changed over time. He left out a lot of texts that could make a big difference in what we teach, possibly dislodging the idea of inerrancy, because if we question inerrancy, we won't have the kind of ministry he wanted. It would disappear."

I think that's when I realized that inerrancy of the Scripture was the bedrock of The Way. Without that assertion, Wierwille would have nothing but his snow story—a thin prop without a perfect Bible.

"Well, who knows," Joe shrugged, turning back to the keyboard. "You probably shouldn't listen to me. You were perfectly happy before."

"Keep talking, Joe. I wasn't as happy as you might think."

My friend pushed his hands through his hair. "Well, what if some books in the Bible were included for political or religious reasons or maybe some were left out for those same reasons? What if some letters were added in that were not 'inspired,' as Wierwille applies the term? We make the claim that God's hand was upon the men making the decisions about which books to include in the Bible, but that is a belief—a nice idea to support what we say."

"I guess there's a lot to learn," I said, feeling more and more inept.

"Yep. But the important thing is to keep life simple. This stuff isn't so significant. Wierwille was a fundamentalist, so of course Walter is, too. These ideas aren't within that framework, so we'd better forget 'em for now."

It is frequently said that cartographers long ago marked the unchartered areas of their maps with the words "Here be dragons."[1] If you ventured out there, those monsters would eat you alive. Joe and I walked in dragon country now.

"Well, I've got another chapter to enter, so—"

"Okay, see you later," I said, and stood up to leave. I happened to glance at the framed drawing of Wierwille's family tree that hung on the wall behind the door. His ancestral crest decorated the top. I never understood why this was in our workroom—maybe to remind us he was watching? At the end of the week, after we'd opened and shut the door countless times, the frame would be crooked, teetering on its nail. I usually straightened it. Not that day.

45

Too Academic

Unfortunately, we began the following year with a dramatic national disaster. In January 1986, the Space Shuttle Challenger exploded, breaking into pieces after liftoff. All seven members of the crew were killed. Someone announced news of the shocking accident at lunch in the dining room. People dropped their forks. Later, my father sent me photos he took from his winter home in Mount Dora, Florida, that documented the orange blast and erratic trail of white smoke, an image that became the symbol of space travel catastrophes. A shroud of grief and disillusionment oppressed the country. Similarly, before long The Way would also detonate and rip apart, likewise sending waves of grief into our hearts. In early March, just before our in-ministry explosion, poisonous gases began seeping into our department.

It began like this. One morning, Walter phoned the research room and summoned Joe to his office. We figured they were merely going over some minor research business, but I jokingly wished Joe good luck as he rushed out the folding doors, straightening his tie. Walter had met with Joe the previous week—along with John, Walter's assistant on the harmony of the Gospels project, and Alvin, the librarian—to discuss responsibilities for the following year. The priority for Joe, of course, was finishing the interlinear. The target completion date was January 1987, nine months from now. By this time, Walter's duties had increased to include other departments and projects. He was overworked, so he announced to our small group that he wanted someone to take over for him as team coordinator—Joe. It was a compliment to Joe, but he declined, explaining he intended to earn a PhD after he finished the interlinear. To do that, he and his family would need to move away, probably back to the University of Chicago, where the previous winter he earned his MA. Joe and Alvin later told me that Walter was disappointed Joe could not accept, but respected his decision—no hard feelings.

Less than five minutes after he'd been summoned to Walter's office, Joe burst through the folding doors again. He looked beat up. His jaw was clenched. The tie he'd been wearing dangled from his hand. He tossed it on a stack of papers and sat down, as dazed as a bloody boxer in his corner of the ring.

"What happened?" I whispered, alarmed. I did not want others in the room to notice that there was trouble.

"Hey, Joe," I said in my normal tone of voice. "I'm supposed to check the status of those copies downstairs in the Print Shop. They need you to sign off on them, remember? Can you go with me now?" I tilted my head at the back door. The others didn't look up, accustomed to our running up and down the stairs. I walked ahead of my friend past the coffeepot and pushed open the heavy door. We stepped onto the staircase landing high above the dark warehouse and I let the door slam closed.

"Hurry," I said. *Clang, clang, clang.* Our shoes echoed as we dashed down the steel stairs. At the bottom, I grabbed his arm, making him stay by the railing. The nearby door to the Print Shop was open. Someone inside might hear us.

"Joe, tell me what happened."

"I … I … I think I just got fired." He heaved a sigh, holding the railing as if he might fall.

"Fired?"

"Yeah. Walter fired me." He winced as if he'd been stabbed and looked away.

I clutched the railing. "Why?"

"He said Craig talked to him." Joe's tone sounded as if he were hypnotized. "Evidently Craig told Walter to inform me that by this August, there would no longer be a job for me here. I can work until August. Then I go."

"That's ... that's crazy." My insides were flapping like a bird. "Why, Joe, why?"

"We're getting too academic, Craig said."

"What the hell?"

"I guess maybe ... somebody might have said something about me—"

"Not me."

"I know that." He shot me a don't-be-stupid look. "I thought it might be T. J.—I've told him stuff about research when we go jogging at lunchtime."

T. J. was Craig's assistant. His attitude often irked me. Joe, T. J., and their wives had been through the Corps training together in Emporia, Kansas, where the guys had bonded during the running program. They'd even raced in the New York City Marathon. A couple of years earlier, out of the three hundred or so Corps trained at Emporia, T. J. had been specially chosen by Craig.

"Joe, T. J. adores Craig. He might be your friend, but he's way more loyal to Craig. He'd tattle about research problems in a heartbeat if he suspected you were not completely loyal."

My friend shook his head back and forth. We wondered aloud what T. J. might have blabbed to Craig, if he had. What was going on? Only last week Walter had asked Joe to oversee the team.

"Oh, I can't believe this," I whined. "You've done absolutely nothing wrong. Didn't Walter stick up for you? Don't they know we need you here?"

"Look, we've gotta stay calm. Let's just try and figure out how to finish the interlinear before I leave." He paced around for a minute, and then started to walk away.

"God, I hope we can," I said. "Do you think we can? August is only five months away."

He whirled around. "I don't know. I just don't. I can't think straight. I told Walter he'd kicked me in the gut. We'll talk about it later." He turned toward the open warehouse door and said he'd see me after lunch.

"Something will work out," I called after him. "It has to." I watched him exit, a bowed silhouette against the blinding sunlight.

Ed was waiting for me in the dining room, so I dashed through the Print Shop to get there. My husband would never understand this situation, and I wasn't going to tell him now.

The next morning, I waited until no one was watching and headed to Walter's office.

Walter greeted me from his desk, pointing to a chair across from him. His smile was hesitant, his voice weary. I quickly glanced down at the notes I'd made the night before so that I wouldn't forget anything I wanted to say.

"I need to talk to you about Joe, Walter. He told me he's supposed to leave in August."

My boss folded his hands on top of an open book in front of him. First, I reminded Walter that my primary task in the department was the interlinear, since I had delegated other tasks, with his permission, to our part-time helper. He looked as if he'd forgotten.

"If Joe leaves in August," I said, "and if we haven't finished the interlinear by then, I don't know what to do. Bernita is having a fit over this. Today she stayed home. Do you know she says we've got to get the interlinear done before Joe leaves or else we're hung?"

"No." He gulped.

"Well, nobody can do the translating but Joe, not even Bernita, and she knows it. I'm so confused," I said, choking up. "Why is it that one week Joe is offered the job of team coordinator and the next week he's fired?"

"I don't know."

What do you mean, you don't know? You're the boss.

"Well, who made that decision?" I asked, clenching my teeth.

"Craig."

"Were you there when he made it?" My ire was up. I could hardly believe myself, but I didn't care that I might sound like Perry Mason.

"Yes."

"Did you tell him Joe had already planned to leave when we completed the interlinear?"

"Yes. I thought it was right for Joe to finish the project before he left."

"But did you tell Craig no one else is trained and can take responsibility for the final translation if Joe doesn't finish by August? No one else can do it."

"Yes, but he said we'll have to train somebody else."

"Who?"

"Well, I was hoping you could finish it."

"Me?" I laughed out loud. But Walter was not laughing. Not a tiny bit. Deadpan, he stared at me. Indignation flamed across his face.

"Walter, *I* can't do it. I don't know enough." In no uncertain terms I made it clear that I did not have the knowledge or expertise for such a task. I thought he knew my capabilities.

"I don't think you give yourself enough credit," he said.

No doubt about it now. Walter Cummins and I inhabited different realities.

Our interlinear team was in the Rare Book Room for a weekly status report. On the table was Joe's list of deadlines for our tasks; the pen in his hand was shaking.

"We're on target, looks like," Joe said, "based on finishing next January. But I need to tell you guys that things have changed. I'll be leaving this August." He fixed his eyes on the report. I heard a communal gasp.

"Let's do our best to finish everything before I go."

Until now, Bernita and I were the only ones who knew Joe had been fired. The three others on the team were our computer services guy, a woman who helped part-time, and the director of the Translations Department, a graduate of the First Way Corps. He oversaw our Spanish, French, and German translations of Wierwille's teachings and conferred with Joe on translation issues. Regardless of the language, modern Spanish or ancient Syriac, translating was a unique field with specific requirements and vexations. Joe and the translations director understood perhaps better than anyone besides Bernita and Walter that translations were *approximations*, not *reproductions*. Words were not "accurate" in the way Wierwille used the term. Bernita knew this, but left Wierwille to his jargon. Walter knew it, but kowtowed to Wierwille. From training and experience, Joe and his translations friend understood profoundly what Johann Wolfgang von Goethe, the German poet, wrote: "Whatever one may say about the inadequacy of translation, it remains one of the most important and praiseworthy activities in the general traffic among nations."[1]

Joe did not say why he was leaving, nor did anyone ask at that meeting. (They respectfully approached him later.) Bernita barked, "I don't know how we can finish it by August." She huffed and puffed, and fidgeted in her chair, and when we finished, she left the room before anyone else. After that, Joe drove off to The Way College of Emporia in Kansas to teach figures of speech to The Way Corps, and I racked my brain trying to solve the mystery behind his getting fired. If Wierwille were still alive, he never would have let Craig fire the person bringing this piece of the Aramaic project to completion.

Worries overtook me. If someone as competent as Joe could be told to leave, I could easily be next, especially since I'd told Walter flat out that I could not finish the interlinear.

I could feel in the atmosphere—in the hallways, in the stairwells, and in Walter's body language—that something serious was underway. Foreboding weighed me down.

In April, the Satellite Research Group convened for a week in the BRC down the road near the old Corps trailers. About a hundred people were there. I sat alone in the back row. At the last session, Walter made a disturbing announcement. "For the time being," he said, "the focus group for the History of the Text is disbanded."

Muffled sounds of protest rose. We all knew how important that topic was. We needed facts about the various texts to evaluate their reliability. Not only was Walter's decision unimaginable, but also it was shocking that he chose to tell us now. We all knew that Joe was in charge of that focus group and he'd just left for Emporia.

"I know, I know," Walter said, raising his hand, "but this is in keeping with the general policy about putting new research away for six months to get perspective on it before addressing it again and publishing it. We need to stay united on the issues we agree on, and set aside new issues until we learn more."

We'd heard this before, but surely it couldn't apply to the history of the text, which was textual investigation, not a Bible topic to set aside. Walter himself had written, in no uncertain terms, about the importance of this topic: "The study of the text in connection with its meaning and application cannot be neglected. Textual criticism, hermeneutics [the study of the general principles of biblical interpretation] and practical Christian living cannot be separated."[2]

I suspected the group was shut down because it dealt with uncomfortable questions about texts, like older readings preserved within more recent versions, and about issues related to families of manuscripts.

These concerns were important if we were a research ministry, but apparently that's not really what we were. By this time, I had seen enough evidence that showed we never had been. We were a machine churning out Wierwille's own ideas and cherry-picked doctrines and selling his unending classes.

Alone in the back row, I surmised that the newly defunct focus group was thinking, like I was, that texts lay at the heart of the ministry's purpose—if we weren't learning about their history, which could help determine their reliability, then what were we doing?

Walter looked pale and nervous. Puzzle pieces were coming together. Craig said we were getting too academic, so canceling this group made sense, but why was Walter letting Craig pull the strings of research? Why had Craig fired Joe for the very reason he was hired: being a Corps grad with specific academic training? We were confused and hurt, not yet knowing the reason for this sea change. Wierwille had often encouraged Corps grads, if they showed interest and aptitude, to attend college and get training in biblical languages to help with research. Had Wierwille not really intended to expand the Research Department like many of us thought?

The pressure on Joe to find a job elsewhere, while at the same time being expected to put his heart into his work here and in Emporia, was ludicrous. Few people knew of his predicament, since Walter had not announced it and Joe was not the kind of man to broadcast his problems. We may as well have been trapped in M. C. Escher's *House of Stairs* for our inability to make sense of our topsy-turvy situation.[3]

When Joe returned from Emporia, he found me distraught over the discontinued History of the Text group, struggling with Aramaic research papers, and trying to calm Bernita. She wandered in and out of the research room, repeatedly asking why Joe had to leave. Walter wasn't saying. I could not help her. Joe himself honestly wasn't sure. Bernita kept up her chant: "If Joe doesn't finish the interlinear before August, we're hung."

A sense of doom weighed on me. Research was falling apart and I could not understand why. I reflected back on previous years when other researchers had left and decided to investigate. One night while Ed was at choir practice and Rachel was asleep, I pulled my file box from the back of the closet and in a folder marked Letters from VPW to Way Corps, I found the letter I wanted. Dated October 20, 1978, it said, in part:

> … I allowed [one named Marty McRae, and two others] of the Eighth Corps, for their four-hour-a-day responsibility [at The Way College of Emporia], to start in research … In giving them this privilege I made a mistake … All three of these men are good men, but all three got tricked by the Adversary, unknowingly I trust. But once you get tricked you are certain that you are right.[4]

Doctor's accusatory voice flooded my memory. That ugly incident years ago probably lay behind Frank's message on my first day about our need to protect the Word. Doctor then quoted from a letter one of those "traitors" had sent to The Way Corps: "Power for Abundant Living materials or Wierwille are wrong … the reason we had to leave was because we were faced with a monster … error upon error …"[5]

Now that monster stared at me.

I put the letter back in the file box and went downstairs. The kitchen curtains hung open, and I watched a spray of stars blinking in the Ohio sky. A dog barked in someone's yard, and I began to cry like I hadn't cried in years, weeping over everything—my threadbare marriage, the madness at work, and those researchers who'd been silenced and publicly shamed. I now knew for myself that they were right. As I climbed the stairs to bed, I vowed to watch my words. Ed still hoped for promotion. I couldn't let him know my doubts, not yet. He might blab. If Walter found out, he could indict me like Wierwille had those others, and it was frightening the way it could go, as Doctor's letter said: "These three men are perhaps heading down the road of 2 Timothy 3: [they] would become 'traitors, heady, high-minded ...'" I knew that was not true of me, but I had to protect myself.

46

President's Men

On April 23, 1986, at our weekly Way Corps meeting at Headquarters, hundreds of us filled the auditorium, and with no warning witnessed the decimation of The Way as we knew it. At about 6:50 p.m., I pulled open the door of the Word Over the World Auditorium and stepped inside, feeling as safe as I would upon entering my own home.

I took a seat next to Bernita. About five hundred Way Corps graduates and interim Corps on staff that year filled row upon row of the red velvet theatre chairs. Other Corps grads were settled in their trailers on the compound to watch the meeting on closed-circuit television or listening on their telephones from other Way Corps training locales around the country, making a total of a couple of thousand people. We expected Craig Martindale on stage any minute to deliver introductory remarks, followed by Walter, who would teach another installment of his word-by-word examination of 2 Thessalonians, the epistle of Saint Paul we were studying that year. Our team had helped him write the literal translation according to usage—the literal, as we called it—for the Scripture he would scrutinize that night, as we did every week. Smiling ushers handed photocopies of that translation to Corps entering the auditorium.

Bernita and I, tucked in our cushy chairs, saved a seat for Joe. He was late. Unusual. The rest of the research team—refreshed from dinner at home, now wearing ties and jackets—filled our row. Minutes ticked by. When Walter taught at Corps nights, he relied on Joe, not Bernita, for Aramaic expertise. Where was Joe? While Bernita and I waited for him to join us, we commiserated, dreading the moment Walter might call out for Joe's help, only to hear he was absent. When the organ music stopped, Joe was still nowhere in sight. Craig, looking unusually haggard, appeared on stage.

"Tonight, instead of Rev. Walter Cummins," Craig said, looking down, avoiding our expectant faces, "Rev. Christopher Geer will handle the meeting." Then Craig faded like a wavering shadow to the back of the stage and sat in a straight-backed chair.

What was Geer doing here? Evidently he had flown over from Scotland, but we hadn't known it. Usually visiting leaders show themselves in the dining room or hallways. My stomach knotted with tension. Why was he taking over Corps night? What about the Bible verses Walter was supposed to teach? Where *was* Walter?

Geer entered from the side curtain and walked toward Walter's desk. He currently directed the European Way Corps, but he had also been Wierwille's most trusted confidant for more than a decade, serving Wierwille's every wish. Whenever I had seen Geer, he was accompanying Wierwille, the two of them looking as if they'd just hatched a scheme or knew things none of the rest of us could fathom.

Geer sat in Walter's chair. He looked pompous and sour. I'd heard that Geer had been the key instigator behind our 1976 paranoia when Wierwille ordered each of us to buy a rifle, stockpile dried food, and prepare to flee to the woods or underground bunker in the event that the Communists, the Illuminati, or some other evil entity took over the country on the Fourth of July. Tonight, eight years later, we sat under this bodyguard's ominous gaze. His mouth twitched. His eyes were sunken and dark.

"I have written a paper I call 'The Passing of a Patriarch,'"[1] he boomed, "setting forth Doctor Wierwille's last conversations with me in Scotland, shortly before he died."

This document would prove to be far more than just a paper.

"It's as close to a transcription as I could write of everything Doctor told me about the present condition of the ministry," he said, puffing out his chest. "It is dated February 15, 1986, because that was when I delivered it to the current Board of Trustees: Craig Martindale, Don Wierwille, and Howard Allen. I did not intend to read this tonight, but I believe I must. The contents have been leaked."

Leaked?

"No one is allowed to leave the auditorium until we finish here," he said. "The doors are now locked."

Adrenaline rushed through me. Wierwille used to do this—lock the doors at Corps night—but only when he had a crisis on his hands. Locked doors signified we were firmly in his grip, physically *and* psychologically, with no way out. I wanted to run, but Geer scared me. No one in that room moved. No one budged for the next two and a half hours while he read his paper aloud at Walter's desk and controlled the room like a train wreck dominates the six o'clock news.

First, a litany of his accomplishments at Gartmore: repairing the property, running classes, and worrying over Wierwille's declining health during his last visit. This sounded more like a five-star review of Geer than a last will and testament from Wierwille. And the raves went on for at least ten pages before he got around to Wierwille's alleged statements:

"Son, what would you say if I told you I was going to die?" After a moment I responded: "Sir, every day that I have been with you I have always been mentally and physically prepared to accept and deal with your death … You know that I have literally covered your body with mine when there were situations that demanded it. I have also pushed my mind to accept and carry [*sic*] any last-minute instructions that you might give me. I have known that they might be the last directions for the Ministry." He hesitated and looked across the horizion [*sic*]... Finally he spoke again, "Well, I am dying."[2]

This sounded like Wierwille's way of talking, but how did I know he really said this? I didn't. But Geer's reputation for loyalty and devotion to Wierwille gave him credibility. Craig, at the back of the stage in his chair, stared at the floor; his shoulders slumped.

In the end I am almost alone. I am reminded of Paul [the Apostle]. My last days have been so lonely. You see, son, I have two earthly sons. Today I cannot really talk to either one of them. J. P. [John Paul, Wierwille's younger son] is a nice guy, but spiritually he just doesn't have it; he's weak. The hardest to face, though, is Donnie [Donald, Wierwille's older son and vice president of The Way]. Despite everything that I have tried, he is not a spiritual man. I knew years ago that he had tremendous administrative abilities. That I have never questioned. I had really thought that if he was with us he would grow and make a commitment spiritually, but he hasn't. He is governed by facts, sense knowledge, and has basically neglected the spirit of God in his life. Perhaps he has done more to harm this Ministry than any other single man in its entire history. ... You see, when I first got sick Father [God] had already told me by then that I couldn't change the things that were happening in the Ministry, but I kept thinking that I could get Don to change and live as a spiritual man, that I could get things back on the right track. ... I do know that I was aware before I gave up the Presidency. I saw things starting and then what I said was rejected. Then things started going worse faster and faster.[3]

Oh my God, what did Geer think he was doing? These familiar vague accusations—"…governed by facts … neglected the spirit of God in his life"—led nowhere productive, I knew. They were disparaging beyond belief, and always unsubstantiated. What's worse, now it seemed that Wierwille made them about his own sons.

Geer continued reading. According to his account, Wierwille had also voiced strong thoughts about Howard Allen, his former pal as well as The Way's general manager and current secretary-treasurer. "Today he [Howard] is not the man he once was spiritually and certainly not the man he could have been if he had stayed faithful."

Good heavens. I looked around the auditorium. A mask of distress covered every face. Wierwille's vindictiveness, laid bare by this syco-phant, shocked us all. If Geer's recollections were to be believed, with those comments Wierwille had just wiped out the credibility of two trustees responsible for the organization.

> You know, son, there is only one man who could have handled Europe, that's you. In my heart there were only two men who could handle the Presidency, you and Craig. Right now there is only one man who can save the Ministry, that's you. You and Craig are the only ones left … The only hope that is left as far as I can see it is for you to get to Craig somehow and talk to him. I have not been able to.[4]

Ah, so that's it. Now it's up to Geer to straighten out Craig and save the ministry. Craig, still in his chair, didn't flinch. He looked dazed and dis-tant, as if wondering when this would be over. People around me were aghast with disbelief. Geer had launched a volcanic eruption and there was nowhere to flee.

Geer continued detailing assertions he claimed Wierwille made about top Way leaders (even more were attacked). The broadsides were so unspecific and vicious—mostly centering on valuing facts over being spiritual—that I dismissed them as the rantings of a sick and dying man who wouldn't own up to his own failings. He took no responsibility for the organization, offered no solutions, and blamed his top men for ruining it. Mass confusion surely lay ahead.

Minutes ticked by. Sweat trickled from under my arms. My mouth grew dry. If this really was Wierwille's last will and testament, it was shameful. It was more like Wierwille's last act of revenge. He had appointed those leaders and it sickened me that he denigrated them like this, even if they had failed. In doing so, he clearly showed what a mean, bitter, and self-centered man he was. I felt even sicker about Geer hijacking Corps night to spew this self-serving tirade.

The worst part was when he said:

See, son, even the research work is being affected. It is still accurate but not vital like it should be. It is only a matter of time until it loses its integrity too. Walter is already kowtowing to Donnie. Donnie has no right to be involved in the research; he hasn't got the spirituality or the integrity to touch it. His kind of management will kill it. … Unless things change drastically, our research work will suffer very quickly. Donnie will push to have things done that will impress the academic world. I have nothing against impressing the academic world. Son, we have to work the Word to stand approved before HIM. It's HIS Word. If it impresses the brains or not, it's still HIS Word. When we lose sensitivity of listening to that Word, then we will be a denomination. That's the only route it can go. … I spiritually feel that all these boys that are translating my class into all these languages are not accurate. For some Greek words there may be as many as seven English words and you have to translate it accurately or you don't have the Word ...[5]

This was it! No more stunning indictment of Wierwille's ignorance about research and translations could have been made, and ironically, he made it himself. He stupidly accused translators for doing what translators do.

You are right, Doctor. Those translations are not accurate because accuracy does not even exist. Translating is not an accuracy business. It is an attempt at approximation.

I knew better than most in that auditorium that research *was* an academic enterprise. What else could it be? Guesswork? And how would it "suffer quickly"? Per Wierwille's *modus operandi*, no details were given to validate his idiotic smears. Wierwille just couldn't admit that the people he had put in charge of translations, in both modern and ancient languages, were doing their best. He tore them down to maintain his position of sole authority in all ministry business, this included. But he was an ignorant bully, and his words, delivered by the pompous Mr. Geer, could not fool or rattle me. What freaked me out was the appearance of Geer in a space he should not occupy, in a position of power he should not have. But that night, Geer's pronouncements succeeded in pulling off his corporate coup d'état. He pushed The Way organization over the balcony, and it died on impact. He coldheartedly grabbed control over a multimillion-dollar business by claiming it was really Wierwille's voice speaking to us.

Around me, people's faces bore creased brows, turned-down mouths, and tears, spelling fear in capital letters. What should be done? Accusations about research upended what The Way Corps deemed the integrity of the Word, accusations against leaders destroyed the organization that was supposed to promote that Word. Corps members near me appeared as hardened casts, like the hollow figures in Pompeii discovered buried after Mt. Vesuvius erupted, some curled in the fetal position.

Before Geer ordered Bless Patrol—the armed security guards—to unlock the auditorium doors, he told us to go home and "keep our heads in the Word." We were not to speak to anyone about the letter. We were to not to think, either, he said—only pray and read the Bible. *Don't think? What kind of leader would say that?*

I eased out of my chair, feeling dizzy, drained, struck by a pounding headache. Bernita buttoned up her sweater and muttered, "Hurry." I fell in step behind her as we pushed through the crowded aisle. People were spilling into the lobby and fumbling out the doors like town folk fleeing rivers of fiery lava. I felt nauseated, but I could not imagine how Don, Craig, Howard, and Walter must feel. They may have made mistakes, but Geer was worse—he'd just turned Headquarters into an obliterated landscape of fear, panic, and helplessness. He had us where he wanted us. Upset and confused. Ripe for abuse.

I did not always admire the trustees or the things they did—like firing Joe for no apparent reason—but I didn't understand why they'd let Geer do this. Amazingly, they had each signed a statement admitting that this letter's account of their failures was correct. Craig had written "I've read this several times. I believe it to be the truth. It must be adhered to for the survival of this ministry. I stand with The Teacher [Wierwille] and the truth of his last words. I love you."

As it turned out, Craig and Geer would duel for years over rights to their man of God's legacy. Former followers told me many years later that Craig—whipped, confused, and paranoid—called that period "the fog years," until he finally extricated himself from Geer and demanded a written statement of loyalty from Corps and staff. Rather than obey, many left, and some formed their own Bible-based cults.

My mind was racing as I left the auditorium. I wondered whether the derogatory statements about biblical research were the reason Joe was dismissed. Geer said he first read this paper to the trustees in February, and Joe was fired in March. But why was he the scapegoat? Why not fire Walter, who was responsible for research? Walter had told me that Craig ordered him to release Joe, but it might have been Geer. Had he been pulling all the strings since February? Where, by the way, *was* Walter? Had he known of tonight's takeover?

Ed found me in the crowd on the way to the parking area, whispered he'd see me at home, and drove off. Despite the number of people streaming out of the building, I heard no one talking. The only sounds were hundreds of footsteps crunching across the gravel. People bore their shock silently, following Geer's orders.

I located my red Chevy wagon, settled behind the wheel, and started driving home. The five minutes it took felt like an hour. Over the years, I'd witnessed many reproof sessions—in Corps meetings, in the Fireplace Room, in the woods, in the dining room, or anywhere Wierwille felt like lashing out with accusations. Sometimes the offender was present, other times not. Afterward, friends rejected friends, sure that the offenders were under the influence of the Devil. Wierwille, just as he was to me after the Toledo escapade, could be degrading and harsh. Even so, the accusations Geer had just relayed were unprecedented.

At home, Rachel, almost eleven years old, was getting ready for bed after coming home from her babysitting job. I tucked her in, and we snuggled a few minutes, talking about her homework and her dance class after school. I didn't dare tell her what Geer had done. She was too young to understand the politics. I snapped off her light and trudged downstairs, wondering what sort of life we were giving her, mired in this organization.

Ed was in the kitchen poking around in the refrigerator, and our housemate, Penny—secretary to Earl, my old mentor from Greenville, who was now a top administrator—was coming in the back door. The three of us ended up at the kitchen table, snacking on chips and onion dip.

"You guys want a drink?" Ed asked. I was ready for a beer, but he was breaking open a new bottle of Jack Daniels. Ed's drinking had increased lately.

"Sure," we said. Ed poured some in three juice glasses, adding Coca-Cola and ice. He and Penny started speculating, ignoring Geer's directive not to discuss his paper. They wondered what the trustees might do to straighten out the ministry, but I couldn't formulate anything to say. The more they hashed out the meeting, the wider the gap between us grew. They assumed Geer's letter was truthful from beginning to end. They accepted the idea of spiritual problems to be solved, even though those problems were not fully described nor any solutions offered other than the nebulous "get back to the Word."

Insanity. In my own kitchen.

Geer was frightening. Although he was no longer a bodyguard, he often carried a gun. (Clergy, at a meeting Geer conducted in the BRC solely for them, later spoke of seeing Geer with a gun at the podium.) Now he appeared to be in charge of Bless Patrol. I vowed to avoid him. Whether The Way got fixed or not was not my problem. The concordance was finished. That was good enough, although I clung to a pea-sized hope of our completing the interlinear by August. Beyond that, I couldn't resolve my looming doubts about Wierwille's fundamentalism and wrong teachings.

Ed stopped gulping his drink to hypothesize about what Don Wierwille had done wrong, and Penny tried to guess what Craig might do to redeem himself. I daydreamed about getting into my Chevy wagon with Rachel and driving to the nearest East Coast beach before anything else dreadful happened. Ocean City called loud and long. I took another swallow of whiskey, imagining a lounge chair with me in it, mindlessly gazing at the deep green sea for the rest of my life. A few more sips. Wonder what happened to Rob, my surfing Jesuit? More sips. Why hadn't I listened to him? Ed refilled my glass. Had my father been right? Was this the gutter he once predicted?

"So, Charlene, what do you think about tonight?" asked Penny. She sat beside Ed, looking like his twin—worry lines creased both faces. I was determined not to show any trace of my dissatisfaction with the ministry. Earl, Penny's boss, had become a close friend of Walter's, and I was afraid that anything I said would eventually reach my own boss's ears. I focused on Rachel, sleeping innocently upstairs. She depended on her parents. If I caused trouble, we would land on the street with no paycheck.

Maybe it was cowardly of me, but looking back, I am thankful I laid low.

"Amazing. Couldn't have guessed *that* would happen tonight."

Ed chimed in. "Whenever anything big happens, Charlene goes quiet."

As out of sync as he was with me, at least he knew that.

Soon Penny said good night and plodded down the hall to her room. A few minutes later, Ed said he was turning in. He left and went upstairs.

"I can't sleep yet," I called. "I'll stay here awhile." I listened until he settled down, then I fled into my thoughts, shoving my fingers through my hair, now a tangled mess from doing that all night. Cool April air flowed through the open window, and, except for a hoot owl in the barn, I heard nothing. I took another sip of Jack, wondering whether Ed still coveted a promotion after tonight. Every Way leader was henceforth under close examination. How could anyone trust anyone after this?

Another sip. The reason we moved here was now a sick joke. A spiritual boost? What a laugh. What I dreamt would be Paradise had degenerated into Purgatory, and tonight it turned into Hell.

Joe. How could I explain this calamity to him? The one time he missed a Corps meeting and this happened. Maybe he'd been locked out of the auditorium. The plastic wall clock above the stove told me it was eleven fifteen. I gulped my drink, moved to the wall phone, and dialed his number. As I waited for him to pick up, I stood by the screened-in back door and peered outside. Shadows marked the lawn in a hundred distorted patterns. Our cat, Solomon, meowed by the barn; he was probably hunting down a rat. Too bad he couldn't sniff out the human rats and do away with them, too. Another sip …

Joe and his wife were among the few good people I knew. Now they were leaving. They'd already sold their house in New Bremen and were staying with Joe's parents in another town about an hour and a half away. He drove all those miles back and forth every day.

"Hello?" Joe's voice was groggy.

"Joe. It's Charlene. Are you okay?" I set my glass on the hutch by the door.

"Yeah, what's up?"

"Where were you tonight?" Solomon meowed at the door, and I let him in.

"Oh. I went shopping."

"Shopping? For heaven's sake—"

"Well, I gotta get new clothes for interviews. Besides, Walter doesn't need me anymore."

I let that sink in—hard to argue with a guy who's been kicked in the head.

"Sorry to wake you, but I thought you should know what happened tonight. You won't believe it." I gave him the gist, along with my opinions on fallout we might face in the morning. I fully expected Walter to shoulder the blame for ruining research, whatever that meant. I could easily see him accepting unsubstantiated indictments supposedly handed down from Wierwille.

Joe took the story in stride, told me to get some rest, and we hung up. I stood in the hall a minute, feeling angrier than ever with Craig for firing my friend. Craig (maybe at Geer's insistence) had ripped the work we loved right out of our hands. I sank into a kitchen chair, admitting with deep sadness that I had also betrayed myself. I had ignored all the warnings from people who cared about me—not only my father but also many others. "Wierwille's just another preacher," Rob had said, "out for power over you." His words stung now like my first sip of whiskey. How could I have been so wrong about God leading me here?

I refilled my glass, moved into the living room, turned on the television, and burrowed into the sofa. An old movie was on. Robert Redford's face, ruddy and angled, filled the screen, his strawberry-blond hair and dreamy eyes close enough to touch. The character Redford played, I wasn't sure who, sat at a desk piled with bulging folders. He whispered into a telephone, glanced up and down, and tapped his pencil on a notepad. The camera pulled back and a busy newsroom came into view, revealing a long-haired Dustin Hoffman typing fast and blinking faster. *All the President's Men.*

I shuddered. This was us, our failed leaders, our paranoia, Geer's volcanic eruption—All President Wierwille's Men. The booze overtook me. When the television station signed off with a rousing rendition of the "Star Spangled Banner," I jerked awake.

47

Bowing Out

A few days later, in the real world, across the Atlantic and over a continent or two, the Soviet Union's power station in Chernobyl blew up and created a catastrophic nuclear meltdown that alarmed the entire world. In Wayworld, we were too preoccupied to notice it, careening in the aftermath of our own meltdown. The top leaders—even Walter—were under suspicion for not doing what they should have, although what exactly that was remained a mystery, at least to us. Evidently it was no mystery to them, because Geer said they admitted their guilt by writing their signatures on the last page of his paper. Did they know what they were doing? I had no idea.

The morning after Geer's coup, Joe and I watched from our adjoining desks as our team members filed in, quiet as frightened mice. Walter wandered into the room, looking lost in his own library. He gave no explanation of his part in this nightmare, simply repeating, as if under orders, Geer's directive to keep our heads in the Word. Then he wandered out.

Soon, another shockwave hit. Orders came from the top: shut down every project at Headquarters, no matter how critical. This affected about two-thirds of the approximately six hundred staff members. Chris

Geer decreed—with the agreement of the Board of Trustees—that everything was under reexamination until further notice. Printing presses stopped. Way Productions performances ceased. Building plans were left on the drawing board. Of necessity, food services, maintenance, and day-to-day services continued, like the switchboard and Bless Patrol. Unimaginably, work on our interlinear was suspended.

The chance, as slim as it had been, of meeting the August deadline had vanished. As the days went by, I suffered from frequent headaches and bouts of nausea. A cloud of mourning settled over our research room, driving Bernita to hibernate in her office. Joe made phone calls to set up job interviews in an Olympian effort to resurrect his teaching career, abandoned years before to enter The Way Corps. Geer convened meetings in the auditorium to hash things out, but I feared him and did not attend. He also met daily with leaders, including Walter, in Wierwille's old motorcycle shed. Their goings-on were secret.

Geer's directive to keep our heads in the Word was infuriating. First of all, my spiritual life was my business, and I knew that going back to Wierwille's plagiarized, manipulative teachings was not going to help me. But the official policy was that the answers to all our questions were to be found in Wierwille's Power for Abundant Living materials. We should reread them even during work hours. Thankfully, Walter did not enforce that rule. To stay busy, I reviewed Syriac grammar and tried to work my way through Moisés Silva's *Biblical Words and Their Meanings*, a highly regarded new lexical tool for Bible scholars. I didn't understand much, but I tried. No one else on staff read books such as that, although Bernita and Walter ordered them for research use and shelved them in the library. Staff and Corps were too busy to read much of anything.

For the following year, Walter was scheduled to teach Romans to the Corps, and we assumed that was still on. In preparation for writing literals with him, I diagrammed chapter after chapter of verses in Romans and chewed pack after pack of gum while doing so. I remembered Sister

351

Margaret Mary coaching us in diagramming back in Catholic school—I had forgotten how important it could be to clarifying exactly what I read. All those years later, it helped me understand what each verse was about, independent of Wierwille's theology. In the process, it strengthened my skepticism of Wierwille's teachings.

Soon I tired of waiting to find out what the leaders were deciding for the ministry's future and decided to do something about my own. I still hoped, foolishly (unlike Joe, who was realistic and sensed his involvement with the project was over), that the on-hold rule might be reversed for the interlinear, and that Joe could stay past August to finish it. We'd promised the book not only to our followers but also to scholars around the world, even the authoritative Society for Biblical Literature. It would be disappointing and embarrassing if we didn't produce. With a last gasp of idealism, I composed a letter to Craig Martindale:

> ... Now [Joe] has been told he is to leave in August regardless of how much is done on the interlinear, and let someone else finish ... I told Walter I was very disappointed about [Joe's] leaving then and that if he [Walter] was thinking I could finish it I could not. I did say I would do all I could to help finish it before [Joe] left. I am very concerned, knowing what is involved in producing this book.

I ended by asking Craig for a meeting. I copied Walter—I wanted my boss in the loop. Days came and went with no response. Joe kept job-hunting. At Headquarters, an Aramaic class began for about two hundred Corps students; Joe had been assigned to teach it, with me assisting. Bernita, agitated over the status of our interlinear, had been glad to get away and teach Aramaic at our Indiana Campus.

Class was an alternate reality. Joe and I made our own fun in spite of the pressure. We played jitterbug music during breaks and let students eat snacks at their tables. We stayed after hours to tutor them in vocabulary and on how to use the new concordance. When they asked about the interlinear, we told them the truth: it was suspended, like every other project. When our class ended, Craig still had not answered me.

I had let my husband read my letter to Craig. I told him I was writing a second.

"You're making too big a deal out of this, Charlene," Ed said. He wagged his head, as if scolding a child. "Joe's problems are not your business."

That might have been true, but the interlinear *was* my business. As far as I was concerned, Way leaders would be fools to waste believers' money to train someone else for the job. I could not shake my sense of injustice over Craig ousting Joe, no matter how many miles down the country roads I marched, or bike rides I took with Rachel, or glasses of Jack Daniels I drank. Someone had to listen to me.

I wrote Craig:

> ... I believe it is only right to tell you that if your decision is final to train someone else to take his [Joe's] responsibility, then the only honest thing I can do is to ask for a change in my job assignment.

I shook as I signed my name. As far as I knew, my request was unprecedented. No other member of the research team at Headquarters had ever resigned *and* in the same breath asked for reassignment to another department. Flags would surely go up. Past loyal researchers came and went to complete projects, but dissatisfied ones were either fired for openly disagreeing with Wierwille's research or quit before they got fired and immediately moved away. I did not yet possess the courage to tell my husband about my desire to leave the ministry. After Geer's letter, he'd told me he wanted to help fix it. Given we had no money and no

Plan B for where to go if we left, I could not bring myself to cause an uproar. Ed and I had agreed to three years of staff service; one more year remained, during which we'd prepare for an approved field assignment—likely not a paid position—and then could leave without ugly confrontations with our bosses, our leaders. Out in the field, somehow I'd manage to drop out and Ed could do whatever he wanted. It was a risky plan, I knew, and one that might even break up our marriage, but I couldn't come up with anything better. Resigning from the research team if Walter hired someone else to finish the interlinear would be my baby step toward disassociation.

I had copied Walter on my second letter. To appease me, I think, he offered me a plum task for the coming year: I could coordinate the Satellite Research Group conference and oversee Corps research papers. I told him I'd think about his offer but knew I would refuse. I took to dodging him whenever I saw him coming down the hall. By mid-June, I'd still not heard from Craig Martindale, and Joe was preparing to leave. If by some chance he was allowed to finish the interlinear, I could justify staying in the Research Department; otherwise, I wanted out.

For comfort, I turned to my father. When I called him, he assured me that I'd tried to do my best at The Way. I shouldn't worry over it. We'd both changed since 1970—that was certain. He sent a note:

… [Since] you found things have undergone some changes I guess with your idealism it has been a letdown after so many years, but knowing you, you will bounce back in good shape, remain flexible. There are many things in life that one cannot control and sometimes it is difficult to adjust, but I'm sure you will succeed.

Until later – Love you, Dad"[1]

I locked Dad's letter in my file box, grateful we had not abandoned each other.

With no answer from Craig, one afternoon I knocked on Walter's door.

"Walter, I need to talk with you about next year." It began in only two months.

Walter was slumped in his chair holding an unlit pipe, not doing anything, only sitting. On the desk other cold pipes lay in a glass ashtray.

"With everything that's happened," I said, "I think it's best for me to request a different staff assignment, as I said in my last letter. I think you know Ed and I agreed to work here three years, then return to the field. For next year, I was thinking that since I have experience with children's fellowship, I could help in the Child Care Department." That was our preschool, conducted in a mobile unit down the road near the barn.

Walter had bags under his eyes. He was exhausted, I was sure, from continual meetings and the insecurity of daily life unimaginable when we'd met in that Orlando restaurant and he expressed excitement over my return here. I could hardly believe the change in the ministry and in each of us since. He pulled himself forward, studying my face.

"I understand, Charlene," he said. Tears moistened his eyes. "I know you've been through a lot. I hope you're not too hurt." He covered his mouth with his hands.

"Thanks, Walter, I just need a change." I couldn't get sentimental. I was too mad. I murmured clichés about appreciation for what I had learned from him and the team and got up to leave. "See you later, then."

I followed the maze of halls like a mouse and hid in the computer room to pull myself together. I needed perspective before I could face Bernita. My mother often told me not to quit, to keep on trying. She had told me that when I was afraid at my swimming lessons, frustrated by my math homework, daunted by complex sewing projects. But wasn't there a limit to trying? I could not change the confines of Wierwille's fundamentalism. I could not fix his flawed research. I could not make Walter stop kowtowing to Craig. I could not reverse Craig's decisions about Joe and the interlinear. I could not change anyone or anything but myself. The Way suffocated me and left me no alternative but to abandon it as soon as I could. This didn't *feel* like quitting. I *felt* like I was making a good decision for my own mental, spiritual, and emotional health, so I made myself march across the library and down the hall to Bernita's office before I lost my gumption.

She was standing by her glass-front bookcase—an antique I coveted—with her hands shoved in her sweater pockets, lost in thought. She turned when I entered the doorway.

"Bernita, I need to talk, something important has happened. I was just in Walter's office. I resigned."

"I see," she said, keeping her hands in her pockets.

"I'm sorry, Bernita. I don't feel I can contribute to the department anymore. I need to do something different, and I'm sorry if you feel I'm letting you down."

"I understand," she said. She gave me a tired look, but said no more.

If she resented my leaving, I never knew. If she even envied it, I could not tell. I thought she might be angry, say I was breaking my commitment to the project, but instead she drew a Kleenex from her pocket—a gesture I'd seen a thousand times—wiped her eyes, and hugged me.

Fall 1986. Charlene with little ones from the Child Care program in the pumpkin patch at Way Headquarters. She was given this part-time job after resigning from the biblical research team in July 1986. Background: the Outreach Services Center (OSC), a small city under one roof where about 600 staff, mostly Way Corps, worked during the 1980s.

Summer 1987. The branch campus of The Ohio State University in Lima, Ohio, where Charlene resumed her college education in the fall of 1986 after resigning from the biblical research team and taking a part-time job at Way Headquarters. She took six classes at OSU before her escape from The Way in August 1987.

Part 8
Rejection

48

Turning the Tide

"Hop in," I said. Joe opened the passenger door of my Chevy wagon at the curb of the OSC building, still in his work clothes. Staff men were required to mow the compound's lawns that day. We sped to the branch campus of The Ohio State University in Lima, about forty-five minutes away, for an appointment with his brother, an admissions counselor. I might be able to return to college. This wild turn of events came about not long after I resigned.

"Try it out, see what happens," Joe had said. "You might like it."

"Yeah, right." At first, picking up the pieces of my abandoned education and returning to college was unimaginable and intimidating. How could I possibly add classes and homework to the demands of a job and family? But the idea brewed like tea in a pot, and before long I let myself think it would be worth trying. I'd gain what no one could take away—education. Since I was stuck at Headquarters for another year, at least I could begin earning college credits.

"What do you think, Ed? I'd like to try," I'd said, "if they'll accept me. I've worked so much with kids, I could major in elementary education."

"I guess so, if you want to." Ed was noticeably unenthusiastic. He had other things to worry about, he said, like the status of the ministry.

361

That was probably true, but I'd seen two empty bottles of Stroh's beer on the kitchen counter, and he had another one in his hand. Discussing college was bad timing, I saw, but Joe had already contacted his brother and arranged an interview for me. I'd wanted to set that appointment before Joe moved away.

"It'll be a lot of work," I said, vying for Ed's attention, "so I'll need your support. I think I can get half of my tuition paid by The Way. That's part of our benefits."

I was sure Ed felt shut out. He had little respect for college. After another gulp of beer, he said sure, why not? When I told Rachel I was headed to college, her eyes grew round with surprise—her mother was going to school like her!

I knew it wouldn't be easy. Sixteen years had passed since I'd walked out on my history professor's offer of another chance. My sister had returned to college late in life. Comparatively, I was still young—thirty-four. The more I thought it over, the more I *felt* excited. *Felt* happier. *Felt* better. I'd circled back to believing that it wasn't wrong to *feel* whatever I felt, that feelings made us human. Wierwille had been wrong to deny their value.

Denial of feelings had become such a habit, it's a wonder I broke it at all. For starters, I was now doing what Shakespeare put so well: "To thine own self be true, and it must follow, as the night the day, thou canst not then be false to any man."

Joe and I arrived in Lima, where his brother interviewed me and gave me hope that I could succeed. He answered my questions and handed me application forms to begin my journey away from propaganda back to education. Touring the campus, I felt more secure—maybe it was the combination of solid brick buildings, scented flowery air, and students with backpacks and determined looks, unlike Way staff who were flocking to doctors for anxiety treatments. Bad moods there spiraled into depression. Thanks to Joe, I had something positive in the making.

After the appointment, Joe and I headed back home.

"I'm sure my grades from East Carolina will be a problem," I said, driving slowly in Lima's rush hour.

"That was a long time ago. Not so worrisome."

"But I left with a GPA of only 1.8. I blew off half my finals. I'm so embarrassed."

"Yeah, well, take the evaluation tests. See how you do. You've got nothing to lose other than a little time and money for the application. With your story, I'll bet they give you a chance."

I fell silent, considering the fortune I'd spent on The Way—sixteen years of my mind, my love, and my life. Compared with that, applying to college cost nothing.

The great thing was that finally my attention shifted from the ministry's turmoil to options for my own life. Instead of thinking in terms of right with God or wrong with God, I was thinking in terms of what paths might be good. Self-trust was growing; insecurity was melting away. Wasn't that what God wanted for me?

Joe, to our great relief, soon secured a teaching job in another state, returning to his interrupted career. Looking back, I realize that those last weeks before he left turned the tide and made my eventual escape possible.

Some OSU classes were held at night, so I assured Ed that I would keep working on staff for a paycheck. Walter had submitted my request for reassignment to Child Care, and they accepted me after a brief interview. Hanging out with kids again would be refreshing and fun—a good change, even if OSU did not accept me. I took the evaluation tests and waited.

To distract myself, I joined Rachel for bike rides after work and spring-cleaned the house. I also wrote my father about OSU, and he was more than proud, having been deeply concerned ever since I'd called to say the ministry was falling apart and I wanted to get out as fast as I could. He sent me money to celebrate and visit Marie, my sister, so in June I got time off, sent Rachel to day camp, and prepared to fly to Oklahoma City, where she lived. The last time we had seen one another was in 1983 when she and her family visited our family in Orlando for Christmas. With seven of us crowded into our apartment, we had little privacy and spent most of our time at Disney World and with Dad and Gabrielle, snowbirds wintering in nearby Mount Dora. Marie and I had been separated so long—by our seven-year age gap, by religious differences, and by geography—that we were nearly strangers. When I called her about coming to visit, I briefly explained my crisis, told her that we'd probably be in Ohio another year, and let her know that I'd applied to college. She wanted to see me. As I planned my trip, I grew eager to reunite with her and escape tensions with Ed and the chaos at Headquarters. I was sick of sneaking around to avoid people. One reason for sneaking was a novel I kept hidden at home.

On the flight to Oklahoma, I took my secret reading material: a novel called *The Word*, by Irving Wallace. Despite the title, it had nothing to do with The Way. I'd borrowed the book from the St. Marys Community Public Library after Joe mentioned having read it in Chicago while taking Syriac courses. It was about a manuscript said to be a gospel written by James, the Lord Jesus's brother. When he read it, Joe said, it prompted him to consider textual research issues in ways he hadn't before—particularly how texts can be altered and forged. I was wildly intrigued.

I settled in my window seat, reveling in the luxury of a vacation all to myself, and got reabsorbed in the story. Soon a man stopped at the end of the row, said hello, and took his seat on the aisle. The middle seat remained empty. The plane took off.

The stranger had the open-faced look of Andy, the Sheriff of Mayberry on a popular TV show, but I avoided chitchat. Poring over a book was the perfect barrier.

I felt rebellious about reading a novel. Many of us in The Way didn't read fiction at all. Our attitude was that fiction—which described things that had not happened—was simply lies, whereas truth was actual reality, with nothing made up. It baffles me how anyone with a degree in English literature could have converted to The Way, but they did. Our ideas about fiction, I learned later, were tied to our understanding of biblical inerrancy. James Barr, in his book *Fundamentalism*, puts it this way, "The inerrancy of the Bible means that its statements correspond to sequences of actual events, or to relations between actual existing realities."[1] We did not think novels did that. As I read Irving Wallace's novel, I was learning we'd been wrong.

Sitting on that plane was the first time I'd relaxed in months. Unfortunately, the stranger in the suit noticed my book's cover and crashed through my literary barricade.

"Do you mind if I ask what your book's about?" He turned in his seat to face me.

"Oh, a publishing project goes haywire. There's an ancient text, an investigator, and a whole lot of money. I'm about halfway through. Can't wait to find out what happens next," I said, without looking up from the page. I hoped he'd take the hint.

"So, where are you going today?" he asked.

I lowered the book. Reluctantly, I told him. He said he was going to L.A. on business after stopping in Oklahoma.

"So, do you work in Ohio?" he asked.

I almost lied and said I was a stay-at-home mom, but something about his face and my novel and my rebellious mood brought out my inner risk-taker.

"I work at The Way International." The look on his face was unmistakable. It said *Oh my God.*

"How do you like it?" he asked.

"I don't. I'm leaving as soon as I can." I felt my courage gaining momentum. "The Way is not what it claims to be," I ventured to say.

Nodding in a sympathetic way, he said he had heard of "that cult." I cringed at the label. It was more than embarrassing. It was degrading. He asked more questions, I gave more answers, and before I realized it, I'd done the unimaginable: confided about recent despicable Way events to a complete stranger. It was one of the best days of my life.

"It's too bad these groups get away with taking advantage of people," he said. We nodded to each other, and when the plane landed in Oklahoma City, we said good-bye. I entered the terminal with new feelings of relief, freedom, and strength. Having unburdened myself like that, I'd taken another step on the road to release and recovery. Telling someone outside the group about its true nature made me feel less isolated. I'd thrown a rope, and the hook at its end held firm for me to climb.

Oklahoma was dry and hot and flat. Marie, full of good cheer, greeted me at the airport, and I imagined people could tell we were sisters. We had the same hazel eyes and freckled skin as our mother and the petite build that ran in the family. I felt a pang of nostalgia for Mom. I thought she would be happy, like Dad, about my leaving The Way and attempting to resume my education. If only she could see this day.

The next afternoon, Marie and I took a swim in the pool at her apartment complex, lingering in the shallow end, intending to talk heart to heart. But as I relaxed in the water, a wave of exhaustion from months of stress hit me and the thought of rehashing the painful events that preceded this trip was the last thing I wanted to do. But I must talk to her. I'd just told my emotional story to a total stranger on the plane; my own sister should hear it, too. For a few minutes we swam in silence and watched a young mother help her little boy practice flutter kicks. Maple trees along the fence partly shaded us from the blazing sun. We sipped sodas from plastic cups, and I moved around so the sun could do its magic on my arms and my attitude. Soon I unraveled the story, trying to convey the depth of my disillusionment, anger, and fear.

"I just want you to know that I'm shocked over this," Marie said. "The Way was your whole life. I thought you'd never leave."

"Yeah, me neither."

"You were so involved for so long. I can see how shaken up you are."

My body ached all over from fatigue; my nerves were frazzled. I literally shook as I rehashed the chaotic events aloud.

"Yeah, I've even quit believing there is any such thing as 'the accuracy of the Word.' It was only a sales pitch Wierwille made up."

"Wow, you have had a rough time," she said. Her eyes narrowed. "Remember when I took the PFAL class, and I thought it was pretty good?"

"Sure." Ed, Rachel, and I had been living in desolate Bakersfield, California, then—a lifetime ago. I splashed my feet in the lukewarm pool.

"But then believers started pestering me for sponsorship money so they could go in The Way Corps. That bugged me. And I had questions that nobody listened to," she said.

"Like what?" I took a sip of soda.

"Well, for one thing, why is there violence in the Old Testament? God is love. Right?"

"I don't understand the violence, either," I said. "Wierwille explained it away by saying God had a different relationship with mankind during that era. He had a chosen people to protect. But now I'm not sure what to believe about that. Anyway, you never told me you had questions like this, only that people bugged you for money. Too bad we didn't talk more over the years." I sighed and paddled around in the pool. "We've let so much go unsaid, haven't we?"

"Yeah, but now that you're getting out, I hope we communicate more. You must realize that I can hardly get over your decision to leave it all behind. Amazing, just shocking."

She said she hoped I'd get accepted into OSU. "That'll help you a lot," she added.

"What was it like for you," I asked, "going back to college after so many years?" I rested my head on the edge of the pool, stretched out my legs, and watched them float to the surface as I listened to her share enlivening experiences.

For the rest of my visit, we discussed her classes and reminisced about growing up in Salisbury. To my surprise, she confided about how worried she'd been when I had dropped out of college and run off to Ohio. At the time, I was so absorbed by The Way, I failed to see how distressed my sister really was; I'd held her at arm's length. All I could say was that I regretted rejecting my family and friends and hoped to make up for lost time. By paying for my plane ticket, our father had given us a chance to repair our relationship, and I was grateful.

But when I boarded the flight for home, my heart tumbled under a wave of anxiety. The plane was a time machine, returning me to a shattered past.

49

The Stairwell

The July afternoon when Craig, our president (under twenty-four-hour surveillance from Chris Geer), found me alone in the research room, he scared me to death. It was another staff outdoor workday, but not for me. I was dillydallying at my desk, cleaning out drawers before leaving to take Rachel to the dentist. I felt no compunction to reschedule that to do my employer's yard work. Just as I was about to go, I heard footsteps approach our folding doors, and then Craig Martindale was there, standing in the doorway in a white nylon running suit. He looked nervous, burdened, and heavy in his shoes.

"Hi, Craig." I did not stand up. That in itself let him know how I felt. You were supposed to stand up immediately whenever your leader, a man of God, entered the room.

"How's come you're in here? It's an outside work day." He fumbled with his nylon jacket and tugged it off. I wondered why he, too, was here, since he must have expected all of us to be outside mowing and pulling weeds. Why would he bother to come to an empty room?

"I know, I know … everyone else is out there today," I said, and waved around the office, "but I've got to take Rachel to the dentist." I stood up and grabbed my purse.

"Well, I hear you resigned. I want to make sure your reasons are healthy. How 'bout we step outside, have a little talk?" He nodded toward the back door, and I wondered why we couldn't talk right there. Later, a reliable source would tell me that our room was probably bugged by Bless Patrol officers to record anything suspicious. Craig, as president, would have known that.

The term *healthy* was Way jargon for spiritually right with God, and his use of it let me know my behavior was flying in his face. A resignation from anyone in the inner circle of trusted researchers—whose loyalty was assumed as locked tight, whose knowledge-base was rare, and whose skills were highly valued—would draw attention. Also, as an elder Corps, I knew lots of Way followers, and the possibility that I could spread my dissatisfactions about research was real.

"Sure, and yes, I did resign, and I think my reasons are healthy. I just feel like I need to change everything in my life."

Oh no, I didn't mean to say that. Would he ask what "change everything" meant? No, he was distracted, scanning the room, checking out the bookcases, stacks of papers, and materials laying around.

I waited until he said, "Let's go."

I reached the back door first. We stepped onto the staircase landing, the door clicked shut behind us, and I had the sensation of dangling in space, each of us spinning on strings like figures on an Alexander Calder mobile, never meeting, always turning. I grabbed the railing and glanced downward through the diamond-shaped patterns of the grate. One of my high heels had gotten stuck in a hole.

The warehouse was vacant except for a few sparrows circling overhead lights. A lawn mower roared near one of the huge open doors, spreading noxious exhaust. Craig was too tall for me to look in the face as he began talking at me, not with me, in a babbling stream—he and the trustees were meeting all the time, he'd read my letters, I wasn't ignored, they would reevaluate Joe, they would decide whether or not to finish the Aramaic project, they might let Joe work from the field after he left, maybe I could help, nothing was certain.

I listened with my lips pressed tight, unable to tell whether he was lying or really meant Joe might be involved from the field.

"We'll see what Joe does," he said. "He's had attitudes a long time, so I want you to think over everything he's ever told you and line it up with what the Word says, got that?"

"Uh huh." I fought the bile that rose from my throat. So that was the real reason for this talk: to warn me against my friend. But Craig had just revealed his own true colors—ignorance, arrogance, jealousy, and paranoia. His Wayspeak—"line it up with the Word"—was Wierwille propaganda meaning that if something didn't match Way teachings, reject it. Joe's "attitudes"—also Wayspeak—meant the Devil influenced him.

Craig was damaged more than I'd imagined. Panic struck me hard. He still had power. I had next to none. Craig was waiting for me to fly to Joe's defense; I knew that. Then he could justify getting rid of me, too. But I was determined to go on my own terms.

Since I didn't argue, Craig petered out of things to say and the talk was over. I tried to open the door, forgetting it had locked. No one answered when I knocked, and no Bless Patrol officers were around with keys.

"I'm sorry, Craig. We have to go downstairs and reenter the building through the Print Shop." I was more anxious than embarrassed, and after tugging my shoe out of the grate, I started down the stairs ahead of him and rushed through the Print Shop into the main hall where we split off, without any more talk, and went our separate ways. In the reception lounge, I paused a minute to rest. Flopping onto a couch, I stared into the vast black fireplace.

That encounter had done more than upset me over Joe, the project, and Craig's mental health. It had cheered me on. I'd survived it. I'd not caved in. I'd taken the unbearable heat and seen through the farce Craig called a "little chat." The stairwell meant one more step toward an inner independence that I would never give back.

The next morning, I knocked on Walter's office door to report on my conversation with Craig. The bags under Walter's eyes were worse than ever.

"What did Craig mean, 'watch what Joe does'?" I asked.

"Well, Joe and I have had things we've disagreed about, and you've seen some of that yourself, but I still think Joe is a great person."

My warning bells went off. Walter was not in the slightest bit fazed or indignant over Craig's "chat." He didn't even raise his eyebrows. Maybe, just maybe, Walter agreed with Craig. The realization was as shocking as if someone said the food I'd just swallowed was poisoned.

Or maybe it was the other way around. Maybe Craig got his warped ideas about Joe from Walter. Omigod. Was it possible? Walter, I reminded myself, had started with The Way at an even younger age than I had. By this time, the stakes must be too high for him to risk defending someone Craig wanted to fire. Walter had a wife and children and their college funds to protect. His reputation as the inheritor of Wierwille's research was still intact, despite Chris Geer's letter, although Geer had his foot on Walter's throat.

I just wanted to get out of there. "I don't understand why Craig would say that about Joe, but I guess it doesn't matter. Joe is leaving soon enough." I wadded up my notes.

"Look, Charlene, I don't want to see you leave the department hurt or angry."

"Thanks, I'm just trying to understand what's happening around here."

"I guess everyone feels like that."

Walter gave me a grim look, and I got up and left. No doubt, he was hiding information from me, but I was doing the same thing. On opposite sides of the Way fence, we each schemed to survive. The question was—which side did God take? Either one? I felt sure I was on the right track for me, but God's place in all this was a mystery. My previous precious beliefs were being hammered by ugly reality. All I could do was act on what I thought was good and let the chips fall. It wasn't long before I got around to thinking like someone I'd eventually study, Baruch Spinoza, the seventeenth-century philosopher. Spinoza's attitude is described by another philosopher, J. Thomas Cook:

> ... to say that God acts in order to achieve some purpose or to fulfil some desire of his, is to say that God lacks something and desires it. But an infinite [and all powerful] being cannot lack anything.[1]

Without the notion that God has plans for people, or needs us to do something for Him, my own courage grew. I would make my own plans, despite the turmoil I sensed was not over yet.

50

Good-byes

It was the best of times, and the worst. Joe and I were in the research office, aware it was one of the last days either of us would spend in it—ever. The men on staff were told to work outside that day, and Joe was going to join them after he finished a few office tasks, but he was in no hurry. At our adjoining desks, my friend balanced a pencil on his finger, and I sat there feeling like a bird peering over a cliff.

"This application stuff takes time," Joe said, twirling the pencil like a tiny baton. "Academic institutions work slowly and sometimes in a disorganized way, but they can't find a more eager student than you."

"Thanks, that helps. I'm scared, you know."

I was brooding. Walter had betrayed us, Geer had hijacked the ministry, Craig had disparaged Joe's good name, and the power-hungry trustees held hostage our beloved Aramaic project. My husband still clung to hope that he might help save the ministry, which was ludicrous, but delusional or not, Ed was my husband, we had a child to support, and we were stuck in Ohio for another year. With no acceptance letter from The Ohio State University yet, I couldn't hide my self-pity.

Considering the seismic shifts I had undergone, disorientation was normal. I'd dropped the conviction that Wierwille was "our man of

God," that the Bible was perfect, and that God had a plan for me. Rethinking those issues was exactly what I needed to do, but doing it was like scraping my fingernails across a chalkboard twenty-four hours a day. Reevaluating what I'd done and why I'd stuck around so long—out of duty and a desire to find "the truth"—exhausted me. I lost weight. I neglected my nails. I let housework go.

Pivotal events—dropping out of college, going into the Corps, and marrying Ed—all decisions I had once perceived as directives from God, were freshly laid open for examination like a corpse in a forensics lab. I blinked under the bright lights. What had made those gashes on the neck? What about the stab wound in the chest? What exactly was the cause of death?

"C'mon. Let's get outside; we can talk more there," Joe said. We went down the back stairs and left through the warehouse door at the end of the building, walking down the lane where no one was around. Under the summer sun, I continued to unburden myself, confessing omissions and commissions. I'd alienated family and friends for the sake of The Way. I'd lost an adoring boyfriend. I'd dismissed warnings against dropping out of college. I'd influenced idealistic believers to commit to this ministry and to enter The Way Corps, placing them right in Wierwille's manipulative hands. I'd let simplistic either-or thinking dominate my mind. For the most part, I had not loved people for who they were, but for being like-minded with me on the Word—which isn't love at all. At times, I'd felt that way with my husband. Worst of all, I'd steered my child into believing The Way was the best ministry in the world.

"Good God, Joe, what have I done?" I cried. "I've made a mistake that's lasted all these years." I stopped walking and covered my face with my hands.

"Hey, take it easy. Breathe." My friend's empathy was palpable.

I quieted down, but kept thinking how I'd let Wierwille run my life. What did I have to show for it? A tattered marriage, a phony biblical research career, a nightmare I couldn't wake up from, and no way to escape.

I was beginning to understand that my association with Wierwille had been complicated and codependent, among a whole lot of other things. His narcissism demanded control over earnest followers like me, and I needed certainty, which is what he promised. This unhealthy relationship between leader and follower lies at the heart of many people's experience in any sort of cult.

I soon lost steam and calmed myself, wiped the tears off my face.

"You're right, Charlene. You spent a lot of years in this ministry. I hope you'll see they aren't wasted. Try to remember all the things you've learned and the people you've helped one way or another. All the friends you've made. Hold on to the good. Leave the rest." He admitted he had to follow that advice himself.

For a few minutes we settled into the comfort of our friendship. I knew how awful I must sound. Joe had gone to the trouble and his own expense of gaining a university education for the Aramaic project. That wasn't cheap.

"You know, I'm disappointed, too," he said. "It's time you got back to the office. I'll go with you for a minute. I want to show you something that really shook me up."

In the office, he slid open his desk drawer and pulled out a manila folder.

"Prepare yourself for a shock," he said as he handed it to me.

Inside was a newsletter: *Personal Freedom Outreach*, Jan/March 1983. The cover article, by John P. Juedes, was titled "Wierwille Borrows: A Challenge to the Originality of His Teaching on *Receiving the Holy Spirit*." [1] The article reported Wierwille's meeting with J. E. Stiles, author of *The Gift of the Holy Spirit*, in Tulsa, Oklahoma. Stiles helped Wierwille speak in tongues. I had heard that from Wierwille himself, and it is repeated in Elena Whiteside's *The Way: Living in Love*. What I'd had no way of knowing was that Wierwille had copied much of Stiles's book word for word, as the newsletter made clear with examples.

> … one wonders why Wierwille never mentions Stiles' publications in footnotes or anywhere else. The similarities between portions of Stiles' *The Gift of the Holy Spirit* [1948] and Wierwille's *Receiving the Holy Spirit Today* (First edition, 1954) suggest one reason for the silence. We invite you to examine the following excerpts from these two books with an eye for similarities in ideas and terminology.[2]

The article cited about twenty-five instances of Wierwille copying Stiles, in most cases nearly word for word.

"Oh my God, Joe," I whispered. "I have Stiles's book at home. Ed got it in Los Angeles."

"What?"

"I've had Stiles's book on a shelf for years. I just never read it."

"Wow … my mother sent me that article," Joe said. "I showed it to Walter, but he said Doctor learned from lots of people. That's the standard defense against plagiarism. You've heard it. He says the same thing every time we get letters complaining Doctor copied from men like Bullinger, Pillai, Lamsa—"

"I've got to get home and find that book."

Joe said I could go ahead and copy the article, so I ran downstairs to the Print Shop, nonchalantly photocopied it without anyone noticing, and returned the original to Joe.

"See you tomorrow," I said and rushed out the door.

When Ed came home, I was in our room with Stiles's book and Wierwille's book open side by side. In one hand I held the newsletter with pencil marks where I'd underlined pertinent statements. In the other hand, I held a half-full bottle of Stroh's beer. Fading sunlight made the wooden floor look lit from the inside, on fire, just like me.

I summarized the situation for my husband and swept my arm over the undeniable black-and-white evidence in front of us.

"I don't care," Ed said. "Plagiarism is just academic mumbo jumbo. So what if Wierwille put his name on his own Holy Spirit book? He wrote it. So what if he learned some stuff from Stiles? Truth belongs to everybody, not just Stiles."

"How do you know that Stiles's book *is* the truth?"

Ed stood still, looking at me.

"Even if Stiles wrote the truth, which we can't be sure of, Doctor had no right to copy it and then claim *he* wrote it. He said he learned it all directly from God. But he *stole* it."

"Oh, come on—"

"Ed, you're looking right at the evidence, same as me." I pointed at all of it. "And another thing—Doctor made money selling his plagiarized Holy Spirit book. It's outrageous."

"You're hysterical, Charlene. Quit freaking out about all your research stuff, will ya? I've gotta eat and get back for choir practice. Stop making a federal case out of everything."

It was clear that if I were going to escape this place with any sanity and with my family intact, I needed to change how I talked with my husband. Leaning back on the bed, I remembered the time when Ed had told Wierwille we had Stiles's book.

One afternoon in 1974, Ed and I were in downtown Los Angeles, crammed in a hotel elevator with Wierwille and Howard Allen, descending to the first floor for a big meeting of believers from all over the state. Wierwille faced the elevator doors, his back to Ed. I was behind Howard, studying his fresh haircut. It looked expensive, and aftershave wafted off his collar. I listened while Ed recounted his trip to Stiles's church and how he'd been given a copy of Stiles's book about the Holy Spirit, wasn't that amazing? Doctor's posture tensed, but otherwise he showed no surprise or curiosity about our being given this important book by the man who supposedly instigated an enormous change in his own spiritual life by showing him how to speak in tongues.

"The old man's dead now, right?" Wierwille asked, glancing sideways at Howard.

"No, sir," said Ed. "I don't think so." (Stiles died in 2002.)

We reached the first floor, the elevator door slid open, Wierwille hurried out with Howard at his heels, and they went briskly down the hall away from us. Later, Ed and I shared our puzzlement over Doctor's lack of excitement about our remarkable story. We could only assume he'd had no time for chitchat.

In our New Knoxville home, this alarming article I held in my hand explained Wierwille's rush down that hall. He'd *deliberately* avoided further talk of Stiles. How different our lives might have been if only I had paid attention and questioned Doctor's reaction.

That day I also got honest about my own attitudes over the years. As Joe mentioned, I'd known that Wierwille had been criticized for plagiarism. His usual comeback was that he "learned from others." I'd been aware of it for years, but I hung in a cloud of denial about it, just like Ed, accepting Wierwille's rationalizations:

> Lots of the stuff I teach is not original. Putting it all together so that it fit—that was the original work. I learned wherever I could, and then I worked that with the Scriptures. What was right on with the Scriptures, I kept; but what wasn't, I just dropped.[3]

In academic circles, plagiarism is *not* tolerated. It is stealing. When I first took the PFAL class in Greenville, I overheard Earl mention that Wierwille used E. W. Bullinger's *How to Enjoy the Bible* to help him create the PFAL class, but I didn't imagine Wierwille literally copied anything. We accepted that Wierwille was just making the pieces of God's teachings fit together, like God wanted him to do. All of us were too far over the moon to own up to the seriousness of Wierwille's plagiarism. And it was serious. With it, he gained power and made millions of dollars. In 1971, Wierwille published a book version of the PFAL class, which spread his plagiarism further. Although attendee numbers for the PFAL class were not always accurately logged, tens of thousands of people worldwide had taken the class by 1985, and that year The Way reported $30 million in income from donations, class fees, and bookstore sales.[4] As a tax-exempt organization, The Way made a fortune.

With the article about Stiles's book as evidence, I gave up the rationalizations I'd made in the past for Wierwille's "borrowing" and got honest about what he really was: a willful plagiarist.

Word got around that I was leaving the research team. Walter knew how much inside information I had, that I was upset he fired Joe, and that I was disillusioned over the interlinear now on hold. He probably surmised (correctly) that I didn't support Craig anymore either, so I didn't doubt he would keep his eye on me. It's an understatement to say he would not like it if I went around blabbing about research problems. Not only was Walter's reputation at stake, but also Wierwille's credibility and that of the Word he taught. I knew too much.

Damage control ensued. One weekend before Joe left Ohio for his new job, the telephone rang in my kitchen.

"Charlene, hi. It's Nancy." Earl's wife, my old mentor, was the one who'd told me to stay in the Corps even if I didn't understand what was going on. I wasn't sure whether she still felt that way, or whether she thought the place was as messed up as I did. I didn't know anything about what she thought, or why she would even call me.

"Hey, I heard you resigned from research."

"Yes." Earl and Walter were friends. Word *had* spread.

"I just want to make sure you're okay. Honestly, Charlene, I'm concerned about you. I hope you're not mad at Walter."

"I'm okay. Walter understands I need a change." That was true, absent the underlying drama. This call meant one thing: I *was* being monitored. I'd never discussed my work on the research team with Nancy or any events leading to my resignation. Our children were school friends, but as parents, we didn't socialize.

"Well, I hope so. You know, we all need to stand together on the Word, especially now, with so much going on."

I hurried to agree with her and we hung up. She never contacted me again. After that, I made more of an effort to avoid people I knew. Corps week annual meetings started, but I did not attend. Thousands of Corps members arrived and stayed for the Rock of Ages festival afterward, renting every available room in motels and pitching tents at campgrounds on or near Way property, but I stayed away. Some were desperate to hear Chris Geer read his "Passing of a Patriarch" paper, hoping to understand what the chaos was about. Others, who had already heard it, listened again. Ed told me that the yellow-and-white-striped circus tents were filled to overflowing.

Walter and the research team's schedules were so irregular during that time that no one tracked my activities. With the rest of the research team under the big top, I helped Joe empty his office bookshelves and pack his files and coffee cups. I cleaned out my desk, too, and carried my things home. No one organized a going-away party for Joe or anything for me. I bought a box of donuts and the two of us ate them in the upended research room.

Finally, only days before Joe left, an envelope arrived from The Ohio State University. I'd been accepted! But only on a provisional basis until my grades showed I could do the work. I wept with happiness, Joe clapped me on the back, and Rachel danced around the kitchen, but I saw through Ed's forced smile.

When the time came, I drove Joe and his family to Neil Armstrong Airport, a cluster of hangars and landing strips named for the astronaut born in Wapakoneta, a neighboring town. Armstrong had walked on the moon. After OSU's letter, I felt as if I'd landed there myself.

We unloaded suitcases from my car while a private plane—a Cessna—piloted by a relative of Joe's waited on the sizzling tarmac. The scent of sweet corn drifted around and the airplane's roaring engine told us we had one last minute to say good-bye, and so we did.

The Cessna gained altitude fast. I watched its silhouette against lavender clouds rippling through the sky as it left me perched on the bumper of my red Chevy wagon, engulfed in tears, cornfields, and the splintering mess of my life. I saw only one good thing: along with those skyward pastels, hope lay on the horizon, thanks to my friend in that plane.

51

Billboard

Changes, most beyond my control, would not stop. I may as well have been a billboard for what most people know, but what Wierwille, with his authoritarian fundamentalism, denied: "The only thing certain is change."

Right after Joe left, the house our family rented was sold, so with Penny, our housemate (and Earl's secretary), we moved to a ranch-style place owned by Wierwille's nephew—the reliable workhand who'd whisked Debbie and me, and later Rose, to the Lima bus station after our supposed spiritual failures. He gave us a discount on the rent, which was generous, but I worried that if he discovered I had turned, trouble would ensue—I must keep my mouth shut and watch my behavior carefully for the entire next year. We piled our belongings into a Way truck and unloaded them in that nephew's house on Botkins Angle Road in New Knoxville, a five-minute drive from Headquarters. Leafy trees and a split-rail fence framed the yard. A Holstein dairy farm was across the street. I would grow to love those black-and-white cows, as I'd often wander down that dusty road to think.

My assignment in Child Care surrounded me with preschoolers whose sweet, high-pitched voices greeted me every morning and whose imaginations delighted me during art hour as they drew flowers, pets, and huge-eyed mothers. Without trying, those children salved my torn-up heart and I felt joy again. To some degree, I even reclaimed the vitality of spontaneity—grossly lacking in adults around there. On some days, I read my little friends stories—preapproved books with positive messages about helpful children and friendly animals, not the frightening fairy tales I had loved as a child. We played Simon Says and hopscotch, and when winter came, we bundled up and went sledding in the yard. We shared hours of laughter, challenges, and surprises.

My workmates refrained from asking questions about my quitting the research team. They were probably scared. Geer's paper planted serious doubts about loyalty in my former department. They speculated over whether their jobs were at risk, unsure of which leader to follow—Chris Geer or Craig Martindale—and shrank from upset parents who argued right in front of the children over which leader God wanted for us. Somehow, for the sake of the little ones, we created a haven of peace for a few hours a day and tried to enjoy it ourselves.

My other haven was in Lima. In my first class at OSU, Psychology 100, I felt like a bird freed from its cage. We examined the mind, a good place to start for someone leaving a fundamentalist cult. I took a front-row seat in the oatmeal-colored lecture hall, thinking now I could hear another side of the story.

My professor, a small man with wire-rimmed glasses, was convinced by Pavlov, the behavioral psychologist who trained dogs to salivate at the sound of a bell, that humans were no more than trained animals themselves. I wasn't sure I agreed, doubting that our cat, Solomon, reflected on his life as I did mine. It was easy, though, to identify ways Wierwille had conditioned me to think and behave, like reinforcing the belief that if we remained faithful to the household of Way believers, we would earn rewards in heaven. If not, Satan would ruin us. That fear I'd now rejected. I was a new me—a happy student. We continued studies in human motivation, emotions, and behavior, reading works by other giants in the field, like B. F. Skinner, Freud, Jung, and Maslow. I pondered their perspectives as I sorted out my cult experience. I told no one in class where I lived or worked and hid behind labels of homemaker and mother, ashamed of my connection to The Way. Even though I'd broken my ties—at least in my heart—The Way was known in those parts, and I feared that my classmates, possibly new friends, would think I was weird—literally—and consider me mentally unstable, even fear me, if I disclosed my past. I did not want to sabotage my transition into mainstream society. I wanted only to blend in.

As for my attitude toward outsiders, I relearned that people could and should be valued for who they are, not as people to recruit. Appreciating others meant no strings attached—no agenda. A healthy sense of humanity grew alongside my intellectual development.

At the compound, I was the invisible woman. I skipped lunch in the dining room to do homework. I easily avoided leaders since the Child Care unit was at the other end of Wierwille Road from the OSC building where they worked. I skirted Sunday services and Corps night teachings, and no one confronted me. With their own jumbled schedules and scattered activities, no one seemed to notice my whereabouts, and Ed didn't judge my actions, at least aloud. I did not visit the research room or Walter or Bernita, even though they'd urged me not to be a stranger. My heart told me to stay away. Confusion had installed itself in the OSC. Six months had passed since Geer had read his nightmarish letter, and still leaders at Headquarters floundered. Ed would tell me of dining room announcements about leaders in the field who left to form their own offshoots of The Way. They circulated letters saying they'd left a corrupt organization, but they'd "gotten away with the gold" of Wierwille's teachings.

Melodrama ensued, made of unimaginable backstabbings, confessions, severed friendships, and damning words. Numbed, I tried to let the farce and fuss spin past me, like traffic in another lane. I thought I was beyond caring about the ministry's fate—until Walter Cummins made me realize that part of me still did.

52

Interlinear Fiasco

The unimaginable persisted like an incurable disease—Walter replaced Joe. He hired a loyalist from the Satellite Research Group to finish our interlinear, and I was sick about it. A serious devotee, Bart (not his real name) had taken the PFAL class as a teenager, graduated from The Way Corps, gotten married, taken some classes at the University of Chicago, and worked for a time with Bernita before I returned in 1984. Now, because of his undying fidelity, he'd been rewarded.

I'd last seen Bart the previous year at our research conference at Headquarters shortly after Walter had fired Joe. In the research room one day, Joe met with Bart to show him an example from the Peshitta NT in Syriac that illustrated why discovering the history of the Peshitta text was vital. It illustrated the ball of wax Joe and I wanted to avoid with the Corps students' research papers. I stood nearby and observed as Joe explained the notated group of three-by-five cards he'd created and laid on our conference table. Each card contained a verse from the King James Version of the Bible that had the word *love* in it and the corresponding Syriac and Greek words from which the word *love* was translated. This made plain the problem Joe and I had discussed more than once: The Syriac and the Greek words for *love* did not correspond perfectly. They couldn't. Greek had several words. Syriac had two. Did this matter? For Way believers, it did. It raised questions about Syriac speakers' views of love but more importantly to us, it meant that the Syriac text could not substantiate Wierwille's teachings based on Greek. What value, then, was the Syriac text?

Wierwille claimed that to arrive at the "accurate Word," we must know "how to find the accuracy of the Hebrew, Greek, *and* Aramaic texts." This was even stated in The Way's marketing materials. So how could we do that? For the Way ministry student fixated on the notion that there even existed an accurate Word of God, the question was, which text was accurate? Or perhaps, how do we determine the accurate Word by *comparing* these texts? This was the foundation of The Way, the belief that propelled the entire organization, like a rocket booster, shooting Wierwille's ministry into orbit. No accurate Word meant no Way ministry.

I watched as Joe presented the disturbing evidence to Bart, who got defensive and insisted that the Greek, not the Peshitta, must be accurate—because it was more stable.

"But what if the Peshitta," Joe said, "preserves, in some parts, a translation from an early Greek manuscript that we don't have access to anymore? Maybe that Greek manuscript was destroyed or lost?" He pointed to the cards. "In that case, the Syriac text, not the Greek, might be closer to the long-lost original, right?"

Bart fell silent.

"Look," Joe said. "We know how families of manuscripts are a crisscrossed web of connections we don't always know how to untangle. We can't just pick which text we like best or change a text whenever we feel like it."

That's when dissension, like an undertow, pulled those two apart. When Walter later canceled the History of the Text focus group, I wondered whether that conversation was the reason.

When Bart was hired to replace Joe, I was mad all over again and

slumped in disappointment. I suspected Bart would change Joe's translation if it suited him or if someone pressured him to do it to match
Wierwille's teachings.

Despite my distraction over Bart, I did not regret leaving the Research Department, not for one minute. Its foundation in fundamentalism—with its nonnegotiable assertion of scriptural inerrancy—could
never be changed.

The interlinear was published in 1988. My suspicions proved true. Joe's
translation was changed to bring it more in line with Wierwille's teachings. The most glaring example was the *e-li, e-li* verse. Wierwille had
taught it meant, "for this purpose I was spared." Bart, perhaps along
with Bernita and Walter, had come up with: "for what purpose have you
spared me?"—Wierwille's interpretation but in the form of a question
rather than a statement—which was in contrast to Joe's "for what purpose have you left me?" I'd seen Joe's translation myself, and it was reflected in the concordance, too. I do not know under what circumstances the change was made—maybe jobs depended on it. Regardless, the
interlinear was out of sync with the concordance. This was completely
unacceptable, not only for purposes of studying at The Way, but also
because scholars around the world would scoff. It showed utter lack of
care, consistency, and academic integrity.

Controlling, manipulative sects like The Way conduct business hidden
from public scrutiny and sometimes get away with more disturbing behavior than changing Syriac translations to favor their leader's teachings.
A few months after Bart arrived, I learned something more terrible
about Wierwille. It struck me like a tsunami, and I reeled in its wake for
months … I still do.

53

Spilling Secrets

In the spring of 1987, I ran into Warren, the older brother of one of my girlfriends. We were in the IGA grocery store near my house, and he approached me in a tired way, as though he bore an inescapable, incurable burden. Lines I'd never seen before encircled his eyes.

"Hey, Warren. You all right?"

"No, actually, I'm not." He leaned against a counter.

"What's wrong? Want to talk?"

"I would … but not here." He glanced around. "Any chance you could meet me for coffee at Adolph's? I've got to talk to somebody. You love Trudy as much as I do. It's about her."

"Sure. Three o'clock? Today?"

"Perfect," he whispered, and left the store.

Warren, a Corps grad, worked at Headquarters. His sister Trudy was my friend. She had graduated from the Corps a few years after me, and we'd worked together at the Rock several times.

In the back of Adolph's that afternoon, Warren was waiting, a blue baseball cap low over his eyes. As always, the ancient restaurant, with display cases full of candy, cigars, and junky odds and ends, stank of hamburger grease and cigarette smoke. A few locals, probably old farmers, were playing checkers near the bar. Adolph soon appeared, his trademark dollar bill clipped to the front of his shirt with a ballpoint pen, his order pad in hand. We asked for coffee. He delivered two steaming cups and left us alone.

"Prepare yourself, Charlene," said Warren. "This is the worst of all the crap that's gone down since Geer read his damn patriarch paper."

I pressed my hands on the table.

Warren looked me square in the eyes. "Wierwille had a lot of women."

"Huh?"

"Had, like screwed. Hundreds, according to my source … who is a leader you know, but I can't tell you who it is. I promised."

"What?" Fear shot through my veins. I shook a little. I blinked a lot. I felt as if I were back in the research room hearing The Comment—the whisper that changed everything—again. I wanted to deny this, of course; I wanted to say it was impossible.

"Trudy was one of those girls, Charlene. She told me herself last week."

Dumbfounded, shocked, disoriented, I thought I'd been living in hell already, but this … my head spun.

"Some Corps girl that Wierwille got his hands on before Trudy recruited her 'to help take care of the man of God,' as they put it. There was a whole secret sex ring doing this. Wierwille charmed the girls and they brought in more girls to see Wierwille, day and night. They kept their secret in a lockbox—you know that term, Wierwille used it for other stuff, too. If any of them got to be a problem—protested or said they'd tell—he threatened to deny everything. It would be their word against his." Warren pulled his cap down his brow. "Scumbag."

Shock makes people slow down and feel dislocated, as if they are somewhere other than in the chair they are sitting in. That was me.

"Is Trudy … is she … is she okay?" I tore at my paper napkin. "I mean, of course … I don't know what I mean. Hundreds? Trudy? It's—" I glanced around the room, hoping no one heard us.

391

"It's insane. Yeah. But true. And my own sister."

I felt as sick as I had when Ed told me he was in love with someone else. I'd entered *The Twilight Zone* again.

"I know Trudy like nobody else," Warren said, sighing into his coffee. "She's got no reason to make this up. No reason." His voice was getting hoarse. "She broke down at home but didn't tell our folks. Only me. She'd heard about the fiasco with Geer saying that Craig Martindale and the trustees were failures and the ministry was off-track, so she thought she should tell me about her and Wierwille and that some top leaders pimped for him all the time. Now *that's* off-track. She says some of them had girls, too. They're bastards, Charlene, predators and fakes." Warren frowned at the table. "Trudy says some of those women are finally feeling guilty over what they did, ashamed about what other girls talked them into doing, but get this ... some aren't sorry at all, they're proud they 'served the man of God.' You won't believe who some of them are, either. Trudy told me some names." He sputtered out a few.

"Oh my God." Where had I been? Why hadn't I realized? Memories flooded me with hints of who else might have been involved, but I was only guessing. Did Mrs. Wierwille know? Did Wierwille's kids suspect?

"He got away with this shit until the day he died. Think about any girl who worked with V. P., you know, on projects and stuff. She could have been one of his bunnies."

I pushed my cup away.

"I'm sorry, I shouldn't have dumped this on you so fast. Please don't tell Trudy you know. And don't tell Ed, either. He'll blab."

"I won't. I'm so sorry ..."

When I was about four years old, one summer day at the beach in Ocean City, my mother and my sister stood on either side of me at the water's edge. I wasn't yet used to fast-moving surf or the relentless roar of the ocean, but I was curious. The three of us held hands like a string of paper dolls and waded into the small waves that ran up on the sand, bubbled, hissed, and slid back into the sea. I jumped up and down.

"Slow down, honey. Careful now," Mom said.

Not a minute later, a rogue wave curled overhead and crashed, knocking me over and tearing me out of my mother's and sister's hands, the undertow dragging me out to tumble in the green-gray water as if in a washing machine. I could not tell which way was up. Powerful currents tangled seaweed around my arms and kept me from wiggling free to find the sky. Before the worst, my mother and sister pulled me out.

54

Clampdown

A month later, in October, Warren telephoned me at home with another torrent of bad news.

"They fired John. Somebody called me a minute ago and told me."

"Oh, shit."

John Schoenheit, a former research team colleague whose specialty was Old Testament history and Eastern customs, had worked closely with Walter Cummins and was his friend. John and Walter had pioneered the Harmony of the Gospels project, trying to show, as Wierwille always taught, that the gospels fit together and scriptural inerrancy was true; there were no contradictions in the Bible, they were only in our minds. This is one of the major beliefs of fundamentalists.

Warren had gotten a copy of a recent research paper that John wrote about adultery.[1] People wrote research papers all the time on various topics, so this was not unusual. What was unusual was the topic. Why adultery? John had sent the paper to selected friends who passed it around, which is how Warren ended up with it. Warren passed it on to me. I read it in minutes.

"Apparently, John is a wreck," Warren said. "He told a friend of mine that Geer, Craig, Howard Allen, Don [Wierwille's son], and—get this—

Walter Cummins, his buddy, grilled him in Doctor's old motorcycle shed about this adultery paper. Sounds like they raked him over the coals for doing new research, which is supposed to be on hold like everything else around here. But what's new about the Bible saying adultery is wrong?"

"Nothing."

"Sounds like Walter didn't even try to defend John," Warren said, "didn't give one stinking word of support, after all those years John slaved away in that department."

I felt sorry for John, and very worried about my own situation. If discovered, I too would be considered a heretic. I was still under the radar—but for how long? If I slipped up, I could be ostracized and my family hurt like John's.

The next afternoon after working at Child Care, I snuck over to John's house. He looked like a ragged fugitive who hadn't eaten in days. We sat in the living room while he talked and talked despite his blood-shot eyes and fingers that kept strumming his knee. He was shell-shocked, like Joe had been when he was fired, only John, sitting across from me, visibly shaken, had been thrown out on the spot.

"The weird thing is," he said, "they would not say *why* they were firing me. They just kept saying, 'You know the reason.'" In his paper, he had not mentioned Wierwille's name or anyone else's. The material was mostly Bible verses about adultery to show it was wrong. John knew he'd hit a secret nerve.

After Geer had read his "Passing of a Patriarch" paper, several women, married and unmarried, had approached John for clarification about what the Bible said about adultery. Some revealed affairs with married Way leaders, including Wierwille, explaining they'd been told that flesh did not matter to God, only spirit mattered, so they could have sex with anyone as long as they did it with love.[2] He was shocked.

In his paper, John had compiled verses on the topic, and pointed out that Wierwille often interpreted the word adultery in the Bible as *spiritual* adultery—whoring after false gods instead of worshipping the true God. I'd heard those teachings and thought the contexts could support Doctor's interpretation, so I did not question them. Besides, I'd believed that Doctor was "the man of God"—he had special understanding. John's compilation, though, made it clear that the Bible said it was against God's will to have sex with someone other than your spouse. What could be more incredible or ironic than for pointing out that the Bible says adultery is wrong, John Schoenheit was kicked out of The Way?

Now out of a job, John had no plan B. His wife was fired by default. They received no severance pay to help with their mortgage. They had little savings, and young children in tow. My heart ached for them, and for the women who'd been used by leaders they'd trusted. It ached for all of us who'd believed in Wierwille. We'd let idealism blind us to manipulators, sexual predators, and false prophets. We'd been deaf to our own inner voices.

As I scoured my memories for signs I'd missed, the past took on unsettling, deeply disturbing interpretations. I recalled the winter vacation in 1974 when Wierwille and Howard had spent a week in Squaw Valley with us Corps stationed in California. That moment Wierwille had sidled up to me—what was that, really? What was really going on when he asked "Your man taking good care of you, honey?" Perhaps rather than a pastoral care moment, it had been a proposition. I felt stupid about my naiveté, but when a person is looking through one kind of interpretive glasses, it is impossible to see through any other.

More memories tumbled out of storage. Corps women in Trailer Six—had any of them been caught in Wierwille's sex trap? Was Rose's sudden shutdown precipitated by an incident with Doctor? I did not know. I thought about each of my Corps sisters, considering times when Wierwille had summoned one or two to his motor coach or to his house when Mrs. Wierwille was visiting her sister. I felt like a fool. I ended up vomiting in the bathroom, not only because of the sex abuse, but also the fake research and my teetering marriage. A rash broke out on my arms. A local doctor said it was nerves.

I was ashamed to think that the sex ring had existed in the Corps right under my nose, and I had been too preoccupied with my own business—Ed and my absorbing Aramaic job—to notice. I'd missed the signals. Obviously, I had been foolish to think of Wierwille as our "father in the Word," incapable of screwing my friends. I recalled that night in the Fireplace Room when he'd fumed about the newspaper interview with the disgruntled ex-follower who accused him of inappropriate relations with women. No wonder he'd denied it so vehemently.

Ed's reaction, when we talked about the sex-ring revelations, was: "What a hypocrite, condemning me for screwing around."

The Way as we'd known it was gone. After John was fired, more leaders abandoned their posts on the field; some forming spin-off groups that perpetuated Wierwille's teachings under different names. Newer Corps grads replaced them, and some older Corps stepped up. Ed, still working in the Shipping and Receiving department, kept putting himself forward as someone who could help fix the ministry's problems, which were still not articulated by anyone—unsurprisingly, the adultery issue was never publicly admitted. For a short while, Ed was considered for a Branch leader position, but in the end he was passed up. He became despondent, with no idea of how lucky he was. I was totally relieved.

The Way, like a rotten building, fell to pieces before our eyes. Corps grads left, one after another. Before Christmas of 1986, the much-admired director of the Way Corps at Headquarters at that time, Rev. Ralph Dubofsky, left with his family. Ralph had held many top leadership positions since the late '70s and had a reputation for speaking up.

On December 10, 1986, Ralph read his resignation statement to The Way Corps, and he and his family soon vanished. Not until I left The Way did I find out from Ralph what had happened. Ralph had confronted Christopher Geer, Craig and Donna Martindale, Howard Allen, Don Wierwille, Earl Burton, Walter Cummins, and two new trustees, Johnny Townsend and Ricardo Caballero, over misdeeds. By this time, Geer had taken control of Bless Patrol—The Way's private security police. They carried handguns. Geer installed one armed Bless Patrol guard (and a Doberman Pinscher) inside Ralph's mobile home and assigned more to keep watch on him and his family for two weeks while arrangements were made for them to leave. They drove away December 14th. Imprisoned in his mobile home, right across the yard from the Child Care unit where I worked, he was incommunicado. I had no idea, even though I was close by, that such outrageous actions were underway. Ralph's departure was more than disturbing. It was a clear sign to me that no hope for change was left.

Mixed feelings plagued me. How much of this chaos had been our own making? We participated. We followed. We fed the predator, supplied him in every way, yet he had deceived us from the start. Wierwille as cult leader and Wierwille as fundamentalist biblical researcher created a powerful force that overcame the vulnerable, and vulnerable people cannot always flee.

55

Sleeping Beauty

Friends turned on friends; others could not hear one another. Maybe they couldn't help it. One night Ed and I visited another staff couple—a longtime buddy of Ed's and his wife—at their house in New Knoxville. We'd dropped Rachel off at one of her schoolmates in town so we could have time with Zack, an ordained Corps grad, and his wife, Cheri. They were dependable, loyal, hospitable folks. They'd worked on staff long enough to have purchased their house. But soon I realized their stability was their downfall, and that denial about Wierwille's manipulations—of people and Scripture—had not only been my problem, but it also plagued most every salaried staff person at The Way. We had more at stake than a Way believer in the field who attended a fellowship once a week. Those followers had integrated lives in the hubbub of the world. Not us. Dependent on stability in the organization, we dangled from a line of tenuous filament called loyalty.

At Zack's, the men headed for the den to hash over ministry rumors, and Cheri and I sipped wine in the living room and caught up on our kids, her part-time job at Headquarters, and my college classes. With their children asleep upstairs, the house was peaceful, and I thought that perhaps Cheri, a dear friend these past three years, might listen to me, might realize we'd been duped. When I thought the moment was right, I pried open the can of research sludge I carried everywhere. "I've been wondering, Cheri. Do you have any questions about my resigning from the research team? I'd be happy to talk about it."

"Oh, that's your private business," she said, "but I was concerned. It's such an honor to be in that group. I guessed things had changed or something, so you left."

Cheri was one of the few friends I had. With her, I intended to stay off the adultery topic, knowing I'd have to prove it with names, and I couldn't reveal my source, not even to Cheri.

"Things did change," I said. "Not to upset you, but the fact is that I came face to face with some deliberately wrong research in Doctor's work, even in the PFAL class." I took a sip of wine, bracing myself for an outburst of protest or alarm, or at least a serious question.

"Well," said Cheri, smoothing her skirt, "I'm sure Walter will fix everything, sort it all out. I think we should try to focus on the basics of the Word, like Craig says." My friend raised her glass in salute despite the barricade she'd just erected.

I may as well have said that the trouble in research was that the room needed a paint job. Obviously, my friend liked her life as Sleeping Beauty. It required nothing of her. To her, the Biblical Research Department was disconnected from "the basics" in the PFAL class. She could not grasp that the basics came from sloppy, inept, and outright wrong so-called research to begin with. If I'd told her much was also plagiarized, well, I imagined she'd say the same thing Ed had—that's just silly, sense-knowledge talk, and no one cares.

"So, you're out of that department now," she said with a smile. "Enjoy college."

"Sure." I wanted to cry. In a perverted way, her denial was beautiful protective gauze preventing her from the kind of breakdown I was having. The purity of her intention was as breathtaking as spring rain but as

400

heartbreaking as a flash flood. Like her, I'd left those messy little details to Walter to sort out—and look what happened. The game was fixed. But Cheri was not interested in the game. She'd not yet realized it *was* a game.

Cheri's optimism was denial in disguise, and I knew it because she did not take seriously our leaders' instability, evidenced every day. I guessed that since she had a nice family, lived in a lovely home in a quiet neighborhood, grew veggies in a garden, and believed she was part of a ministry spreading God's Word, that she was too insulated to think. The noxious cult's diseases had not yet infiltrated her space. I was beginning to see that most people don't change until they have a personal crisis, and my research crisis was not personal to Cheri.

My dear friend wouldn't listen, so why bother anyone else? I shut up after that, did my job and my homework, and took care of my family. I also wrote to Joe. Thanks to him, I was where I could breathe. By this time it was January 1987, six months after I'd resigned from the stifling research team. It seemed they had forgotten me—until one night a friendly phone call told me they had not.

56

Ambiguous Mission

Sometimes divergent pathways reconnect, and when they do, expectations often fail. One morning, the telephone rang in my kitchen. It was Alvin, the research librarian.

"I want to talk with you about the department," he said. "So much has happened since you left, and I want to share some really neat things the team is doing." He had me cornered. Besides being the librarian, Alvin—an ordained Third Corps graduate and Walter's long-time assistant—evidently was tasked with calling wayward researchers like me.

It was a snowy day in January 1987, and I had to hurry to Lima for class, but thinking it might appear suspicious if I declined a cozy chat, I agreed to meet him for lunch. I'd known Alvin a long time. When I was in the Second Corps, he entered the Third Corps, and when Wierwille put Second Corps in charge of small groups of Third Corps—to make sure they stuck with the program—Alvin was in my group. I gave him the same advice I'd gotten from my Corps mentor, Nancy: Dr. Wierwille knows what he's doing; just stay, you will be blessed. I cringed (and still do) over passing that along to Alvin. This telephone call was payback.

We agreed to meet at Pizza Hut in St. Marys, not far from my route to Lima. Alvin was already at a table and waved at me when I opened the door. It was a bitter cold day, and I was starved after a busy morning in Child Care. The restaurant smelled of hot cheese and burnt crust and the lunchtime crowd was buzzing. When I reached Alvin, he hugged me and helped me with my chair, acting charming but looking as if he'd forgotten to shave that day. We ordered pizza slices and salads, and I asked for a Coca-Cola. He ordered a beer. Right away, I told him I had exactly one hour because I had to get to class on time. Snow was forecast. Driving could be dicey.

"I understand." He sniffed.

I chatted about college a little too fast, trying to deflect talk about the department or ministry gossip—about Geer's paper, or about Craig, our inept president, or about spin-off groups being formed by people like John Lynn, former state leader of North Carolina and former Way Corps coordinator, or about John Schoenheit getting fired after distributing his research paper about adultery. As far as I knew, Alvin was unaware I'd hopped the fence of loyalty and now gauged him from the other side. He glanced around as if to say I should hurry up and let him talk. Our cheerful waitress soon placed our food on the table.

"I wanted to catch you up on what's happening in the department," he said and took a long draw on his beer. "It's going good, but it's not the same without you. So, you happy in Child Care?"

I couldn't tell what he wanted. Was he fishing for bad attitudes I might have about the research? Secret yearnings to return to the research team? Regrets? Heretical beliefs?

"Sure, the kids are great, so funny and smart. I love them." I figured that the best way to get through this encounter was to relax and take whatever Alvin said at face value.

With another furtive glance around, he said the team was "getting back to the basics of the Word," like Chris Geer, leading the coup for control, had ordered everyone to do. I nodded politely and chewed a pepperoni. Those so-called basics were what had gotten us into this fix.

How on earth could they save us now?

Alvin said they listened to old tapes of Wierwille's Sunday night teachings. I raised my eyebrows and kept chewing. They wanted to return to the simple truths Doctor taught, he said with tears in his eyes, especially in the PFAL class. New research was canceled. I wasn't surprised he left other developments out of his story, like Walter hiring Bart to finish Joe's job and firing John for telling the truth about the meaning of adultery in the Bible.

"Hearing Doctor's voice on those old tapes reminds me of the Word in all its simplicity." He paused at this nostalgia, waiting for my agreement, but he may as well have been talking to the waitress. I knew Alvin and I knew he would not understand, much less accept, my changed opinion of Wierwille, so I did not risk a hint of that.

It's striking how ideologues like Alvin (and my former self) assume their listeners are as enthralled with what they say as they are. They fail to understand that by assuming listeners love their rhetoric, they become bereft of empathy for what might be inside their listeners' hearts. No real conversation takes place.

"You know," I said, "I'm so busy with college and everything else I don't have much time to think about research." I rattled on some more to deflect any more propaganda. Soon, Alvin's blank stare at the plate of pizza told me his reconnaissance mission was over—whatever its purpose had been. I said good-bye and rushed off to my new class: Sociology 101.

57

Cures and Calamity

Sociology 101 handed me a bundle of unexpected relief that continued with its gifts for years. The kindness of Dr. Schaffer, my professor, was something I encountered repeatedly in college, but her special effort to teach a session about cults, done for me personally, was *exceptional*. It clarified the new and often frightening understanding I was gaining about my years in The Way. Wierwille had used me for his own gain. I accepted that. His teachings were fundamentalist propaganda to keep me bound to the group. I accepted that, too, although it was embarrassing. I recognized the twofold nature of the experience: the cult attraction fueled by Wierwille's snow story, and the fundamentalist inerrancy appeal based on willfully ignorant views of the Bible. I had lost time, money, and energy in service to a cult leader, but I was one of the lucky ones who had the good fortune to resume real education before I left Headquarters and had to face the outside world. I was free in new ways. But I wasn't out yet. And sometimes I was scared. Could I escape? Anything could happen, given the unpredictability of the men in control at Headquarters.

Until this time, my opinions had carried no weight anywhere. Not at home with Ed. Not at work in research. Not with longtime friends like Cheri. But the spring term at OSU brought a surprise I've never forgotten. It happened when I took a writing class. One day the instructor asked us to brainstorm ideas for an essay about music. What were our opinions on popular tunes? Opinions? I could not remember the last time anyone asked me for my opinion, not since Joe left. Students around me had no trouble speaking up. Our teacher, a gentle young woman who also taught high school, wrote their ideas about bands and singers on the board, not excluding anything, not censoring anyone. I loved the process, although I refrained from getting involved. After class, the teacher scrunched into the desk next to mine. She was so close I could smell the mints she had in her mouth.

"Charlene," she whispered in a friendly way, "this is a remedial class working at ninth-grade level. What are you doing in here?" She fingered her ponytail, tied with a silk ribbon, waiting and wondering. "Your journals prove you are working well beyond that."

"It's okay," I said. "I love your grammar lessons and all your help. Please let me stay. I need to recover so much that I've lost."

She looked puzzled but said that if I was happy, she was too. The truth was, when I had taken the university's placement tests, I was so stressed out that I could not think straight. Even the most basic rules of grammar, like matching pronouns with the right nouns, had confused me. This lovely teacher's patience calmed me. She helped me learn in a protective atmosphere, and her supportive comments in the margins of my journals made me come alive. Soon I was writing fairly upbeat entries, a sign I was on the mend.

Ed didn't seem worried about our financial stability, despite the ministry uproar, but I was nervous every time I registered for a college course. I knew that if the wrong Way people found out I'd given up on the ministry, we could be fired like John and sent away, ending my education abruptly during an unfinished term. We would have little savings and nowhere to go but to our parents, temporarily. I worried about

Rachel, now in sixth grade. She was eleven years old, and some of her Way friends were registered to take the Power for Abundant Living class, twelve being the qualifying age. They were nudging her in that direction. She would be twelve in June. I had only months to thwart them.

College saved me. Any time I had a spare minute on the OSU campus, I ran to the library. One day, browsing around in the religion section, I discovered *The Gnostic Gospels* by Elaine Pagels, a study of newly discovered ancient texts, some of which were older than the New Testament gospels, that gave a different accounting of Jesus's life and words. Documents other than ones in the KJV fascinated me. I wondered what would have happened if they'd been included as Scripture. Who knew? Pagels's book led me to another one that explained the mysterious Q source that I'd overheard Joe whispering about with his friend in the research room not long after I joined the team. After I read about Q source, I understood why they'd whispered: they could not talk openly about it. The information strikes at the very heart of Wierwille's premise that the Bible was authored by God, not men. I already knew from Wierwille that Mark was the first gospel written. But what I'd never learned until that day in the OSU library was that Matthew and Luke share a lot of the same information that is in Mark because they used Mark to write their own Gospels! There is also material that Matthew and Luke share that is *not* in Mark. It's *that* material scholars called the Q source. We don't know exactly what Q was—a document or an oral tradition—but the writers of Matthew and Luke used it in their accounts of Jesus's life.

This was more than important information about writing gospels. It overturned my view of Scripture. It directly contradicted what I had believed for seventeen years in The Way—no wonder Joe kept it quiet. Q source uprooted the foundation of Wierwille's fundamentalist teaching—that God is the author of the Bible and he told each writer what to write, instead of them deciding that for themselves. It was critical evidence, at least to me, for understanding the Bible in a new and different way—one that appealed to me.

At Way Headquarters, in the spring of 1987, I was reminded that privately owned farm properties like The Way abide by their own rules of operation when my path ran counter to Wayworld procedures. I did it again—resigned. Supervisors had failed to install a fence around the Child Care playground. Shocking to me was that the fence had been bought (before my time) but stored in the warehouse, apparently forgotten. Reminders from Child Care personnel went ignored. That wasn't all. The snow-sledding hill was also unprotected. Safety first? By spring I'd had enough. I sent my resignation letter, citing the hazards and questioning our possible non-compliance with county ordinances, to the man in charge, who was also a clergyman and father of kids in my care.

The next afternoon, he visited the Child Care unit and called me to the tiny office behind the kitchen. He still wore denim overalls and muddy work boots from morning farm inspections.

"You're overreacting, Charlene," he said, "and putting unnecessary stress on people." His voice rose with each word. "Look, I don't care if I go to jail," he added, sticking his nose in the air. "That'll give me more time to read the Bible."

Yikes. I'd expected to be intimidated, but I didn't expect this insanity. I was sure my coworkers could hear through the walls; they must be alarmed.

"And I'm telling you that I'm not willing to be responsible for other people's children in this environment."

No more talk. He scribbled his signature on my assignment-change request form for the Multi-Services Department and left me alone in the room. What a pity. His child was among my favorites.

I said good-bye to the children and my wonderful coworkers, wishing them the best, but I was profoundly worried about them. My immediate supervisor knew the contents of my letter; now things were up to her. I couldn't solve all the problems at The Way, but I felt better knowing that at least I'd tried to fix one. Later I heard things improved.

It was March, but still cold. The Multi-Services Department—The Way's clearinghouse for day laborers—soon arranged an assignment for me. At the door of an aluminum shed near the barn, a guy in jeans handed me a yellow raincoat and black galoshes. He also gave me a power hose. Every morning I scrubbed windshields and tires and vacuumed car interiors to the blare of country music, scouring muddy cars and spotless cars alike. The cleanest car I serviced belonged to Craig's wife, Donna, who drove it only to go shopping. I laughed to ward off crying. A few weeks later, the coordinator called me. "I see on your skills list that you know how to sew," he said. "Can you help make draperies?"

Part 9
Escape

58

Hanging Threads

In the enormous OSC building at Headquarters, on the second floor, at the opposite end from the Research Department down the hall, a sewing machine waited for me. It was May 1987. Ed and I had been at Headquarters for almost three years, and I was now being sent to the fourth job of my "spiritual boost." The sewing room was windowless, like the research room, and large. Exit stairs to the warehouse were out in the hall around the corner. If I still had to be blockaded at the Alamo, this was a good last stand.

My manager, an intense but pleasant woman from New Jersey, had a large sheet of plywood set on saw horses where she spread yards of fabric that we marked, pinned, cut, folded, and hauled over to the machines. She kindly instructed me on the fine points of lining drapes, creating pleats, and finishing them with a professional look. I'd found a haven, it seemed, even though confusion swirled like low-hanging fog throughout the building.

It was almost a year since Joe had left, and I'd safely landed in college. Bad memories of my research issues with Walter, the Aramaic project, Geer's power grab, and the sickening revelation of Wierwille's sex ring floated in the background … for a while.

Then one day in the sewing room, as I prepared to leave work and stop off at home before driving to OSU, an interoffice envelope arrived. My boss handed it to me. The sender was Bart, Joe's replacement. Ugh. Inside was a photocopy of a recent letter addressed to Bart from a member of the Satellite Research Group.[1] At the top, Bart had written a little note in red ink indicating he was sending it to me because he imagined it would bless me. He also expressed his gratitude for my work and quoted an appropriate Scripture verse, signing off by telling me he loved me.

That sounded nice, but my gut began to churn. Bart and I had not spoken about work since his arrival. Why seek me out? I stuck the letter in my purse, gathered my things, and said good-bye to my boss. At home in the kitchen, I read the letter. The author indicated that those of us who had learned Aramaic should comply with what Wierwille taught, even if and when we saw that the Aramaic text did not support Wierwille's teachings. According to this letter, I understood the author to say we were too immature and not skilled enough to question Wierwille. Wierwille knew best. This was in line with standard operating procedures that Walter passed on to all researchers. What bugged me most was that Bart had never taken time to speak to me about why I left the department, nor approached me for a meaningful conversation, but he clearly thought he had the right to reprove and warn me by using the content of this letter. My blood boiled. I stashed the letter in my trusty file box, got in my car, and hit the road. Rock and roll on the radio soon got me laughing over Bart's note in red about the letter blessing me. It did. It gave me another twig to toss on the bonfire of twisted Wayspeak.

59

Exodus

"Well, my dear ones," he said, looking at us with tears in his eyes, "I'm beside myself with concern about all this disruption and hurt. It's a shame it's all gone sour." Ed's father, in his sixties but radiating the energy of a forty-year-old man, spoke in the gentle ways of the pastoral minister and searched our eyes to find our hearts. It was a spring day in 1987. We drank tea with him in our living room in New Knoxville and shed more of Wierwille's influence, even while in the shadow of Headquarters down the road. I think Ed's heart was freer to open to his father now; more light was getting through. While I'd been taking college classes, Ed had realized that no place existed for him in the chaotic hallucination called The Way. I was so relieved I cried when Ed decided to leave and telephoned our families. When I spoke with my father-in-law, he seemed to understand, without much explanation, the unimaginable gravity of our situation. The next week he arrived at our house.

"I can help you start over," he said. "Simply tell me what you need."

Ed had already called his former boss in Florida and gotten his old sales job back. We were being airlifted off the flaming shipwreck.

We discussed the practicalities of our new situation that day, and then he set down his teacup.

415

"I need to tell you something," he said, "but it is disturbing. I could hardly believe it myself."

One of Ed's former high school friends, Kristen, a Way Corps grad married to a Way clergyman, had left the ministry the previous year, returned with her children to her mother's home in Rye, New York, and divorced her husband. We'd heard rumors about this but no details. Over the years we'd fallen out of touch with Kristen. Ed's father struggled to find polite words to describe her personal circumstances. As soon as he said Kristen had been seduced by Wierwille, I understood—the secret sex ring. I was shocked.

In 2008, Kristen Skedgell would publish her disturbing memoir, *Losing the Way,* a gut-wrenching story of her seduction by Wierwille.

My thoughts hurried to my conversation with Warren about his sister, my old friend Trudy, being a victim, and then, of course, the women in the sex ring that John Schoenheit told me about when I visited him at his house the day after the trustees fired him. I felt dizzy with fury that Wierwille got away with his abuses, sexual and otherwise, and died without answering for them. I still remember my father-in-law's final words that day: "It's heartbreaking, isn't it?"

Just when I thought I'd heard the worst, that August I was in my kitchen with my longtime girlfriend, Tillie, who'd served as a WOW Ambassador. Now she was married, and for the past couple of years, during Corps Week and the Rock of Ages, she and her husband, Ted, a Corps grad, stayed with us so they could attend those events. This time their sweet company was an especially welcome reprieve from the black hole we called the ministry. But that evening, Tillie was distant; her usual good cheer had vanished.

"Charlene, I need to talk to you," she said. "Ted and I don't have a choice. We can't stay here anymore—"

"What?"

"You guys are too negative. We can't be around you anymore so we're going to stay at Headquarters. Got a room in the Corps dormitory and we need to leave now. They even got a crib for the baby."

It took me a few seconds to process this, to grasp that she was rejecting us. I was blindsided. For one thing, Ed and I had not said much about current events compared with what we could have. Tillie and Ted had only been with us two days, they'd been jetlagged and busy tending to their fussy baby, and with everyone's hectic schedules, no heart-to-heart talk had taken place. Ed had spent a few minutes commenting on Craig's deplorable confusion and Chris Geer's crazy takeover and I'd agreed with him, but I'd steered clear of research issues and other serious problems. We certainly hadn't announced our plan to break from The Way. To prepare our friends for those shocks required more time.

"We think you and Ed should, you know, be alone," Tillie said. "You guys are wrong about Craig. The Devil is tricking you so we don't want to hear any more negatives about him, or Chris Geer, or anything."

"Tillie—"

"We're standing with this ministry, Charlene, until God tells us different."

My old friend looked away and picked up her baby bag. I knew Tillie, and when she made up her mind, it was pointless to argue. I had no idea whether she had come to this decision herself or if someone had told her to shun us. Given the mass confusion at Headquarters, even if she had told someone about us, word of our disloyalty did not reach upper leadership. No one called or came over to confront us.

I heard Ted clicking suitcases shut and then dragging them into the hall. Rachel, thank goodness, was at camp, far from this awful scene.

Before I said something regrettable, I moved past Ted to our bedroom down the hall and made myself not slam the door. Through the walls, I heard the kitchen door bang open and Ed's voice asking what was going on.

I was hurt. I was mad. I was disgusted. But I knew I couldn't blame Tillie. I blamed Wierwille. He perpetrated hateful divisions like this from the beginning, demanding loyalty, frightening us with ruination from the Devil if we left his group, conflating himself with the Apostle Paul, indoctrinating us to reject friends who quit following his interpretation of the Bible. He hammered us all the time with the phrase, "You have no friends when it comes to the Word." I knew the path to reach Tillie was now blocked. Until she cleared it in her own time (if she ever did), I should leave her alone like she wanted me to.

Ed knocked on our bedroom door and came in. "I'll drive them to Headquarters, be back soon." What else could he do? He obliged them, delivered them to a place they mistakenly believed was spiritually safer than their own friends' home. Before I ventured back to the kitchen, I waited for the crunch of tires over the pebble driveway, and then got busy to calm myself. I picked up a sponge and wiped the counters. I grabbed the dirty aluminum frying pan and plunged it under steaming water. I pushed hair out of my eyes and broke down in tears. Through the window above the sink, I saw blue jays fight in the half-empty birdbath, splashing rainwater onto the ground. Beyond them, in the clump of woods past our yard, our cat, Solomon, dashed into the underbrush, chasing a mole or rabbit or squirrel that he would show no mercy and drop on our doorstep, as if the dead creature were a gift. I scrubbed the frying pan harder and harder, cursing Wierwille, Walter, Craig, and Geer, all of them who'd made this whirling evil mess. And hadn't I been helping them do it? I cursed myself, too. Every second my anger grew as I obsessed over the whole rotten system of The Way—its bigotry, deception, and abuse committed in the name of God. Before I realized what I was doing, I raised the frying pan and flung it to the floor, falling on my knees beside it, shaking and sobbing and hating myself for ever getting involved with The Way, for rejecting everyone who'd warned me against it, for wasting my youth.

A bird sang from the birdbath. I couldn't help but realize that betrayal like Tillie's was inevitable. Without the ability to see through Wierwille, she could only stay with him. I might have also stayed if I'd not experienced what I had during the last three years. But part of me still blamed her. She judged me to be deceived by the Devil without hearing my story.

I think now that all of us in The Way bear some sort of responsibility for what happened. For the rest of our lives, we will carry whatever Way experiences we had—good and bad and unending in their complications—like faded scars on our backs.

I heard tires on the gravel again. Ed was home. I grabbed the frying pan, scrambled to my feet, and feeling nauseated, leaned against the counter. Ed opened the door.

"What happened to you? Look at that frying pan—"

The side was bashed in. I tried to explain.

"It's okay," Ed said. "Look, before I dropped them off, I told Tillie that she'll never know how much she hurt you."

I thanked him for that, feeling better he'd stood up for me. Maybe our marriage was on an upswing after all.

What do I make of friendship now, when Way friends split away from me without a second thought? Because I lost so many friendships to the stronghold of The Way, each new one since is a second chance.

After the Tillie episode, Ed and I went for a walk down Botkins Angle Road in front of our house. Holsteins, fenced in across the street, mooed and stirred around in their pasture. A familiar sight. We'd been sorting junk for a yard sale, eager to get going. Months earlier I had started packing photographs, letters, and off-season clothes. Our lives were unpredictable, overshadowed by infighting and paranoia among Way leaders and staff. I had to be ready for the unexpected. If we said the wrong thing to the wrong person, we could be booted to the curb at any time, like John was after his adultery paper hit the fan.

With help from my father-in-law, we were buying a condo in Orlando, Florida, the area we'd left three years earlier.

"It'll be great to get back there," Ed said, "I can do without Ohio winters."

Cows near the fence, hearing Ed's voice, turned to stare.

"I even look forward to my old job."

The Rock of Ages was in full swing at the compound only a few miles down Highway 29. When the wind was right, I heard faint singing from the crowds—there were about eighteen thousand believers that year—and imagined them in hundreds of rows of blue plastic chairs under the towering circus tents. I was glad to be with the cows.

After the Rock, we had our moving sale on a Saturday. Not only was it time for selling, it was time for buying back my life from Wierwille. After the sale, on Monday, we planned to drive to New England and visit our folks before heading down to Florida where we'd meet The Way's moving truck.

If I can just get out of here before anything else happens ...

On my kitchen calendar, I had marked off, in blood-colored ink, every passing day until we left. We had only two more to go. Meanwhile, our front yard was filled with tables not set for dinner but with things to purge. Ed hawked them like a pro. Grass, sweet with Ohio sunshine and rain, lay in small green rows from Ed's mowing job the day before. Humidity seeped through my T-shirt as I scavenged in the garage for a lawn chair, obsessing that I'd sacrificed half my life for Wierwille. At thirty-five, I felt old.

Rachel, now twelve years old, ran around the yard helping her dad, innocent of the complex reasons underlying our move. She'd been raised in The Way's doctrines, and I knew it might take a long time to rear her out of them. So many beliefs were divisive and arrogant, like thinking anyone who dismissed our teachings did not please God. Re-teaching my daughter was going to be a strange and difficult task. I cringed when I thought about it.

I found the lawn chair and dragged it under the sweeping tree by the driveway. My part in preparing for the sale—choosing what to sell, marking price tags, organizing tables—was over. Now I could rest. Lounging, I watched puffy clouds heap into shapes: an elephant, a mushroom, a rat. A pang of longing hit me. Oh, to be as far away from here as they were. I watched Rachel, in shorts and a yellow T-shirt, straighten clothes hanging from a line Ed had strung between the trees and arrange items on a card table: flower vases, mixing bowls, and my green-and-gold Way Corps coffee cup. My final day in the research room, I'd used that cup for the last time, as well as a purse-sized Bible with my notes correcting verses to match Way teachings. Only a loyal Way follower would value those things now.

Moving gave us the chance not only to untangle ourselves from a corrupt ministry, but also to solve a serious problem regarding Rachel. She and her friends wanted to see the video version of Wierwille's Power for Abundant Living class at someone's house. It would start soon. All thirty-six hours of it. They'd each have to pay the hundred-dollar fee. That class. It was that class of Wierwille's plagiarized fundamentalist Bible teaching that lured me into this cult when I was a teenager, a mere six years older than Rachel was.

"We can talk about that later, honey," I told her, intending not to.

I have to get my child away …

The best news was that the PFAL class would not start until after we left. Without that to look forward to, Rachel let us know she was unhappy about moving. We were taking her from her friends and the village where she rode her bike all over in safety and freedom. I explained the reasons, but she was too young to grasp them. The unraveling of a mother from her life's purpose is impossible to expect any child to comprehend. She did warm to the idea of resuming dancing classes in Florida, but she would face the challenge of making new friends. I was sorry about that. Each of us had that daunting task.

The demands of moving had made Ed unaware of Rachel's hounding me to take the PFAL class, and I hadn't told him. I'd been afraid to. Although he was ready to leave the organization, I wasn't sure he'd rejected Wierwille's teachings. But the tipoff came the day of our recent walk.

"I want to run a fellowship in Florida," he'd said. "At our house. It won't be associated with The Way but ... you know, I just want to help people."

"Well, you'll have to count me out, Ed. I don't know what I believe about the Bible anymore." My admission surprised us both, like a release valve sprung open, revealing truth to the light of day. I think that's when he realized, or at least heard, where my inner life had taken me. No one makes a disbelieving, negative, tricked-by-Satan statement like that in an environment like ours and goes unrebuked. But by this time, Ed was as out of the ministry as I was and far from calling the kettle black, and he did not chastise me.

What seemed that day on Botkins Angle Road—while the cows stared at us and the crowd sang in the distance and Ed muttered about the future—to be an admission of the darkest confusion proved to be a step toward wholeness. I didn't know what the Bible was, but I would try to find out. I had come full circle and returned to the path I'd not taken when Doug witnessed to me at ECU. Back then, I could've made a beeline to Joyner Library to get information about the Bible myself, but I took the easy route and landed in Wierwille's trap. I paid a high price. My youth was gone, my education delayed, my marriage dysfunctional, my goals proven to be illusions—but at least I was awake, as awake as I could be given the circumstances. The dream was over, and I'd found myself anew. Sometimes I felt elated; other times I felt terrible, scared, spun around, but I was grateful that The Comment spoken in the research room had shaken me up enough to admit Wierwille's fallibility. The Comment had saved me. I had hope.

Now, in the lawn chair, I closed my eyes behind my dark glasses and rested, listening to Rachel chatting with her dad. Leaves above me rustled; a truck drove by blasting a popular movie theme, the singer lamenting over something taking her breath away. What had taken my breath away was out-of-proportion weariness from marking white price tags and pasting them on blazers, dresses, and high heels I never wanted to see again—sad reminders of working on the research team. What was supposed to have been one of the great privileges of my life had turned into one heartbreaking disaster after another.

The irony of my whole Way experience was that the biblical research that had pulled me into The Way was the catalyst for my exit.

If only I could vanish into thin air ...

Cars pulled into our driveway. Ed waved them into parking spots, directing people, chatting them up for a look at our hand-me-downs. Shoppers arrived from their mobile homes at Headquarters, embracing my husband and child. I heard them gush "Bless you" with every hug. I shrank from greeting them, afraid of questions about our move. We had worked with hundreds of those like-minded believers at the compound, and we knew hundreds more spread around the country, but I would miss only a few—ones who had already left.

Bargain hunters, nervous birds, picked through our things. The female organist bought the formal gown I'd worn in a Way wedding in California in the '70s. A young mother, her little girl holding her hand, bought Rachel's old bike. Someone bargained with Ed for a sofa. I wanted to sell every last thing, to rid myself of every reminder of my Way-soaked life as if it were infected. Even if it had all burned to cinders, I would not have cared. I fantasized about dumping the contents of our house on the lawn and driving off. This particular house had been problematic. It belonged to Wierwille's nephew, and I'd spent that whole year worrying he might find out I'd turned. Two more days and I could forget about that!

I observed Way followers buy things that had once belonged to me and wondered whether they would have paid their money if they knew we were not leaving to take another Way ministry assignment but leaving the ministry for good. With beliefs about the evils of deserting—viewed as turning your back on God—devoted staffers would consider our *stuff* spiritually contaminated.

Thankfully, the yard sale ended without anyone questioning me. Neither Walter nor Bernita had sought me out to say good-bye—nor had any other research team member. And I had not gone looking for them. It felt better that way. Like all staff and their supervisors, Ed and I had already met with our bosses to sign forms stating our intentions for the following year. We were vague in our statements about new jobs and school schedules, and since we kept our mouths shut, they assumed our loyalty was intact, and that we'd probably run a Twig fellowship—the very least every Corps grad was expected to do.

It was a sultry August morning when we left. The air, thick with haze, floated like covers over a dream. Ed steered our green sedan out of the driveway, and I followed in my red Chevy with Rachel in the passenger's seat. I heard the tires crunch that gravel for the last time as I gave a final sweeping glance over the graceful trees, the split-log fence, the wide green yard, and the house where so much had happened, where we'd argued, loved, broken down, and survived.

We turned our cars onto the blue ribbon of Highway 29 in the opposite direction from the compound. I bid farewell to the Holsteins on the corner and we rolled past the IGA grocery store. When we passed Adolph's Restaurant, I thought of the secrets spoken there. The door was greasy, as always, but faintly golden as the sun began its skyward climb to warm the day and guide us east. I rolled down my window and smelled whiffs of wet and heavy soybean plants and the good, sweet earth below them.

On black lines of telephone wire, sparrows hopped over one another, twittering as we drove underneath. The monotonous hum of tires on blacktop filled the car, and an inner silence, the kind engendered by relief, gave me comfort I desperately needed. In the trunk, returning the same way it arrived, was my file box full of Way papers and college assignments—witnesses of my vexing adventures and newer, better ones.

I settled against the padded driver's seat. Next to me, Rachel was quiet, squinting in the sunshine, watching farmland stream by. She turned for a close look as we passed a girlfriend's house, and I sensed how hard it was for her to leave her friends. They loved her. They'd even thrown her a surprise good-bye party. My girl was so brave at such a tender age. I hoped I could be as brave as that, trust the goodness in the universe, and, over time, help her understand that leaving The Way was the best thing for us.

We drove by her school, the churches, the little public library. We passed neat rows of streets coming to life with men opening office doors, women hanging laundry on droopy clotheslines, dogs barking at kids on bikes, and endless rows of cornstalks fanning out into the distance that filled our vistas all those years. These townspeople were unaware of the drama we carried as we drove past them. When the last house of the village was reflected in my rearview mirror, I knew I'd cleared certain teeth in the road, the kind that, if you back up after you cross them, will rip your heart wide open.

END

Afterword

Our new and completely different life began. We moved into a comfortable condo near Orlando, Florida, close to a good school for Rachel. She resumed dancing classes and in time made new friends, although her anger with us for taking her away from her Ohio buddies took a while to subside. At work, Ed made new connections. In 1988, I resumed college at what was then Valencia Community College, right after skin cancer surgery on my face. An attentive hair stylist had identified the telltale sign that I had ignored for years, praying it would go away, believing God would heal me. It took leaving the cult to get healed.

I was at loose ends at first, living without The Way lifestyle—no mandatory meetings, no pastoral care moments, no singing or speaking in tongues or listening to Wierwille's recorded Bible teachings. The tether that had tied me to the mother craft was severed, and I floated in deep space. I did not open a Bible for a long time. Instead, I read library books about the Bible's history and about Christian fundamentalism. I spoke to no Way loyalists. I joined no church. Neither did Ed. I did not hesitate to reject invitations to join offshoot groups whose former Way leaders believed they'd "gotten away with the gold" of Wierwille's teachings, even while acknowledging many were plagiarized. I was grateful I'd gotten away *from* his fundamentalist faux gold.

Before long, Ed gave up on hosting his own fellowship and focused on his job. We took Rachel to the beach on weekends and recovered in our own ways. Education, formal and informal, was my therapy. In 1990, I earned an associate of arts degree at Valencia. Marital counseling, the little we tried, was a spectacular failure. Ed and I divorced in 1991. Soon Rachel finished high school and eventually graduated from college, creating her own life. She is the great gift from my years of cult involvement.

I finally graduated—*summa cum laude*—from Rollins College with a bachelor's degree in English literature in 1994. Rollins, a liberal arts college, offered me a place to freely think, question, explore, and gain the knowledge and understanding essential to challenging fundamentalism and cults that spawn it.

My father and I made amends. His was a dry and corny sense of humor. On July 4, 1997, my sister, stepmother, and I were together when, as fireworks exploded around midnight, the call came from the hospital—Dad had passed. At every skyward boom, I imagined he would have chuckled, "I wanted to go out with a bang."

Thirteen years after escaping The Way, I found the love of my life, Dr. Hoyt Edge, a professor of philosophy. We met at Rollins, married, and enjoy traveling, having visited more than twenty countries, learning from each culture. I blog about our adventures. The world, once my so-called enemy, is in truth a fascinating teacher.

In 2012, forty-two years after Rob, my surfing Jesuit, warned me against The Way, I found him through the Internet. Hoyt and I have had lovely visits with Rob, affording me a chance few people have to thank a person who tried to help. I found out my 1973 wedding invitation had never reached him. (I never figured out what happened to it.) His 1974 visit in L.A. was a last gasp attempt at romance.

The only Way leader mentioned in this book who is still with The Way International is Howard Allen, a retired trustee. Walter J. Cummins, my research boss, left The Way a few years after I did but continues Wierwille-style biblical research and teaching. Others I worked with in the Biblical Research Department also left or were fired during the 1980s and 1990s. Christopher Geer formed his own Bible-based outreach using materials from Wierwille's classes. Craig Martindale's presidency ended in 2000 when he faced his second lawsuit for sexual harassment and was dismissed. Bernita Jess passed away in 2012, having supported The Way until she died. Doug, my recruiter, is also deceased.

The Way International, as of this writing, still exists and is run by a Board of Directors at its New Knoxville, Ohio, headquarters. Some former Way leaders conduct offshoot ministries, including John Lynn and John Schoenheit. Victor Paul Wierwille's grandson (and namesake) formed a similar group called S.O.W.E.R.S.

To this day, Joe Wise (who flew off in that tiny plane into the sunset) and I remain friends. I like to think I was his best student ever.

Notes

Preface

1. Author Karl Kahler states, "Cult numbers are notoriously hard to pin down, and are often inflated by anti-cult writers more concerned with sounding the alarm than checking the facts. Many writers have claimed The Way had 100,000 members, as if everyone who ever took the class were still a member. Around 1982, when [Craig] Martindale [second president of The Way International] was marching in Ontario and Way leaders were talking to the press, I heard consistently that we were claiming to have 40,000 members." Karl Kahler, *The Cult That Snapped: A Journey into The Way International* (Los Gatos, CA: Karl Kahler, 1999), 110.
   See also: Zay N. Smith, "The Way—40,000 and Still Growing," *Chicago Sun-Times*, Aug. 17, 1980.

2. Elena S. Whiteside, *The Way: Living in Love.* (New Knoxville, Ohio: American Christian Press, 1972), 142–149.

3. James Barr, *Fundamentalism* (Philadelphia: The Westminster Press, 1978) 37.

4. The definition of *cult* is taken from "Cults: Theory and Treatment Issues," a paper presented by Rutgers University professor Benjamin Zablocki at a conference on May 31, 1997; cited in Michael D. Langone, "Cults, Psychological Manipulation, and Society: International Perspectives—

An Overview," *Cultic Studies Journal* 18 (2001), 1–12. http://www
.icsahome.com/articles/cultspsymanipsociety-langone.

Chapter 1: *Hiding in Plain Sight*

1. These and other traits of cults or high-control groups are expounded in
many books about the topic. One of my favorites is *Combatting Cult Mind
Control* by Steven Hassan.

Chapter 4: *Enticed*

1. *The Myth of the Six Million* by Prof. David L. Hoggan promotes denial of the
Holocaust. Wierwille shared that view. Karl Kahler reports, "In a mailing to
students of the 1979 Advanced Class [on Power for Abundant Living], The
Way recommended that students read *The Hoax of the Twentieth Century*
and *The Myth of the Six Million*, which claim that the Nazi Holocaust either
never happened or was grossly exaggerated by Zionist propagandists in order to win sympathy for Jews." Kahler, *The Cult That Snapped*. 119.
2. From a one-page marketing flyer used for a brief time by The Way in the
1980s.
3. Victor Paul Wierwille, *Power for Abundant Living*. (New Knoxville, Ohio:
American Christian Press, 1971) 19.

Chapter 5: *The Way for Me*

1. This account appears in Whiteside's, *The Way: Living in Love*. (New Knoxville, Ohio: American Christian Press, 1972) 145–146. In the coming
years, Gerald, Earl, and Doug each entered the Way Corps, were ordained
by Wierwille, became Limb leaders, and afterwards served in higher positions of authority.

Chapter 7: *Snow Story*

1. Whiteside, *The Way: Living in Love,* 178.
2. Ibid. 180-181.

3. An account of the crash, which took place on November 14, 1970, can be found at http://www.history.com/this-day-in-history/plane-crash-devastates -marshall-university

Chapter 10: *The Class*
1. Wierwille, *Power for Abundant Living*, 5.

Chapter 11: *No Defense*
1. In the early 1970s, Wierwille organized The Way like a tree. Way followers were leaves. Home fellowships of three or more leaves were Twigs. Several Twigs made a Branch, a group of Branches was an Area. A Limb was a state, a Trunk was a country, and Headquarters and the other Way Corps training locations (in Kansas, Indiana, Colorado, and Gartmore, Scotland) were Root locales that fed The Way Tree with the Word.

Chapter 15: *Addicted to the Ministry*
1. Mr. John R. M. Lawrence, librarian at the Joyner Library at East Carolina University, provided me with a scanned copy of the article in the college newspaper. Pat Crawford, "The Mall Replaces Downtown Greenville as Prime Area of Student Recreation," *Fountainhead*, Supplement Issue Number 2 (Greenville, North Carolina), April 5, 1971.

Chapter 18: *Becoming Corps*
1. Bruce Benson, "Cults Can Spring Up from Anywhere," BlueRidgeNow. com Times-News Online, May 31, 2014. http://www.blueridgenow.com/ article/20140531/ARTICLES/405311000.
2. "The Way Corps Principles," *The Way Magazine*, January/February 1984, 13.

Chapter 20: *Nothing Is Perfect*
1. I knew Rev. Walter J. Cummins personally and learned much of this

information from personal conversations with him over the years. A number of biographical details also appear in Whiteside's, *The Way: Living in Love.* (New Knoxville, Ohio: American Christian Press, 1972) 108–117, and in Penny Marchand's article in *The Way Magazine.* Penny Marchand, "Walter J. Cummins," Leadership Profiles, *The Way Magazine*, January/February 1986, 22–23.

2. Rev. Walter J. Cummins describes his trips to institutes in Germany in his article "In Search of the God-breathed Original," *The Way Magazine*, March/April 1976, 8–11.

Chapter 23: *Family Disconnections*

1. Jane Howard, "The Groovy Christians of Rye, N.Y.—Youngsters Go on a Religion Trip and Leave Many Parents Baffled," *Life* 70, no. 18, May 14, 1971, 78–86.

Chapter 24: *Me, Lazy?*

1. Part of Ed's story appears in Whiteside, *The Way: Living in Love,* 28–34.

2. We called baby blessing ceremonies "baby dedications." At such events, a Way clergyman said a prayer that dedicated the baby's life to the service of the Lord. The parents promised to raise the child in the Word.

Chapter 25: *The Aramaic Dream*

1. Leading modern New Testament scholars, foremost among them Bart Ehrman, disagree with Lamsa. Ehrman says, "Although there have been scholars from time to time who thought that the Gospels may originally have been written in Aramaic, the overwhelming consensus today, for lots of technical linguistic reasons, is that the Gospels [Matthew, Mark, Luke, and John] were all written in Greek." Bart Ehrman, *Jesus, Interrupted: Revealing the Hidden Contradictions in the Bible (and Why We Don't Know About Them).* (New York: HarperOne, 2009), 106.

Chapter 29: *California Shocks*

1. Whiteside, *The Way: Living in Love*, 199–200.

Chapter 30: *Climbing the Way Tree*

1. Kahler. *The Cult That Snapped*, iii.
2. Ibid.

Chapter 31: *A Graceless Fall*

1. I quote from my father's journal with permission from my sister and my daughter, my co-inheritors of his estate. Joseph Lamy, private journal in the possession of the Author.

Chapter 34: *A Rabbit Hole in London*

1. Manuscript Add. 14425 described at: http://www.bl.uk/onlinegallery /sacredtexts/syriacbib.html. Access date: September 4, 2016.

Chapter 36: *The Hub of the Word*

1. Karl Kahler, *The Cult That Snapped*, iv.

Chapter 37: *Not So Good*

1. Victor Paul Wierwille, "Ordained of God," *The Way Magazine*, July/ August 1981, 4–5.

Chapter 38: *Dust to Dust*

1. Jack Gilbert, "Michiko Dead," *The Great Fires: Poems 1982–1992* (New York: Alfred A. Knopf, 1994), 61.

Chapter 39: *Research and Loyalty*

1. This paper titled "Household and Family" is in the Author's collection.
2. "A Believer's Pledge of Allegiance," *The Way Magazine*. July/August 1984, Table of Contents page.

Chapter 41: *The Call that Changed It All*

1. Victor Paul Wierwille's death certificate is available online on an empirenet.com website maintained by Dr. John Juedes, a Lutheran pastor and board member of Personal Freedom Outreach, who conducts extensive research on The Way International. http://www.empirenet.com/~messiah7/vp_DEATH.htm.

Chapter 42: *Book Baby*

1. The names of authors or editors typically appear on the cover and title page of a book. The words "Edited by The Way International Research Team" appear only at the bottom of page v, below the dedication. The Way International Research Team, eds., *The Concordance to the Peshitta Version of the Aramaic New Testament* (New Knoxville, Ohio: American Christian Press. The Way International), 1985.
2. Ibid., ix.
3. Wierwille, *Power for Abundant Living*, 155–156.
4. Ibid., 156. The George Lamsa translation of the Peshitta translates Matthew 27:46 as, "My God, my God, for this I was kept!" http://www.studylight.org/bible/glt/matthew/27.html#copyright.
5. Frank Herron, ed., "Introducing Our New Concordance," *The Way Magazine*, July/August 1985, 28–30.
6. Bernita Jess had a microfilm of Schaaf's concordance. Carolus [Carolo] Schaaf, *Lexicon Syriacum Concordantiale: omnes Novi Testamenti Syriaci voces, et ad harum illustrationem multas alias Syriacas & linguarum affinium dictiones complectens : cum necessariis indicibus, Syriaco & Latino, ut & catalogo nominum propriorum ac gentilium N.T. Syr.* Lugduni Batavorum: Typis Joh. Mulleri, Joh. fil., 1709. See https://archive.org/details/Schaaf-LexiconSyriacumConcordantiale1709.

Chapter 44: *Trust and Trepidation*

1. "Dragons in History," GenesisPark.com, accessed May 2016. http://www

.genesispark.com/exhibits/evidence/historical/dragons/
For another perspective, see Robinson Meyer, "No Old Maps Actually Say 'Here Be Dragons.'" *The Atlantic*, December 12, 2013, accessed September 3, 2016. http://www.theatlantic.com/technology/archive/2013/12/no-old-maps-actually-say-here-be-dragons/282267/.

Chapter 45: *Too Academic*

1. This quote is from a letter Goethe wrote to Thomas Carlyle, dated July 20, 1827, in Erik Redling, ed., *Traveling Traditions: Nineteenth-Century Cultural Concepts and Transatlantic Intellectual Networks* (Berlin: De Gruyter, 2016), 6. https://books.google.com/books?id=T5zUCwAAQBAJ&pg=PA6&lpg=PA6&dq=Goethe+%26+%22the+inadequacy+of+translation%22&source=bl&ots=-mo6l3tgWv&sig=e8ESpRY2OvpX-2qR_4iMRO5CjacQ&hl=en&sa=X&ved=0ahUKEwia4fGq17fOAhWI-eSYKHfUeDrM4ChDoAQgbMAA#v=snippet&q=traffic&f=false

2. Walter's article appeared in a GMIR insert in *The Way Magazine*. GMIR comes from Aramaic for "to perfect, accomplish, mature, complete." We used the term to refer to Biblical research studies "designed to present the necessary documentation of the inherent and inerrant accuracy of the Scriptures." Rev. Walter J. Cummins, "A Fresh Look at Biblical Literature," GMIR, A Biblical Research Study insert, *The Way Magazine*, July/August, 1983. (There were no page numbers on GMIR inserts.)

3. See M. C. Escher's "House of Stairs" at the MCEscher.com website: http://www.mcescher.com/gallery/back-in-holland/house-of-stairs/.

4. The October 20, 1978 letter from Wierwille was mass mailed to all Way Corps members. Marty McRae's name is cited with permission. The letter is stored (although upside down) on the Internet at: https://docs.google.com/viewer?a=v&pid=sites&srcid=ZGVmYXVsdGRvbWFpbnxjb3Jw-c25ld3NsZXR0ZXJzfGd4OjYxNDNkNTBmNmZiNjk5MWU U

5. Ibid.

Chapter 46: *President's Men*

1. Christopher C. Geer's "The Passing of a Patriarch" letter is published at Grease Spot Café, a website generously provided by Michael Duffy for former Way followers: http://www.greasespotcafe.com/main2/waydale/waydale-miscellaneous/passing-of-the-patriarch.html. Access date: May 21, 2007 (As of October 31, 2016, the link is not working. To retrieve the document, search the main website, www.greasespotcafe.com. It is also published by Spirit & Truth Fellowship International on the Christian Educational Services web site run by John Schoenheit. http://www.christian-educational.org/monthlyletters/misc/pop.htm. Access date: September 2016. See also the review of "The Passing of a Patriarch" by Dr. John P. Juedes. Juedes reports: "Geer published it ["The Passing of a Patriarch"] about 1986 through the European Christian Press of The Way of Great Britain, which Geer headed." The Way of Great Britain has since disbanded, Geer moved back to the United States, and he is no longer associated with The Way International. John Juedes, "The Passing of a Patriarch by Christopher C. Geer," http://www.empirenet.com/~messiah7/rvw_patriarch.htm. See also Dr. Juedes's comments on "Chris Geer—PFAL Piracy" at http://www.empirenet.com/~messiah7/rec_geerclone.htm.
2. Ibid.
3. Ibid.
4. Ibid.
5. Ibid.

Chapter 47: *Bowing Out*

1. I quote from my father's letter with permission from my sister, my co-inheritor of his estate. Joseph Lamy, private journal in the possession of the Author.

Chapter 48: *Turning the Tide*

1. James Barr, *Fundamentalism* (Philadelphia: The Westminster Press, 1978), 55.

Chapter 49: *The Stairwell*

1. J. Thomas Cook, *Spinoza's Ethics: A Reader's Guide* (New York: Continuum, 2007), 44.

Chapter 50: *Good-byes*

1. Dr. John P. Juedes, "Wierwille Borrows ... A Challenge to the Originality of His Teaching on 'Receiving the Holy Spirit,'" *Personal Freedom Outreach* 3, no. 1, January/March 1983, 1.
2. Ibid., 11.
3. Whiteside, *The Way: Living in Love,* 209.
4. Income reported by Karl Kahler. Kahler, *The Cult That Snapped,* iv.

Chapter 54: *Clampdown*

1. John Schoenheit's "Research Paper on Adultery" can be found at: http://www.christianeducational.org/monthlyletters/misc/Adultery.htm. John W. Schoenheit is no longer associated with The Way International. His own ministry is Spirit & Truth Fellowship International.
2. Some women's accounts would later appear in Karl Kahler's *The Cult That Snapped.*

Chapter 58: *Hanging Threads*

1. This letter is in the collection of the Author. The person who wrote it did not give permission to quote it; therefore, it is paraphrased. Also, "Bart" is an alias. As of this writing, neither person is associated with The Way International.

Acknowledgments

No book is an island. Neither is a writer. My deepest gratitude for help in bringing this story into the world goes to a star-studded group of talented and loving people, beginning with Dr. Lezlie Laws and Kären Love Blumenthal, editors of my first published essay about The Way, "An Affinity for Windows." Special thanks go to Team *Undertow*, whose dedication and skill are every writer's dream: Mary Ann de Stefano, Alice Peck, and Ruth Mullen, spectacular editors at various stages of this book's development, and Duane Stapp, the book's creative designer, who went the extra mile. I thank many generous readers who gave me their time, attention, and insight as they provided valuable feedback on the emerging manuscript over the years, especially: Robyn Allers, Morin Bishop, Stacey Boo, Dr. Rita Bornstein, Rachel and Adam Chase, Dr. Philip F. Deaver, Janice Decker, Ralph Dubofsky, Michael Duffy, Kim Fields, Melissa Goings, Arthur Goldwag, Ann Hellmuth, Dr. Bethany Hicok, Virginia Higgins, Sharalee Jorgensen, Karl Kahler, Dr. Lezlie Laws, Dr. Susan Libby, Dr. Rachel Newcomb, Marty McRae, Steve Muratore, Dr. Jonathan Miller, Karen Ozolnieks, Robert Rochefort, Robert Ruff, Richard Russell, Sara Schlossman, Patricia Simmons, Kristen Skedgell, Jeff Stevenson, Rene Townsend, Joe Wise, and Dr. Timothy Yocum. Gratitude goes to innumerable other friends and writers for empathetic support, including: Dr. Barbara Carson, Patricia Charpentier, Dr. Persis Coleman, Dr. Thomas Cook, Jodi Garceau, Suzannah Gilman, Don Glenn, Linda Goddard, Darlyn Finch Kuhn, Susan Lilley, Elizabeth Maupin, Micki Meyer, Dr. Robert Moore, Darla Moore, Jamie Morris, Dr. Thomas Ouellette, Dr. Jay Yellen, the Rollins College English Department faculty, and members of the Rollins Women's Association. I want to highlight my appreciation of Dr. Rita Bornstein, President Emerita of Rollins College, who introduced me to author Joanie Schirm, who recommended editors Alice and Ruth, through whom I found Duane, *Undertow*'s designer—this string of talent made real the motto, "It takes a village." Heartfelt thanks goes to Michael Duffy, the founder and tireless administrator of greasespotcafe.com—an online community of former Way followers—for his invaluable assistance and kindness, and for publishing my work at GSC. His courage, and that of GSC members, has healed many lives for many years. Special thanks also goes to Michael D. Langone, PhD, Executive Director of the International Cultic Studies Association, and to other healers at ICSA, for encouraging me and publishing my work in the *ICSA Today* magazine. Educators like Todd French, PhD, Yudit Greenberg, PhD, and Eric Smaw, PhD, of the Rollins College Department of Philosophy and Religion contributed to the book's value by having me share my Way story with their students. During the years I worked on the manuscript, annual wisdom flowed from the Rollins Winter with the Writers literary festival and the Florida Writers Association. Special help came from librarians at East Carolina University's Joyner Library who found documentation of my student protest escapade. Yoga instructor David Walsh, LMHC, Leslie Lynch, LMT, and hair stylist Lauren Barnes each provided healing energy. I'm indebted to dear friends Dr. Roger Casey and Robyn Allers, whose bigheartedness allowed me to sneak to their beachside condo for weeks at a time to write. All through the years, my family members extended their love and faith in me. My sister cheered me on, as did my nieces, my cousins, my uncle, my brother-in-law, and my stepdaughter, Shannon. Rachel Chase, my daughter and yoga teacher, and my son-in-law, Adam, faithfully shined the light of their love on this most personal memoir, gave me strength to keep writing, and in countless ways infused me with joy. My deepest gratitude, beyond calculation, absolutely goes to my husband and love of my life, Dr. Hoyt Edge, who understood that I needed to tell this story, informed it with his wisdom, read drafts and improved them, lifted roadblocks, cooked meals, assuaged fears, and whose steady love, patience, and support in every way made this book possible.

Bibliography

"A Believer's Pledge of Allegiance." *The Way Magazine*, July/August 1984.

Barr, James. *Fundamentalism*. Philadelphia: The Westminster Press, 1978.

Benson, Bruce. "Cults Can Spring Up from Anywhere." BlueRidgeNow.com Times-News Online, May 31, 2014. http://www.blueridgenow.com/article /20140531/ARTICLES/405311000.

Cook, J. Thomas. *Spinoza's Ethics: A Reader's Guide*. New York: Continuum, 2007.

Crawford, Pat. "The Mall Replaces Downtown Greenville as Prime Area of Student Recreation." *Fountainhead* Supplement Issue Number 2 (Greenville, North Carolina), April 5, 1971.

Cummins, Rev. Walter J. "A Fresh Look at Biblical Literature." GMIR, A Biblical Research Study [Insert]. *The Way Magazine*, July/August 1983.

———. "In Search of the God-breathed Original." *The Way Magazine*, March/April 1976.

Ehrman, Bart. *Jesus, Interrupted: Revealing the Hidden Contradictions in the Bible (and Why We Don't Know About Them)*. New York: HarperOne, 2009.

Geer, Christopher C. "The Passing of a Patriarch." Accessed May 2007. http://www.greasespotcafe.com/main2/waydale/waydale-miscellaneous /passing-of-the-patriarch.html. See also: http://www.christianeducational. org/monthlyletters/misc/pop.htm. Accessed September 4, 2016.

Gilbert, Jack. *The Great Fires: Poems 1982–1992*. New York: Alfred A. Knopf, 1995.

Hassan, Steven. *Combatting Cult Mind Control*. Rochester, Vermont: Park Street Press, 1988.

Herron, Frank, ed. "Introducing Our New Concordance." *The Way Magazine,* July/August 1985.

History.com staff. "Plane Crash Devastates Marshall University." History. com. 2009. Accessed 2012. http://www.history.com/this-day-in-history/ plane-crash-devastates-marshall-university.

Hoggan, David L. *The Myth of the Six Million*. Los Angeles: Noontide Press, 1969.

"Household and Family." Unpublished, undated one-page statement in the Author's collection.

Howard, Jane. "The Groovy Christians of Rye, N.Y.—Youngsters Go on a Religion Trip and Leave Many Parents Baffled." *Life* 70, no. 18. May 14, 1971.

Juedes, John P. "Chris Geer—PFAL Piracy." 1999, revised 2007. http://empirenet.com/~messiah7/rec_geerclone.htm.

——. "'The Passing of a Patriarch' by Christopher C. Geer: Review." 1997. http://www.empirenet.com/~messiah7/rvw_patriarch.htm.

——. "Wierwille Borrows … A Challenge to the Originality of His Teaching on 'Receiving the Holy Spirit.'" *Personal Freedom Outreach* 3, no. 1. January/March 1983.

Kahler, Karl. *The Cult That Snapped: A Journey into The Way International.* Los Gatos, CA: Karl Kahler, 1999.

Marchand, Penny. "Walter J. Cummins." Leadership Profiles. *The Way Magazine*, January/February 1986.

Meyer, Robinson. "No Old Maps Actually Say 'Here Be Dragons.'" *The Atlantic.* December 12, 2013. Accessed September 3, 2016. http://www.theatlantic.com/technology/archive/2013/12/no-old-maps-actually-say-here-be-dragons/282267/.

Redling, Erik, ed. *Traveling Traditions: Nineteenth-Century Cultural Concepts and Transatlantic Intellectual Networks.* Berlin: De Gruyter, 2016.

Schaaf, Carolus. *Lexicon Syriacum concordantiale: omnes Novi Testamenti Syriaci voces, et ad harum illustrationem multas alias Syriacas & linguarum affinium dictiones complectens : cum necessariis indicibus, Syriaco & Latino, ut & catalogo nominum propriorum ac gentilium N.T. Syr.* Lugduni Batavorum: Typis Joh. Mulleri, Joh. fil. 1709.

Schoenheit, John W. "Research paper on Adultery." Unpublished manuscript, 1986. http://www.christianeducational.org/monthlyletters/misc/Adultery.htm.

Shakespeare, William. http://www.brainyquote.com/quotes/quotes/w/william sha106104.html

Smith, Zay N. "The Way—40,000 and Still Growing," *Chicago Sun-Times*, Aug. 17, 1980.

"The Way Corps Principles." *The Way Magazine*, January/February 1984.

"The Way International." Marketing flyer in the Author's collection. New Knoxville, Ohio: American Christian Press, ca. 1980.

The Way International Research Team, eds. *The Concordance to the Peshitta Version of the Aramaic New Testament.* New Knoxville, Ohio: American Christian Press, 1985.

Whiteside, Elena S. *The Way: Living in Love.* New Knoxville, Ohio: American Christian Press, 1972.

Wierwille, Victor Paul. "Ordained of God." *The Way Magazine,* July/August 1981.

——. *Power for Abundant Living.* New Knoxville, Ohio: American Christian Press, 1971.

Zablocki, Benjamin. "Cults: Theory and Treatment Issues." In Langone, Michael D. "Cults, Psychological Manipulation, and Society: International Perspectives—An Overview." *Cultic Studies Journal* 18 (2001): 1-12. http://www.icsahome.com/articles/cultspsymanipsociety-langone.